CLYMER®

KAWASAKI

KSF250 • 1987-2000

The world's finest publisher of mechanical how-to manuals

INTERTEC PUBLISHING

P.O. Box 12901, Overland Park, Kansas 66282-2901

Copyright ©2000 Intertec Publishing

FIRST EDITION
First Printing October, 2000

Printed in U.S.A.

CLYMER and colophon are registered trademarks of Intertec Publishing.

ISBN: 0-89287-765-0

Library of Congress: 00-108273

MEMBER

MOTORCYCLE
INDUSTRY
COUNCIL, INC.

Technical illustrations by Steve Amos and Robert Caldwell.

Technical photography by Ron Wright.

COVER: Photographed by Mark Clifford, Mark Clifford Photography, Los Angeles, California.

PRODUCTION: Susan Hartington.

INTERTEC BOOK DIVISION

President Cameron Bishop
Executive Vice President of Operations/CFO Dan Altman
Senior Vice President, Book Division Ted Marcus

EDITORIAL

Director of Price Guides
Tom Fournier

Senior Editor
Mark Jacobs

Editors
Mike Hall
Frank Craven
Paul Wyatt

Associate Editors
Robert Sokol
Carl Janssens
James Grooms

Technical Writers
Ron Wright
Ed Scott
George Parise
Mark Rolling
Michael Morlan
Jay Bogart
Ronney Broach

Inventory and Production Manager
Shirley Renicker

Editorial Production Supervisor
Dylan Goodwin

Editorial Production Assistants
Greg Araujo
Dennis Conrow
Susan Hartington
Shara Meyer

Technical Illustrators
Steve Amos
Robert Caldwell
Mitzi McCarthy
Michael St. Clair
Mike Rose

MARKETING/SALES AND ADMINISTRATION

General Manager, Technical and Specialty Books
Michael Yim
General Manager, AC-U-KWIK
Randy Stephens
Advertising Production Coordinator
Kim Sawalich
Advertising Coordinator
Jodi Donohoe
Advertising/Editorial Assistant
Janet Rogers
Advertising & Promotions Manager
Elda Starke
Marketing Assistant
Melissa Abbott
Associate Art Director
Chris Paxton
Sales Manager/Marine
Dutch Sadler
Sales Manager/Manuals
Ted Metzger
Sales Manager/Motorcycles
Matt Tusken
Sales Coordinator
Paul Cormaci
Telephone Sales Supervisor
Joelle Stephens
Telemarketing Sales Representative
Susan Kay
Customer Service/Fulfillment Manager
Caryn Bair
Fulfillment Coordinator
Susan Kohlmeyer
Customer Service Supervisor
Terri Cannon
Customer Service Representatives
Ardelia Chapman
Donna Schemmel
Kim Jones
April LeBlond

The following books and guides are published by Intertec Publishing.

CLYMER SHOP MANUALS
Boat Motors and Drives
Motorcycles and ATVs
Snowmobiles
Personal Watercraft
**ABOS/INTERTEC/CLYMER BLUE BOOKS
AND TRADE-IN GUIDES**
Recreational Vehicles
Outdoor Power Equipment
Agricultural Tractors
Lawn and Garden Tractors
Motorcycles and ATVs
Snowmobiles and Personal Watercraft
Boats and Motors
AIRCRAFT BLUEBOOK-PRICE DIGEST
Airplanes
Helicopters

AC-U-KWIK DIRECTORIES
The Corporate Pilot's Airport/FBO Directory
International Manager's Edition
Jet Book
I&T SHOP SERVICE MANUALS
Tractors
INTERTEC SERVICE MANUALS
Snowmobiles
Outdoor Power Equipment
Personal Watercraft
Gasoline and Diesel Engines
Recreational Vehicles
Boat Motors and Drives
Motorcycles
Lawn and Garden Tractors

CONTENTS

QUICK REFERENCE DATA

VEHICLE HISTORY

MODEL:_____ YEAR_____
VIN NUMBER:_____
ENGINE SERIAL NUMBER:_____
CARBURETOR SERIAL NUMBER OR I.D. MARK:_____

Record the numbers here for reference

TIRE SPECIFICATIONS

Front tire	
Type	Knobby/trail tubeless
Size	AT21 x 7.0-10
Manufacturer	Dunlop KT846
Rear tire	
Type	Knobby/trail tubeless
Size	
1987-1989	AT22 x 11.00–10
1990-on	AT22 x 10.00–10
Manufacturer	Dunlop KT847
Inflation pressure (cold)*	
Front	25 kPa (3.6 psi)
Rear	21 kPa (3.0 psi)
Maximum tire pressure	
(cold, to seat beads when installing tire)	
Front	250 kPa (36 psi)
Rear	
1987	210 kPa (30 psi)
1988-on	250 kPa (36 psi)

*Tire inflation pressure for original equipment tires. Aftermarket tires may require different inflation pressures; refer to aftermarket manufacturer's specifications.

RECOMMENDED LUBRICANTS AND FLUIDS

Fuel	Regular unleaded
Octane	87 [(R + M)/2 method] or research octane of 91 or higher
Capacity	8.3 L (2.2 U.S. gal. [1.8 Imp. gal])
Engine oil	
Grade	API SE, SF or SG
Viscosity	SAE 10W-30, 10W-40, 10W-50, 20W-40, or 20W-50
Capacity	
Oil change	1.8 L (1.9 U.S. qt. [1.6 Imp. qt.])
Oil and filter change	2.0 L (2.11 U.S. qt. [1.75 Imp. qt.])
Brake fluid	DOT 3 or DOT 4
Cooling system	
Capacity (engine, radiator, reservoir)	1.45 L (1.53 U.S. qt. [1.28 Imp. qt.])
Coolant ratio	50% soft water, 50% coolant
Chain lubricant	SAE 90 gear oil

REPLACEMENT BULBS

Item	Voltage/wattage
Headlight (high/low beam)	12V 45/45W
Taillight	12V 8W
Reverse indicator (1990-on)	12V 3.4W

MAINTENANCE AND TUNE-UP SPECIFICATIONS

Spark plug	
US and CA models	NGK DP8EA-9 or ND X24EP-U9
Canadian models	NGK DPR8EA-9 or ND X24EPR-U9
European models (1990-on)	NGK DPR8EA-9 or ND X24EPR-U9
Spark plug gap	0.8-0.9 mm (0.031-0.035 in.)
Ignition timing	10° BTDC at 1300 rpm
Ignition advance	35° BTDC at 3000 rpm
Idle Speed	Slowest smooth idle speed
Pilot air screw	1 3/4 turns out
Valve clearance	
Intake	0.20-0.24 mm (0.008-0.009 in.)
Exhaust	0.20-0.24 mm (0.008-0.009 in.)
Cylinder compression	480-785 kPa (70-114 psi)
Brake pad thickness	4.5 mm (0.177 in.)
Brake pad wear limit	1.0 mm (0.039 in.)
Brake pedal height	To suit rider preference
Throttle lever free play	2-3 mm (0.08-0.12 in.)
Choke cable free play	2-3 mm (0.08-0.12 in.)
Clutch lever free play	2-3 mm (0.08-0.12 in.)
Reverse cable free play	2-3 mm (0.08-0.12 in.)
Parking brake cable free length	42-44 mm (1.65-1.73 in.)
Drive chain 20-link length	
Standard	317.5-318.2 mm (12.50-12.52 in.)
Service limit	324 mm (12.76 in.)
Drive chain slack	40-50 mm (1.58-1.97 in.)
Cooling system test pressure	103 kPa (15 psi)
Radiator cap relief pressure	73.5-103 kPa (11-15 psi)

MAINTENANCE AND TUNE UP TIGHTENING TORQUES

Item	N•m	in.-lb.	ft.-lb.
Coolant drain bolt	7.8	69	–
Engine		–	
Oil drain bolt	15	–	11
Oil passage bolt	15	–	11
Oil pipe banjo bolt	20	–	15
Spark plug	14	–	10
Brake bleed valve	7.8	69	–
Brake hose banjo bolt	23	–	17
Brake caliper mounting bolts	25	–	18
Parking brake adjuster locknut (1987 models)	18	–	13
Rear master-cylinder-pushrod locknut	18	–	13
Spark plugs	14	–	10

(continued)

MAINTENANCE AND TUNE UP TIGHTENING TORQUES (continued)

Item	N•m	in.-lb.	ft.-lb.
Valve adjusting screw locknut	25	–	18
Wheels			
Wheel nut	34	–	25
Rear hub nut	145	–	107
Front hub nut	34	25	
Rear axle locknut	160	–	118
Swing-arm clamp bolt	37	–	27

CHAPTER ONE

GENERAL INFORMATION

This detailed, comprehensive manual covers the KSF250 Mojave from 1987-on. The expert text gives complete information on maintenance, tune-up, repair and overhaul. Hundreds of photos and drawings provide a guide through every step.

A shop manual is a reference. As in all Clymer books, this one is designed with the reader in mind. All chapters are thumb tabbed. Important items are extensively indexed at the rear of the book. All procedures, tables and illustrations in this manual are designed for the reader who may be working on the ATV for the first time or using this manual for the first time. All the most frequently used specifications and capacities are summarized in the *Quick Reference Data* pages at the front of the book.

Keep this book handy in a tool box. It will help to better understand how the ATV operates, to lower repair costs and to generally improve satisfaction with the ATV.

Kawasaki uses a letter and numeral designation in the model number to identify the model year of their ATVs. **Table 1** at the end of this chapter lists the letter-to-year designation information and the VIN numbers. Record this information in the *Quick Reference Data* section and have it available when purchasing replacement parts.

Table 1 lists model coverage and serial numbers.

Table 2 lists general vehicle dimensions.

Table 3 lists vehicle weight.

Table 4 lists decimal and metric equivalents.

Table 5 lists standard torque specifications.

Table 6 lists conversion tables.

Table 7 lists technical abbreviations.

Table 8 lists metric tap and drill sizes.

Tables 1-8 are at the end of this chapter.

MANUAL ORGANIZATION

All dimensions and capacities in this manual are expressed in standard U.S. units and in metric units.

This chapter provides general information and discusses equipment and tools useful for both preventive maintenance and troubleshooting.

Chapter Two provides methods and suggestions for quick and accurate diagnosis of problems. Troubleshooting procedures discuss typical symptoms and logical methods to pinpoint the trouble.

Chapter Three explains all periodic lubrication, maintenance and recommended tune-up procedures to keep the ATV running well.

Subsequent chapters describe specific systems such as the top end, lower end, clutch, transmission, fuel, exhaust, suspension and brakes. Each chapter provides disassembly, repair and assembly procedures in simple step-by-step form.

If a repair is impractical for a home mechanic, it is so indicated. It is usually faster and less expensive to take such repairs to a dealership or competent repair shop. Specifications concerning a particular system are included at the end of the appropriate chapter.

Some of the procedures in this manual require special tools. In most cases, the tool is illustrated either in actual use or alone. Well equipped mechanics may find they can substitute similar tools already on hand or fabricate a substitute.

NOTES, CAUTIONS AND WARNINGS.

The terms NOTE, CAUTION and WARNING have specific meanings in this manual. A NOTE provides additional information to make a step or

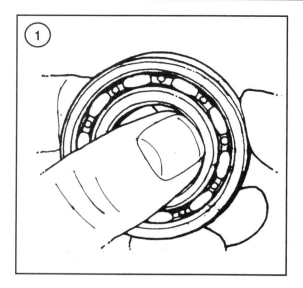

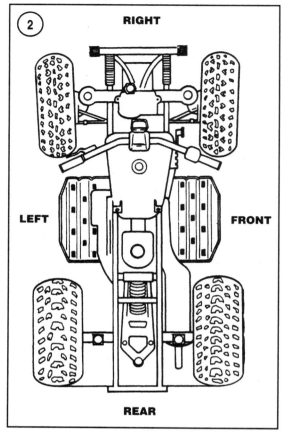

procedure easier or clearer. Disregarding a NOTE could cause inconvenience but would not cause equipment damage or injury.

A CAUTION emphasizes areas where equipment damage could result. Disregarding a CAUTION could cause permanent mechanical damage, however, injury is unlikely.

A WARNING emphasizes areas where injury or even death could result from negligence. Mechanical damage may also occur. Take WARNINGS *seriously.* In some cases, serious injury or death has resulted from disregarding similar warnings.

SAFETY FIRST

Professional mechanics can work for years and never sustain a serious injury. By observing a few rules of common sense and safety, most accidents can be avoided. Ignoring these rules can result in personal injury and/or damaged equipment.

1. Never use gasoline as a cleaning solvent.

2. Never smoke or use a torch in the vicinity of flammable liquids, such as cleaning solvent, in open containers.

3. If welding or brazing is required on the ATV, remove the fuel tank and shock absorbers to a safe distance away form the vehicle, (at least 50 feet or 15 meters).

4. Use the correct tool for the task.

5. When loosening a tight or stuck nut, be guided by what would happen if the wrench should slip. Be careful, and protect yourself accordingly.

6. When replacing a fastener, make sure to use one with the same measurements and strength as the old one. Incorrect or mismatched fasteners can result in damage to the ATV and possible injury. Beware of fastener kits filled with poorly made nuts, bolts, washers and cotter pins. Refer to this chapter for additional information.

7. Keep all hand tools and power tools in good condition. Wipe greasy and oily tools after using them. They are difficult to hold and can cause injury. Replace or repair worn or damaged tools.

8. Keep the work area clean and uncluttered.

9. Wear safety goggles during all operations involving drilling, grinding, the use of a cold chisel or anytime there is an uncertainty about the safety of the eyes. Wear safety goggles when using solvent and compressed air to clean parts.

10. Keep an approved fire extinguisher nearby. It must be rated for gasoline (Class B) and electrical (Class C) fires.

11. When drying bearings or other rotating parts with compressed air, never allow the air jet to rotate

the bearing or part. The air jet is capable of rotating them at faster speeds than those for which they were designed. The bearing or rotating part is very likely to disintegrate and cause serious injury and damage. To prevent bearing damage when using compressed air, hold the inner bearing race by hand (**Figure 1**).

SERVICE HINTS

Most of the service procedures covered are straightforward and can be performed by anyone reasonably handy with tools. However, consider your capabilities carefully before attempting any operation involving major disassembly of the engine assembly.

Take the time and do the job right. Do not forget that a newly rebuilt engine must be broken-in the same way as a new one. Refer to the break in procedure described in Chapter Five.

1. Front, as used in this manual, refers to the front of the ATV; the front of any component is the end closest to the front of the ATV. Left and right refer to the position of the parts as viewed by a rider sitting on the seat facing forward. For example, the throttle control is on the right side of the handlebar. These rules are simple, but confusion can cause a major inconvenience during service. See **Figure 2**.

2. Whenever servicing the engine or clutch, or when removing a suspension component, secure the ATV in a safe manner.

3. Tag all similar internal parts for location, and mark all mating parts for position. Record shim number, thickness and alignment when removed. Identify and store small parts in plastic bags (**Figure 3**). Seal and label them with masking tape.

4. Place parts from a specific area of the engine—like the cylinder head, cylinder, clutch and shift mechanism— into plastic boxes to keep them separated.

5. When disassembling transmission shaft assemblies, use an egg flat (See **Figure 3**). Set the parts from a shaft in one of the depressions in the same order in which it was removed.

6. Label all electrical wiring and connectors before disconnecting them. Again, do not rely on memory alone.

7. Protect finished surfaces from physical damage or corrosion. Keep gasoline, brake fluid and coolant off painted surfaces.

8. Use penetrating oil on frozen or tight bolts, and strike the bolt head a few times with a hammer and punch (use a screwdriver on screws). Avoid the use of heat where possible. It can warp, melt or affect the temper of parts. Heat also damages paint and plastic.

9. Unless specified in the procedure, parts should not require unusual force during disassembly or assembly. If a part is difficult to remove or install, determine the cause before continuing.

10. To prevent debris from falling into the engine, cover all exposed openings.

11. Read each procedure *completely* while inspecting the actual parts before starting a job. Make sure each step is thoroughly understood, and follow the procedure step by step.

12. Recommendations are occasionally made to refer service or maintenance to a Kawasaki dealership or a specialist in a particular field. In these cases, a professional may perform the procedures more economically

13. In procedural steps, the term *replace* means to discard a worn or defective part and to install a new or exchange unit in its place. *Overhaul* means to remove and disassemble a major system or assembly, inspect all its parts, and then replace worn or defective parts as required during reassembly and reinstallation.

14. Some operations require using a hydraulic press. It would be wiser to have these operations performed by a shop equipped for such work rather than trying to perform the job with makeshift equipment that may damage the machine.

15. Repairs go much faster and easier if the machine is clean before work is begun. There are many special cleaners on the market, like Bel-Ray De-

greaser, for washing the engine and related parts. Follow the manufacturer's directions on the container for the best results. Clean all oily or greasy parts with cleaning after they are removed.

> *WARNING*
> *Never use gasoline as a cleaning agent. It presents an extreme fire hazard. Be sure to work in a well-ventilated area when using cleaning solvent. Always have a fire extinguisher, rated for gasoline fires, on hand.*

> *CAUTION*
> *If using a car wash to clean the ATV, do **not** direct the high pressure water at steering bearings, carburetor hoses, suspension components, wheel bearings or electrical components. High-pressure water will flush grease out of the bearings or damage the seals.*

16. Many of the dealership labor charges are for the time involved during the removal, disassembly, assembly, and reinstallation of other parts to reach the defective part. It is frequently possible to perform the preliminary operations yourself and then take the defective unit to the dealership for repair at considerable savings.

17. When special tools are required, obtain them before starting. It is frustrating and time-consuming to start a job and then be unable to complete it.

18. Make diagrams (or take a Polaroid picture) wherever similar-appearing parts are found (like crankcase bolts, which often are not the same length). It might seem easy to remember where everything came from, but mistakes are costly. You may be sidetracked, not return to work for days or even weeks, and the carefully laid out parts may become disturbed.

19. When assembling parts, be sure all shims and washers are installed exactly as they came out.

20. Whenever a rotating part contacts a stationary part, look for a shim or washer. Use new gaskets if there is any doubt about the condition of the old ones. A thin coating of oil on non-pressure type gaskets may help them seal more effectively.

21. Use heavy grease to hold small parts in place if they tend to fall out during assembly. However,

keep grease and oil away from electrical and brake components.

WASHING THE VEHICLE

Regular cleaning of the ATV is an important part of its overall maintenance. After riding the ATV in extremely dirty areas, clean it thoroughly. Doing this makes maintenance and service procedures quick and easy. More important, proper cleaning prevents dirt from falling into critical areas undetected. Failing to clean the ATV or cleaning it incorrectly will add to your maintenance costs and shop time because dirty parts wear out prematurely. It is unlikely that your ATV will break because of improper cleaning, but it can happen. When cleaning the Kawasaki, use shop rags, scrub brush, bucket, liquid cleaner and access to water. Many riders use a coin-operated car wash. Coin-operated car washes are convenient and quick. Improper use of the high water pressures, however, can do more damage than good to the ATV.

> *NOTE*
> *Simple Green is a safe biodegradable, non-toxic and non-flammable liquid cleaner that works well for washing ATVs and for removing grease and oil from the engine and suspension parts. Simple Green can be purchased at some supermarkets, hardware and garden stores, and discount supply houses. Follow the directions on the container for recommended mixing ratios.*

When cleaning the ATV, and especially when using a spray type degreaser, remember that what goes on the ATV rinses off and drips onto the driveway or

into the yard. If it is possible, use a degreaser at a coin-operated car wash. If the ATV is being cleaned at home, place thick cardboard or newspapers underneath the ATV to catch the oil and grease deposits as they are rinsed off.

CAUTION
Some of the steps in this procedure relate to an ATV that has been subjected to extremely dirty conditions, like mud or excessive road dirt. To avoid surface damage, carefully scrub the frame plastic side covers with a soft sponge or towel. Do not use a brush on these covers. The surfaces will scratch.

1. Place the ATV on level ground, and set the parking brake.
2. Check the following before washing the ATV:
    a. Make sure the gas filler cap (**Figure 4**) is on tight.
    b. Make sure the engine oil filler cap (**Figure 5**) is tight.
    c. Cover the muffler opening.

d. Remove the front fender cover, and cover the snorkel duct (**Figure 6**) opening with plastic or duct tape.
3. Wash the ATV from top to bottom with soapy water. Use the scrub brush to get excess dirt out of the wheel rims and engine cavities. Concentrate on the upper controls, engine, side panels, and gas tank during this wash cycle. Do not forget to wash dirt and mud from underneath the fenders, suspension and engine crankcase.
4. Concentrate the second wash cycle on the frame tubes and suspension.
5. Direct the hose underneath the engine and suspension. Wash these areas thoroughly.
6. The final wash is the rinse. Use cold water without soap, and spray the entire ATV again. Use as much time and care when rinsing the ATV as when washing it. Built up soap deposits quickly corrodes electrical connections and removes the natural oils from tires, causing premature cracks and wear. Make sure the ATV is thoroughly rinsed off.
7. Rock the ATV from side to side to allow any water that has collected on horizontal surfaces to drain off.
8. Remove the plastic cover or duct tape from the snorkel duct.
9. Uncover the muffler opening.
10. Start the engine, and let it idle so the engine burns off any internal moisture.
11. Before placing the ATV into the garage, wipe it dry with a soft terry cloth or chamois. Inspect the machine while drying it for further signs of dirt and grime. Make a quick visual inspection of the frame and other painted components. Paint any worn-down spots with touch-up paint to prevent rust from forming.

SPECIAL TIPS

Because of the extreme demands placed on an ATV, several points should be kept in mind when performing service and repair. The following items are general suggestions that may improve the overall life of the machine and help avoid costly failures.
1. Use a threadlocking compound such as ThreeBond No. TB1342 (blue) or Loctite No. 242 (blue) on all bolts and nuts, even if they are secured with lockwashers. This type of locking compound does not harden completely and allows easy removal of the bolt or nut. A screw or bolt lost from an

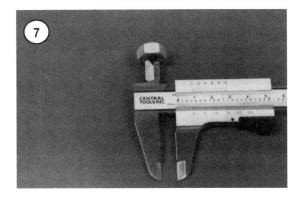

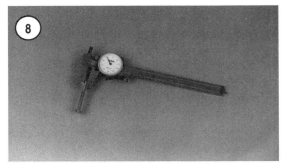

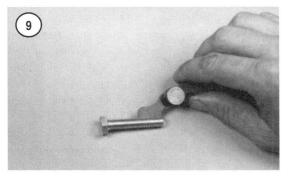

engine cover or bearing retainer could easily cause serious and expensive damage before its loss is noticed. Make sure the threads are clean and free of grease and oil. Clean the threads with contact cleaner before applying a small amount of locking compound. If too much locking compound is applied, it can work its way down the threads and bond together parts that should not be bonded to one another.

2. Use a hammer-driven impact tool to remove all bolts and screws, particularly engine cover screws. This tool helps prevent the rounding off of bolt heads.

3. When replacing missing or broken fasteners (bolts, nuts and screws), especially on the engine or frame components, always use Kawasaki replacement parts. They are specially designed for each application.

4. When replacing engine gaskets, always use Kawasaki replacement gaskets *without* sealer, unless otherwise indicated. These gaskets are designed to swell when they come in contact with oil. Gasket sealer prevents the gaskets from swelling as intended, which can result in oil leaks. Kawasaki gaskets are cut from material of the precise thickness. Installation of a too thick or too thin gasket in a critical area could cause engine damage.

TORQUE SPECIFICATIONS

The materials used in the manufacture of a Kawasaki may be subjected to uneven stresses if the fasteners used to hold the subassemblies are not installed and tightened correctly. Improper bolt tightening can cause cylinder head warpage, crankcase leaks, premature bearing and seal failure, and suspension failure from loose or missing fasteners. Use

an accurate torque wrench (described in this chapter) together with the torque specifications listed at the end of most chapters.

Torque specifications throughout this manual are expressed in Newton-meters (N•m) and foot-pounds (ft.-lb.).

Torque wrenches calibrated in meter kilograms can be used by converting Newton-meters to meter kilograms. Move the decimal point one place to the right; for example, 35 N•m = 3.5 m-kg. The exact mathematical conversion is 3.5 m-kg = 34.3 N•m.

To convert foot-pounds to Newton meters multiply the foot pounds specification by 1.3558. For example 150 ft.-lb. × 1.3558 = 203 N•m.

Refer to **Table 5** for standard torque specifications for various size screws, bolts and nuts not listed in the respective chapter tables. To use the table, first determine the size of the bolt or nut. Use a vernier caliper and measure the inside dimension of the threads of the nut (**Figure 7**) and across the threads for a bolt (**Figure 8**).

FASTENERS

The materials and designs of the various fasteners used on a Kawasaki are not arrived at by chance or accident. Fastener design determines the type of

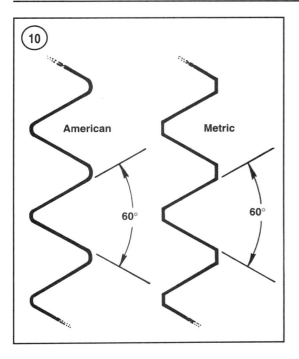

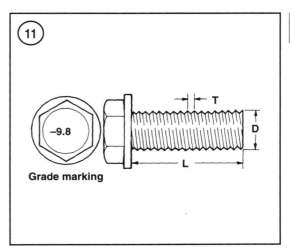

tool required to work the fastener. Fastener material is carefully selected to decrease the possibility of physical failure.

Nuts, bolts and screws are manufactured in a wide range of thread patterns. To join a nut and bolt, the diameter of the bolt and the diameter of the hole in the nut must be the same. It is just as important that the threads on both be properly matched.

The best way to tell if two fastener threads match is to turn the nut onto the bolt (or the bolt into the threaded hole in a piece of equipment) by hand. Be sure both pieces are clean. When excessive force is required, check the thread condition on each fastener. If the thread condition is good but the fasteners jam, the threads are not compatible. A thread pitch gauge (**Figure 9**) can be used to determine pitch. Kawasaki motorcycles are manufactured with ISO (International Organization for Standardization) metric fasteners. The threads are cut differently than those of American fasteners (**Figure 10**).

Most threads are cut so that the fastener must be turned clockwise to tighten it. These are called right-hand threads. Some fasteners have left-hand threads. These must be turned counterclockwise to be tightened. Left-hand threads are used in locations where normal rotation of the equipment would tend to loosen a right-hand threaded fastener.

ISO Metric Screw Threads (Bolts, Nuts and Screws)

ISO (International Organization for Standardization) metric threads come in three standard thread sizes: coarse, fine and constant pitch. The ISO coarse pitch is used for almost all common fastener applications. The fine pitch thread is used on certain precision tools and instruments. The constant pitch thread is used mainly on machine parts and not for fasteners. The constant pitch thread, however, is used on all metric thread spark plugs.

Metric screws and bolts are classified by length (L, **Figure 11**), nominal diameter (D) and distance between thread crests (T). A typical bolt might be identified by the numbers 8—1.25 × 130, which indicates that the bolt has a nominal diameter of 8 mm, the distance between thread crests is 1.25 mm and bolt length is 130 mm.

WARNING
Do not *install screws or bolts with a lower strength grade classification than what was installed originally by the manufacturer. Doing so may cause engine or equipment failure and possible injury.*

The measurement across two flats on the head of the bolt (**Figure 12**) indicates the proper wrench size to use. **Figure 13** shows how to measure bolt diameter. When buying a bolt from a dealer or parts store, it is important to know how to specify bolt length. The correct way to measure bolt length is by measuring from underneath the bolt head to the end of the bolt (**Figure 14**). Always measure bolt length in this manner to avoid buying bolts that are too long.

Machine Screws

There are many different types of machine screws. **Figure 15** shows a number of screw heads requiring different types of turning tools. Heads are also designed to protrude above the metal (round) or slightly recessed in the metal (flat).

Nuts

Nuts are manufactured in a variety of types and sizes. Most are hexagonal (6-sided) and fit on bolts, screws and studs with the same diameter and pitch. **Figure 16** shows several types of nuts. The common nut is generally used with a lockwasher. A self-locking nut has a nylon insert that prevents the nut from loosening. No lockwasher is required. Wing nuts are designed for fast removal by hand. Wing nuts are used for convenience in non-critical locations.

To indicate the size of a metric nut, manufacturers specify the diameter of the opening and the thread pitch. This is similar to bolt specifications but without the length dimension. The measurement across two flats on the nut indicates the proper wrench size to be used (**Figure 17**).

Self-Locking Fasteners

Several types of bolts, screws and nuts incorporate a system that develops an interference between the bolt, screw, nut or tapped hole threads. Interference is achieved in various ways: by distorting threads, coating threads with dry adhesive or nylon, distorting the top of an all-metal nut, using a nylon insert in the center or at the top of a nut, etc.

Self-locking fasteners offer increased holding strength and vibration resistance. Some self-locking fasteners can be reused if in good condition. Others, like the nylon insert nut, form an initial locking condition when the nut is first installed. The nylon forms closely to the bolt thread pattern, and thus reduces any tendency for the nut to loosen. For maximum safety, *always discard* previously

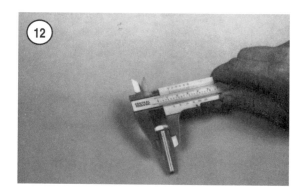

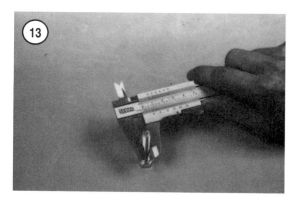

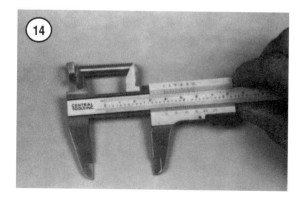

used self-locking fasteners, and install new ones during reassembly.

Washers

There are two basic types of washers: flat washers and lockwashers. Flat washers are simple discs with a hole to fit a screw or bolt. Lockwashers are designed to prevent a fastener from working loose due to vibration, expansion and contraction. Washers can be used in the following functions:

    a. As spacers.

1

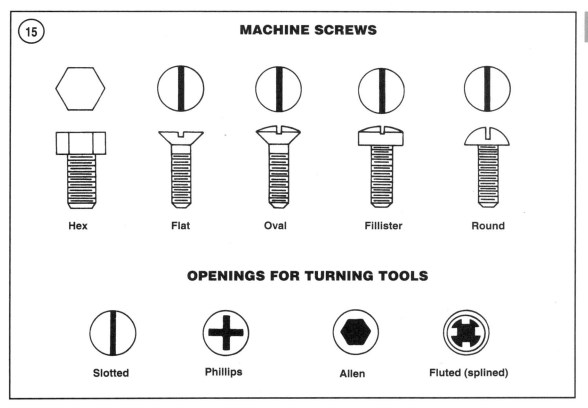

MACHINE SCREWS

Hex   Flat   Oval   Fillister   Round

OPENINGS FOR TURNING TOOLS

Slotted   Phillips   Allen   Fluted (splined)

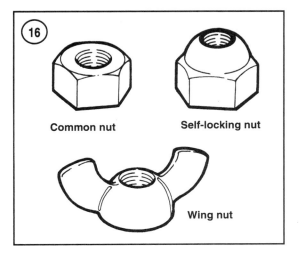

Common nut   Self-locking nut

Wing nut

ing surface. This allows the fastener to be turned easily with a tool.

b. To prevent galling or damage of the equipment by the fastener.

c. To help distribute fastener load during torquing.

d. As seals.

Note that flat washers are often used between a lockwasher and a fastener to provide a smooth bear-

CAUTION
As much care should be given to the selection and purchase of washers as that given to bolts, nuts and other fasteners. Beware of washers that are made of thin and weak materials. These will deform and crush the first time they are used in a high torque application.

Cotter Pins

Cotter pins (**Figure 18**) are used to secure special kinds of fasteners. The threaded stud, bolt or axle must have a hole in it. The nut or nut lock piece, on the other hand, must have castellations around which the cotter pin ends wrap. Do not reuse cotter pins.

Circlips

Circlips can be internal or external design. They are used to retain items on shafts (external type) or within tubes (internal type). In some applications, circlips of varying thickness are used to control the end play of assemblies. These are often called selective circlips. Replace circlips during installation because removal weakens and deforms them.

Two basic styles of circlips are available: machined and stamped circlips. Machined circlips (**Figure 19**) can be installed in either direction (shaft or housing) because both faces are machined, thus creating two sharp edges. Stamped circlips (**Figure 20**) are manufactured with one sharp edge and one rounded edge. When installing stamped circlips in a thrust situation (transmission shafts, fork tubes, etc.), the sharp edge must face away from the part producing the thrust. When installing circlips, observe

the following:

   a. Compress or expand circlips only enough to install them.

   b. After the circlip is installed, make sure it is completely seated in its groove.

   c. Transmission circlips become worn with use and increase side play. For this reason, always use new circlips whenever a transmission is reassembled.

LUBRICANTS

Periodic lubrication helps ensure long life for any type of equipment. The type of lubricant used is just as important as the lubrication service itself, although in an emergency the wrong type of lubricant is better than none at all. The following paragraphs describe the types of lubricants most often used on ATVs. Be sure to follow the manufacturer's recommendations for lubricant types.

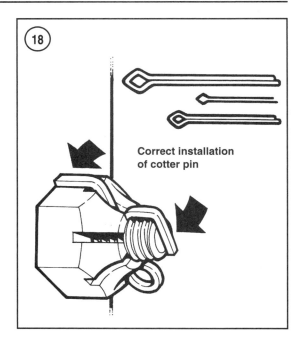

Correct installation of cotter pin

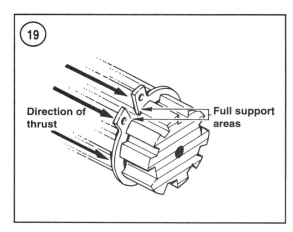

Direction of thrust

Full support areas

Generally all liquid lubricants are called oil. They may be mineral-based (including petroleum bases), natural-based (vegetable and animal bases), synthetic-based or emulsions (mixtures). Grease is an oil to which a thickening base has been added so that the end product is semi-solid. Grease is often classified by the type of thickener added; lithium soap is commonly used.

Engine Oil

Engine oil is classified by two standards, the American Petroleum Institute (API) service classification and the Society of Automotive Engi-

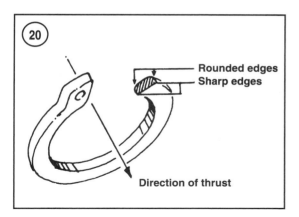

neers (SAE) viscosity rating. This information is on the oil container label. Two letters indicate the API service classification. The number or sequence of numbers and letter (10W-40 for example) is the oil's viscosity rating. The API service classification and the SAE viscosity index are not an indication of oil quality.

The service classification indicates that the oil meets specific lubrication standards. The first letter in the classification, *S*, indicates that the oil is for gasoline engines. The second letter indicates the standard the oil satisfies. The classificaton started with the letter *A* and is currently at the letter *J*.

Always use an oil with a classification recommended by the manufacturer. Engine damage can occur by using an oil with a classification different than that recommended.

Kawasaki models described in this manual require oil with a SE, SF or SG classification.

Viscosity is an indication of the oil's thickness. Thin oils have a lower number while thick oils have a higher number. Engine oils fall into the 5 to 50-weight range for single-grade oils.

Most manufacturers recommend multigrade oil. See **Table 3** in Chapter Three. These oils perform efficiently across a wide range of operating conditions. Multigrade oils are identified by a *W* after the first number, which indicates the low temperature viscosity.

Engine oils are most commonly mineral (petroleum) based; however synthetic and semi-synthetic types are used more frequently. Follow the manufacturer's recommendation for type, classification and viscosity when selecting engine oil.

Grease

Greases are graded by the National Lubricating Grease Institute (NLGI). Greases are graded by number according to the consistency of the grease; these range from No. 000 to No. 6, with No. 6 being the most solid. A typical multipurpose grease is NLGI No. 2. For specific applications, equipment manufacturers may require grease with an additive such as molybdenum disulfide (MoS_2).

RTV GASKET SEALANT

Room temperature vulcanizing (RTV) sealant is used on some pre-formed gaskets and to seal some components. RTV is a silicone gel supplied in tubes and can be purchased in a number of different colors.

Moisture in the air causes RTV to cure. RTV has a shelf life of one year and will not cure properly when the shelf life has expired. Check the expiration date on an RTV tube before using it. Always replace the cap on the tube as soon as possible, and keep partially used tubes tightly sealed.

Applying RTV Sealant

Clean all gasket residue from mating surfaces. Surfaces should be clean and free of oil. Remove all RTV gasket material from bolt holes. If left in place, it can cause a "hydraulic" effect and influence bolt torque.

Apply RTV sealant in a continuous bead. Circle all mounting holes unless otherwise specified. Torque mating parts within 10 minutes of application.

GASKET REMOVER

Stubborn gaskets can present a problem during engine service. They can take a long time to remove, and incorrect use of gasket scraping tools can damage the gasket mating surfaces. To quickly and safely remove stubborn gaskets, use a spray gasket remover. Spray gasket remover can be purchased through automotive parts houses. Follow the manufacturer's directions for use.

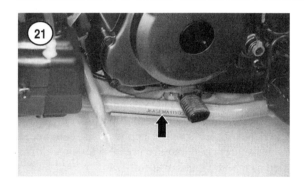

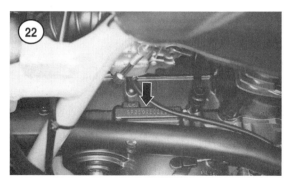

THREADLOCKING COMPOUND

Use a threadlocking compound to help secure many of the fasteners on the ATV. Threadlocking compound locks fasteners against vibration loosening and seal against leaks. The following thread locking compounds are recommended for many threadlock requirements described in this manual.

    a. ThreeBond No. 1342 (blue): low strength, frequent repair.
    b. Loctite No. 242 (blue): low strength, frequent repair.
    c. ThreeBond No. 1360 (green): medium strength, high temperature.
    d. ThreeBond No. 1333B (red): medium strength, bearing and stud lock.
    e. ThreeBond No. 1303 (orange): high strength, frequent repair.
    f. Loctite No. 271 (red): high strength, frequent repair.

EXPENDABLE SUPPLIES

Use certain expendable supplies during maintenance and repair work. These include grease, oil, gasket cement, rags and cleaning solvent. Ask the dealership for the special locking compounds, silicone lubricants and other products that make ATV maintenance simpler and easier. Cleaning solvent or kerosene is available at some service stations, paint or hardware stores.

Be sure to follow the manufacturer's instructions and warnings listed on the label of any product. Some cleaning supplies are very caustic and are dangerous if not used properly.

WARNING
Reduce the risk of fire by storing shop rags used to absorb oil, grease and

chemical solvents in a sealed metal container until they can be washed or properly discarded.

NOTE
To prevent solvent and other chemicals from being absorbed into your skin, wear a pair of petroleum-resistance gloves when cleaning parts. These can be purchased through industrial supply houses or hardware stores.

SERIAL NUMBERS

Kawasaki makes frequent changes during a model year, some minor, some relatively major. When ordering parts from the dealership or other parts distributor, always order by frame and engine serial numbers. The vehicle identification number is stamped on the left-side lower frame member (**Figure 21**). The engine number is stamped on the right side of the crankcase (**Figure 22**). The carburetor identification number is stamped on the right side of the carburetor body (**Figure 23**).

Record these numbers and have them available when purchasing parts. Compare new parts to old

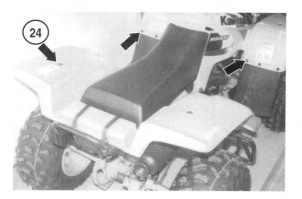

before buying them. If they are not alike, have the parts manager explain the difference. **Table 1** lists VIN and engine serial numbers for the models covered in this manual.

WARNING AND INFORMATION LABELS

A number of warning labels have been attached on the Kawasaki. These labels contain information that is important to safety when operating, transporting and storing the ATV. Refer to information labels on the fenders (**Figure 24**), air filter housing (**Figure 25**) and other places on the vehicle. Refer to the Owner's Manual for a description and location of each label. If a label is missing, order a replacement label from a Kawasaki dealership.

BASIC HAND TOOLS

Many of the procedures in this manual can be carried out with simple hand tools and test equipment familiar to the average home mechanic. Keep tools clean and in a tool box. Keep them organized with

the sockets and related drives together, the open-end combination wrenches together, etc. After using a tool, wipe off dirt and grease with a clean cloth and return the tool to its correct place.

High quality tools are essential. When starting to build a tool collection avoid poor grade tools. They are usually made of inferior materials that wear quickly and are uncomfortable to use.

Quality tools are made of alloy steel and are heat treated for greater strength. They are lighter and better balanced than poorly made ones. Their surface is smooth, making them a pleasure to work with and easy to clean. The initial cost of good tools may be more, but they are economical in the long run.

Screwdrivers

The screwdriver is a very basic tool, but if used improperly it will do more damage than good. The slot on a screw has a particular dimension and shape. A screwdriver must be selected to conform to that shape. Use a small screwdriver for small screws and a large one for large screws or the screw head will be damaged.

Two basic types of screwdriver are required: common (flat-blade) screwdrivers (**Figure 26**) and Phillips screwdrivers (**Figure 27**).

Screwdrivers are available in sets, which often include an assortment of common and Phillips blades. If you buy them individually, buy at least the following:

    a. Common screwdriver-5/16 × 6 in. blade.
    b. Common screwdriver-3/8 × 12 in. blade.
    c. Phillips screwdriver-size 2 tip, 6 in. blade.
    d. Phillips screwdriver-size 3 tip, 6 and 10 in. blades.

Use screwdrivers only for driving screws. Never use a screwdriver for prying or chiseling metal. Do not try to remove a Phillips or Allen head screw with a common screwdriver (unless the screw has a combination head that accepts either type); the head can be damaged so that the proper tool will be unable to remove it. Keep screwdrivers in the proper condition and they will last longer and perform better. Always keep the tip of a common screwdriver in good condition. **Figure 28** shows how to grind the tip to the proper shape if it becomes damaged. Note the symmetrical sides of the tip.

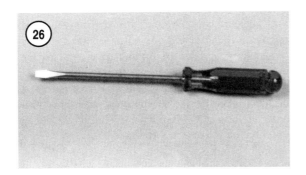

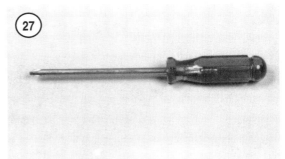

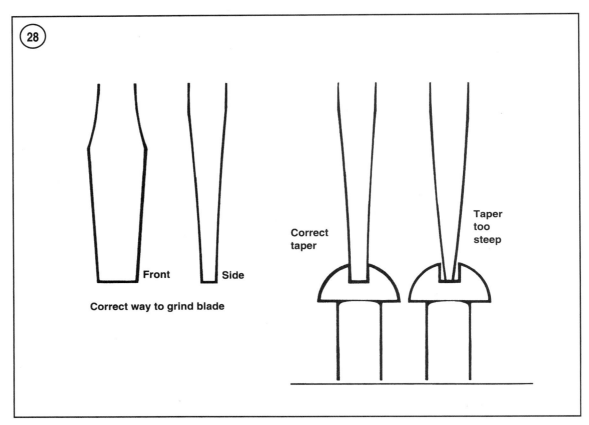

Front   Side

Correct way to grind blade

Correct taper

Taper too steep

Pliers

Pliers come in a wide range of types and sizes. Pliers are useful for cutting, bending and crimping. Do not use them to cut hardened objects or to turn bolts or nuts. **Figure 29** shows several pliers useful in motorcycle repair. Each type of pliers has a specialized function. Slip-joint pliers are general purpose pliers. Use these for holding things and for bending.

Needlenose pliers are used to hold or bend small objects. Adjustable pliers hold various sizes of ob- jects; the jaws remain parallel to grip around objects uch as pipe or tubing. There are many more types of pliers. The ones described here are most suitable for ATV repairs.

Locking Pliers

Locking pliers or vise-grips (**Figure 30**) are used to hold objects very tightly like a vise. Avoid using them unless necessary since their sharp jaws will permanently scar any objects they hold. Locking

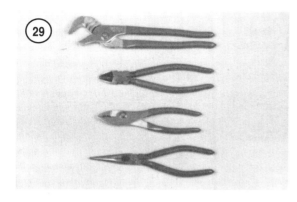

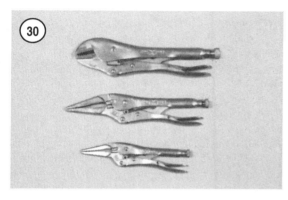

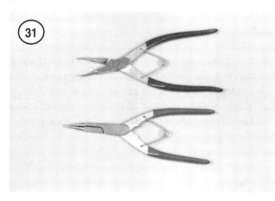

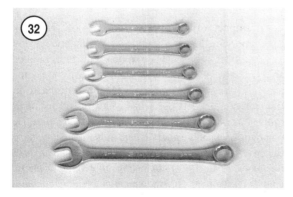

pliers are available in many types (**Figure 30**) for more specific tasks.

Circlip Pliers

Circlip pliers (**Figure 31**) are made for removing and installing circlips. External pliers (spreading) are used to remove circlips that fit on the outside of a shaft. Internal pliers (squeezing) are used to remove circlips which fit inside a gear or housing.

> *WARNING*
> *Always wear safety glasses when removing and installing circlips. They may slip and fly off.*

Box, Open-end and Combination Wrenches

Box-end, open-end and combination wrenches are available in sets or separately in a variety of sizes. On open- and box-end wrenches, the number stamped near the end refers to the distance between two parallel flats on the bolt head or nut. On combination wrenches, the number is stamped near the center.

Box-end wrenches require clear overhead access to the fastener but can work well in situations where the fastener head is close to another part. They grip on all six edges of a fastener for a very secure grip. They are available in either 6-point or 12-point. A 6-point wrench has superior holding power and durability, but it requires a greater swing radius. A 12-point wrench works better in situations where the swing radius is limited.

Open-end wrenches are fast and work best in areas with limited overhead access. Their wide flat jaws make them unstable for situations where the bolt or nut is in a bore or close to the edge of a casting. These wrenches grip only two flats of a fastener so if either the fastener head or the wrench jaws are worn, the wrench may slip off.

Combination wrenches (**Figure 32**) have an open-end on one side and a box-end on the other with both ends being the same size. These wrenches offer the greatest versatility.

Adjustable (Crescent) Wrenches

An adjustable or crescent wrench can be adjusted to fit nearly any nut or bolt head that has clear ac-

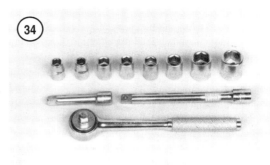

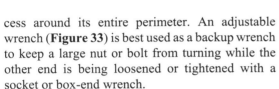

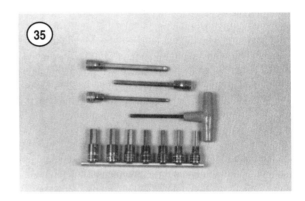

cess around its entire perimeter. An adjustable wrench (**Figure 33**) is best used as a backup wrench to keep a large nut or bolt from turning while the other end is being loosened or tightened with a socket or box-end wrench.

Adjustable wrenches have only two gripping surfaces which make them more subject to slipping off the fastener, damaging the part and possibly causing personal injury. The fact that one jaw is adjustable only aggravates this shortcoming.

These wrenches are directional; the solid jaw must be the one transmitting the force. If the adjustable jaw is used to transmit the force, it will loosen and possibly slip off.

Socket Wrenches

This type is the fastest, safest and most convenient wrench to use. Sockets, which attach to a ratchet handle, are available with 6-point or 12-point openings and with 1/4, 3/8, 1/2 and 3/4 in. drives. The drive size indicates the size of the square hole which mates with the ratchet handle (**Figure 34**).

Allen Wrenches

Allen wrenches are available in sets or separately in a variety of sizes. These sets come in SAE and metric sizes. Allen bolts are sometimes called socket bolts. Sometimes the bolts are difficult to reach, and it is suggested that a variety of Allen wrenches be purchased (like the socket driven, T-handle and extension type) as shown in **Figure 35**.

Torque Wrench

A torque wrench is used with a socket to measure how tightly a nut or bolt is installed. They come in a wide price range and with either 1/4, 3/8 or 1/2 in. square drives (**Figure 36**). The drive size indicates the size of the square drive that mates with the socket.

Impact Driver

An impact driver makes removal of fasteners easy and eliminates damage to bolts and screw slots. Impact drivers (**Figure 37**) and interchangeable bits are available at most large hardware, motorcycle or auto parts stores. Do not purchase an inferior one. It will not work as well and requires more force than a good one. Sockets can also be used with a hand impact driver; however, make sure that the socket is designed for use with an impact driver or air tool. Do not use regular hand sockets. They may shatter during use.

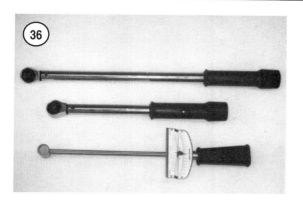

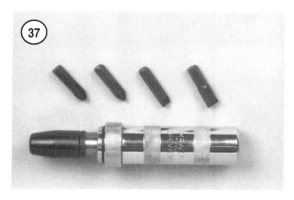

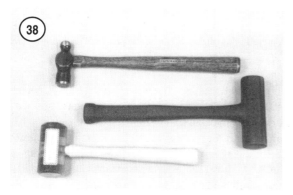

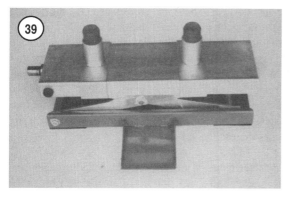

Hammers

The correct hammer (**Figure 38**) is necessary for repairs. A soft-faced hammer (rubber or plastic) or a soft-faced hammer filled with leadshot is sometimes necessary during engine disassembly. Never use a metal-faced hammer on engine or suspension parts. Excessive damage results in most cases. The same amount of force can be produced with a soft-faced hammer. Use a metal-faced hammer when using a hand impact driver.

Support Jacks

The correct type of support jack is necessary for many routine service or major component replacement procedures on the ATV. When it is necessary to raise either the front or rear of the vehicle, the Centerstand Scissor Jack available through Kawasaki dealerships from K&L Supply, Santa Clara, CA (**Figure 39**) is suitable for most service procedures. It is adjustable and is very stable for use with the frame configuration of this vehicle.

PRECISION MEASURING TOOLS

Accurate measurement is important when performing mechanical service. Many of the service procedures in this manual require accurate measurements. These include basic checks such as engine compression and spark plug gap to the more complex, involving internal engine and transmission assemblies.

Precision measuring tools are expensive. If the proper tools are not available, have the checks and measurements performed at a Kawasaki dealership, good motorcycle repair shop or a machine shop as required. As skill and desire to perform more in depth service work increase, it may prove economical to purchase these specialized tools.

Feeler Gauge

Feeler gauges come in assorted sets and types (**Figure 40**). The feeler gauge is made of either a piece of flat or round hardened steel of a specified thickness. Wire gauges are used to measure spark plug gap. Flat gauges are used for other measurements. Feeler gauges are also designed for special-

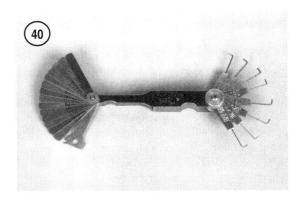

ized uses. For example, the end of a gauge is usually small and angled to facilitate checking valve clearances.

Vernier Caliper, Dial Caliper and Digital Electronic Caliper

These are valuable tools for reading inside, outside and depth measurements with semi-close precision. The vernier caliper is shown in **Figure 41**. Although this type of tool is not as precise as a micrometer, they allow reasonable, non-close tolerance measurements, typically to within 0.025 mm (0.001 in.). Common uses of a vernier caliper are measuring the length of the clutch springs, the thickness of clutch plates, shims and thrust washers, brake pad or lining thickness or the depth of a bearing bore. The jaws of the caliper must be clean and free of burrs at all times in order to obtain an accurate measurement. There are several types of vernier calipers available. The standard vernier caliper has a highly accurate graduated scale on the handle (**Figure 42**) in which the measurements must be calculated, following the manufacturer's instructions. A dial indicator caliper is equipped with a small dial and needle that indicates the measurement reading. The digital electronic type, however, uses an LCD display that shows the measurement on a display screen. Some vernier calipers must be zeroed prior to making a measurement to ensure accuracy. Refer to the manufacturer's instructions for this procedure.

Outside Micrometers

An outside micrometer is a precision tool used to accurately measure parts using the decimal divi-

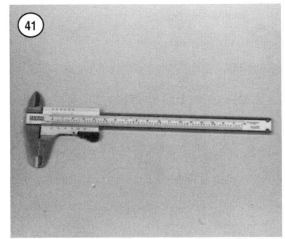

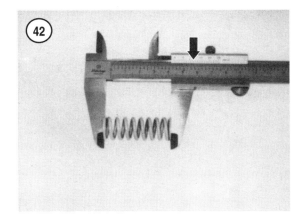

sions of the inch or meter (**Figure 43**). While there are many types and styles of micrometers, this section describes steps on how to use the outside micrometer. The outside micrometer is the most common type of micrometer used when servicing an ATV. It accurately measures the outside diameter, length and thickness of parts used on these vehicles. These parts include pistons, piston pins, crankshaft, piston rings, transmission shafts and various shims. The outside micrometer is also used to measure the dimension taken by a small hole gauge or a telescoping gauge described later in this section. After the small hole gauge or telescoping gauge has been carefully expanded within the bore of the component, carefully remove the gauge and measure the outer dimension of the gauge with the outside micrometer.

Other types of micrometers include the depth micrometer and screw thread micrometer. **Figure 44**

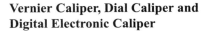

43

DECIMAL PLACE VALUES*

0.1	Indicates 1/10 (one tenth of an inch or millimeter)
0.010	Indicates 1/100 (one one-hundreth of an inch or millimeter)
0.001	Indicates 1/1,000 (one one-thousandth of an inch or millimeter)

*This chart represents the values of figures placed to the right of the decimal point. Use it when reading decimals from one-tenth to one one-thousandth of an inch or millimeter. It is not a conversion chart (for example: 0.001 in. is not equal to 0.001 mm).

44

STANDARD INCH MICROMETER

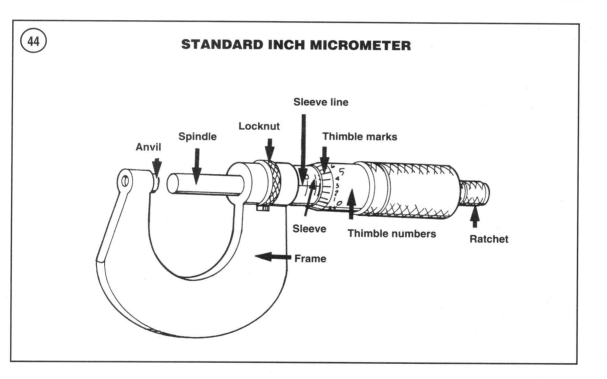

Sleeve line
Locknut
Spindle
Thimble marks
Anvil
Sleeve
Thimble numbers
Ratchet
Frame

identifies the various parts of the outside micrometer.

Micrometer Range

A micrometer's size indicates the minimum and maximum size of a part that it can measure. The usual sizes are: 0-1 in. (0-25 mm), 1-2 in. (25-50 mm), 2-3 in. (50-75 mm) and 3-4 in. (75-100 mm). These micrometers use fixed anvils.

Some micrometers use the same frame with interchangeable anvils of different lengths. This allows the installation of the correct length anvil for a particular job. For example, a 0-4 in. interchangeable micrometer is equipped with four different length anvils. While purchasing one or two micrometers to cover a range from 0-4 in. or 0-6 in. is less expen-

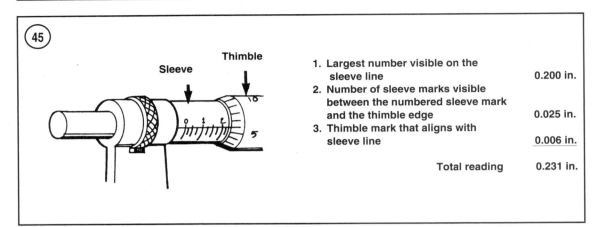

(45)

Sleeve   Thimble

1. Largest number visible on the
   sleeve line   0.200 in.
2. Number of sleeve marks visible
   between the numbered sleeve mark
   and the thimble edge   0.025 in.
3. Thimble mark that aligns with
   sleeve line   0.006 in.

                        Total reading   0.231 in.

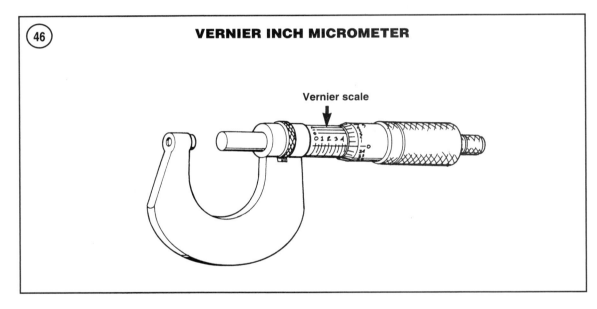

(46)   **VERNIER INCH MICROMETER**

Vernier scale

---

sive, its overall frame size makes it less convenient to use.

How to Read a Micrometer

When reading a micrometer, numbers are taken from different scales and then added together. The following sections describe how to read the standard inch micrometer, the vernier inch micrometer, the standard metric micrometer and the metric vernier micrometer.

Standard inch micrometer

The standard inch micrometer is accurate up to one-thousand of an inch. (0.001 in.). The heart of

the micrometer is its spindle screw with 40 threads per inch. Every turn of the thimble moves the spindle 1/40 of an inch or 0.025 in..

Before learning how to read a micrometer, study the markings and part names in **Figure 44**. Turn the micrometer's thimble until its zero mark aligns with the zero mark on the sleeve line. Now turn the thimble counterclockwise and align the next thimble mark with the sleeve line. The micrometer now reads 0.001 in. (one one-thousandths) of an inch. Thus, each thimble mark is equal to 0.001 in. Every fifth thimble mark is numbered to help with reading: 0, 5, 15 and 20.

Reset the micrometer so that the thimble and sleeve-line zero marks align. Then turn the thimble counterclockwise one complete revolution and

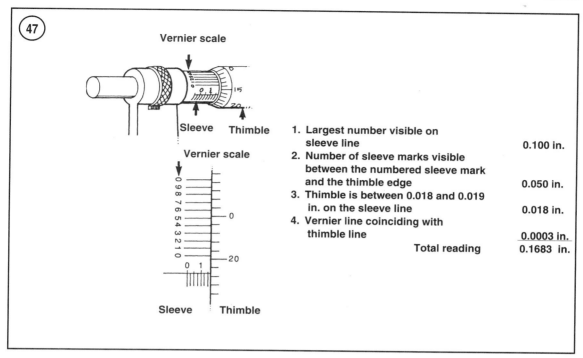

1. Largest number visible on sleeve line	0.100 in.
2. Number of sleeve marks visible between the numbered sleeve mark and the thimble edge	0.050 in.
3. Thimble is between 0.018 and 0.019 in. on the sleeve line	0.018 in.
4. Vernier line coinciding with thimble line	0.0003 in.
Total reading	0.1683 in.

align the thimble zero mark with the first line in the sleeve line. The micrometer now reads 0.025 in. (twenty-five thousandths) of an inch. Thus each sleeve line represents 0.025 in.

Now turn the thimble counterclockwise while counting the sleeve line marks. Every fourth mark on the sleeve line is marked with a number ranging from 1 through 9. Manufacturers usually mark the last mark on the sleeve with a 0. This indicates the end of the micrometer's measuring range. Each sleeve number represents 0.100 in. For example, the number 1 represents 0.100 in. and the number 9 represents 0.900 in.

When reading a standard micrometer, take the three measurements described and add them together. The sum of the three readings is the measurement in a thousandth of an inch. (0.001 in.).

To read a micrometer, perform the following steps and refer to the example in **Figure 45**.
1. Read the sleeve line to find the largest number visible-each sleeve number mark equals 0.100 in.
2. Count the number of sleeve marks visible between the numbered sleeve mark and the thimble edge-each sleeve mark equals 0.025 in. If there is no visible sleeve mark, go to Step 3.
3. Read the thimble mark that aligns with the sleeve line-each thimble mark equals 0.001 in.

NOTE
If a thimble mark does not align exactly with the sleeve line but falls between two lines, estimate the fraction or decimal amount between the lines.

4. Adding the micrometer readings in Steps 1, 2 and 3 gives the actual measurement.

Vernier inch micrometer

A vernier micrometer can accurately measure in ten-thousandths of an inch. (0.0001 in.). While it has the same markings as the standard inch micrometer, a vernier scale scribed on the sleeve (**Figure 46**) makes it unique. The vernier scale consists of 11 equally spaced lines marked 0-9 with a 0 on each end. These lines run parallel on the top of the sleeve where each line is equal to 0.0001 in. Thus, the vernier scale divides a thousandth of an in. (0.001 in.) into ten-thousandths of an inch. (0.0001 in.).

To read the vernier micrometer, perform the following steps and refer to the example in **Figure 47**:
1. Read the micrometer in the same way as on the standard inch micrometer. This is the initial reading.
2. If a thimble mark aligns exactly with the sleeve line, reading the vernier scale is not necessary. If a

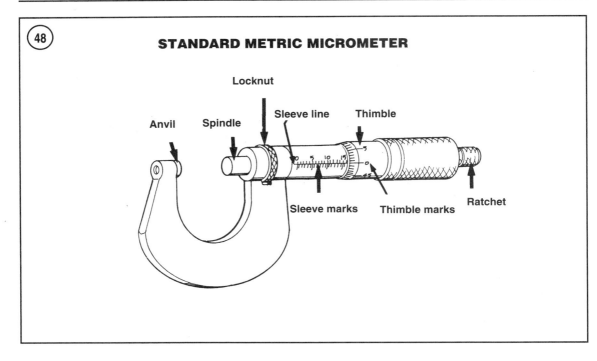

STANDARD METRIC MICROMETER

Locknut

Anvil   Spindle   Sleeve line   Thimble

Sleeve marks   Thimble marks   Ratchet

thimble mark does not align exactly with the sleeve line, read the vernier scale in Step 3.

3. Read the vernier scale to find which vernier mark aligns with the one thimble mark. The number of that vernier mark is the number in ten-thousandths of an inch to add to the initial reading taken in Step 1.

Metric micrometer

The metric micrometer is very similar to the standard inch micrometer. The differences are the graduations on the thimble and sleeve as shown in **Figure 48**.

The standard metric micrometer accurately measures to one one-hundredths of a millimeter (0.01 mm). On the metric micrometer, the spindle screw is ground with a thread pitch of one-half millimeter (0.5 mm). Thus, every turn of the thimble moves the spindle 0.5 mm.

The sleeve line is graduated in millimeters and half millimeters. The marks on the upper side of the sleeve line are equal to 1.00 mm . Every fifth mark above the sleeve line is marked with a number. The actual numbers depend on the size of the micrometer. For example, on a 0-25 mm micrometer, the sleeve marks are numbered 0, 5, 10, 15, 20 and 25. On a 25-50 mm micrometer, the sleeve marks are

numbered 25, 30, 35, 40, 45 and 50. This numbering sequence continues with larger micrometers (50-75 and 75-100). Each mark on the lower side of the sleeve line is equal to 0.5 mm.

The thimble scale is divided into fifty graduations where one graduation is equal to 0.01 mm. Every fifth graduation is numbered to help with reading from 0-45. The thimble edge is used to indicate which sleeve markings to read.

To read the metric micrometer, add the number of millimeters and half-millimeters on the sleeve line to the number of one one-hundredth millimeters on the thimble. To do so, perform the following steps and refer to the example in **Figure 49**:

1. Take the first reading by counting the number of marks visible on the upper sleeve line. Record the reading.

2. Look below the sleeve line to see if a lower mark is visible directly past the upper line mark. If so, add 0.50 to the first reading.

3. Now read the thimble mark that aligns with the sleeve line. Record this reading.

NOTE
If a thimble mark does not align exactly with the sleeve line but falls between the two lines, estimate the decimal amount between the lines.

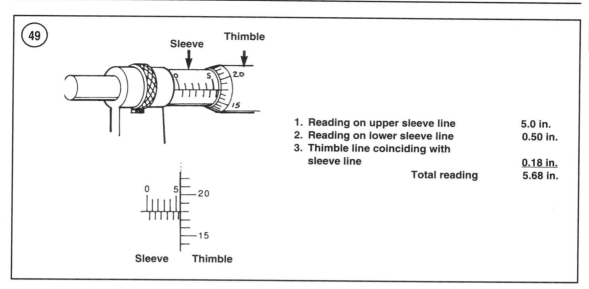

1. Reading on upper sleeve line		5.0 in.
2. Reading on lower sleeve line		0.50 in.
3. Thimble line coinciding with sleeve line		0.18 in.
	Total reading	5.68 in.

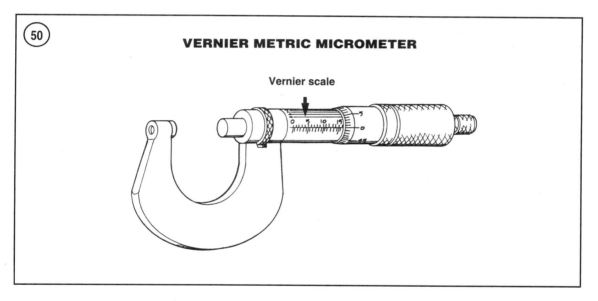

VERNIER METRIC MICROMETER

Vernier scale

4. Adding the micrometer readings in Steps 1, 2 and 3 gives the actual measurement.

Metric vernier micrometer

A metric micrometer can accurately measure to two thousandths of a millimeter (0.002 mm). While it has the same markings as the standard metric micrometer, a vernier scale scribed on the sleeve (**Figure 50**) makes it unique. The vernier scale consists of five equally spaced lines 0, 2, 4, 6 and 8. These lines run parallel on the top of the sleeve where each line is equal to 0.002 mm.

To read the metric vernier micrometer, perform the following steps and refer to the example in **Figure 51**:

1. Read the metric vernier micrometer the same way as with the metric standard micrometer. This is the initial reading.

2. If a thimble mark aligns exactly with the sleeve line, reading the vernier scale is not necessary. If a thimble line does not align exactly with the sleeve line, read the vernier scale in Step 3.

3. Read the vernier scale to find which mark aligns with one thimble mark. The number on the vernier

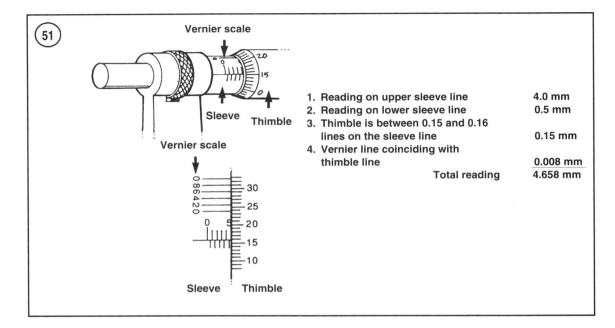

1. Reading on upper sleeve line   4.0 mm
2. Reading on lower sleeve line   0.5 mm
3. Thimble is between 0.15 and 0.16
   lines on the sleeve line   0.15 mm
4. Vernier line coinciding with
   thimble line   0.008 mm
          Total reading   4.658 mm

scale is the number in thousands on a millimeter to add to the initial reading taken in Step 1.

Micrometer Accuracy Check

Before using a micrometer check its accuracy as follows:

1. Make sure the anvil and spindle faces are clean and dry.

2. To check a 0-1 in. (0-25 mm) micrometer, perform the following:

  a. Turn the thimble until the spindle contacts the anvil. If the micrometer has a ratchet stop, use it to ensure that the proper amount of pressure is applied against the contact surfaces.

  b. Read the micrometer. If the adjustment is correct, the 0 mark on the thimble will be aligned exactly with the 0 mark on the sleeve line. If the 0 marks do not align, the micrometer is out of adjustment.

  c. To adjust the micrometer, follow the manufacturer's instructions provided with the micrometer.

3. To check the accuracy of a micrometer above the 1 in. (25 mm) size, perform the following:

  a. Manufacturers usually supply a standard gauge with their micrometers. A standard is a steel block, disc or rod that is machined to an exact size to check the accuracy of the mi-

crometer. For example, a 1-2 in. micrometer is equipped with a 1 inch standard gauge. A 25-50 mm micrometer is equipped with a 25 mm standard gauge.

  b. Place the standard gauge between the micrometer's spindle and anvil, and measure the outside diameter or length in the same manner as measuring a component from a vehicle. Read the micrometer. If the adjustment is correct, the 0 mark on the thimble will be aligned exactly with the sleeve line. If the 0 marks do not align, the micrometer is out of adjustment.

  c. To adjust the micrometer, follow the manufacturer's instructions provided with the micrometer.

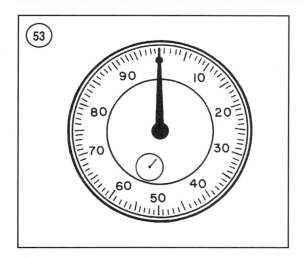

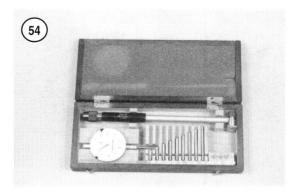

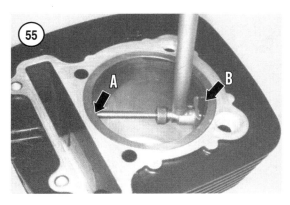

Proper Care of a Micrometer

Because the micrometer is a precision instrument, it must be used correctly and with great care. When using and storing a micrometer, refer to the following:

1. Store a micrometer in its box or in a protected place where dust, oil and other debris cannot come in contact with it. Do not store micrometers in a drawer with other tools or hang them on a tool board.

2. When storing a 0-1 in. (0-25 mm) micrometer, the spindle and anvil must not contact each other. If they do, rust may form on the contact ends or the spindle will be damaged from temperature changes.

3. Do not clean a micrometer with compressed air. Dirt forced under pressure into the tool can cause premature damage.

4. Occasionally lubricate the micrometer with light weight oil to prevent rust and corrosion.

5. Before using a micrometer, check its accuracy as previously described in this section.

Dial Indicator

A dial indicator (**Figure 52**) is a precision tool used to check dimensional variations, both radial and axial runout, of machined parts such as transmission shafts and to check crankshaft runout and end play. A dial indicator may also be used to locate the piston at a specific position when checking ignition timing. For ATV service procedures, select a dial indicator with a continuous dial (**Figure 53**). Several different mounting types are available, including magnetic stands that attach to iron or steel surfaces, a clamp that can be attached to various components and a spark plug adapter that locates the probe of the dial indicator through the spark plug hole. See *Magnetic Stand* in this chapter. The text in each chapter indicates the type of mount necessary for each specific measuring procedure.

Cylinder Bore Gauge

The cylinder bore gauge is a very specialized precision tool. The gauge set shown in **Figure 54** consists of a dial indicator, handle and a number of different length adapters for different bore sizes. The bore gauge is used to make cylinder bore measurements such as bore size, taper and out-of-round. Depending on the bore gauge, it can sometimes be used to measure brake caliper and master cylinder bore sizes. In some cases, an outside micrometer must be used together with the bore gauge to determine bore dimensions.

Select the correct length adapter (A, **Figure 55**) for the size of the bore to be measured. Zero the bore gauge according to manufacturer's instructions and insert the bore gauge into the cylinder. Carefully move the gauge around in the bore to make sure it is centered and that the gauge foot (B, **Figure 55**) is sitting correctly on the bore surface. This is necessary in order to obtain a correct reading. Refer to the manufacturer's instructions for reading the actual measurement obtained.

Small Hole Gauges

Use a set of small hole gauges (**Figure 56**), to measure a hole, groove or slot. A small hole gauge measures the smallest holes. A telescoping gauge, on the other hand, measures slightly larger holes (see below). A small hole gauge is required to measure rocker arm bore and brake master cylinder bore diameters. The small hole gauge does not have a scale for direct readings. Use an outside micrometer together with the small hole gauge to determine the bore dimension.

Carefully insert the small hole gauge into the bore of the component to be measured. Tighten the knurled end of the gauge to carefully expand the gauge fingers to the limit within the bore (**Figure 57**). *Do not overtighten* the gauge. It has no built-in release feature. If tightened too much, the gauge fingers can damage the bore surface. Carefully remove the gauge, and measure the outside dimension of the gauge with a micrometer (**Figure 58**) as described in this chapter.

Telescoping Gauges

Use a telescoping gauge (**Figure 59**) to measure hole diameters from approximately 8 mm (5/16 in.) to 150 mm (6 in.). For example, it could be used to measure brake caliper bore and cylinder bore diameters. Like the small hole gauge, the telescoping gauge does not have a scale for direct reading. Use an outside micrometer together with the telescoping gauge to determine the bore dimension.

Select the correct-size telescoping gauge for the bore to be measured. Compress the movable side of the gauge post and carefully install the gauge into the bore, and release the movable post against the bore. Center the gauge by carefully moving it around in the bore. Tighten the knurled end of the gauge to hold the movable gauge post in this posi-

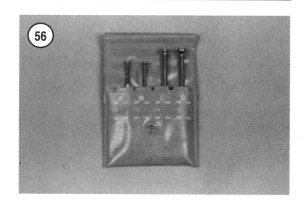

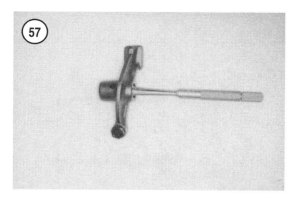

tion. Carefully remove the gauge and measure the outside dimension of the gauge posts with a micrometer as described in this chapter.

Compression Gauge

An engine with low compression cannot be properly tuned and does not develop full power. A compression gauge (**Figure 60**) measures engine compression. The one shown has a flexible stem with an extension for holding while cranking the en-

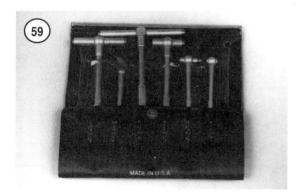

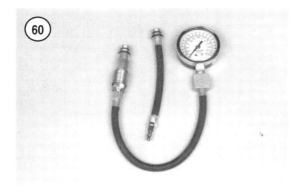

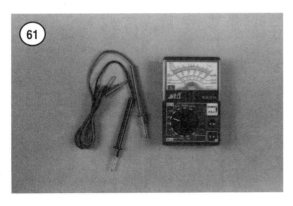

gine over. Open the throttle all the way when checking engine compression as described in Chapter Three.

Multimeter

A mulitmeter is a valuable tool for all electrical system troubleshooting (**Figure 61**). The voltage application is used to indicate the voltage applied or available to various electrical components. The ohmmeter portion of the meter is used to check for

continuity and to measure the resistance of a component. Some tests are easily accomplished using a meter with a sweeping needle (analog), but other tests require a digital multimeter.

In some electrical tests, the internal design of a meter affects the test readings. In these instances, the vehicle's manufacturer instructs the use of a specific meter because another meter may produce inaccurate results. The text in this book notes if a particular meter should be used to perform a test.

To measure voltage

> *NOTE*
> *Make sure the negative (–) or ground surface that will be used is clean and free of paint and/or grease. If possible, use a non-painted bolt that is attached directly to the frame.*

1. Make sure the meter's battery power source is at full power. If its condition is doubtful, install a new battery(s).
2. Select the meter voltage range to *one scale higher* than the indicated voltage value of the circuit to be tested.
3. Touch the red test probe to the *positive* (+) end and the black test probe to the *negative* (–), or ground, end of the circuit.
4. Refer to the appropriate procedure in the chapter to determine what switch(s) must be either turned ON or OFF within the circuit being tested.
5. With the switch(s) in the correct position, read the position of the needle on the VOLTS or VOLTAGE scale of the meter face or the digital readout, and refer to the specified voltage listed in the test procedure. Refer to the manufacturer's instructions for any special conditions relating to the meter being used.

To zero an analog ohmmeter

> *NOTE*
> *Every time an analog ohmmeter is used to measure resistance, it must be zeroed in order to obtain a correct measurement. Most digital ohmmeters are not equipped with a zero ohms adjust feature; when turned on they are automatically set at zero (provid-*

ing the meters battery is at full power).

1. Make sure the meter's battery power source is at full power. If its condition is doubtful, install a new battery(s).

2. Make sure the test probes are clean and free of corrosion.

3. Touch the two test probes together and observe the meter needle location on the OHMS scale on the meter face. The needle must be on the 0 mark at the end of the scale.

4. If necessary, rotate the ohms adjust knob on the meter, in either direction, until the needle is directly on the 0 mark on the scale. The meter is now ready for use.

To measure resistance

1. Zero the analog meter as previously described.
2. Disconnect the component from the circuit.

> *NOTE*
> *Polarity is not important when measuring the resistance of a component. Either test probe can be placed at either terminal of the component.*

3. Place the test probes at each end of the component, read the position of the needle on the OHMS scale of the meter face or the digital readout, and refer to the specified resistance in the test procedure.

4. If the component is not within specification, replace it.

5. If the component is within specification, reinstall it in the circuit.

Continuity test

A continuity test is used to determine the integrity of a circuit, wire or component.

Continuity is indicated by a low resistance reading, usually zero ohms, on the meter. No continuity is indicated by an infinity reading. A broken or open circuit has no continuity. A complete circuit has continuity. A continuity test is also useful to check components for a short to ground. A shorted component has a complete circuit (continuity) between the component and ground.

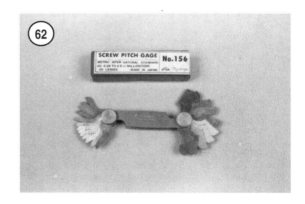

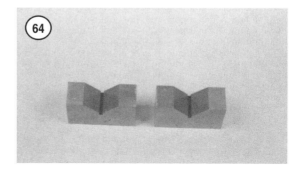

> *NOTE*
> *Every time an analog ohmmeter is used for a continuity check, it must be zeroed in order to obtain a correct reading.*

1. Zero the analog meter as previously described.

> *NOTE*
> *Polarity is not important when making a continuity check on a component or circuit. Either test probe can be placed at either terminal of the component or circuit.*

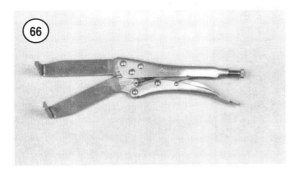

2. Place the test probes at each end of the component or circuit and read the position of the needle on the OHMS scale of the meter face, or digital readout.

3. If there is *continuity (low resistance)*, the meter will indicate zero or a low amount of resistance. In this test the resistance value is not important. Use this test to determine if the circuit is complete or not.

4. If there is *no continuity (infinite resistance)*, the meter needle will not move and will stay at the infinity symbol or the digital readout will indicate infinity.

5. If the component is not within specification, replace it.

6. If the component is within specification, reinstall it in the circuit.

Screw Pitch Gauge

A screw pitch gauge (**Figure 62**) determines the thread pitch of bolts, screws, studs, etc. The gauge is made up of a number of thin plates. Each plate has a thread shape cut on one edge to match one thread pitch. When using a screw pitch gauge to determine

a thread pitch size, try to fit different blade sizes onto the bolt thread until both threads match.

Magnetic Stand

A magnetic stand (**Figure 63**) is used to hold a dial indicator securely when checking the runout of a round object or when checking the end play of a shaft.

V-Blocks

V-blocks (**Figure 64**) are precision machined blocks used to hold a round object when checking its runout or condition. In ATV repair, Use V-blocks when checking the runout of such items as transmission shafts, crankshaft, wheel axles and other shafts and collars.

Surface Plate

Use a surface plate (**Figure 65**) to check the flatness of parts. While industrial quality surface plates are quite expensive, the home mechanic can improvise. A piece of thick, flat metal or plate glass can sometimes be used as a surface plate. The quality of the surface plate affect the accuracy of the measurement being taken. The surface plate can have a piece of fine grit paper mounted on its surface to assist in cleaning and smoothing a flat surface of a part. The machined surfaces of the cylinder head, cylinder, crankcase and other close fitting parts may require a very good quality surface plate to smooth nicked or damaged surfaces.

SPECIAL TOOLS

A few special tools may be required for major service. These are described in the appropriate chapters and are available either from a Kawasaki dealership or other manufacturer as indicated.

This section describes special tools unique to this type of ATV's service and repair.

The Grabbit

The Grabbit (**Figure 66**) is a special tool used to hold various parts when loosening and tightening fasteners.

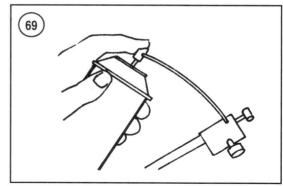

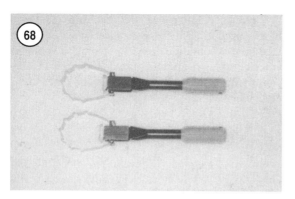

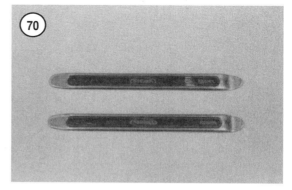

Rotor Puller

A rotor puller (**Figure 67**) is required to remove the magneto rotor (flywheel) from the end of the crankshaft. There is no satisfactory substitute for this tool. Because the rotor is a taper fit on the crankshaft, makeshift removal often results in crankshaft and rotor damage.

Piston Ring Compressor Tools

Use a the piston ring compressor tool (**Figure 68**) to compress the piston rings during cylinder installation and prevent piston ring damage.

Pressure Cable Lube Tool

Use a cable lube tool to force cable lubricant throughout a control cable.

This tool (**Figure 69**) (Kawasaki part No. K56019-021) is attached to one end of a control cable. It has a tube fitting that forces pressurized cable lubricant throughout the length of the cable.

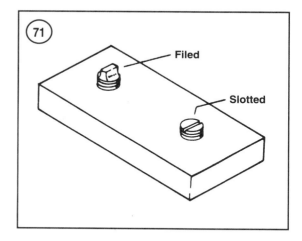

Tire Levers

When changing tires, use a good set of tire levers (**Figure 70**). Never use a screwdriver in place of a tire lever. Refer to Chapter Ten for tire lever use. Before using a tire lever, check the working end of the tool and remove any burrs with a file. Do not use a tire lever for prying anything but tires.

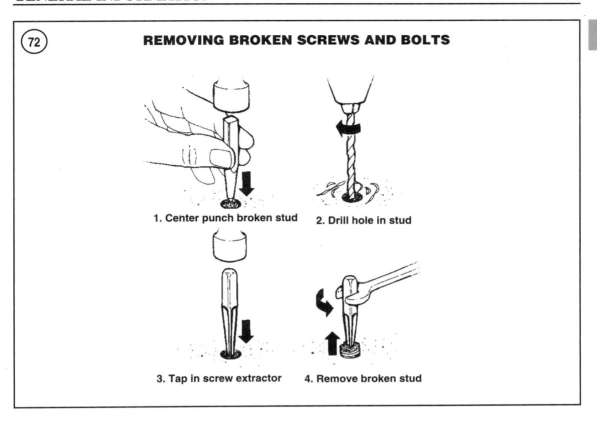

REMOVING BROKEN SCREWS AND BOLTS

(72)

1. Center punch broken stud

2. Drill hole in stud

3. Tap in screw extractor

4. Remove broken stud

FABRICATING TOOLS

Some of the procedures in this manual require the use of special tools. The resourceful mechanic can, in many cases, think of acceptable substitutes for special tools. This can be as simple as using a few pieces of threaded rod, washer and nuts to remove or install a bearing or fabricating a tool from scrap material. If a special tool can be designed and safely made, but it requires some type of machine work, contact a local community college or high school that has a machine shop curriculum. Some shop teachers welcome outside work that can be used as practical shop applications for students.

MECHANIC'S TIPS

Removing Frozen Nuts and Screws

When a fastener cannot be removed, several methods may be used to loosen it. First, apply penetrating oil such as Liquid Wrench or WD-40 (available at hardware or automotive supply stores). Apply it liberally, and let it penetrate for 10-15 min-utes. Rap the fastener several times with a small hammer. Do not hit the fastener hard enough to cause damage. Reapply penetrating oil if necessary.

If the fastener is too damaged to use this method, grip the head with locking pliers and twist the screw out.

Avoid applying heat unless specifically instructed. The heat may melt, warp or remove the temper from parts.

Removing Broken Screws or Bolts

When the head breaks off a screw or bolt, several methods are available for removing the remaining portion. If a large portion of the remainder projects out, try gripping it with locking pliers. If the projecting portion is too small, file it to fit a wrench or cut a slot in it to fit a screwdriver. See **Figure 71**.

If the head breaks off flush, use a screw extractor. To do this, centerpunch the exact center of the remaining portion of the screw or bolt. Drill a small hole in the screw and tap the extractor into the hole. Back the screw out with a wrench on the extractor. See **Figure 72**.

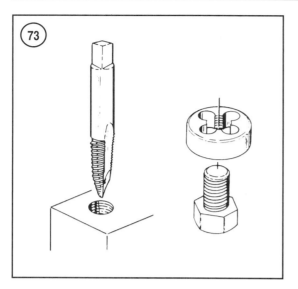

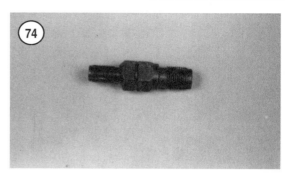

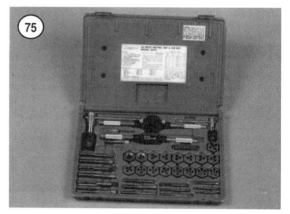

Remedying Stripped Threads

Occasionally, threads are stripped through carelessness or impact damage. Often the threads can be repaired by running a tap (for internal threads on nuts) or die (for external threads on bolts) through the threads. See **Figure 73**. To clean or repair spark plug threads, use a spark plug tap (**Figure 74**).

NOTE
*Tap and dies can be purchased individually or in a set as shown in **Figure 75**.*

If an internal thread is damaged, it may be necessary to install a Helicoil (**Figure 76**) or some other type of thread insert. Follow the manufacturer's instructions when installing the insert.

If it is necessary to drill and tap a hole, refer to **Table 8** for metric tap and drill sizes.

BEARING REPLACEMENT

Bearings (**Figure 77**) are used throughout the engine and drive assembly to reduce power loss, heat and noise resulting from friction. Because bearings are precision-made parts, they must be properly lubricated and maintained. When a bearing is damaged, replace it immediately. However, when installing a new bearing, care should be taken to prevent damage to the new bearing. While bearing replacement is described in the individual chapters

where applicable, the following should be used as a guideline.

NOTE
Unless otherwise specified, install bearings with the manufacturer's marks or number facing outward.

Bearing Removal

While bearings are normally removed only when damaged, there may be times when it is necessary to remove a bearing that is in good condition. However, improper bearing removal will damage the bearing and maybe the shaft or case half. Note the following when removing bearings.

WARNING
Failure to use proper precautions will probably result in damaged parts and may cause injury.

1. Before removing the bearings, note the following:
   a. Remove any seal(s) that interfere with bearing removal. Refer to *Seals* in this chapter.

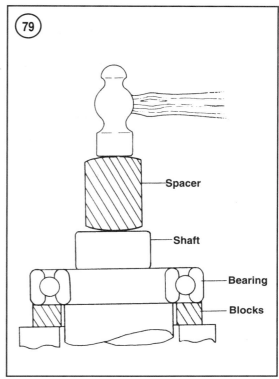

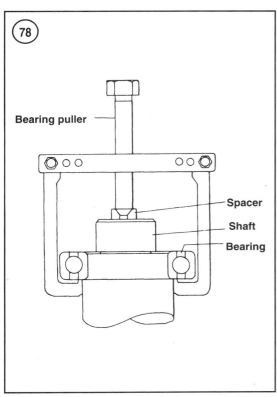

b. When removing more than one bearing, identify the bearings before removing them. Refer to the bearing manufacturer's numbers or marks on the bearing.

c. Record the direction in which the bearing marks face for proper installation.

d. Remove any set plates or bearing retainers before removing the bearing.

2. When using a puller to remove a bearing from a shaft, take care that the shaft is not damaged. Always place a piece of metal between the end of the shaft and the puller screw. In addition, place the puller arms next to the inner bearing race. See **Figure 78**.

3. When using a hammer to remove a bearing from a shaft, do not strike the shaft with the hammer. Instead, use a brass or aluminum spacer between the hammer and shaft (**Figure 79**). Make sure to support both bearing races with wooden blocks as shown.

4. A hydraulic press is the ideal tool for bearing removal. However, certain procedures must be followed or damage may occur to the bearing, shaft or bearing housing. Note the following when using a press:

a. Always support the inner and outer bearing races with a suitable size wood or aluminum ring (**Figure 80**). If only the outer race is supported, pressure applied against the balls and/or the inner race will damage them.

b. Always make sure the press arm (**Figure 80**) aligns with the center of the shaft. If the arm is not centered, it may damage the bearing and/or shaft.

c. The moment the shaft is free of the bearing, it will drop to the floor. Secure or hold the shaft to prevent it from falling.

5. Use a blind bearing remover to remove bearings installed in blind holes (**Figure 81**).

Bearing Installation

1. Before installing the new bearing(s), perform the following:

a. Clean and inspect the bearing bore or shaft.

b. Remove any burrs from the bearing bore or shaft.

c. Compare the old and new bearings to make sure the correct bearing is being installed.

2. When installing a bearing into a housing, apply pressure to the *outer* bearing race (**Figure 82**). When installing a bearing onto a shaft, apply pressure to the *inner* bearing race (**Figure 83**).

3. When installing a bearing as described in Step 2, some type of driver will be required. Never strike the bearing directly with a hammer or the bearing will be damaged. When installing a bearing, use a piece of pipe or a socket with a diameter slightly smaller than the bearing race. **Figure 84** shows the correct way to use a socket and hammer when installing a bearing onto a shaft.

4. Step 2 describes how to install a bearing into a case half and over a shaft. However, when installing a bearing over a shaft and into a housing at the same time, both outer and inner bearing races must be supported. In this situation, use a spacer installed underneath the driver tool so that pressure is applied evenly across both races. See **Figure 85**. If the outer race is not supported as shown in **Figure 85**, the balls will push against the outer bearing track and damage it.

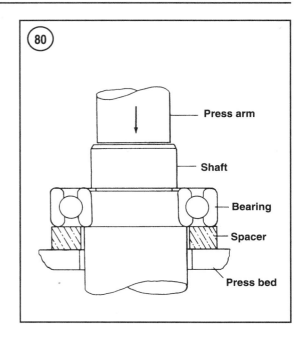

Shrink Fit

1. *Installing a bearing over a shaft:* When a tight fit is required, the bearing inside diameter will be smaller than the shaft. In this case, driving the bearing onto the shaft using normal methods may cause bearing damage. Instead, the bearing should be heated before installation. Note the following:

a. Secure the shaft so it is ready for bearing installation.

b. Clean all residue from the bearing surface of the shaft. Remove burrs with a file or sandpaper.

c. Fill a suitable pot or beaker with clean mineral oil. Place a thermometer (rated higher than 120° C [248° F]) in the oil. Support the thermometer so that it does not rest on the bottom or side of the pot.

d. Remove the bearing from its wrapper, and secure it with a piece of heavy wire bent to hold it in the pot. Hang the bearing in the pot so it does not touch the bottom or sides of the pot.

e. Turn the heat on and monitor the thermometer. When the oil temperature rises to approximately 120° C (248° F), remove the bearing from the pot and quickly install it. If necessary, place a socket on the inner bearing race and tap the bearing into place. As the bearing chills, it will tighten on the shaft so work

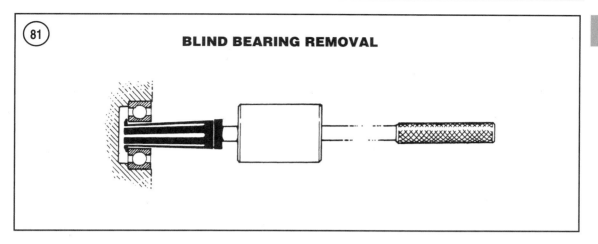

BLIND BEARING REMOVAL

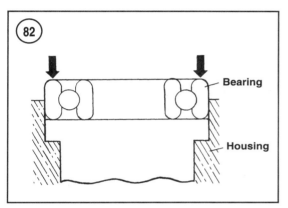

Bearing

Housing

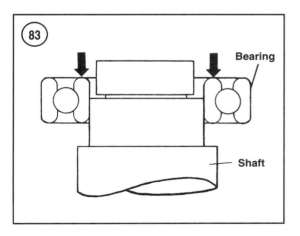

Bearing

Shaft

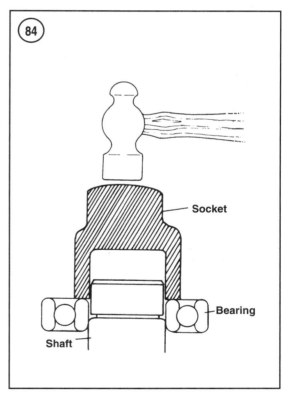

Socket

Bearing

Shaft

quickly when installing it. Make sure the bearing is installed all the way.

2. *Installing a bearing into a housing*: Bearings are generally installed in a housing with a slight interference fit. Driving the bearing into the housing using normal methods may damage the housing or cause bearing damage. Instead, the housing should be heated before the bearing is installed. Note the following:

CAUTION
Before heating the crankcases in this procedure, wash the cases thoroughly with detergent and water. Rinse and rewash the cases to remove all traces of oil and other chemical deposits.

a. Heat the housing to a temperature of approximately 100° C (212° F) in an oven or on a hot plate. An easy way to check temperature is to drop tiny drops of water on the case. If they sizzle and evaporate immediately, the temperature is correct. Heat only one housing at a time.

CAUTION
Do not heat the housing with a torch. Never bring a flame into contact with the bearing or housing. The direct heat destroys the case hardening of the bearing and may likely warp the housing.

b. Remove the housing from the oven or hot plate. The housing is hot. Hold onto it with heavy welding gloves or kitchen pot holders.

NOTE
A suitable sized socket and extension works well for removing and installing bearings.

c. Hold the housing with the bearing side down and tap the bearing out. Repeat for all bearings in the housing.

d. Prior to heating the bearing housing, place the new bearing in a freezer, if possible. Chilling a bearing slightly reduces its outside diameter while the heated bearing housing assembly is slightly larger due to heat expansion. This makes bearing installation much easier.

NOTE
Always install bearings with the manufacturer's marks or number facing outward.

e. While the housing is still hot, install the new bearing(s) into the housing by hand, if possible. If necessary, lightly tap the bearing(s) into the housing with a socket placed on the outer bearing race (**Figure 82**). Do not install new bearings by driving on the inner bearing race. Install the bearing(s) until it seats completely.

SEALS

Seals (**Figure 86**) are used to contain oil, water, grease or combustion gasses in a housing or shaft.

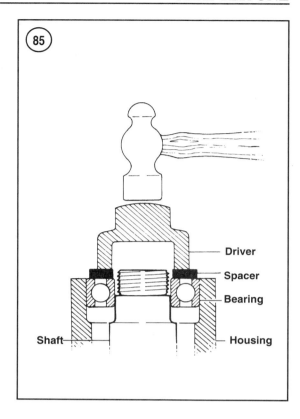

Improper removal of a seal can damage the housing or shaft. Improper installation can damage the seal. Note the following:

a. Prying is generally the easiest and most effective method of removing a seal from a housing. However, always place a rag underneath the pry tool to prevent damage to the housing.

b. Pack waterproof grease into the seal lips before the seal is installed.

c. Seals are usually installed with the manufacturer's numbers or marks facing out, however, this is not always the case. In situations where a double sided seal is used, record the markings on the side of the seal that faces out. In some instances, the seal may be marked on both sides: for example OUTSIDE and INSIDE. Look for these marks, and install the seal correctly.

d. Seals can be installed by hand or may require the use of force. If using force, use a bearing driver or socket placed on the outer portion of the seal and drive it squarely into its bore (**Figure 87**). Never install a seal by hitting the top of the seal with a hammer.

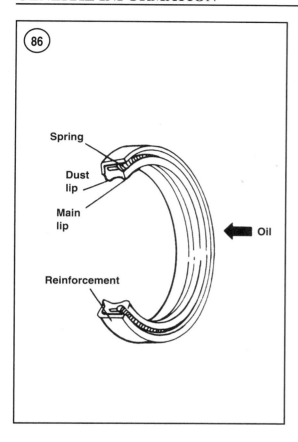

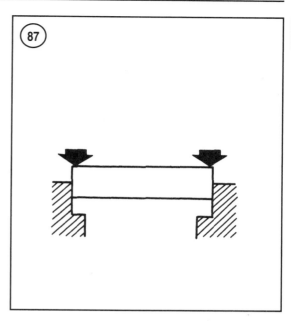

RIDING SAFETY

General Tips

1. Read the owner's manual and know the machine.

2. Check the throttle and brake controls before starting the engine.

3. Know how to make an emergency stop.

4. Never add fuel while anyone is smoking in the area or when the engine is running.

5. Never wear loose scarves, belts or boot laces that could catch on moving parts.

6. Always wear eye protection, head protection and protective clothing to protect the entire body.

7. Riding in the winter months requires a good set of clothes to keep dry and warm, otherwise the entire trip may be miserable. If dressed properly, moisture will evaporate from the body. Even mild temperatures can be very uncomfortable and dangerous when combined with a strong wind or traveling at high speed.

8. Never allow anyone to operate the ATV without proper instruction.

9. Ride with another vehicle or in a group when on long trips, in case a problem develops.

10. Never attempt to repair the machine with the engine running except when necessary for certain tune-up procedures.

11. Check all the machine components and hardware frequently, especially the wheels and the steering.

Operating Tips

1. Never operate the machine in crowded areas or steer it toward people.

2. Avoid dangerous terrain.

3. Cross highways (where permitted) at a 90° angle after looking in both directions. Post traffic guards if crossing in groups.

4. Do not ride the vehicle on or near railroad tracks. Engine and exhaust noise can drown out the sound of an approaching train.

5. Keep the headlight and taillight free of dirt, and never ride at night unless the headlight and taillight are ON.

6. Do not ride the ATV without the seat and fenders in place.

7. Always steer with the hands.

8. Be aware of the terrain and avoid operating the ATV at excessive speed. Hidden obstructions,

hanging tree limbs, unseen ditches, and even wild animals and hikers can cause injury and damage the ATV.

9. Do not panic if the throttle sticks. Turn the engine stop switch to the OFF position.

10. Do not tailgate. Rear end collisions can cause injury and machine damage.

11. Do not mix alcohol or drugs with riding.

12. Keep both feet on the footrests. Do not let your feet hang out to stabilize the machine when making turns or in near spill situations. Broken limbs could result.

13. Check the fuel supply regularly. Do not travel so far when there is insufficient fuel to return.

14. Make sure the parking brake is completely released while riding. If left on, the rear brake pads will be damaged.

Table 1 INITIAL SERIAL NUMBERS

Year/model	VIN number	Engine number
1987 KSF250-A1	JKASFMA1·HB500001	SF250AE000001
1988 KSF250-A2	JKASFMA1·JB508601	SF250AE009001
1989 KSF250-A3	JKASFMA1·KB511901	SF250AE009001
1990 KSF250-A4	JKASFMA1·LB515000	SF250AE012501
1991 KSF250-A5	JKASFMA1·MB516101	SF250AE012501
1992 KSF250-A6	JKASFMA1·NB517301	SF250AE012501
1993 KSF250-A7	JKASFMA1·PB518201	SF250AE012501
1994 KSF250-A8	JKASFMA1·RB519501	SF250AE012501
1995 KSF250-A9	JKASFMA1·SB521201	SF250AE012501
1996 KSF250-A10	JKASFMA1·TB522851	SF250AE012501
1997 KSF250-A11	JKASFMA1·VB524101	SF250AE012501
1998 KSF250-A12	JKASFMA1·WB525501	SF250AE012501
1999 KSF250-A13	JKASFMA1·XB526801	SF250AE012501
2000 KSF250-A14	JKASFMA1·YB527101	SF250AE012501

Table 2 GENERAL VEHICLE DIMENSIONS

Overall length	1735 mm (68.3 in.)
Overall width	1090 mm (42.9 in.)
Overall height	
1987	1020 mm (40.2 in.)
1988-on	1035 mm (40.7 in.)
Wheelbase	1125 mm (44.3 in.)
Track	
Front	855 mm (33.7 in.)
Rear	830 mm (32.7 in.)
Ground clearance	215 mm (8.5 in.)
Seat height	
1987	745 mm (29.3 in.)
1988-on	755 mm (29.7 in.)

Table 3 VEHICLE WEIGHT

Dry weight	
1987	165 kg (363.8 lb.)
1988	169 kg (372.6 lb.)
1989-on	172 kg (379.2 lb.)

(continued)

1

Table 3 VEHICLE WEIGHT (continued)

Curb weight	
1987	
Front	85.5 kg (188.5 lb.)
Rear	89.5 kg (197.3 lb.)
1988 & 1989	
Front	87.5 kg (192.9 lb.)
Rear	91.5 kg (201.7 lb.)
1990-on	
Front	88.5 kg (195.1 lb.)
Rear	93.5 kg (206.1 lb.)

Table 4 DECIMAL AND METRIC EQUIVALENTS

Fractions	Decimal in.	Metric mm	Fractions	Decimal in.	Metric mm
1/64	0.015625	0.39688	33/64	0.515625	13.09687
1/32	0.03125	0.79375	17/32	0.53125	13.49375
3/64	0.046875	1.19062	35/64	0.546875	13.89062
1/16	0.0625	1.58750	9/16	0.5625	14.28750
5/64	0.078125	1.98437	37/64	0.578125	14.68437
3/32	0.09375	2.38125	19/32	0.59375	15.08125
7/64	0.109375	2.77812	39/64	0.609375	15.47812
1/8	0.125	3.1750	5/8	0.625	15.87500
9/64	0.140625	3.57187	41/64	0.640625	16.27187
5/32	0.15625	3.96875	21/32	0.65625	16.66875
11/64	0.171875	4.36562	43/64	0.671875	17.06562
3/16	0.1875	4.76250	11/16	0.6875	17.46250
13/64	0.203125	5.15937	45/64	0.703125	17.85937
7/32	0.21875	5.55625	23/32	0.71875	18.25625
15/64	0.234375	5.95312	47/64	0.734375	18.65312
1/4	0.250	6.35000	3/4	0.750	19.05000
17/64	0.265625	6.74687	49/64	0.765625	19.44687
9/32	0.28125	7.14375	25/32	0.78125	19.84375
19/64	0.296875	7.54062	51/64	0.796875	20.24062
5/16	0.3125	7.93750	13/16	0.8125	20.63750
21/64	0.328125	8.33437	53/64	0.828125	21.03437
11/32	0.34375	8.73125	27/32	0.84375	21.43125
23/64	0.359375	9.12812	55/64	0.859375	22.82812
3/8	0.375	9.52500	7/8	0.875	22.22500
25/64	0.390625	9.92187	57/64	0.890625	22.62187
13/32	0.40625	10.31875	29/32	0.90625	23.01875
27/64	0.421875	10.71562	59/64	0.921875	23.41562
7/16	0.4375	11.11250	15/16	0.9375	23.81250
29/64	0.453125	11.50937	61/64	0.953125	24.20937
15/32	0.46875	11.90625	31/32	0.96875	24.60625
31/64	0.484375	12.30312	63/64	0.984375	25.00312
1/2	0.500	12.70000	1	1.00	25.40000

Table 5 STANDARD TORQUE SPECIFICATIONS

Fastener size or type	N•m	in.-lb.	ft.-lb.
5 mm screw	4	35	–
5 mm bolt and nut	5	44	–

(continued)

Table 5 STANDARD TORQUE SPECIFICATIONS (continued)

Fastener size or type	N•m	in.-lb.	ft.-lb.
6 mm screw	9	80	–
6 mm bolt and nut	10	88	–
6 mm flange bolt			
(8 mm head, small flange)	9	80	–
6 mm flange bolt			
(10 mm head) and nut	12	106	–
8 mm bolt and nut	22	–	16
8 mm flange bolt and nut	27	–	20
10 mm bolt and nut	35	–	26
10 mm flange bolt and nut	40	–	29
12 mm bolt and nut	55	–	41

Table 6 CONVERSION TABLES

Multiply	By	To get equivalent of
Length		
Inches	25.4	Millimeter
Inches	2.54	Centimeter
Miles	1.609	Kilometer
Feet	0.3048	Meter
Millimeter	0.03937	Inches
Centimeter	0.3937	Inches
Kilometer	0.6214	Mile
Meter	3.281	Mile
Fluid volume		
U.S. quarts	0.9463	Liters
U.S. gallons	3.785	Liters
U.S. ounces	29.573529	Milliliters
Imperial gallons	4.54609	Liters
Imperial quarts	1.1365	Liters
Liters	0.2641721	U.S. gallons
Liters	1.0566882	U.S. quarts
Liters	33.814023	U.S. ounces
Liters	0.22	Imperial gallons
Liters	0.8799	Imperial quarts
Milliliters	0.033814	U.S. ounces
Milliliters	1.0	Cubic centimeters
Milliliters	0.001	Liters
Torque		
Foot-pounds	1.3558	Newton-meters
Foot-pounds	0.138255	Meter-kilograms
Inch-pounds	0.11299	Newton-meters
Newton-meters	0.7375622	Foot-pounds
Newton-meters	8.8507	Inch-pounds
Meters-kilograms	7.2330139	Foot-pounds
Volume		
Cubic inches	16.387064	Cubic centimeters
Cubic centimeters	0.0610237	Cubic inches
Temperature		
Fahrenheit	(F – 32) 0.556	Centigrade
Centigrade	(C × 1.8) + 32	Fahrenheit
Weight		
Ounces	28.3495	Grams
Pounds	0.4535924	Kilograms

(continued)

Table 6 CONVERSION TABLES (continued)

Multiply	By	To get equivalent of
Weight (continued)		
Grams	0.035274	Ounces
Kilograms	2.2046224	Pounds
Pressure		
Pounds per square inch	0.070307	Kilograms per square centimeter
Kilograms per square centimeter	14.223343	Pounds per square inch
Kilopascals	0.1450	Pounds per square inch
Pounds per square inch	6.895	Kilopascals
Speed		
Miles per hour	1.609344	Kilometers per hour
Kilometers per hour	0.6213712	Miles per hour

Table 7 TECHNICAL ABBREVIATIONS

ABDC	After bottom dead center
ATDC	After top dead center
BBDC	Before bottom dead center
BDC	Bottom dead center
BTDC	Before top dead center
C	Celsius (Centigrade)
cc	Cubic centimeters
cid	Cubic inch displacement
CDI	Capacitor discharge ignition
cu. in.	Cubic inches
DOHC	Dual overhead camshaft
F	Fahrenheit
ft.	Feet
ft.-lb.	Foot-pounds
gal.	Gallons
H/A	High altitude
hp	Horsepower
in.	Inches
in.-lb.	Inch-pounds
I.D.	Inside diameter
KACR	Kawasaki automatic compression release
kg	Kilograms
kgm	Kilogram meters
km	Kilometer
kPa	Kilopascals
L	Liter
m	Meter
MAG	Magneto
ml	Milliliter
mm	Millimeter
N•m	Newton-meters
O.D.	Outside diameter
oz.	Ounces
psi	Pounds per square inch
PTO	Power take off
pt.	Pint
qt.	Quart
rpm	Revolutions per minute

Table 8 METRIC TAP AND EQUIVALENT DRILL SIZE

Metric tap (mm)	Drill size	Decimal equivalent	Nearest fraction
3 × 0.50	No. 39	0.0995	3/32
3 × 0.60	3/32	0.0937	3/32
4 × 0.70	No. 30	0.1285	1/8
4 × 0.75	1/8	0.125	1/8
5 × 0.80	No. 19	0.166	11/64
5 × 0.90	No. 20	0.161	5/32
6 × 1.00	No. 9	0.196	13/64
7 × 1.00	16/64	0.234	15/64
8 × 1.00	J	0.277	9/32
8 × 1.25	17/64	0.265	17/64
9 × 1.00	5/16	0.3125	5/16
9 × 1.25	5/16	0.3125	5/16
10 × 1.25	11/32	0.3437	11/32
0 × 1.50	R	0.339	11/32
11 × 1.50	3/8	0.375	3/8
12 × 1.50	13/32	0.406	13/32
12 × 1.75	13/32	0.406	13/32

TROUBLESHOOTING

Diagnosing mechanical and electrical problems is relatively simple if orderly procedures are used and a few basic principles are kept in mind. The first step in any troubleshooting procedure is to define the symptoms closely and to localize the problem. Subsequent steps involve testing and analyzing those areas that could cause the symptoms. A haphazard approach may eventually solve the problem, but it can be very costly in terms of wasted time and unnecessary replacement of parts.

Proper lubrication, maintenance and periodic tune-ups as described in Chapter Three reduces the necessity for troubleshooting. Even with the best of care, however, all vehicles may require troubleshooting.

Never assume anything. Do not overlook the obvious. If the engine does not start, the engine stop switch or start switch may be shorted out or damaged. When trying to start the engine, the engine may have flooded.

If the engine suddenly quits, what sound did it make? Consider this and check the easiest, most accessible areas first. If the engine sounded as if it ran out of fuel, check if there is fuel in the tank. If there is fuel in the tank, is it reaching the carburetor? If not, the fuel tank vent hose may be plugged, preventing the flow of fuel from the tank to the carburetor.

If nothing obvious turns up in a quick check, look a little further. Learning to recognize and describe symptoms makes repairs easier for you or a mechanic at the shop. Describe problems accurately and fully.

Gather as much information as possible to aid in diagnosis. Note whether the engine lost power gradually or all at once, what color smoke came from the exhaust and so on. Remember, the more complicated a machine is, the easier it is to troubleshoot because symptoms point to specific problems.

After defining the vehicle's symptoms, test and analyze areas that could cause the problem. Guessing at the cause of a problem may provide the solution, but it can easily lead to frustration, wasted time and a series of expensive, unnecessary replacement of parts.

Expensive equipment or complicated test gear is not needed to determine whether repairs can be attempted at home. A few simple checks could save a large repair bill and lost time while the ATV sits in a dealer's service department. On the other hand, be realistic and do not attempt repairs beyond your abilities. Service departments tend to charge heavily for reassembling someone else's work, most will not even take on such a job. Use common sense so that you do not get in over your head.

OPERATING REQUIREMENTS

An engine needs three basic requirements to run properly: correct air/fuel mixture, compression and a spark at the right time (**Figure 1**). If one basic requirement is missing, the engine will not run. Four-stroke engine operating principles are described in Chapter Four.

If the ATV has not been in use for a period of time and refuses to start, check and clean the spark plug. If the plug is not fouled, inspect the fuel delivery system. This includes the fuel tank, fuel valve, in-line fuel filter (if used) and fuel line. If the ATV sat for a while with fuel in the carburetor, fuel deposits may have gummed up carburetor jets and air passages. Gasoline tends to lose its potency after long periods. Condensation may contaminate the fuel. Drain the old gas, and try starting with a fresh tankful.

TROUBLESHOOTING INSTRUMENTS

Chapter One describes the instruments needed and provides instruction on their use.

STARTING THE ENGINE

If the engine refuses to start, the following outline is a guide for basic starting procedures. In all cases, make sure there is an adequate supply of fuel in the tank.

Starting a Cold Engine

1. Shift the transmission into NEUTRAL.
2. Move the fuel valve to the ON position (**Figure 2**).
3. Move the choke lever (**Figure 3**) to its fully on position.
4. With the throttle completely closed, operate the kickstarter.
5. When the engine starts, work the throttle slightly to keep it running.
6. Idle the engine for approximately one minute or until the throttle responds cleanly, then release the choke. The engine should be sufficiently warmed to prevent stalling.

Starting a Warm or Hot Engine

1. Shift the transmission into NEUTRAL.
2. Move the fuel valve to the ON position (**Figure 2**).
3. Make sure the choke lever (**Figure 3**) is in the off position.
4. Open the throttle slightly, and operate the kickstarter.

Starting a Flooded Engine

If the engine does not start and there is a strong gasoline smell, the engine may be flooded. If so, open the throttle all the way and operate the

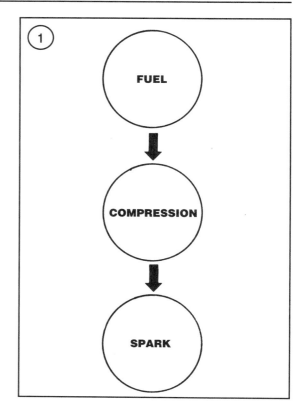

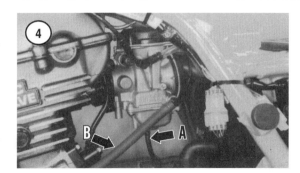

kickstarter. Make sure the choke is in the off position. Holding the throttle open allows more air to reach the combustion chamber.

> *NOTE*
> *If the engine refuses to start, check the carburetor overflow hose (A, **Figure 4**) attached to the fitting at the bottom of the float bowl. If fuel runs out the end of the hose, the float is stuck open, allowing the carburetor to overfill.*

STARTING DIFFICULTIES

If the engine cranks over but is difficult to start, go down the following list step by step. Check each item while remembering the three engine operating requirements described earlier in this chapter.

If the engine still does not start, refer to the appropriate troubleshooting procedures that follow in this chapter.

1. Is the choke lever in the correct position? Move the choke lever (**Figure 3**) to its fully on position for a cold engine and turn it off for a warm or hot engine.

2. Is there fuel in the tank? Fill the tank if necessary. Has it been a while since the engine was run? If in doubt, drain the fuel tank, and fill it with fresh

fuel. Check for a clogged fuel tank vent tube (**Figure 5**). Remove the tube from the filler cap. Wipe off one end, and blow through it. Remove the filler cap and check for a plugged hose nozzle.

> *WARNING*
> *Do not use an open flame to check in the tank. A serious explosion is certain to result.*

3. Pull the fuel line (B, **Figure 4**) from the carburetor and insert the end of the hose into a container. Turn the fuel valve on (**Figure 2**) and see if fuel flows freely. If fuel does not flow out and there is a fuel filter installed in the fuel line, remove the filter and turn the fuel valve on again. If fuel flows, the filter is clogged and must be replaced. If no fuel comes out, the fuel valve may be shut off, blocked by foreign matter, or the fuel tank vent hose (**Figure 5**) may be plugged.

4. If there is suspicion that the cylinder is flooded, or there is a strong smell of gasoline, open the throttle all the way and operate the kickstarter. If the cylinder is severely flooded (fouled or wet spark plug), remove the spark plug and dry the base and electrode (**Figure 6**) thoroughly with a soft cloth. Reinstall the plug and attempt to start the engine.

5. Check the carburetor overflow hose on the bottom of the float bowl (A, **Figure 4**). If fuel is running out of the hose, the float is stuck open. Turn the fuel valve off, and tap the carburetor a few times. Then turn on the fuel valve. If fuel continues to run out of the hose, remove and repair the carburetor as described in Chapter Eight. Check the carburetor vent hoses to make sure they are clear. Check the end of the hoses for contamination.

> *NOTE*
> *Even though fuel is reaching the carburetor, the fuel system could still be*

the problem. The jets (pilot and main) could be clogged or the air filter could be severely restricted. However, before removing the carburetor, continue with Step 6 to make sure that the ignition provides an adequate spark.

6. Make sure the engine stop switch is not stuck or working improperly. Also make sure the switch wires are not broken or shorted. If necessary, test the engine stop switch as described in Chapter Nine.

> *NOTE*
> *If an aftermarket kill switch was installed, check the switch for proper operation. This switch may be defective.*

7. Is the spark plug cap (**Figure 7**) on tight? Push it on and slightly rotate it to clean the electrical connection between the plug and the connector. Push or screw the plug cap into the high-tension lead.

> *NOTE*
> *If the engine still does not start, continue with the following.*

8. Perform the spark test described in *Engine Fails to Start (Spark Test)* in this chapter. If there is a strong spark, perform Step 9. If there is no spark or if the spark is very weak, test the ignition system as described in this chapter.

> *NOTE*
> *If the fuel and ignition systems are working properly, the one remaining area to check is the mechanical system. Unless the engine seized, mechanical problems affecting the top end generally occur over time, depending on maintenance and vehicle use. Isolate the mechanical problem to one of these areas: top end, bottom end, clutch or transmission. Engine top and bottom end components are covered in Step 9. Clutch and transmission problems are covered elsewhere in this chapter.*

9. Check the cylinder compression as follows:
   a. Turn off the fuel valve.

> *CAUTION*
> *To prevent damage to the ignition system, ground the spark plug when performing the following steps.*

   b. Remove and ground the spark plug against the cylinder head as shown in **Figure 8**.

   c. Place a finger *over* the spark plug hole.

   d. Operate the kickstarter. When the piston comes up on the compression stroke, pressure in the cylinder should force your finger from the spark plug hole. If this is the case, the cylinder probably has sufficient compression to start the engine.

> *NOTE*
> *There still may be a compression problem even though it seems good with the previous test. Check engine compression with a compression gauge as described in Tune-up in Chapter Three.*

ENGINE STARTING TROUBLES

An engine that refuses to start or is difficult to start is very frustrating. More often than not, the problem is minor and can be found with a simple and logical troubleshooting approach.

The following items show a beginning point from which to isolate engine starting problems.

Engine Fails to Start (Spark Test)

Perform the following spark test to determine if the ignition system is operating properly.

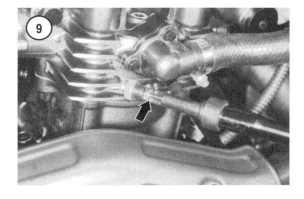

CAUTION
Before removing the spark plug in Step 1, clean all debris away from the plug base. Dirt that falls into the cylinder causes rapid engine wear.

1. Disconnect the plug cap (**Figure 7**) and remove the spark plug.

NOTE
A spark tester is a useful tool when checking the ignition system. **Figure 9** *shows the Motion Pro Ignition System Tester (part No. 08-122). Insert this tool into the spark plug cap and set its base against the cylinder head to provide a ground. The tool's air gap is adjustable, and it allows the spark to be seen and heard while testing the intensity of the spark. This tool is available through most motorcycle dealerships.*

NOTE
Set the air gap on the spark tester to 6 mm (1/4 in.).

2. Insert the spark plug (or spark tester) into its cap and touch the spark plug base against the cylinder head to ground it (**Figure 8**). Position the spark plug so the electrode can be seen.

WARNING
If the engine is flooded, do not perform this test. The spark plug could ignite fuel that is ejected through the spark plug hole.

WARNING
Do not hold the spark plug, wire or connector. Serious electrical shock may result.

3. Turn the ignition switch on, and crank the engine with the kickstarter. A fat blue spark should be evident across the spark plug electrode. Note the following:
  a. If the spark is intermittent, weak (white or yellow in color) or if there is no spark at all, continue with Step 4.
  b. If the spark is good, proceed to Step 6.

4. Make sure the engine stop switch is not stuck or working improperly. Disconnect the engine stop switch leads and recheck the spark. Note the following:
  a. If there is a spark, the engine stop switch or stop-switch circuit is damaged. Replace the switch and retest.
  b. If there is still no spark, test the engine stop switch as described in Chapter Nine. If the switch tests good, reconnect it to the wiring harness and continue with Step 5.

WARNING
If the engine stop switch is defective, install a new switch as soon as possible. It is not safe to ride the ATV with a missing or disconnected engine stop switch.

5. A loose, corroded or damaged spark plug terminal is a common source of ignition system malfunctions, especially intermittent malfunctions. Test the plug cap and terminal by performing the following:
  a. Disconnect the spark plug cap from the spark plug. Hold the plug wire and try to turn the cap. The cap must fit tightly on the wire. If there is any looseness, the terminal inside the cap may be pulled away from the plug wire.

b. Install the spark plug into the plug cap. The terminal ring inside the plug cap should snap tightly onto the spark plug when connecting the parts together.

c. If there is a problem, remove the plug cap from the plug wire. If used, cut the plastic tie securing the cap to the plug wire.

d. Check the metal terminal for corrosion or other damage. Remove any corrosion with a file or sandpaper. Check the terminal where it connects to the plug wire.

e. Check the wire strands in the end of the plug wire for corrosion or other damage.

f. Check the plug wire at the end of is outer rubber cover for excessive looseness or play, which may indicate a weak or broken plug wire. The plug wire can be damaged from vibration or mishandling.

g. Hold the plug wire, without the spark plug cap and terminal, 6 mm (1/4 in.) from the cylinder head as shown in **Figure 10**. Have an assistant crank the engine. If there is a good spark, the spark plug cap terminal is faulty or the terminal was not making good contact with the plug wire.

h. Cut off approximately 6 mm (1/4 in.) from the end of the plug wire to provide new wire for a good electrical contact. If attempting to cut just the insulator (rubber part only) to expose more of the wire core, do not cut into the wire core itself.

i. Pack the plug cap or the plug wire end with dielectric grease to keep moisture from entering the cap and interrupting the spark.

j. Install the spark plug cap securely onto the wire. Make sure there is good contact between the plug wire core and the spark-plug-cap terminal.

k. Repeat the spark test. If there is still no spark, proceed to Step 6.

6. If the spark plug cap was not the problem, test the ignition system as described in *Ignition System* in this chapter.

7. If the spark is good, perform the test described in *Engine is Difficult to Start* in this chapter.

ENGINE IS DIFFICULT TO START

If the engine is difficult to start, check for one or more of the following malfunctions.

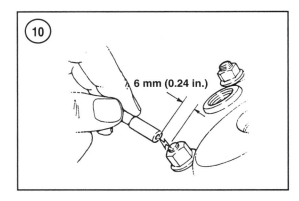

1. Incorrect air/fuel mixture:
   a. Excessively dirty or blocked air filter element.
   b. Incorrect carburetor adjustment.
   c. Plugged pilot jet.
   d. Plugged pilot passage.
2. Engine flooded:
   a. Incorrect starting procedure.
   b. Incorrect fuel level (too high).
   c. Worn fuel valve and seat assembly.
   d. Fuel valve stuck open or leaking.
   e. Damaged float.
3. No fuel flow:
   a. No fuel.
   b. Fuel valve (**Figure 2**) turned off.
   c. Plugged or restricted fuel valve.
   d. Plugged fuel line (B, **Figure 4**).
   e. Plugged fuel filter (if used).
   f. Plugged fuel tank cap vent hose (**Figure 5**).
4. Weak spark:
   a. Fouled or wet spark plug.
   b. Loose or damaged spark plug cap connection.
   c. Loose or damaged plug wire-to-spark plug cap connection.
   d. Defective ignition coil.
   e. Defective CDI unit.
   f. Corroded stator or rotor pickup surfaces.
   g. Damaged stator coils.
   h. Sheared rotor Woodruff key.
   i. Loose rotor nut.
   j. Loose or dirty electrical connections (**Figure 11**).
5. Low engine compression:
   a. Loose spark plug or missing spark plug gasket.
   b. Stuck piston ring.
   c. Excessive piston ring wear.

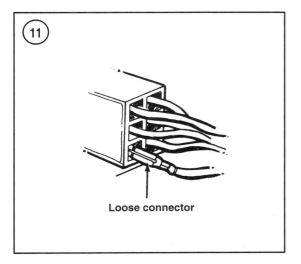

Loose connector

d. Excessively worn piston and/or cylinder.
e. Loose cylinder head fasteners.
f. Cylinder head incorrectly installed and/or tightened.
g. Warped cylinder head.
h. Damaged head gasket.
i. Damaged base gasket.
j. Loose cylinder fasteners.
k. Broken or weak valve spring.
l. Bent valve.
m. Carbon accumulation on valve seat.
n. Compression release mechanism worn or stuck open.

Engine Will Not Turn Over

If the engine does not turn over because of a mechanical problem, check for one or more of the following malfunctions:

NOTE
*After checking the following items, refer to **Drive Train Noise** later in this chapter for additional information.*

1. Defective kickstarter and/or gear.
2. Broken kickstarter return spring.
3. Damaged kickstarter ratchet gear.
4. Seized or damaged idler gear.
5. Seized or damaged piston.
6. Seized engine bearings.
7. Broken connecting rod.
8. Seized rocker arm.
9. Seized camshaft.

10. Seized primary drive/clutch assembly.
11. Seized transmission gear or bearing.
12. Seized balancer gear.

POOR IDLE SPEED PERFORMANCE

If the engine starts but idle performance is poor, check the following malfunctions.
1. Incorrect air/fuel mixture:
   a. Excessively dirty or blocked air filter element.
   b. Incorrect carburetor adjustment.
   c. Restricted pilot jet.
   d. Plugged air passage.
   e. Loose or cracked airbox boot or duct.
   f. Loose carburetor hose clamps.
   g. Plugged fuel tank cap vent hose (**Figure 5**).
   h. Starter plunger stuck open.
   i. Incorrect fuel level.
2. Weak spark:
   a. Fouled or wet spark plug.
   b. Incorrect spark plug heat range.
   c. Loose or damaged spark plug cap connection.
   d. Loose or damaged plug wire at the spark plug cap or at the ignition coil.
   e. Defective ignition coil.
   f. Defective CDI unit.
   g. Defective stator coils.
   h. Defective pickup coil.
   i. Loose or dirty electrical connections (**Figure 11**).
   j. Incorrect ignition timing.
3. Low engine compression:
   a. Loose spark plug or missing spark plug gasket.
   b. Stuck piston ring.
   c. Excessive piston ring wear.
   d. Excessively worn piston and/or cylinder.
   e. Loose cylinder head fasteners.
   f. Cylinder head incorrectly installed and/or tightened.
   g. Warped cylinder head.
   h. Damaged head gasket.
   i. Damaged base gasket.
   j. Loose cylinder fasteners.
   k. Broken or weak valve spring.
   l. Bent valve.
   m. Carbon accumulation on valve seat.
   n. Compression release mechanism worn or stuck open.

4. Other causes of poor idle are:
    a. Incorrect ignition timing.
    b. Carburetor vacuum piston not moving smoothly.
    c. Throttle valve not completely opening.
    d. Engine oil viscosity too high.
    e. Engine overheating.
    f. Brakes dragging.
    g. Clutch clipping.

POOR RUNNING OR HIGH SPEED PERFORMANCE

Check for one or more of the following malfunctions.
1. Incorrect air/fuel mixture:
    a. Excessively dirty or blocked air filter element.
    b. Plugged carburetor vent tube (A, **Figure 4**).
    c. Incorrect or plugged main jet.
    d. Worn jet needle and/or needle jet.
    e. Plugged air jet or air passage.
    f. Loose or cracked air-box boot or duct.
    g. Loose carburetor hose clamps.
    h. Restricted fuel tank cap vent hose (**Figure 5**).
    i. Fuel valve (**Figure 2**) plugged or restricted.
    j. Fuel line (B, **Figure 4**) plugged or restricted.
    k. Fuel filter (if used) plugged or restricted.
    l. Starter plunger stuck open.
    m. Incorrect float level.
    n. Water in the fuel.
2. Engine speed drops off or cuts out abruptly:
    a. Plugged air filter element.
    b. Plugged exhaust system.
    c. Clutch slipping.
    d. Plugged main jet.
    e. Incorrect fuel level.
    f. Starter plunger stuck partially open.
    g. Throttle valve does not open all the way.
    h. Brakes dragging.
    i. Engine overheating.
    j. Water contamination in the fuel.
3. Low engine compression:
    a. Loose spark plug or missing spark plug gasket.
    b. Stuck piston ring.
    c. Excessive piston ring wear.
    d. Excessively worn piston and/or cylinder.
    e. Loose cylinder head fasteners.
    f. Cylinder head incorrectly installed and/or tightened.
    g. Warped cylinder head.
    h. Damaged head gasket.
    i. Damaged base gasket.
    j. Loose cylinder fasteners.
    k. Broken or weak valve spring.
    l. Bent valve.
    m. Carbon accumulation on valve seat.
    n. Compression release mechanism worn or stuck open.

Engine Knocking

If the engine knocks under acceleration, check for the following:
1. Excessive carbon buildup in the combustion chamber (cylinder head and piston surfaces).
2. Spark plug is too hot (see Chapter Three for the correct heat range).
3. Damaged CDI unit.
4. Incorrect ignition timing.
5. Poor quality fuel.
6. Incorrect fuel type.

Engine Overheating

Check for one or more of the following possible malfunctions.
1. Low coolant level. Visually check for leaks in the cooling system.
2. Coolant deterioration:
    a. Engine coolant contains additives to prevent cooling system corrosion. Because these additives weaken over time, replace the coolant to prevent corrosion buildup. Replace the coolant at the intervals specified in Chapter Three.
    b. Coolant has a unique smell that does not change unless contaminated. When the engine is cold, drain some coolant into a clean, clear container (see Chapter Three). If the coolant has an abnormal smell, exhaust gas may be leaking into the engine water jacket.
3. Defective cooling system:
    a. Defective radiator cap.
    b. Defective water pump.
    c. Plugged radiator and engine coolant passages.

2

d. Collapsed coolant hose.

e. Defective thermostat.

f. Defective thermostatic fan switch.

g. Fan damaged or not working.

4. Incorrect air/fuel mixture:

a. Plugged main jet.

b. Fuel level too low.

c. Loose intake manifold.

d. Airbox housing not sealing.

e. Airbox duct loose or leaking.

f. Plugged air cleaner.

5. Other causes of engine overheating are:

a. Excessive carbon buildup in the combustion chamber (cylinder head and piston surfaces).

b. Clutch slippage.

c. Brake drag.

d. Engine oil level too low or too high.

e. Poor engine oil quality.

f. Incorrect oil viscosity.

g. Dirty or improperly gapped spark plug.

h. Incorrect spark plug.

i. CDI failure.

ENGINE

Engine problems generally indicate that something is wrong in another system, such as ignition, fuel or starting systems. If properly maintained and serviced, the engine should experience no problems other than those caused by age and wear.

Preignition

Preignition is the premature burning of fuel and is caused by hot spots in the combustion chamber. The fuel ignites before it is supposed to. Glowing deposits in the combustion chamber, inadequate cooling or an overheated spark plug can all cause preignition. This is first noticed as a power loss but will eventually result in extensive damage to the internal engine parts because of excessive combustion chamber temperatures.

Detonation

Commonly called spark knock or fuel knock, detonation is the violent explosion of fuel in the combustion chamber instead of the controlled burn that takes place during normal combustion. Severe damage can result. Using low octane gasoline is a common cause of detonation.

Detonation can still occur, however, even if a high-octane fuel is used. Other causes are over-advanced ignition timing, lean fuel mixture at or near full throttle, inadequate engine cooling, or the excessive accumulation of carbon deposits in the combustion chamber (causing higher than normal cylinder compression).

Power Loss

Several factors can cause a lack of power and speed. Look for a restricted air filter or a fouled or damaged spark plug. A piston or cylinder that is galled, incorrect piston clearance or worn or sticky piston rings may be responsible. Look for loose bolts, defective gaskets or leaking machined mating surfaces on the cylinder head, cylinder or crankcase. Also check for a seized or damaged compression release mechanism.

Piston Seizure

This is caused by incorrect bore clearance, piston rings with an improper end gap, compression leak, incorrect engine oil, spark plug of the wrong heat range, incorrect ignition timing or lubrication system failure. Overheating from any cause can result in piston seizure.

Piston Slap

Piston slap is an audible slapping or rattling noise resulting from excessive piston-to-cylinder clearance. When allowed to continue, piston slap eventually leads to a shattered piston skirt.

To prevent piston slap, clean the air filter on a regular schedule. If piston slap is heard, disassemble the engine top end and measure the cylinder bore and piston diameter. Replace parts that exceed their wear limit or show damage.

ENGINE NOISES

1. *Knocking or pinging during acceleration*—Can be caused by using a lower octane fuel than recommended or a poor grade of fuel. Incorrect carburetor jetting and a too hot spark plug can cause pinging.

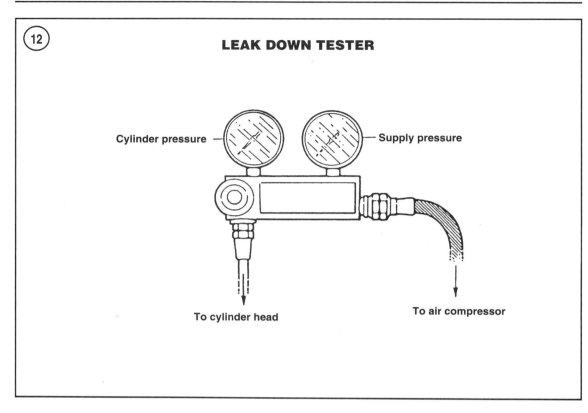

LEAK DOWN TESTER

Cylinder pressure — Supply pressure

To cylinder head   To air compressor

Refer to *Correct Spark Plug Heat Range* in Chapter Three. Check also for excessive carbon buildup in the combustion chamber or a defective CDI unit.

2. *Slapping or rattling noises at low speed or during acceleration*—Can be caused by piston slap from excessive piston-to-cylinder wall clearance. Check also for a bent connecting rod or worn piston pin and/or piston pin bore in the piston.

3. *Knocking or rapping while decelerating*—Usually caused by excessive rod bearing clearance.

4. *Persistent knocking and vibration or other noise*—Usually caused by worn main bearings. If the main bearings are good, consider the following:

    a. Loose engine mounts.

    b. Cracked frame.

    c. Leaking cylinder head gasket.

    d. Exhaust pipe leakage at cylinder head.

    e. Stuck piston ring.

    f. Broken piston ring.

    g. Partial engine seizure.

    h. Excessive connecting rod-to-crankshaft clearance.

    i. Excessive connecting rod side clearance.

    j. Excessive crankshaft runout.

    k. Worn or damaged primary drive gear.

5. *Rapid on-off squeal*—Compression leak around cylinder head gasket or spark plug.

ENGINE LEAK DOWN TEST

Isolate internal engine problems (leaking valve, broken, worn or stuck piston rings) by performing a cylinder leak down test. Perform a cylinder leak down test by applying compressed air to the cylinder and then measuring the percent of leakage. A cylinder leak down tester and an air compressor are required to perform this test (**Figure 12**).

Follow the tester manufacturer's directions along with the following information when performing a cylinder leak down test.

1. Run the engine until it reaches normal operating temperature. Then turn off the engine.

2. Remove the air filter assembly. Secure the throttle in the wide-open position.

3. Set the piston to TDC on the compression stroke. See *Valve Clearance Check and Adjustment* in Chapter Three.

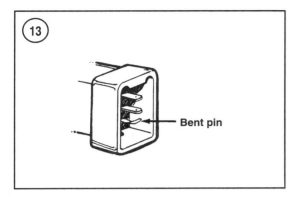

Bent pin

4. Remove the spark plug.

> *NOTE*
> *The engine may turn over when air*
> *pressure is applied to the cylinder. To*
> *prevent this from happening, shift the*
> *transmission into fifth gear and set the*
> *parking brake.*

5. Install the leak down tester into the cylinder spark plug hole.

6. Apply pressure to the cylinder following the tester manufacturer's instructions. Listen for air leaking while noting the following:
   a. Air leaking through the exhaust pipe indicates a leaking exhaust valve.
   b. Air leaking through the carburetor indicates a leaking intake valve.
   c. Air leaking through the crankcase breather tube indicates worn piston rings.

7. A cylinder with 10 percent (or more) cylinder leakage requires further service.

FUEL SYSTEM

Many riders automatically assume that the carburetor is at fault if the engine does not run properly. While fuel system problems are not uncommon, carburetor adjustment is seldom the answer. In many cases, adjusting the carburetor only compounds the problem by making the engine run worse.

Fuel system troubleshooting should start at the fuel tank and work through the system, reserving the carburetor as the final point. Most fuel system problems result from an empty fuel tank, a plugged fuel filter or fuel valve, or contaminated fuel. Fuel system troubleshooting is covered under *Engine Is*

Difficult To Start, Poor Idle Speed Performance and *Poor Running or High Speed Performance* in this chapter.

Check choke operation by moving the choke lever (**Figure 3**) by hand. The choke should move freely without binding or sticking in one position. If necessary, remove the starter plunger as described in Chapter Eight. Inspect its plunger and spring for exessive wear or damage.

ELECTRICAL TROUBLESHOOTING

Without proper information and a suitable plan, electrical troubleshooting can be very time consuming and frustrating. Refer to the wiring diagrams at the end of this book to assist in determining how the circuit operates. Use the wiring diagram to trace the current path from the power source, through the circuit and on to ground.

As with all troubleshooting procedures, analyze typical symptoms in a systematic manner. Never assume anything, and do not overlook the obvious like a separated electrical connector. Test the simplest and most obvious cause first, and try to make tests at easily accessible points on the ATV.

Preliminary Checks and Precautions

Prior to starting any electrical troubleshooting procedure, perform the following:

1. Disconnect the electrical connector in the suspected circuit and check for bent metal pins on the male side of the connector (**Figure 13**). A bent pin creates an open in the circuit.

2. Check each female end of the connector. Make sure the terminal connector on the end of each wire is pushed all the way into the plastic connector. To check this, carefully push them in with a small screwdriver.

3. Check all electrical wires where they enter the metal terminals in both the male and female sides of the connector.

4. Make sure all terminals in the connectors are clean and free of corrosion. Clean, if necessary, and pack the connectors with dielectric grease.

5. Push the connectors together. Make sure they are fully engaged and locked together.

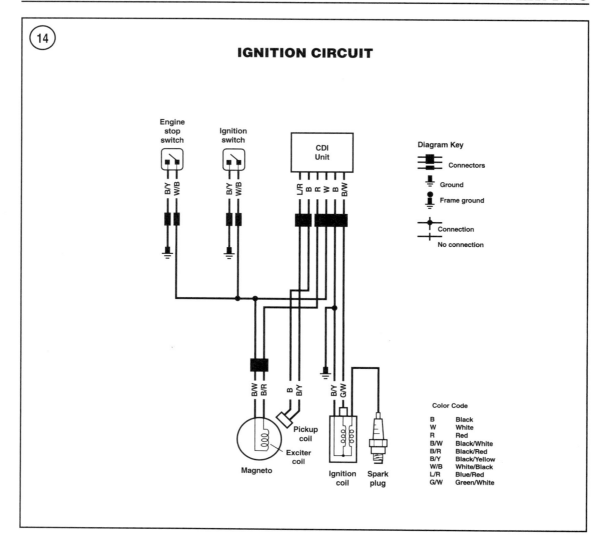

6. Never pull on the wires when disconnecting an electrical connector. Only pull the plastic connector housings.

IGNITION SYSTEM

All models are equipped with a capacitor discharge ignition system (CDI). This solid-state system uses no contact breaker points or other moving parts. **Figure 14** shows a schematic of the ignition system and its components.

Because of the solid-state design, problems with the ignition system are relatively few. However, when problems arise, they cause one of the following symptoms:

1. Weak spark.

2. No spark.

It is possible to check an ignition system that:

1. Does not have spark.

2. Has broken or damaged wires.

3. Has a weak spark.

It is difficult to check an ignition system that malfunctions due to:

1. Vibration problems.

2. Components that malfunction only when the engine is hot or under a load.

Use the troubleshooting procedures in **Figure 15** to quickly isolate an ignition problem.

CLUTCH

The two basic clutch troubles are

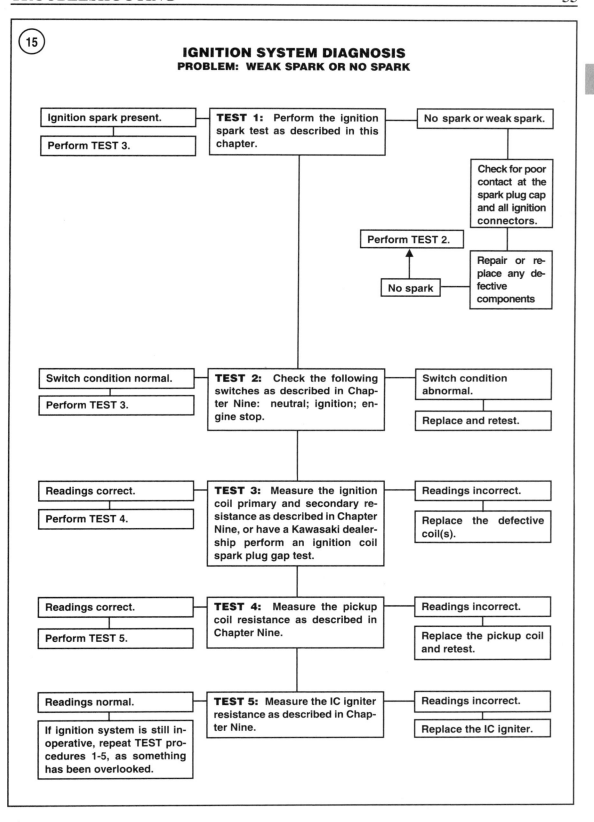

(15)

IGNITION SYSTEM DIAGNOSIS
PROBLEM: WEAK SPARK OR NO SPARK

2

| Ignition spark present. | **TEST 1:** Perform the ignition spark test as described in this chapter. | No spark or weak spark. |

| Perform TEST 3. |

Check for poor contact at the spark plug cap and all ignition connectors.

Perform TEST 2.

No spark

Repair or replace any defective components

| Switch condition normal. | **TEST 2:** Check the following switches as described in Chapter Nine: neutral; ignition; engine stop. | Switch condition abnormal. |

| Perform TEST 3. | | Replace and retest. |

| Readings correct. | **TEST 3:** Measure the ignition coil primary and secondary resistance as described in Chapter Nine, or have a Kawasaki dealership perform an ignition coil spark plug gap test. | Readings incorrect. |

| Perform TEST 4. | | Replace the defective coil(s). |

| Readings correct. | **TEST 4:** Measure the pickup coil resistance as described in Chapter Nine. | Readings incorrect. |

| Perform TEST 5. | | Replace the pickup coil and retest. |

| Readings normal. | **TEST 5:** Measure the IC igniter resistance as described in Chapter Nine. | Readings incorrect. |

| If ignition system is still inoperative, repeat TEST procedures 1-5, as something has been overlooked. | | Replace the IC igniter. |

clutch slipping and clutch dragging.

All clutch troubles, except adjustments, require partial engine disassembly to identify and correct the problem. Refer to Chapter Six for specific procedures.

Clutch Slipping

When the clutch slips, the engine speed increases faster than the actual forward speed indicates. The engine acts like the clutch is being feathered or slipped when it is not. Because the clutch plates are spinning against each other and not engaging, an excessive amount of heat develops in the clutch. This heat causes rapid and excessive clutch plate wear and warping as well as clutch spring failure.

If the clutch slips, check for one or more of the following possible malfunctions.
1. Clutch wear or damage:
   a. Incorrect clutch lever free play.
   b. Loose, weak or damaged clutch springs.
   c. Worn friction plates.
   d. Warped clutch plates.
   e. Severely worn clutch hub and/or clutch housing.
   f. Incorrectly assembled clutch.
   g. Worn or damaged clutch release mechanism.
2. Engine oil:
   a. Low oil level.
   b. Oil additives.
   c. Low viscosity oil.

Clutch Dragging

Clutch drag occurs when the clutch does not slip enough. When shifting into gear with the clutch disengaged, the ATV will jerk or jump forward. Once underway, the transmission is difficult to shift. If this condition is not repaired, the transmission gears will grind and lead to transmission gear and shift fork wear/damage.

If the clutch drags, check for one or more of the following possible malfunctions.
1. Clutch wear or damage:
   a. Warped clutch plates.
   b. Swollen friction plates.
   c. Warped pressure plate.
   d. Incorrect clutch spring tension.
   e. Incorrectly assembled clutch.

   f. Loose clutch nut.
   g. Burnt primary driven gear bushing.
   h. Damaged clutch boss.
   i. Incorrect clutch adjustment.
   j. Damaged clutch release mechanism.
2. Engine oil:
   a. Oil level too high.
   b. High viscosity oil.
   c. Oil deteriorated.

TRANSMISSION AND EXTERNAL SHIFT MECHANISM

The Mojave is equipped with a 5-speed, constant mesh transmission with a reverse gear. Some transmission symptoms are difficult to distinguish from clutch symptoms. For example, if the gears grind during shifting, the problem may be caused by a dragging clutch. However, if the clutch drag problem is not repaired transmission damage will eventually occur.

An incorrectly assembled or damaged external shift mechanism also causes shifting problems. Always investigate the easiest and most accessible areas first. To prevent an incorrect diagnosis, perform the following inspection procedure to troubleshoot the external shift mechanism and transmission. At the same time, check for one or more of the possible malfunctions described in the list below.

The external shift mechanism consists of the shift shaft (A, **Figure 16**), shift cam (B), and the stopper lever (C).

NOTE
The following procedure requires that the transmission be shifted by hand. When trying to shift a constant mesh

transmission, one of the transmission shafts must be turning. To accomplish this easily, have an assistant turn the rear wheel while you shift the transmission.

1. Check that the clutch is properly adjusted. Eliminate any clutch drag or slipping problems. If the clutch is functioning correctly, continue with Step 2.
2. Support the ATV with the rear wheels of the ground.
3. Remove the clutch as described in Chapter Six.

NOTE
Do not allow the shift shaft to back out when shifting the transmission. If necessary, install a plate over the shift shaft to hold it in place.

4. Have an assistant turn the rear wheel while you shift the transmission with the shift lever. Note the following:
   a. Check that the shift shaft return spring straddles the stud as shown in D, **Figure 16**.
   b. If the transmission does not shift properly, remove the shift lever and pull the shift shaft (A, **Figure 16**) from the engine as described in Chapter Seven.
   c. Check the shift shaft for missing parts, incorrect assembly or damage (Chapter Seven).
5. Have an assistant turn the rear wheel while you turn the shift cam (A, **Figure 17**) by hand. As it is being turned, watch the movement of the stopper lever (B, **Figure 17**). Its roller should move in and out of the shift cam detents. Each detent position represents a different gear. The raised detent (C, **Figure 17**) represents neutral.

The stopper lever is held under tight spring tension so the lever roller follows the shift cam surface. When the shift drum turns, it rotates the shift cam. The roller on the shift lever rolls along the rotating shift cam, moving out of one detent and into the next. If this does not happen while shifting the transmission, try to pry the stopper lever out of the detent with a screwdriver. If the stopper lever does not move, it is installed incorrectly.

Remove and reinstall the stopper lever. Try shifting again. If this does not correct the problem, remove the stopper lever and check for damage.
6. Check the shift cam by performing the following:
   a. Shift the transmission into NEUTRAL, and make a mark on the crankcase that aligns with the NEUTRAL detent (C, **Figure 17**) on the shift cam.
   b. While an assistant turns the rear wheels, turn the shift cam to change gears. The transmission should shift into each gear. Each time a shift occurs, a new detent should align with the mark on the crankcase.
   c. If the shift cam cannot be turned or if it locks into a particular gear position, the transmission is damaged. A transmission gear or bearing may be seized, a shift fork could be damaged, or the shift drum could be faulty.
7. Disassemble the engine and remove the transmission as described in Chapter Five.

Difficult Shifting

If the shift shaft does not move smoothly from one gear to the next, check the following.
1. Shift shaft:
   a. Shift fork(s) bent or seized.
   b. Gear(s) binding on shaft.
   c. Shift shaft return spring weak or broken.
   d. Shift pawl spring broken.
   e. Shift shaft return-spring bolt loose.
   f. Shift shaft broken.
2. Stopper lever:
   a. Seized or damaged stopper lever roller.
   b. Broken stopper lever spring.
   c. Loose stopper lever mounting bolt.
   d. Stopper lever incorrectly installed or binding on its pivot.
3. Shift drum and shift forks:
   a. Bent shift fork(s).

b. Damaged shift fork guide pin(s).
c. Seized shift fork (on shaft).
d. Broken shift fork or shift fork shaft.
e. Damaged shift drum groove(s).
f. Damaged shift drum bearing.

Transmission Will Not Stay in Gear

If the transmission shifts into gear but then slips or pops out, check the following.
1. Shift shaft:
    a. Incorrect shift lever position/adjustment.
    b. Stopper lever fails to move or set properly.
2. Shift drum:
    a. Incorrect thrust play.
    b. Excessively worn or damaged shift drum groove(s).
    c. Worn or broken stopper lever spring.
3. Shift fork(s):
    a. Bent shift fork(s).
    b. Worn guide pins.
4. Transmission:
    a. Worn or damaged gear dogs.
    b. Excessive gear thrust play.
    c. Worn or damaged shaft circlips or thrust washers.
    d. Worn splines on main shaft, countershaft, or gear.

Transmission Overshifts

If the transmission overshifts when shifting up or down, check the following.
1. Check for a weak or broken shift shaft return spring.
2. Check for a weak or broken stopper lever spring.

Inoperative Reverse

If the transmission fails to go into or operate in reverse, check the following.
1. Reverse lever:
    a. Incorrect reverse lever adjustment. See *Reverse Cable Adjustment* in Chapter Three.
    b. Stripped reverse lever-to-reverse shift drum splines.
2. Reverse shaft:
    a. Damaged reverse shaft pinion gear thrust play.

b. Excessive reverse shaft pinion gear play.
3. Countershaft.
4. Reverse shift drum and fork:
    a. Damaged reverse shift drum groove.
    b. Bent reverse shift fork.

DRIVE TRAIN NOISE

This section deals with noises restricted to the final drive assembly, clutch and transmission. While some drive train noises have little meaning, abnormal noises are a good indicator of a developing problem. The difficulty involves recognizing the difference between a normal and abnormal noise. One thing that is positive, however, is that by maintaining and riding the ATV, you become accustomed to the normal noises that occur during starting and riding. A new noise, no matter how minor, should be investigated.
1. *Drive train noise*—Investigate any noise that develops in the drive train. Check for the following conditions:
    a. Worn or improperly adjusted drive chain.
    b. Worn or damaged engine sprocket.
    c. Worn or damaged rear sprocket.
    d. Insufficient chain lubrication.
2. *Clutch noise*—Investigate any noise that develops in the clutch. First, drain the engine oil, checking for bits of metal or clutch plate material. If the oil appears normal, remove the clutch cover and clutch (Chapter Six) and check for the following:
    a. Worn or damaged clutch housing gear teeth.
    b. Excessive clutch housing axial play.
    c. Excessive clutch housing-to-friction plate clearance.
    d. Excessive clutch housing gear-to-primary drive gear backlash.
    e. Kickstarter ratchet not disengaging from kick gear.
3. *Transmission noise*—The transmission exhibits more normal noises than the clutch, but like the clutch, a new noise in the transmission should be investigated. Drain the engine oil into a clean container. Wipe a small amount of oil on a finger and rub the finger and thumb together. Check for the presence of metallic particles. Inspect the drain container for signs of water separation from the oil. Transmission associated noises can be caused by:
    a. Insufficient oil level.
    b. Contaminated oil.

c. Oil viscosity too thin. Thin oil will raise the transmission operating temperature.

d. Worn transmission gear(s).

e. Chipped or broken transmission gear(s).

f. Excessive transmission gear side play.

g. Worn or damaged crankshaft-to-transmission bearing(s).

HANDLING

Poor handling reduces overall performance and may cause a crash. If there is poor handling, check the following items.

1. If the handlebars are hard to turn, check for the following:

a. Low tire pressure.

b. Damaged tie rod end.

c. Damaged steering knuckle joint.

d. Bent steering shaft.

e. Damaged steering shaft bearings.

f. Inadequate steering-shaft-bearing lubrication.

2. If there is excessive handlebar shake or vibration, check for the following:

a. Worn tires.

b. Damaged wheel rim(s).

c. Loose steering shaft.

d. Excessive rear axle runout.

e. Worn wheel bearing(s).

f. Loose handlebar clamps.

3. If the handlebar pulls to one side, check for the following:

a. Bent tie rod.

b. Bent steering shaft.

c. Bent suspension arm or swing arm.

d. Damaged rim(s).

e. Bent frame.

f. Incorrect tire air pressure.

g. Damaged shock absorber.

h. Incorrect toe-in adjustment.

4. Shock absorbers—check the following:

a. Damaged damper rod.

b. Leaking damper housing.

c. Sagging shock spring(s).

d. Incorrect shock adjustment.

e. Loose or damaged shock mount bolts.

f. Worn or damaged shock mount bearings.

g. Tire pressure too high.

h. Improperly adjusted shock absorber.

5. Frame—check the following:

a. Damaged frame.

b. Cracked or broken engine mount brackets.

FRAME NOISE

Noises traced to the frame or suspension are usually caused by loose, worn or damaged parts. Various noises that are related to the frame are listed below:

1. *Disc brake noise*—A screeching sound during braking is the most common disc brake noise. Some other disc brake associated noises can be caused by:

a. Glazed brake pad surface.

b. Excessively worn brake pads.

c. Warped brake disc.

d. Loose brake disc mounting bolts.

e. Loose or missing caliper mounting bolts.

f. Damaged caliper.

2. *Shock absorber noise*—Check for the following:

a. Loose shock absorber mounting bolts.

b. Cracked or broken shock spring.

c. Damaged shock absorber.

d. Swing-arm or suspension-arm bearing damaged.

e. Inadequate lubrication in swing-arm or suspension-arm bearing

3. *Other frame-associated noises*—Check for the following:

a. Broken frame.

b. Broken suspension arms.

c. Loose engine mounting bolts.

d. Damaged steering bearings.

e. Loose mounting bracket(s).

BRAKES

The front and rear brake units are critical to riding performance and safety. Inspect the brakes frequently and repair any problem immediately. When replacing or refilling the brake fluid, use only DOT 3 or DOT 4 brake fluid from a sealed container. See Chapter Thirteen for additional information on brake fluid selection and disc brake service. Use the troubleshooting procedures in **Figure 18** to isolate the majority of disc brake troubles.

When checking brake pad wear, check that the brake pads in each caliper contact the disc squarely. If one of the brake pads is wearing unevenly, suspect a warped or bent brake disc or damaged caliper.

⑱ **DISC BRAKE TROUBLESHOOTING**

| Disc brake fluid leakage |

Check:
- Loose or damaged line fittings
- Worn caliper piston seals
- Scored caliper piston and/or bore
- Loose banjo bolts
- Damaged washers
- Leaking master cylinder diaphragm
- Leaking master cylinder secondary seal
- Cracked master cylinder housing
- Too high brake fluid level
- Loose master cylinder cover

| Brake overheating |

Check:
- Warped brake disc
- Incorrect brake fluid
- Caliper piston and/or brake pads hanging up
- Riding brakes during operation

| Brake chatter |

Check:
- Warped brake disc
- Loose brake disc
- Incorrect caliper alignment
- Loose caliper mounting bolts
- Loose front axle nut and/or clamps
- Worn wheel bearings
- Damaged front hub
- Restricted brake hydraulic line
- Contaminated brake pads

| Brake locking |

Check:
- Incorrect brake fluid
- Plugged passages in master cylinder
- Incorrect front brake adjustment
- Caliper piston and/or brake pads hanging up
- Warped brake disc

| Insufficient brakes |

Check:
- Air in brake lines
- Worn brake pads
- Low brake fluid level
- Incorrect brake fluid
- Worn brake disc
- Worn caliper piston seals
- Glazed brake pads
- Leaking primary cup seal in master cylinder
- Contaminated brake pads and/or disc

| Brake squeal |

Check:
- Contaminated brake pads and/or disc
- Dust or dirt collected behind brake pads
- Loose parts

LUBRICATION, MAINTENANCE AND TUNE-UP

ATVs require periodic maintenance to operate efficiently. Neglecting regular maintenance reduces the service life and performance of any vehicle.

This chapter explains the lubrication, maintenance and tune-up procedures required for the Mojave. **Tables 1-5** are at the end of the chapter. **Table 1** is a suggested maintenance schedule. **Table 2** lists tire specifications while **Table 3** lists the recommended lubricants and fluids for the ATV. Maintenance specifications appear in **Table 4**, and tightening torques are in **Table 5**.

PRE-RIDE CHECKLIST

Check the following prior to the first ride of the day.

1. Inspect all fuel lines and fittings for leaks.
2. Make sure the fuel tank is full of fresh gasoline.
3. Make sure the engine oil level is correct; add oil if necessary.
4. Make sure the air filter is clean.
5. Make sure the throttle and the brake levers operate properly with no binding.
6. Check the brake fluid level in the front and rear master cylinder reservoirs; add DOT 3 or DOT 4 brake fluid if necessary.
7. Check the parking brake operation.
8. Check the rear brake pedal height as described in this chapter.

9. Inspect the front and rear suspensions; make sure each has a good solid feel with no looseness.
10. Check the tire pressures; refer to **Table 2**.
11. Check the exhaust system for looseness or damage.
12. Check the tightness of all fasteners, especially engine mounting hardware.
13. Make sure the headlight, taillight and brake light (2000 models) work.
14. Turn the handlebar from side to side to check steering play. Service the steering assembly if excessive play is noted. Also check that the handlebar control cables do not bind.
15. Start the engine, and stop it with the engine stop switch. If engine stop switch does not work properly, test the switch as described in Chapter Nine.

SERVICE INTERVALS

Table 1 lists the recommended service intervals. Strict adherence to these recommendations ensures a long service from the ATV. However, if the vehicle is operated in an area of high humidity, lubricate and service the ATV more frequently to prevent possible rust and corrosion damage. This is particularly true if the vehicle is run through water (especially saltwater) and sand. For convenience when maintaining the vehicle, most of the services shown in **Table 1** are described in this chapter. However,

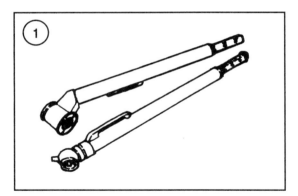

procedures, which require more than minor disassembly or adjustment, are covered in the appropriate chapter of this manual.

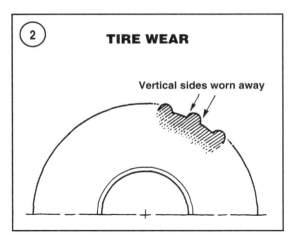

TIRE WEAR

Vertical sides worn away

TIRES AND WHEELS

Tire Pressure

Check and adjust the tire pressure to get the maximum life out of the tire and to ensure good traction and handling. A simple, accurate gauge (**Figure 1**) can be purchased for a few dollars and should be carried in the tool box. Always check the tire pressure when the tires are cold. Tire pressures are listed in **Table 2**.

NOTE
*The tire pressure specifications listed in **Table 2** refer to the original equipment tires. If different tires have been installed, follow the tire pressure recommendations specified by the tire manufacturer.*

WARNING
Always inflate all tires (front and rear) to the correct air pressure. If the vehicle is operated with unequal air pressures, it will pull toward one side, causing poor handling.

CAUTION
Do not overinflate the tires; they will be permanently distorted and damaged. Overinflated tires bulge out along the rim. If this happens, the tire will not return to its original contour.

Tire Inspection

The tires take a lot of punishment due to the variety of terrain they are subject to. Inspect them periodically for excessive wear, cuts, abrasions, etc. If a nail or other object is found in the tire, mark its location with a light crayon prior to removing it. This will help locate the hole for repair. Refer to Chapter Eleven for tire changing and repair information.

To gauge tire wear, inspect the shape of the tread knobs. If the drive knob vertical sides (**Figure 2**) are worn away, replace the tire as described in Chapter Eleven.

WARNING
Do not ride the vehicle with damaged or severely worn tires. Tires in bad condition can cause loss of control. Replace damaged or severely worn tires immediately.

3

Rim Inspection

Frequently inspect the condition of the wheel rims, especially the outer side (**Figure 3**). If the wheel has hit a tree or large rock, rim damage may cause an air leak or knock a wheel out of alignment. Improper wheel alignment can cause excessive vibration and result in an unsafe riding condition.

Make sure the wheel nuts are securely in place on all wheels. If they are loose, the wheel could damage the hub studs or fall off. Tighten wheel nuts to the torque specification in **Table 5**.

LUBRICANTS

Engine Oil

Oil is graded according to its viscosity, which is an indication of its thickness. The Society of Automotive Engineers (SAE) distinguishes oil viscosity by numbers, called weights. Thick (heavy) oils have higher viscosity numbers than thin (light) oils. For example, a 5-weight (SAE 5) oil is a light oil while a 90-weight (SAE 90) oil is relatively heavy. The viscosity of the oil has nothing to do with its lubricating properties.

Grease

Waterproof grease should be used when grease is called for.

CLEANING SOLVENT

A number of solvents can be used to remove old dirt, grease, and oil. See a dealership or an auto parts store.

> *WARNING*
> *Never use gasoline as a cleaning solvent. Gasoline is extremely volatile and contains tremendously destructive potential energy. The slightest spark, from metal parts hitting each other or a tool slipping, could cause a fatal explosion.*

PERIODIC LUBRICATION

Perform the services listed in this section at the maintenance intervals specified in **Table 1**. If the vehicle is exposed to harder than normal use with constant exposure to mud, water, sand, and high humidity, perform the services more frequently.

Engine Oil Level Check

Engine oil level is checked through the oil level gauge mounted in the lower right side of the clutch cover.

1. Start the engine and let it warm up approximately 2-3 minutes.
2. Park the vehicle on level ground and apply the parking brake.
3. Shut off the engine and let the oil settle.
4. View the oil level through the oil level gauge. The oil level should be between the upper and lower lines next to the gauge; see **Figure 4**.
5. If the oil level is low, remove the oil fill cap (**Figure 5**) and add the recommended grade and viscosity oil listed in **Table 3**. Once the oil level is correct, install the oil fill cap.

> *NOTE*
> *Refer to **Engine Oil and Filter Change** in this chapter for additional information on oil selection.*

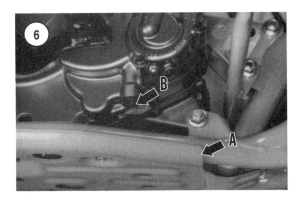

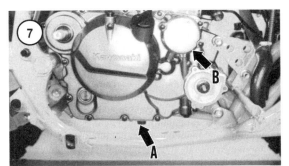

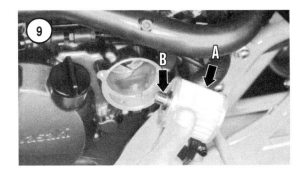

6. If the oil level is too high, remove the oil fill cap (**Figure 5**) and draw out the excess oil with a syringe or suitable pump.

7. Recheck the oil level.

Engine Oil and Filter Change

Regular oil changes contribute more to engine longevity than any other maintenance performed. The recommended oil and filter change intervals are in **Table 1**. This assumes that the vehicle is operated in moderate climates. If it is operated under dusty conditions, the oil will get contaminated more quickly and should be changed more frequently than recommended.

Use only a high-quality, detergent motor oil with an API rating of SE, SF or SG. The rating is printed on the bottle. Refer to **Table 3** for Kawasaki recommended oil viscosity. Try to use the same brand of oil at each oil change.

To change the engine oil and filter use the following:

  a. Drain pan.
  b. Funnel.
  c. Wrench and sockets.
  d. 2-3 quarts of oil (see **Table 3**).
  e. New oil filter.

NOTE
Never dispose of motor oil in the trash, on the ground, or down a storm drain. Many service stations accept used motor oil and waste haulers provide curbside used motor oil collection. Do not combine other fluids with motor oil to be recycled. To locate a recycler, contact

*the American Petroleum Institute (API) at **www.recycleoil.org**.*

NOTE
Warming the engine allows the oil to heat up; thus it flows freely and carries any contaminants out with it.

1. Start the engine and let it warm up to operating temperature.

2. Place the vehicle on level ground and apply the parking brake.

3. Shut the engine off and place a drain pan under the engine.

4. Remove the engine skid plate (A, **Figure 6**).

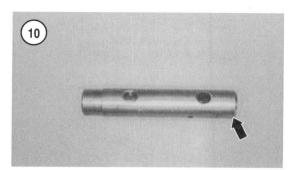

c. Thoroughly clean out the guide pin (**Figure 10**) and filter cavity. If necessary, scrape out any oil sludge.

NOTE
*The guide pin (**Figure 10**) is equipped with a bypass valve. To service the bypass valve, refer to **Bypass Valve Inspection** in this chapter.*

d. Inspect the filter cover and the O-ring. Replace the O-ring if it has become hard or is starting to deteriorate.

e. Lightly wipe both oil filter grommets (**Figure 11**) with clean engine oil.

f. Insert the guide pin through the oil filter (**Figure 12**) and center it.

NOTE
*The guide pin is directional—one end is larger than the other (**Figure 10**). The larger end seats in the crankcase filter cavity. The small end seats in the oil filter cover bore.*

g. Insert the guide pin into the crankcase so the larger outer diameter seats into the crankcase filter cavity (B, **Figure 9**).

h. If removed, install the O-ring into the oil filter cover groove.

i. Install the filter cover so the arrow (**Figure 13**) on the cover points up. The end of the guide pin should fit into the center of the filter cover.

NOTE
If the oil filter cover will not fit into place, the guide pin is installed backward. Remove the oil filter and turn the pin around.

5. Remove the oil drain bolt (A, **Figure 7**) from the bottom of the crankcase. Also remove the oil passage bolt (B, **Figure 6**) from the bottom of the clutch cover.

6. Loosen the oil fill cap. This speeds up the flow of oil.

7. Allow the oil to drain completely.

8. Remove the oil screen (**Figure 8**) from the crankcase.

9. To replace the oil filter, perform the following:

    a. Remove the oil filter cover (B, **Figure 7**) and its O-ring.

    b. Remove the oil filter (A, **Figure 9**) and guide pin (B, **Figure 9**) from the oil filter cavity. Discard the oil filter.

j. Install and tighten the filter cover mounting screws.

10. Clean the oil screen (**Figure 8**) as described in Chapter Five. Install it in place in the crankcase. Replace the screen if necessary.

11. Be sure the gasket is in place on the oil drain bolt and on the oil passage bolt. Replace either gasket as necessary.

12. Install the oil drain bolt (A, **Figure 7**) and the oil passage bolt (B, **Figure 6**). Tighten each to the torque specification in **Table 5**.

13. Insert a funnel into the oil fill hole and fill the engine with the correct weight and quantity of oil. Refer to **Table 3** for refill capacity.

14. Remove the funnel and screw in the oil fill cap (**Figure 5**) securely.

15. Start the engine and let it idle.

16. Check the oil filter cover and drain plugs for leaks.

17. Check the engine oil flow as described in *Engine Oil Flow Inspection* in this chapter.

18. Turn off the engine and allow the oil to settle. Then check the engine oil level as described in this chapter.

> *WARNING*
> *Prolonged contact with oil may cause skin cancer. It is advisable to wash your hands thoroughly with soap and water as soon as possible after handling or coming in contact with motor oil.*

Bypass Valve Inspection

A bypass valve, consisting of a spring and plunger, is installed in the guide pin (**Figure 14**). If the oil filter becomes clogged or damaged to where oil cannot pass through it, pressure buildup in the filter opens the bypass valve. This allows engine oil to bypass the oil filter and go directly to the engine. While the bypass valve is designed to prevent engine damage, the unfiltered oil will cause rapid wear of all moving parts.

> *NOTE*
> *Do not drain the engine oil if only the bypass valve is being serviced.*

1. Remove the oil filter and guide pin as described in this chapter.

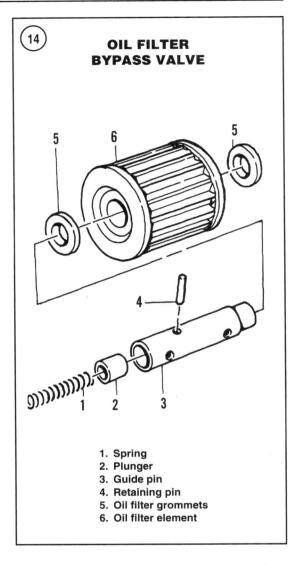

OIL FILTER BYPASS VALVE

1. Spring
2. Plunger
3. Guide pin
4. Retaining pin
5. Oil filter grommets
6. Oil filter element

2. Pull the guide pin from the oil filter, and drive the retaining pin out of the guide pin.

3. Remove the spring and bypass valve plunger.

4. Clean all parts in solvent and dry them thoroughly.

5. Check the plunger for excessive wear or damage. If the plunger is worn, replace the bypass valve assembly.

6. Replace the spring if it is bent or distorted.

7. Install the bypass valve plunger, closed end first, into the guide pin (**Figure 14**).

8. Install the spring into the guide pin. Then compress the spring so it is beyond the retaining pin hole.

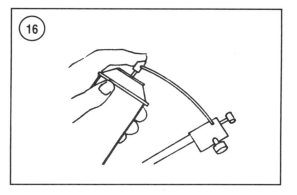

9. Drive the retaining pin into the small hole. The pin should be flush on both sides.

10. Install the oil filter and guide pin as described in this chapter.

Engine Oil Flow Inspection

Use this procedure to check engine oil flow. Perform this procedure after reassembling the engine, when troubleshooting the lubrication system, or if the external oil pipe is removed or replaced.

WARNING
The oil passages deliver engine oil from the oil pump to engine components. Because the oil flowing through these passages is under pressure, do not increase engine speed above idle when checking oil flow in the following step; otherwise, the oil may spray out and cause injury.

1. Check the engine oil level as described in this chapter. Adjust the oil level if necessary.

2. Start the engine and run it at idle.

NOTE
The oil filter housing has been removed for clarity. It is not necessary to remove the housing to access the oil pipe banjo bolt.

3. Loosen, but do not remove, the engine-oil-pipe banjo bolt mounted on the left crankcase; see **Figure 15**. Oil should seep out from around the bolt, indicating that engine oil pressure is present.

4. Turn the engine off.

5. Tighten the banjo bolt to the torque specification in **Table 5**.

6. Wipe up the oil that leaked from the banjo bolt.

7. If no oil leaks from the banjo bolt, remove and inspect the oil filter (this chapter) and the oil screen (Chapter Five). If these components are not at fault, inspect the oil pump and oil pipe as described in Chapter Five.

WARNING
Prolonged contact with oil may cause skin cancer. It is advisable to wash your hands thoroughly with soap and water as soon as possible after handling or coming in contact with motor oil.

General Lubrication

At the service intervals in **Table 1**, lubricate the control cables and drive chain as described below. Also lubricate the following items with the grease:

- a. Throttle cable end.
- b. Throttle lever pivot.
- c. Choke cable.
- d. Parking brake cable end.
- e. Brake pedal shaft.
- f. Reverse cable ends.

Control Cable Lubrication

Clean and lubricate the throttle cable, parking brake cable, choke cable and reverse cable at the intervals indicated in **Table 1**. In addition, the cables should be checked for kinks, excessive wear, damage or fraying that could cause the cables to fail or stick. Cables are expendable items and do not last forever, even under the best of conditions.

A cable lubricator (**Figure 16**) provides the most positive means of control cable lubrication. A can

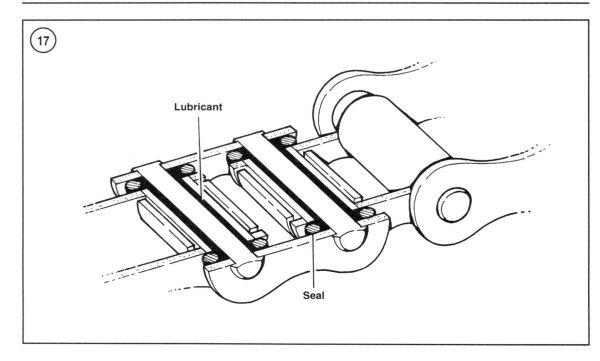

of cable lube or a general lubricant is required. Do not use chain lube as a cable lubricant.

1. Disconnect the cable to be lubricated.

2. Attach a cable lubricator to the end of the cable following its manufacturer's instructions (**Figure 16**).

NOTE
Place a shop cloth at the end of the cable to catch the oil as it runs out.

3. Insert the lubricant can nozzle into the lubricator, press the button on the can and hold it down until the lubricant begins to flow out of the other end of the cable. If the cable lube will not flow out the other end of the cable, remove the lubricator and try at the opposite end of the cable.

4. Disconnect the lubricator.

5. Apply a light coat of grease to the cable ends before reconnecting them. Reconnect the cable and adjust it as described in this chapter.

6. After lubricating the throttle cable, operate the throttle lever at the handlebar. It should open and close smoothly with no binding.

7. After lubricating a brake cable, check brake operation.

Drive Chain Lubrication

Kawasaki recommends SAE 90 oil for chain lubrication. It is less likely to be thrown off the chain than lighter oils. Many of the commercial drivechain lubricants also do an excellent job.

NOTE
*If the drive chain is very dirty, remove and clean it as described under **Drive Chain Cleaning** in this chapter before lubricating it as described in this procedure.*

CAUTION
*The original equipment drive chain is equipped with O-rings between the side plates (**Figure 17**) that seal grease between the pins and bushings. To prevent O-ring damage, only clean the chain with kerosene or diesel oil. Do not use gasoline or other solvents. This causes the O-rings to swell or deteriorate. Refer to the cleaning procedures later in this chapter.*

1. Ride the ATV a few miles to warm up the drive chain. A warm chain increases lubricant penetration.

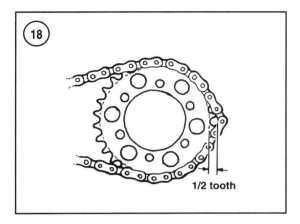

2. Park the ATV on a level surface, and set the parking brake.

3. Shift the transmission into neutral, and support the bike with wooden blocks or a scissors jack so that the rear wheels clear the ground.

4. Oil the bottom chain run with SAE 90 oil or with a commercial chain lubricant *recommended* for use on O-ring drive chains. Concentrate on getting the oil down between the side plates of the chain links (**Figure 17**). Apply oil to the sides of the rollers so oil will seep into the rollers and bushings. Also be sure the O-rings are thoroughly coated with oil.

> *CAUTION*
> *Not all commercial chain lubricants are recommended for use on O-ring drive chains. Read the label carefully before purchasing chain lube. Be sure it is formulated for O-ring chains.*

5. Rotate the chain and continue applying oil until the entire chain has been lubricated.

6. Wipe off any oil or chain lubricant that has dripped onto the swing arm or rear wheel.

UNSCHEDULED LUBRICATION

The services listed in this section are not included in the maintenance schedule (**Table 1**). However, these items should be lubricated on a regular basis. Lubrication and service intervals depend on vehicle use.

Front Control Arms

Remove the front upper and lower control arms (Chapter Eleven) and lubricate the bearings, sleeves, and seals with molybdenum disulfide grease.

Front Hub Wheel Bearings and Seals

The front hub seal lips should be lubricated with high quality wheel bearing grease. The front hub bearings are sealed. They cannot be lubricated. Refer to Chapter Eleven for service.

Swing Arm

Remove the swing arm (Chapter Twelve) and lubricate the needle bearings and seals with molybdenum disulfide grease.

Shock Absorbers

Remove the front shock absorbers (Chapter Eleven) and lubricate the lower pivot spherical bearing and seals with molybdenum disulfide grease.

Remove the rear shock absorber (Chapter Twelve) and lubricate upper pivot needle bearing and seals with molybdenum disulfide grease.

PERIODIC MAINTENANCE

Periodic maintenance intervals are in **Table 1**.

Drive Chain/Sprocket Inspection (Chain Installed)

Inspect the drive chain frequently. Replace the chain if it is excessively worn or damaged. A quick check gives an indication of when to actually measure chain wear. Pull one of the links away from the rear sprocket as shown in **Figure 18**. If the link pulls away from the sprocket by more than half the height of a sprocket tooth, the chain is either excessively worn or adjusted too loosely. Measure drive chain wear by performing the following:

1. Park the ATV on level ground, and set the parking brake. Block the front wheels so the vehicle does not roll in either direction.

2. Raise the rear of the vehicle with a small hydraulic or scissor jack. Place the jack under the frame with a piece of wood between the jack and the frame.

3. Place wooden block(s) under the frame to support the vehicle securely with the rear wheels off the ground.

4. Loosen the clamp bolt on each side of the swing arm (A, **Figure 19**).

5. Insert a drift or other suitable tool into the hole in the bearing housing (B, **Figure 19**).

6. Use the tool to rotate the bearing housing downward until the chain is taut.

7. Tighten each swing arm clamp bolt (A, **Figure 19**) to the torque specification in **Table 5**.

8. Measure the distance between 21 pins (20 links) in the chain's upper run with a vernier caliper (**Figure 20**). Rotate the chain, and measure another 20-link length. Check the chain at several places. If any measurement is greater than the service limit in **Table 4**, replace the drive chain, engine sprocket, and rear sprocket. Never install a new drive chain over worn sprockets or a worn drive chain over new sprockets.

9. Check both the engine sprocket and the rear sprocket for wear (**Figure 21**) or missing teeth. If any wear is noticed on the teeth, replace both sprockets and the drive chain. Never install a new drive chain over worn sprockets or a worn drive chain over new sprockets.

10. Adjust the drive chain tension as described in this chapter.

Drive Chain Cleaning and Inspection

Clean and lubricate the drive chain at the interval in **Table 1** or more frequently if the bike is often ridden in wet, dusty or muddy conditions. A properly maintained chain provides maximum service life and reliability.

1. Remove the drive chain as described in Chapter Twelve.

CAUTION
*The original equipment drive chain is equipped with O-rings between the side plates (**Figure 17**) that seal grease between the pins and bushings. To prevent O-ring damage, only clean the chain with kerosene. Do not use gasoline or other solvents. These cause the O-rings to swell or deteriorate.*

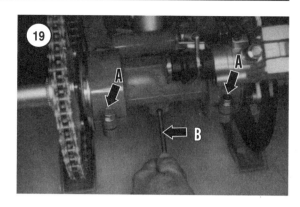

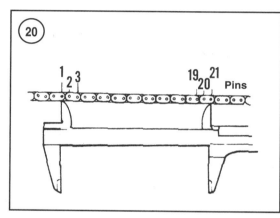

2. Immerse the chain in a pan of kerosene. Let it soak for about 5 minutes. Move the chain around and flex it during this period so the dirt between the pins and rollers works its way out.

3. Scrub the rollers and side plates with a soft brush and rinse away loosened grit. Rinse the chain in fresh kerosene a couple times to make sure all dirt is removed.

4. Immediately dry the chain with compressed air.

5. Stretch out the chain on the workbench, and measure the distance between 21 pins (20 links) of the chain with a vernier caliper (**Figure 20**). If the drive chain is worn to the service limit listed in **Table 4**, replace the drive chain, engine sprocket, and rear sprocket.

NOTE
*Always check both the engine sprocket and the rear sprocket every time the drive chain is removed (**Figure 21**). If any wear is noticed on the teeth, replace both sprockets and the drive chain. Never install a new drive*

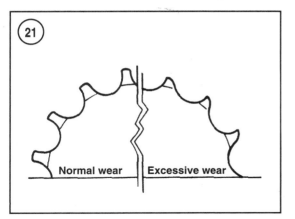

chain over worn sprockets or a worn
drive chain over new sprockets.

6. Lubricate the drive chain with SAE 90 oil or a good grade drive chain lubricant formulated for O-ring chains. Carefully follow the manufacturer's instructions. Make sure all portions of the drive chain are thoroughly oiled.

7. Install the chain as described in Chapter Twelve.

8. Adjust the drive chain tension as described in this chapter.

Drive Chain Tension Inspection

To prevent chain tension related problems, adjust the chain at the intervals specified in **Table 1**. If the ATV is operated at sustained high speeds or if it is repeatedly accelerated very hard, check the drive chain adjustment more often. Drive chain free play that exceeds the wear limit in **Table 4** may damage the frame or swing arm.

1. Park the ATV on a level spot and set the parking brake.

2. Using wooden blocks or a scissor jack, support the ATV so that the rear wheels clear the ground.

NOTE
As the drive chain wears, it becomes tighter at one point. The chain tension must be checked and adjusted at this point.

3. Turn the rear wheel slowly, stop it, and check the chain tension. Continue until the tightest point is located. Mark this spot with chalk, and turn the wheel so that the mark is located over the swing arm upper chain guide at the point shown in **Figure 22**. Check the chain tension at this point.

NOTE
*If the drive chain is kinked or feels tight, it may require cleaning and lubrication. Refer to **Drive Chain Lubrication** in this chapter. If the chain is still tight, it may be damaged due to swollen O-rings, damaged rollers, loose pins or binding links. Refer to Chapter Eleven.*

4. With your thumb and forefinger, lift the chain up and down. Measure the amount of vertical travel in the chain.

5. The vertical travel measurement should be within the drive chain free play specification in **Table 4**. If necessary, adjust the chain as described in the following procedure.

Drive Chain Tension Adjustment

1. Park the ATV on level ground and set the parking brake. Block the front wheels so the vehicle does not roll in either direction.

2. Raise the rear of the vehicle with a small hydraulic or scissor jack. Place the jack under the frame with a piece of wood between the jack and the frame.

3. Place wooden block(s) under the frame to support the vehicle securely with the rear wheels off the ground.

4. Loosen the clamp bolt on each side of the swing arm (A, **Figure 19**).

5. Insert a drift or other suitable tool into the hole in the bearing housing (B, **Figure 19**).

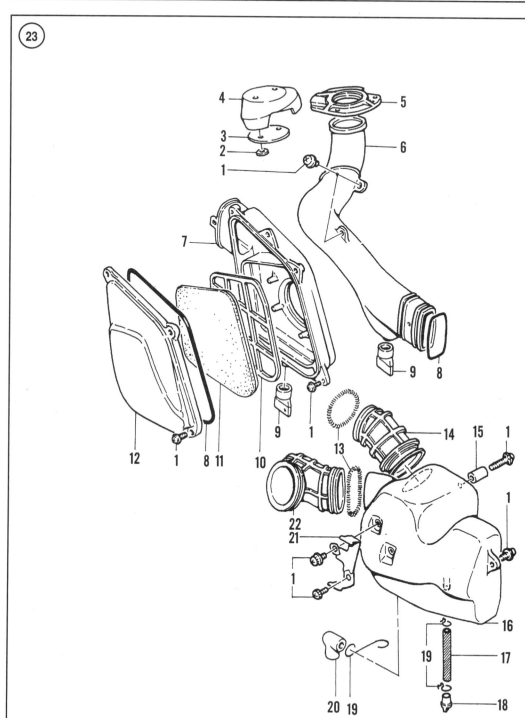

AIR FILTER HOUSING

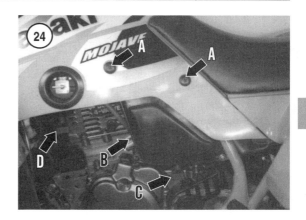

1. Screw
2. Push nut
3. Cap plate
4. Snorkel cap
5. Duct plate
6. Snorkel duct
7. Air filter housing
8. O-ring
9. Drain
10. Air filter base
11. Air filter element
12. Air filter cover
13. Spring
14. Surge tank duct
15. Collar
16. Surge tank
17. Drain hose
18. Drain plug
19. Clamp
20. Breather hose
21 Bracket
22. Housing duct

6. Use the tool to rotate the bearing housing upward or downward until the chain has the amount of free play specified in **Table 4**.

7. Tighten each swing arm clamp nut (A, **Figure 19**) to the torque specification in **Table 5**.

Air Filter

A dirty air filter decreases the efficiency and life of the engine. Never run the ATV without a properly installed air filter. Even minute particles of dust can cause severe internal engine wear and can clog carburetor passages. Refer to **Figure 23** when servicing the air filter.

Removal and installation

1. Remove the plugs (A, **Figure 24**) and remove the brace (**Figure 25**) from behind the fender. This provides access to the upper air filter cover screws.

2. Remove the mounting screws and remove the air filter cover (B, **Figure 24**).

3. Remove the air filter element (A, **Figure 26**) and the air filter base (B, **Figure 26**).

4. Use a flashlight and check the air box-to-housing duct joint for dirt or other contamination that may have passed through the air filter.

5. Wipe the inside of the air box with a clean rag. If it cannot be cleaned while bolted to the frame, remove the air box as described in Chapter Eight. Clean it thoroughly with solvent, with hot soapy water and rinse the air box with water. Thoroughly dry the air box, and reinstall it as described in Chapter Eight.

6. Cover the air box opening with a clean shop rag.

7. Inspect all fittings, hoses and connections from the air box to the carburetor. Check each hose clamp for tightness.

8. Clean and oil the filter as described in this chapter.

9. Squeeze the drain hose (C, **Figure 24**) on the air box and on the snorkel duct (D, **Figure 24**) to drain out water, oil and other debris.

Installation

1. Apply grease to the airbox-to-housing duct joint, the mounting screw holes, the edges of the air filter cover, and the O-ring on the cover.

2. Install the air filter base (B, **Figure 26**) and the air filter element (A, **Figure 26**) into the air box.

3. Fit the cover (B, **Figure 24**) onto the air box and secure it in place with the mounting screws. Be sure the O-ring is in place on the cover.

4. Set the brace (**Figure 25**) in place behind the fender and install the plugs. (A, **Figure 24**) Be sure the arrow on the brace points forward.

Air filter cleaning and oiling

Service the air filter element in a well-ventilated area, away from all sparks and flames.

1. Remove the air filter element as described above in this chapter.

> *WARNING*
> *Do not clean the air filter element with a low flash-point solvent or gasoline. A fire or explosion could occur.*

2. Clean the filter element with the manufacturer's filter solvent or a general high flash-point solvent. Allow the element to air dry.

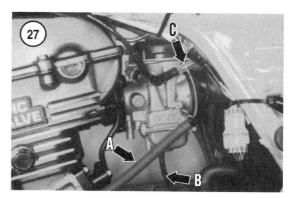

3. Inspect the element carefully. If it is torn or broken in any area, replace the air filter element. If the element is in good condition, continue with Step 4.

4. Fill a clean pan with liquid detergent cleaner and warm water.

5. Submerge the filter into the cleaning solution and gently work the cleaner into the filter pores. Gently soak and squeeze the filter.

> *CAUTION*
> *Do not wring or twist the filter when cleaning it. This harsh action could damage the filter pores or tear the filter loose at a seam. This allows unfiltered air to enter the engine and rapidly cause severe wear.*

6. Rinse the filter under warm water while soaking and gently squeezing it.

7. Repeat Step 5 and Step 6 two or three times or until there are no signs of dirt rinsing from the filter.

8. After cleaning the element, inspect it carefully. If it is torn or broken in any area, replace it. Do not run the engine with a damaged element as it may allow dirt to enter the engine and cause severe engine wear.

9. Set the filter aside and allow it to dry thoroughly.

10. Clean the filter base, air filter cover, and air filter housing in solvent, and dry them thoroughly. If necessary, remove and clean the air filter housing as described above in this chapter.

CAUTION
Make sure the filter is completely dry
before oiling it.

11. Properly oiling an air filter element is a messy job. Use a pair of disposable rubber gloves when performing this procedure. Oil the filter as follows:

    a. Place the air filter into a gallon size storage bag.

    b. Pour foam air filter oil onto the filter to soak it.

    c. Gently squeeze and release the filter so oil will saturate the filter's pores. Repeat this process until the entire filter is completely oiled.

    d. Remove the filter from the bag and check the pores for uneven oiling. This is indicated by light or dark areas. If necessary, soak the filter and squeeze it again.

    e. When the filter oiling is even, squeeze the filter a final time.

12. Install the air filter as described above in this chapter.

13. Pour the leftover filter oil from the bag back into the bottle for reuse.

14. Dispose of the plastic bag.

Fuel Line Inspection

WARNING
Some fuel may spill while performing the procedures in this section. Because gasoline is extremely flammable and explosive, perform these procedures away from all open flames (including pilot lights) and sparks. Do not smoke or allow someone who is smoking into the work area. Always work in a well-ventilated area. Wipe up any spills immediately.

Inspect the fuel line (A, **Figure 27**) from the fuel valve to the carburetor. Replace the fuel line if it is cracked or starting to deteriorate. Make sure the small hose clamps are in place and holding the line securely. Check that the overflow (B, **Figure 27**) and vent hoses (C, **Figure 27**) are in place.

WARNING
A damaged or deteriorated fuel line presents a very dangerous fire hazard to both the rider and machine. A serious problem can occur if fuel should spill onto a hot engine or exhaust pipe.

Fuel Tank Vent Hose

Check the fuel tank vent hose (**Figure 28**) for proper routing. Also check the end of the hose for contamination.

Disc Brake Adjustment

Adjustment of the front and rear disc brakes is not necessary. The hydraulic brakes automatically compensate for brake pad wear as the caliper piston moves outward in its bore. However, if the brake lever or pedal feels spongy or soft when applied, check the brake fluid level in the respective master cylinder reservoir. If air enters the brake system, bleed the brakes as described in Chapter Thirteen.

Brake Pedal Height Adjustment

Adjust brake pedal height to suit rider preference. The adjustment procedure is described below.
1. Park the vehicle on a level surface, and set the parking brake.

2. Loosen the stopper locknut (A, **Figure 29**), and turn the pedal stopper (B, **Figure 29**) until it is completely seated.

3. Loosen the locknut (C, **Figure 29**) on the master cylinder pushrod.

NOTE
If necessary, lightly tighten the pushrod locknut and upper nut together in order to turn the pushrod.

WARNING
*At least 1 mm (0.04 in.) of the pushrod's lower end (A, **Figure 30**) must extend beyond the clevis (B, **Figure 30**). Do not adjust the pushrod so its lower end projection (C, **Figure 30**) is less than 1 mm (0.04 in.).*

4. Use the upper nut (D, **Figure 29**) to turn the pushrod until the brake pedal is at the desired height.

5. Tighten the pushrod locknut down against the clevis, and torque the nut to the specification in **Table 5**.

6. Back out the pedal stopper (B, **Figure 29**) until it rests against the arm on the brake pedal.

7. Tighten the stopper locknut (A, **Figure 29**) securely.

Rear Brake Light Switch Adjustment (2000 models)

2000 model year Mojaves are equipped with front and rear brake light switches. The front brake switch does not require adjustment. The rear switch, however, may. The checking and adjustment procedure is described below.

1. Turn the ignition switch ON.

2. Depress the brake pedal and watch the operation of the brake light. The light should turn on when the pedal has moved approximately 10 mm (0.4 in.).

3. Adjust the brake switch by performing the following:

a. Loosen the locknut (A, **Figure 31**) below the switch bracket.

CAUTION
Be sure the switch does not turn during the adjustment procedure. It could be damaged.

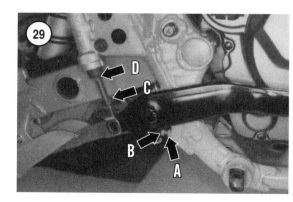

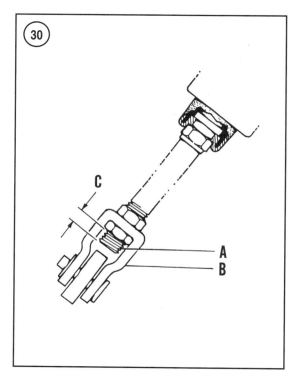

b. Turn the adjust nut (B, **Figure 31**) to move the switch up or down. Moving the switch up turns the brake light on sooner; moving it down, turns the light on later.

c. Tighten the locknut securely against the bracket.

Parking Brake Adjustment (1987 models)

Refer to **Figure 32** when adjusting the parking brake.

1. Loosen the adjuster nuts (A, **Figure 33**) and create plenty of slack in the cable.

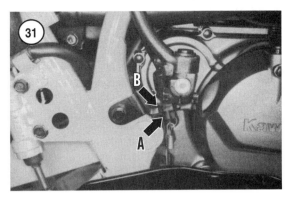

2. Loosen the cam lever locknut (26, **Figure 32**).

3. Turn the parking brake adjuster screw (17, **Figure 32**) in as far as it will go, and then back it out 1/4 turn.

4. Tighten the cam lever locknut securely (26, **Figure 32**).

5. Turn both adjuster nuts (A, **Figure 33**) until the distance from the end of the cable bracket to the center of the cable end is within the range (parking brake cable free length) specified in **Table 4**. See **Figure 34**. If necessary, push the bottom of the cam lever rearward to remove all slack from the cable when making this measurement.

Parking Brake Adjustment (1988-on)

Refer to **Figure 32** when adjusting the parking brake.

1. Turn both adjuster nuts (A, **Figure 33**) until the distance from the end of the cable bracket to the center of the cable end is within the range (parking brake cable free length) specified in **Table 4**. See **Figure 34**. If necessary, push the bottom of the cam lever rearward to remove all slack from the cable when making this measurement.

2. Tighten both adjuster nuts (A, **Figure 33**) securely against the cable bracket.

3. Turn in the parking brake adjuster knob (B, **Figure 33**) in as far as it will go, and then back it out 1/4 turn.

Brake Fluid Level Check/Adjustment

Maintain the brake fluid level in both the front (A, **Figure 35**) and rear (**Figure 36**) master cylinder reservoirs at their maximum levels. If the brake

fluid drops below half-full, add fresh DOT 3 or DOT 4 brake fluid.

NOTE
If the brake fluid level drops rapidly, check the brake hose and fittings for leaking.

1. Park the vehicle on level ground, and set the parking brake.

2. Turn the handlebar so that the front master cylinder reservoir is level.

3. Check the fluid level in the front (A, **Figure 35**) and rear (**Figure 36**) reservoirs.

4. If necessary, add brake fluid by performing the following:

   a. Clean any dirt from the reservoir cover.

   b. Remove the two top cover screws, and remove the cover and diaphragm.

   c. Add fresh DOT 3 or DOT 4 brake fluid from a sealed container until the fluid level is at the upper mark on the reservoir.

WARNING
Use brake fluid clearly marked DOT 3 or DOT 4. Others may vaporize and cause brake failure. Use DOT 3 or DOT 4 brake fluid exclusively. Do not intermix different grades of brake fluid nor different brands. One manufacturer's fluid may not be compatible with another's.

CAUTION
Be careful when handling brake fluid. Do not spill it on plated, painted or plastic surfaces. It will destroy the surface. Wash the area immediately with soap and water, and thoroughly rinse it off.

   d. Reinstall the diaphragm and top cover. Install the screws and tighten them securely.

Disc Brake Hoses

Inspect the brake hoses for cracks, cuts, bulges, deterioration and leaks. Check the metal brake lines for cracks and leaks. Replace any defective brake hoses as described in Chapter Thirteen.

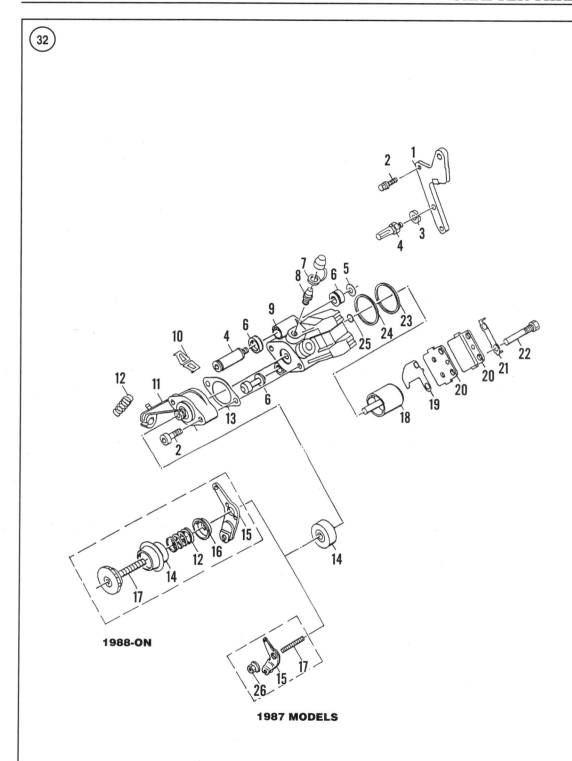

1988-ON

1987 MODELS

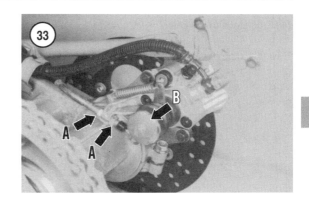

REAR CALIPER

1. Caliper holder
2. Bolt
3. Lockwasher
4. Caliper shaft
5. Beveled washer
6. Friction boot
7. Bleed valve cap
8. Bleed valve
9. Rear caliper
10. Pad spring
11. Parking brake housing
12. Spring
13. Gasket
14. Boot
15. Brake cam lever
16. Plate
17. Parking brake adjuster
18. Piston
19. Wear shim
20. Pad
21. Lockplate
22. Pad holder bolt
23. Dust seal
24. Piston seal
25. O-ring
26. Cam lever locknut

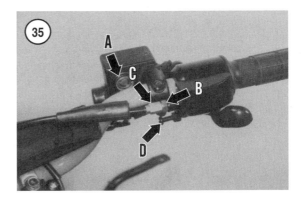

Disc Brake Pad Wear

Replace the brake pads when the lining thickness is worn to the wear limit specified in **Table 4**, when a pad shows uneven wear and scoring, or if there is grease or oil on the friction surface. Refer to Chapter Thirteen.

If the front or rear brake seems to grab and release (pulsate) when using it, check the brake discs for warpage or other damage.

Brake Fluid Change

Every time the reservoir cap is removed, a small amount of dirt and moisture enters the brake fluid. The same thing happens if a leak occurs or if any part of the hydraulic system is loosened or disconnected. Dirt can clog the system and cause unnecessary wear. Water in the brake fluid vaporizes at high temperature, impairing the hydraulic action and reducing the brake's stopping ability.

To maintain peak performance, change the brake fluid every year or when rebuilding a caliper or master cylinder. To change brake fluid, follow the brake bleeding procedure in Chapter Thirteen.

> *WARNING*
> *Use brake fluid clearly marked DOT 3 or DOT 4 only. Others may vaporize and cause brake failure. Dispose of any unused fluid according to local EPA regulations—never reuse brake fluid. Contaminated brake fluid can cause brake failure.*

Clutch Lever Free Play Adjustment

> *NOTE*
> *After adjusting the clutch lever free play, always start the engine and check clutch operation. Improper free play adjustment could lead to clutch slipping.*

1. Pull the dust cover away from the clutch lever.
2. Loosen the locknut (A, **Figure 37**) at the clutch lever and turn the adjuster (B, **Figure 37**) until the gap between the clutch lever and the lever housing is within the range specified in **Table 4**. See (**Figure 38**).

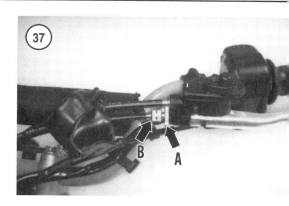

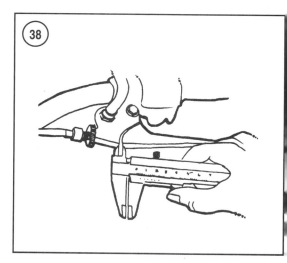

3. Tighten the clutch lever locknut, and reinstall the dust cover.

4. If the free play cannot be set at the clutch lever, loosen the locknuts (A, **Figure 39**) from the clutch cable bracket on the right side.

5. Turn the cable adjuster (B, **Figure 39**) clockwise until it becomes difficult to turn. Tighten the locknuts against the cable bracket.

6. Check the angle formed by the clutch cable and a line drawn between the center of the clutch lever pivot and the center of the cable pivot. The angle (C, **Figure 39**) should be 80-90°.

    a. If the angle is within specification, use the adjuster at the clutch lever, and set the clutch lever free play to the specification listed in **Table 4**. Tighten the locknut.

    b. If the angle is outside the specified range, remove the clutch and inspect the clutch plates and friction discs. Refer to Chapter Six.

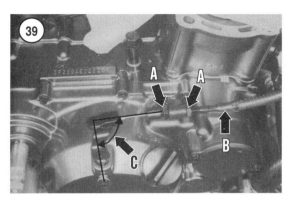

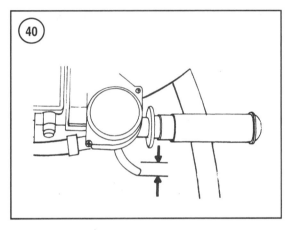

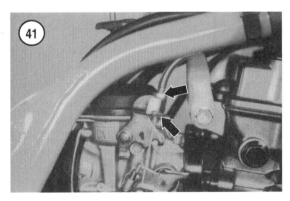

7. Start the engine, and check the operation of the clutch.

Throttle Cable Adjustment and Operation

Check the throttle cable free play at the interval indicated in **Table 1**. The throttle cable free play, measured at the tip of the throttle lever (**Figure 40**), should be within the range specified in **Table 4**.

In time, the throttle cable free play becomes excessive from cable stretch. This delays throttle response and affects low speed operation. On the other hand, if there is no throttle cable free play, an excessively high idle can result.

Minor adjustments can be made at the throttle lever adjuster. Major adjustments must be made at the throttle cable adjuster at the carburetor.

1. At the throttle lever, slide back the throttle cable rubber boot.
2. Loosen the locknut (B, **Figure 35**) and turn the adjuster (C, **Figure 35**) in either direction until the correct amount of free play is achieved.
3. Hold the adjuster and tighten the locknut securely.
4. If the proper amount of free play cannot be achieved at the throttle lever, adjust the free play at the carburetor. Turn the lower adjust nuts (**Figure 41**) in either direction until the correct free play is achieved. Tighten the nuts securely against the bracket.
5. If the throttle cable cannot be adjusted properly, the cable has stretched excessively and must be replaced.
6. Make sure the throttle lever rotates freely from a fully closed to a fully open position.
7. Start the engine and allow it to idle in NEUTRAL. Turn the handlebar from side to side. If the idle increases, the throttle cable is routed incorrectly or there is not enough cable free play.

NOTE
A damaged throttle cable will prevent the engine from idling properly.

Speed Limiter Screw Adjustment

The throttle housing is equipped with a speed limiter screw (D, **Figure 35**) that can be set to prevent the rider from opening the throttle all the way. The speed limiter screw can be set for beginning riders or to control engine rpm when breaking in a new engine.

Varying the length of the speed limiter screw sets the speed limiter adjustment. Turning the screw out increases engine speed and turning the screw in decreases engine speed.

WARNING
Do not operate the vehicle with the speed limiter screw removed from the

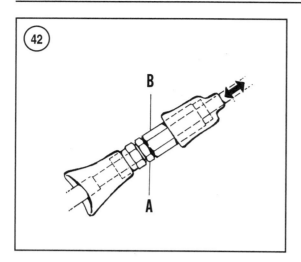

housing. *If the speed limiter is being adjusted for a beginning rider, test ride the vehicle to make sure it is adjusted correctly.*

Choke Cable Free Play Adjustment

1. Pull the dust covers away from the adjuster at the upper end of the choke cable.

2. Grasp the outer clutch cable, and push it in and out. The amount of cable movement equals the choke cable free play. See **Figure 42**.

3. If the free play is outside the range specified in **Table 4**, adjust the free play by performing the following:

    a. Loosen the adjuster locknut (A, **Figure 42**).

    b. Turn the adjuster (B, **Figure 42**) until the free play is within the range specified in **Table 4**.

    c. Tighten the locknut securely, and reinstall the dust covers.

Reverse Cable Free Play Adjustment

Reverse cable free play adjustment takes up slack caused by cable stretch.

1. Park the ATV on level ground and set the parking brake.

2. Shift the transmission into NEUTRAL.

NOTE
Free play is the amount of reverse knob movement before any reverse cable action takes place.

3. Move the reverse knob from side to side and measure free play (**Figure 43**). If the free play is outside the range specified in **Table 4**, continue with Step 4.

4. If necessary, remove the front fender as described in Chapter Fourteen.

5. Slide the dust cover away from the mid-cable adjuster. It is located immediately above the front engine mounting bracket on the left side.

6. Loosen the adjuster locknut (A, **Figure 44**) and turn the cable adjuster (B, **Figure 44**) until the free play is within the range specified in **Table 4**.

7. Tighten the locknut and recheck free play.

Coolant Level Inspection

The coolant level should be checked when the engine is cold.

1. Park the ATV on level ground and set the parking brake.

2. Check the level gauge (A, **Figure 45**) on the coolant reservoir. The coolant should be between the FULL and LOW marks on the gauge.

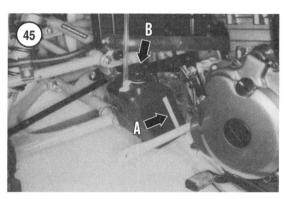

NOTE
Always add coolant through the filler on the coolant reservoir. Do not remove the radiator cap and add coolant to the radiator.

3. If necessary, remove the reservoir filler cap (B, **Figure 45**) and add coolant to the reservoir until the coolant level is at the FULL mark on the gauge. Be sure to add a 50:50 mixture of an antifreeze and distilled water.

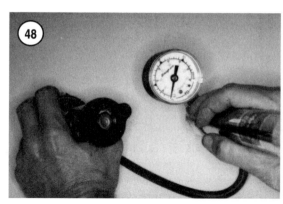

Cooling System Pressure Test

Check the following items at the intervals indicated in **Table 1**. If the test equipment is not available, a Kawasaki dealer, automobile dealer, radiator shop or service station can perform the tests.

WARNING
*Do **not** remove the radiator cap when the engine is HOT. The coolant is very hot and under pressure. Severe scalding could result if the escaping coolant comes in contact with your skin. After the cooling system cools down, slowly loosen the cap to the first detent to safely release any built-up pressure.*

1. Remove the mud guard from the right front wheel as described in Chapter Fourteen. This provides access to the radiator cap.

2. Remove the radiator cap (A, **Figure 46**). Turn the cap counterclockwise to the first detent. Push the cap down and turn it counterclockwise until it is able to be removed.

3. Inspect the rubber sealing washers on the radiator cap (**Figure 47**). Replace the cap if the washers show signs of deterioration, cracking or other damage.

NOTE
Apply water to the rubber washers in the radiator cap prior to installing the cap onto the pressure tester.

4. Test the radiator cap pressure (**Figure 48**). The cap must be able to sustain the relief pressure specified in **Table 4** for a minimum of 10 seconds. Re-

place the radiator cap if it does not hold pressure or if the relief pressure is too high or too low.

CAUTION
Do not exceed the indicated test pressure. If test pressure exceeds the specifications, the radiator may be damaged.

5. Leave the radiator cap off and install the pressure tester onto the cap fitting on the radiator filler neck.
6. Pressure test the entire cooling system. The entire cooling system should be pressurized up to, but not exceeding, the test pressure specified in **Table 4**. If the pressure does not hold steady, check the system for leaks. Replace or repair any component that fails this test.
7. Test the specific gravity of the coolant with an antifreeze tester to ensure adequate temperature and corrosion protection. The system must have at least a 50:50 mixture of antifreeze and distilled water. Never let the mixture become less than 40% antifreeze or corrosion protection will be impaired.
8. Check all cooling system hoses for damage or deterioration. Replace any hose that is questionable. Make sure all hose clamps are tight.
9. Remove the radiator screen.
10. Carefully clean any road debris from the front surface of the radiator core. Use a whisk broom, compressed air or low-pressure water. If the radiator has been hit by a small object, carefully straighten out the fins with a screwdriver.

NOTE
If the radiator has been damaged across approximately 20% or more of the frontal area, replace the radiator as described in Chapter Ten.

11. Install all removed parts.

Coolant Change

The cooling system should be completely drained and refilled at the interval indicated in **Table 1**.

It is sometimes necessary to remove the radiator or drain the coolant from the system to perform a service procedure on some parts of the ATV. If the coolant is still in good condition, the coolant can be reused if it is kept clean. Drain the coolant into a clean drain pan and pour it into a clean, sealable

container like a plastic milk or bleach bottle. This coolant can then be reused if it is still clean.

CAUTION
Antifreeze is poisonous and may attract animals. Do not leave the drained coolant where it is accessible to children or animals.

CAUTION
Use only a high quality ethylene glycol antifreeze specifically labeled for use with aluminum engines and radiators. Do not use an alcohol based antifreeze.

In areas where freezing temperatures occur, make sure the percentage of antifreeze is able to protect the system to temperatures far below those likely to occur.

The following procedure must be performed when the engine is cool.

WARNING
*Do **not** change the coolant or remove the radiator cap while the engine is still hot or even warm. The coolant is very hot and under pressure. Severe scalding could result if the escaping coolant comes in contact with your skin. After the cooling system cools down, loosen the cap slowly to the first detent to safely release any built up pressure.*

CAUTION
Be careful not to spill antifreeze on painted surfaces. Antifreeze damages painted surfaces. Wash a spill immediately with soapy water and rinse the area thoroughly with clean water. Coolant is also slippery. Be sure to clean up any spilled coolant on the ground or on the tires.

1. Park the ATV on a level spot and set the parking brake.
2. Remove the mud guard from the right front wheel as described in Chapter Fourteen.

NOTE
Use a clean drain pan to collect the coolant so the coolant can be inspected for possible internal engine problems after draining is completed.

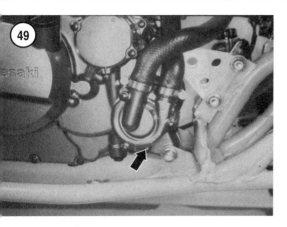

3. Place a clean drain pan under the water pump cover on the clutch cover.

4. Remove the coolant drain bolt (**Figure 49**) from the water pump cover, and drain the coolant from the engine and radiator.

5. Remove the radiator cap (A, **Figure 46**) to speed up the draining process. Turn the cap counterclockwise to the first detent. Push the cap down and turn it counterclockwise until it can be removed.

6. Remove the reservoir hose (B, **Figure 46**) and siphon the coolant from the reservoir.

7. Visually inspect the condition of the coolant.

   a. Sediment in coolant indicates that aluminum parts in the cooling system are corroded.

   b. Brownish color in the coolant indicates that iron parts in the cooling system are rusting.

   c. An abnormal smell from the coolant may indicate an exhaust or combustion leak into the cooling system.

8. If the drained coolant was contaminated or very dirty; flush the cooling system with freshwater. Allow the water to run through the cooling system for approximately 5 minutes. Shut off the water and allow the water to drain out.

9. Install the drain plug (**Figure 49**) with a new gasket. Tighten the plug to the torque specification in **Table 5**.

10. If still removed, attach the reservoir hose (B, **Figure 46**) to the fitting on the radiator filler neck.

11. Refill the cooling system as follows:

    a. Insert a small funnel into the radiator filler neck.

CAUTION
Do not use a higher percentage of coolant-to-water than 50:50. A higher concentration of antifreeze

(60% or greater) actually decreases the performance of the cooling system.

   b. Slowly add a 50:50 mixture of distilled water and antifreeze into the radiator until the fluid level is even with the bottom of the filler neck. Adding the coolant slowly will help rid the system of trapped air.

   c. Use a long-neck funnel and add coolant to the reservoir until the fluid level is even with the FULL line on the coolant gauge (A, **Figure 45**). Install the reservoir cap (B, **Figure 45**).

   d. Install the radiator cap (A, **Figure 46**) and turn it clockwise until it stops turning.

12. Reinstall the removed parts, and start the engine. Let it run at idle speed until the engine reaches normal operating temperature. Shut off the engine.

13. When the engine is cold, check the coolant gauge on the reservoir. If necessary, add coolant (through the reservoir filler) until the level is at the FULL mark on the gauge (A, **Figure 45**).

14. Check for coolant leaks at the drain plug. Tighten if necessary.

15. Test ride the ATV and readjust the coolant level if necessary after the cooling system has cooled down.

Steering System and Front Suspension Inspection

Check the steering system and front suspension at the interval indicated in **Table 1**.

1. Park the vehicle on level ground and set the parking brake.

2. Visually inspect all components of the steering system. Pay close attention to the tie rods and steering shaft, especially after a hard spill or collision. If damage is apparent, repair the steering components. Refer to service procedures described in Chapter Eleven.

3. Check the tightness of the handlebar holder bolts.

4. Make sure the front hub nuts are tight and that the cotter pins are in place.

5. Check that the cotter pins are in place on all steering and suspension components. If any cotter pin is missing, check the nut(s) for looseness. Torque the nut(s) and install new cotter pins.

CAUTION
If any of the previously mentioned bolts and nuts are loose, refer to Chapter Eleven for correct procedures and torque specifications.

6. Check steering shaft play as follows:
   a. To check steering shaft radial play, move the handlebar from side to side (without attempting to move the wheels). If radial play is excessive, the upper steering bearings are probably worn and should be replaced.
   b. To check steering shaft thrust play, lift up and then push down on the handlebar. If excessive thrust play is noted, check the lower steering shaft nut for looseness. If the nut is torqued properly, then the lower steering shaft bearing is worn and should be replaced.
   c. Replace worn or damaged steering shaft parts as described in Chapter Eleven.
7. Check the steering knuckle and tie rod ball joints as follows:
   a. Turn the handlebar quickly from side to side. If there is appreciable looseness between the handlebar and tires, check the ball joints for excessive wear or damage.
   b. Replace worn or damaged steering knuckle and tie rod components as described in Chapter Eleven.

NOTE
When removing cotter pins to check fastener tightness, new cotter pins must be installed.

Spark Arrester Cleaning

Clean the spark arrestor at the intervals indicated in **Table 1**, or sooner if a considerable amount of slow riding is done.

WARNING
To avoid burning your hands, wear heavy gloves if the exhaust system is hot. Work in a well-ventilated area that is free of any fire hazards. Wear safety glasses.

1. Remove the spark arrestor plug (A, **Figure 50**) and the drain plug (B, **Figure 50**) from the muffler.
2. Start the engine.

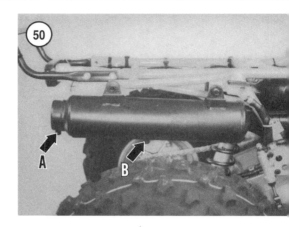

3. Raise and lower the engine speed while tapping the muffler with a plastic mallet. Continue until carbon stops coming out of the opening.
4. Turn the engine off, and reinstall the plugs.

Nuts, Bolts, and Other Fasteners

Constant vibration can loosen many of the fasteners on the vehicle. Check the tightness of all fasteners, especially those on:
   a. Engine mounting hardware.
   b. Cylinder head bracket bolts.
   c. Engine crankcase covers.
   d. Handlebar.
   e. Gearshift lever.
   f. Brake pedal.
   g. Exhaust system.
   h. Front and rear hub nuts.
   i. Wheel nuts

UNSCHEDULED MAINTENANCE

Fuel Valve Cleaning

Periodically remove and clean the fuel valve as described in Chapter Eight.

Carburetor Cleaning

Remove, disassemble and clean the carburetor as described in Chapter Eight.

Exhaust System

1. Inspect the exhaust pipe for cracks or dents which could alter performance.

2. Check all the exhaust pipe fasteners and mounting points for loose or damaged parts.

3. Check for leaks at all fittings in the system. Replace any gaskets as necessary. Refer to Chapter Eight.

Front Hub Bearings

The front hub bearings are sealed and do not require periodic lubrication. However, remove the front hubs and inspect the bearings and seals for excessive wear or damage. Replace the seals if there is excessive grease on the outside of the seal or if there is a deposit of reddish-brown residue around the seal. Refer to Chapter Eleven.

Handlebar

Inspect the handlebar weekly for any damage. Replace a bent or damaged handlebar. The knurled section of the bar should be very rough. Keep the clamps clean with a wire brush. Anytime the bars slip in the clamps, remove and wire brush them to prevent small pieces of aluminum from gathering in the clamps and reducing gripping abilities.

NOTE
If you have installed aluminum bars, make sure you follow the bar manufacturer's directions for installing the bars and clamps.

Handlebar Grips

Inspect the handlebar grips (**Figure 51**) for tearing, looseness or excessive wear. Install new grips when required. Follow the manufacturer's instructions when installing grips.

Frame Inspection

Routinely inspect the frame and brackets for cracks or other damage.

ENGINE TUNE-UP

A tune-up is general adjustment and maintenance to ensure peak engine performance.

The following paragraphs discuss each facet of a proper tune-up, which should be performed in the order given. Unless otherwise specified, the engine should be cold before starting any tune-up procedure.

Have the new parts on hand before beginning.

To perform a tune-up on a Kawasaki, have available the following tools and equipment:
 a. Spark plug wrench.
 b. Socket wrench, assorted sockets and wrenches.
 c. Phillips head screwdriver.
 d. Spark plug feeler gauge (wire type) and gap adjusting tool.
 e. Feeler gauge set.
 f. Timing light.

Cam Chain Adjustment

The Kawasaki ATV is equipped with an automatic cam chain tensioner assembly. No adjustment is required.

Valve Clearance Check and Adjustment

Check and adjust valve clearance with the engine cold. The exhaust valve is located at the front of the engine and the intake valve is at the rear.

1. Park the vehicle on level ground and set the parking brake.

2. Remove the fuel tank as described in Chapter Eight.

3. Remove the cylinder head cover as described in Chapter Four.

4. Remove the timing inspection plug (A, **Figure 52**) and the magneto rotor plug (B, **Figure 52**) from the magneto cover.

5. Remove the spark plug. This makes it easier to turn the engine by hand.

6. The piston must be set to top dead center (TDC) on its compression stroke before checking and adjusting the valve clearance. Perform the following:

a. With a socket on the rotor bolt (A, **Figure 53**), turn the crankshaft counterclockwise and watch the intake valves. After the intake valves open and close, continue turning the crankshaft until the T mark on the magneto rotor aligns with the indexing groove (B, **Figure 53**) in the timing window. See **Figure 54**.

b. When the piston is at TDC on the compression stroke, both rocker arms will have valve clearance, indicating that the intake and exhaust valves are closed. Move each rocker arm by hand. There should be some movement.

7. Check the clearance of both the intake valves and exhaust valves by inserting a flat feeler gauge between the end of the valve stem and the valve adjuster (screw) as shown in **Figure 55**. The correct valve clearances for the intake and exhaust valves are listed in **Table 4**. If the clearance is correct, there will be a slight resistance on the feeler gauge when it is inserted and withdrawn.

8. To adjust the clearance, perform the following:

a. Use a wrench and back off the valve adjuster locknut as shown in **Figure 56**.

b. Use a screwdriver and turn the adjuster in or out so there is a slight resistance felt on the feeler gauge.

c. Hold the adjuster to prevent it from turning and tighten the locknut to the torque specification in **Table 5**.

d. Recheck the clearance to make sure the adjuster did not move when the locknut was tightened. Readjust the valve clearance if necessary.

9. Inspect the cylinder head cover gasket as well as the O-rings in the timing hole plug and the rotor bolt plug. Replace any O-ring that has become hard or is starting to deteriorate.

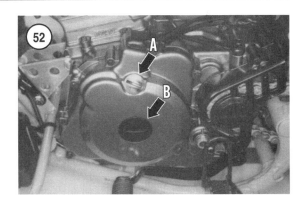

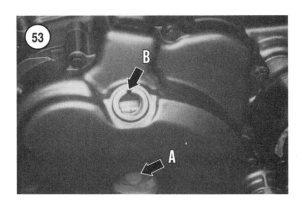

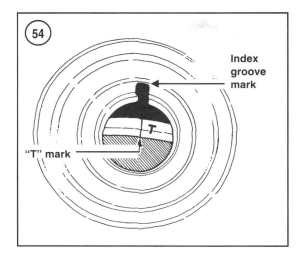

Index groove mark

"T" mark

10. Install the timing inspection plug (A, **Figure 52**) and rotor bolt plug (B, **Figure 52**) into the magneto cover.

11. Install the cylinder head cover as described in Chapter Four.

12. Install the spark plug and reconnect the spark plug cap.

13. Install the fuel tank as described in Chapter Eight.

14. Install the front and rear fenders as described in Chapter Fourteen.

3

Cylinder Compression

A cylinder cranking compression check is one of the quickest ways to check the internal condition of the engine: rings, piston, head gasket, etc. Check compression at each tune-up, record it, and compare it with the reading at the last tune-up. This helps to spot any developing problems.

1. Warm the engine to normal operating temperature. Turn the engine off.

2. Remove the front fender as described in Chapter Fourteen.

3. Remove the spark plug. Insert the plug into the plug cap and ground the plug against the cylinder head (**Figure 57**).

4. Thread or insert the tip of a compression gauge into the cylinder head spark plug hole. Make sure the gauge is seated properly. See **Figure 58**.

> *NOTE*
> *Make sure the engine stop switch is in the OFF position when performing Step 5.*

5. Hold the throttle wide open and sharply turn the engine over with the kickstarter for several revolutions until the gauge gives its highest reading. Record the pressure reading and compare it to the compression specifications in **Table 4**.

6. If the reading is higher than normal:
   a. There may be a buildup of carbon deposits in the combustion chamber or on the piston crown.
   b. The cylinder head gasket or the cylinder base gasket may be too thin.
   c. The compression release spring may be damaged or missing, or the weights are not moving smoothly.

7. If a low reading is obtained, it indicates a leaking cylinder head gasket, valve(s) or piston ring trouble. To determine which, pour about a teaspoon of engine oil through the spark plug hole. Crank the engine over one revolution to distribute the oil, then make another compression test and record the reading. If the compression increases, the valves are good but the rings are worn or damaged. If com-

pression does not increase, inspect the cylinder head gasket. If the gasket is in good condition, the valves probably require service. A valve could be hanging open, but not burned, or a piece of carbon could be on the valve seat.

NOTE
If the compression is low, the engine cannot be tuned to maximum performance. Repair the engine.

8. Remove the compression gauge and install the spark plug and plug cap.

Correct Spark Plug Heat Range

Spark plugs are available in various heat ranges, both hotter and colder than the original equipment plug.

Select a plug of the heat range designed for the loads and conditions under which the ATV will be operating. The incorrect heat range can cause plug fouling or engine overheating, resulting in piston damage.

In general, use a hot plug for low speeds and low temperatures. Use a cold plug for high speeds, high engine loads and high temperatures. The plug should operate hot enough to burn off unwanted deposits, but not so hot that it is damaged or causes preignition. A spark plug of the correct heat range shows a light tan color on the insulator after the plug has been in service.

The reach (length) of a plug is also important. A spark plug that is too short causes excessive carbon buildup, hard starting and plug fouling. A plug that is too long will cause overheating or may contact the top of the piston. Both conditions cause engine damage. See **Figure 59**. If the spark plug is too long, the exposed threads will be coated with carbon and removal of the spark plug will probably damage the threads in the cylinder head.

The standard spark plug for the various models is listed in **Table 4**.

Spark Plug Removal

1. Remove the fuel tank as described in Chapter Eight.

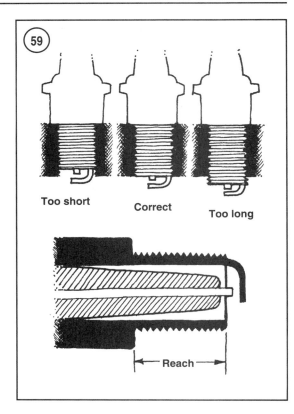

Too short   Correct   Too long

Reach

2. Grasp the spark plug cap (**Figure 60**) as near the plug as possible and pull it off. If the spark plug cap is stuck to the plug, twist it slightly to break it loose.

CAUTION
Whenever the spark plug is removed, dirt around it can fall into the plug hole. This can cause engine damage.

3. Blow away any dirt that has collected around the spark plug.

4. Remove the spark plug with a spark plug socket.

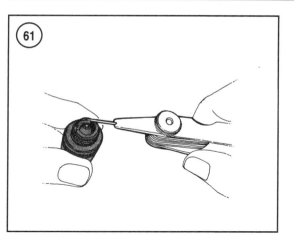

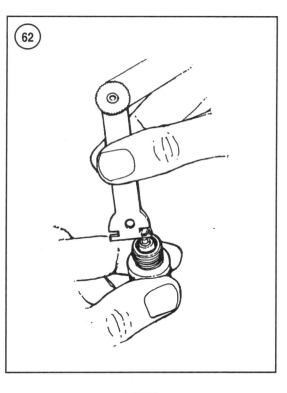

NOTE
If the plug is difficult to remove, apply a penetrating oil, like WD-40 or Liquid Wrench, around the base of the plug and let it soak in about 10-20 minutes.

5. Inspect the plug carefully. Look for a broken insulator, excessively eroded electrodes, and excessive carbon or oil fouling. See *Reading Spark Plugs* in this chapter.

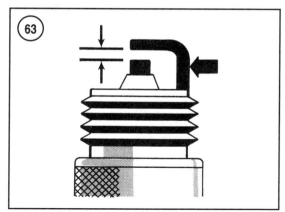

Gapping and Installing the Plug

Carefully gap a new spark plug to ensure a reliable, consistent spark. Use a special spark plug gapping tool and a wire-type feeler gauge.

1. Insert a wire feeler gauge between the center and side electrodes (**Figure 61**). The correct gap is listed in **Table 4**. If the gap is correct, there will be a slight drag felt as the wire is pulled through. If there is no drag, or the gauge won't pass through, bend the side electrode with a gapping tool (**Figure 62**) to set the proper gap (**Figure 63**).

NOTE
Antiseize compound can be purchased at most automotive parts stores.

2. Apply a *small* amount of antiseize compound to the plug threads before installing the spark plug. Do not use engine oil on the plug threads.

3. Screw the spark plug in by hand until it seats. Very little effort should be required. If force is necessary, the plug is cross-threaded or there is carbon on the cylinder head threads. Unscrew it and try again.

NOTE
Do not overtighten the spark plug. This squashes the gasket and destroys its sealing ability.

4. Use a spark plug wrench and tighten the spark plug to the torque specification in **Table 5**. If a torque wrench is not available, tighten the plug an additional quarter to half turn after the gasket has made contact with the head. If installing an old, regapped plug and the old gasket is being reused, only tighten the plug an additional 1/4 turn.

CAUTION
Make sure the spark plug wire is located away from the exhaust pipe.

5. Install the spark plug lead. Make sure the cap is on tight.

Reading Spark Plugs

A significant amount of information about engine and spark plug performance can be determined by careful examination of the spark plug.
1. Remove the spark plug, and compare its firing end to the examples in **Figure 64**.

Normal condition

If the plug has a light tan- or gray-colored deposit and no abnormal gap wear or erosion, good engine, carburetion and ignition conditions are indicated. The plug in use is of the proper heat range and may be serviced and returned to use.

Carbon fouled

Soft, dry, sooty deposits covering the entire firing end of the plug are evidence of incomplete combustion. Even though the firing end of the plug is dry, the plug's insulation decreases. An electrical path is formed that lowers the voltage from the ignition system. Engine misfiring is a sign of carbon fouling. Carbon fouling can be caused by one or more of the following:
   a. Rich fuel mixture.
   b. Spark plug heat range too cold.
   c. Dirty air filter.
   d. Over-retarded ignition timing.
   e. Ignition component failure.
   f. Low engine compression.
   g. Prolonged idling.

Oil fouled

The tip of an oil fouled plug has a black insulator, a damp oily film over the firing end and a carbon layer over the entire nose. The electrodes are not worn. Common causes for this condition are:
   a. Piston rings worn or broken.
   b. Valve guides worn.
   c. Engine not completely broken in.

   d. Spark plug heat range too cold.
   e. Ignition component failure.
Oil fouled spark plugs may be cleaned in an emergency, but it is better to replace them. It is important to correct the cause of fouling before the engine is returned to service.

Gap bridging

Combustion deposits have bridged the gap between the electrodes and created an electrical short. If this condition is encountered, check for an improper oil type or excessive carbon in the combustion chamber. Be sure to locate and correct the cause of this condition.

Overheating

Badly worn electrodes and premature gap wear are signs of overheating, along with a gray or white blistered porcelain insulator surface. Using a spark plug with the wrong heat range (too hot) commonly causes this condition. If the spark plug has not been changed to a hotter one and the plug is overheated, consider the following causes:
   a. Lean fuel mixture.
   b. Over-advanced ignition timing.
   c. Engine running hot.
   d. Intake air leak.
   e. Overtightened spark plug.
   f. No spark plug gasket.

Worn out

Corrosive gases formed by combustion and high voltage sparks have eroded the electrodes. A spark plug in this condition requires more voltage to fire under hard acceleration. Replace with a new spark plug.

Preignition

If the electrodes are melted, preignition is almost certainly the cause. Check for carburetor mounting or intake manifold leaks and over-advanced ignition timing. It is also possible that a plug of the wrong heat range (too hot) is being used. Find the cause of the preignition before returning the engine into service. For additional information on preignition, refer to *Preignition* in Chapter Two.

3

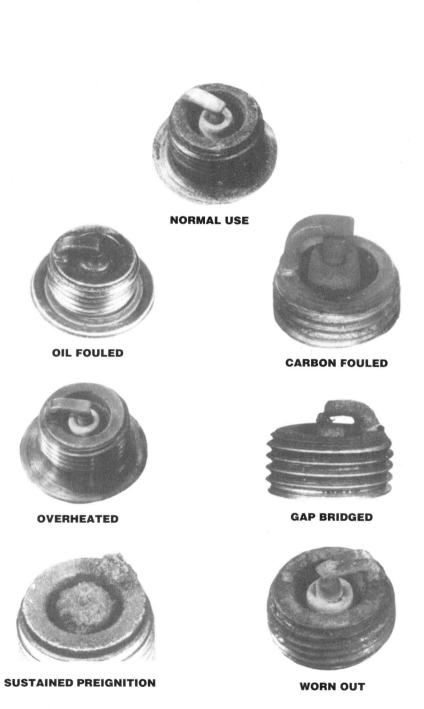

64

SPARK PLUG CONDITIONS

NORMAL USE

OIL FOULED

CARBON FOULED

OVERHEATED

GAP BRIDGED

SUSTAINED PREIGNITION

WORN OUT

Ignition Timing

All models are equipped with a solid state ignition system that requires no adjustments. The fully transistorized system consists of a pickup coil and rotor, CDI unit, ignition coil and spark plug. The pickup coil and rotor are used instead of breaker points to trigger the ignition system. Ignition timing can be checked to ensure that the ignition system is functioning properly.

Incorrect ignition timing can cause a drastic loss of engine performance and efficiency. It may also cause overheating.

Before starting on this procedure, check all electrical connections related to the ignition system. Make sure all connections are tight and free of corrosion. Also check that all ground connections are clean and tight.

1. Start the engine and let it warm up approximately 2-3 minutes.
2. Park the vehicle on level ground and set the parking brake. Shut off the engine.
3. Remove the timing inspection plug (A, **Figure 52**) from the magneto cover.
4. Connect a portable tachometer following its manufacturer's instructions.
5. Connect a timing light following its manufacturer's instructions.
6. Restart the engine and allow it to idle.
7. Aim the timing light at the timing window and pull the trigger while checking ignition timing at the following engine speeds:
    a. At 1300 rpm, the timing is correct if the F mark on the rotor aligns with the index notch on the magneto cover. See **Figure 65**.
    b. At 3000 rpm, the timing is correct if the advanced timing marks on the rotor aligns with the index notch on the magneto cover. See **Figure 65**.
8. If the timing is incorrect, troubleshoot the ignition system as described in Chapter Two.
9. Disconnect the timing light and portable tachometer.
10. Install the timing inspection plug in the magneto cover.

Pilot Air Screw Adjustment

Using a short flat-tipped screwdriver, carefully turn the pilot air screw (**Figure 66**) in (clockwise)

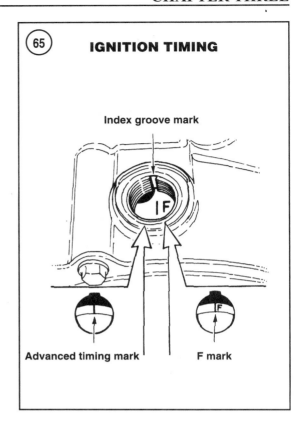

IGNITION TIMING

Index groove mark

Advanced timing mark   F mark

until it *lightly* seats, then back it out (counterclockwise) the number of turns listed in **Table 4**.

Idle Speed Adjustment

Before making this adjustment, the air filter must be clean.

1. Start the engine and let it warm up approximately 2-3 minutes.
2. Park the vehicle on level ground and set the parking brake.
3. Turn the idle speed adjust screw (**Figure 67**) in or out to obtain the slowest smooth idle speed. If it is difficult to obtain a smooth idle speed, make fine adjustments with the pilot air screw (**Figure 66**). To do this, turn the pilot air screw to the point where the idle goes up one way and then drops off when turned the other way. Find the best idle position between these two points, readjusting the idle speed screw if necessary.
4. Open and close the throttle a couple of times; check for variation in idle speed. Readjust if necessary.

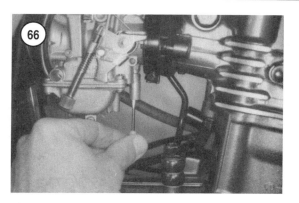

WARNING
With the engine idling, move the handlebar from side to side. If idle speed increases during this movement, the throttle cable needs adjusting or it may be incorrectly routed through the frame. Correct this problem immediately. Do not ride the vehicle in this unsafe condition.

5. Turn the engine off.

STORAGE

Several months of inactivity can cause serious problems and a general deterioration of the ATV's condition. This is especially true in areas of weather extremes. During the winter months it is advisable to prepare the ATV for lay-up.

Selecting a Storage Area

Most riders store their ATVs in their home garages. If a home garage is not available, facilities suitable for long-term ATV storage are readily available for rent or lease in most areas. When selecting a building, consider the following points.

1. The storage area must be as dry as possible. Heating is not necessary, but the building should be well insulated to minimize extreme temperature variations.

2. Avoid buildings with large window areas. Mask the windows if necessary to keep direct sunlight from shinning on the vehicle. This measure may also improve security.

Preparing Vehicle for Storage

Careful preparation minimizes deterioration and makes it easier to return the ATV to service later. Use the following procedure.

1. Wash the vehicle completely. Be sure to remove all dirt in all the hard to reach places like the cooling fins on the head and cylinder. Completely dry all parts of the ATV to remove all moisture.

2. Run the engine for about 20-30 minutes to warm up the oil. Drain the oil, regardless of the time since the last oil change. Refill with the normal quantity and type of oil as described in this chapter.

3. Drain all gasoline from the fuel tank, fuel hose, and the carburetor.

4. Remove the spark plug and add about one teaspoon of engine oil into the cylinder. Reinstall the spark plug and turn the engine over to distribute the oil to the cylinder walls and piston.

5. Lubricate the drive chain and all cables.

6. Remove the battery. Store it in an area where it will not be exposed to direct sunlight, moisture or freezing temperatures. During storage, slowly charge the battery at a rate of 1 amp or less once a month.

7. Tape or tie a plastic bag over the end of the muffler to prevent the entry of moisture.

8. Check the tire pressure. If necessary, inflate the tires to the correct pressure and move the vehicle to the storage area. Place it securely on a stand with all four wheels off the ground.

9. Cover the ATV with a tarp, blanket or heavy plastic drop cloth. Place this cover over the ATV mainly as a dust cover. Do not wrap it tightly, especially any plastic material, as it may trap moisture. Leave room for air to circulate around the ATV.

Inspection During Storage

Inspect the vehicle while in storage. Any deterioration should be corrected as soon as possible. For example, if corrosion is observed, cover it with a light coat of grease or silicone spray.

Crank the engine over a couple of times. Do not start it.

Restoring Vehicle to Service

A vehicle that has been properly prepared and stored in a suitable area requires only light maintenance to restore it to service. It is advisable, however, to perform a tune-up.

1. Before removing the vehicle from the storage area, inflate the tires to the correct pressures. Air loss during storage may have nearly flattened the tires.

2. Remove the cover from the muffler.

3. Refill the fuel tank with fresh gasoline.

4. Install a new spark plug and start the engine.

5. Perform the standard tune-up as described earlier in this chapter.

6. Check the operation of the engine stop switch. Oxidation of the switch contacts during storage may make it inoperative.

7. Clean and test ride the vehicle.

Table 1 MAINTENANCE SCHEDULE

After the first 10 hours of use	Clean the air filter element.
	Check throttle lever free play.
	Check the clutch lever free play; adjust if necessary.
	Clean and regap the spark plug; replace if necessary.
	Change the engine oil and replace the oil filter.
	Inspect the fuel system for contamination or leakage.
	Check the valve clearance.
	Check fasteners for tightness.
	Check all cable adjustments; adjust if necessary.
	Check the radiator hoses and connections for leaks.
	Check steering operation; adjust if necessary.
	Check the front and rear brake pads.
	Check the operation of the brake light switches (2000 models).
Every 10 days of use	Clean the air filter element.
	Check throttle lever free play.
	Check the clutch lever free play; adjust if necessary.
	Check the front and rear brake fluid levels.
	Check all cable adjustment; adjust if necessary.
	Check fasteners for tightness.
Every 30 days of use	Perform general lubrication.
	Check the front and rear brake pads.
	Check the operation of the brake light switch.
Every 90 days of use	Clean and regap the spark plug; replace if necessary.
	Change the engine oil and replace the oil filter.
	Inspect the fuel system for contamination or leakage.
	Check the valve clearance.

(continued)

Table 1 MAINTENANCE SCHEDULE (continued)

Every 90 days of use (continued)	Check steering operation; adjust if necessary.
	Inspect the drive chain, the engine sprocket and the rear sprocket.
	Check the radiator hoses and connections for leaks
Every year	Clean the spark arrester.
	Change the brake fluid.
Every two years	Change the coolant.

3

Table 2 TIRE SPECIFICATIONS

Front tire	
Type	Knobby/trail tubeless
Size	AT21 x 7.0-10
Manufacturer	Dunlop KT846
Rear tire	
Type	Knobby/trail tubeless
Size	
1987-1989	AT22 x 11.00–10
1990-on	AT22 x 10.00–10
Manufacturer	Dunlop KT847
Inflation pressure (cold)*	
Front	25 kPa (3.6 psi)
Rear	21 kPa (3.0 psi)
Maximum tire pressure (cold, to seat beads when installing tire)	
Front	250 kPa (36 psi)
Rear	
1987	210 kPa (30 psi)
1988-on	250 kPa (36 psi)

*Tire inflation pressure for original equipment tires. Aftermarket tires may require different inflation pressures.

Table 3 RECOMMENDED LUBRICANTS AND FLUIDS

Fuel	Regular unleaded
Octane	87 [(R + M)/2 method] or research octane of 91 or higher
Capacity	8.3 L (2.2 U.S. gal. [1.8 Imp. gal])
Engine oil	
Grade	API SE, SF or SG
Viscosity	SAE 10W-30, 10W-40, 10W-50, 20W-40, or 20W-50
Capacity	
Oil change	1.8 L (1.9 U.S. qt. [1.6 Imp. qt.])
Oil and filter change	2.0 L (2.11 U.S. qt. [1.75 Imp. qt.])
Brake fluid	DOT 3 or DOT 4
Cooling system	
Capacity (engine, radiator, reservoir)	1.45 L (1.53 U.S. qt. [1.28 Imp. qt.])
Coolant ratio	50% distilled water, 50% coolant
Chain oil	SAE 90

Table 4 MAINTENANCE AND TUNE-UP SPECIFICATIONS

Spark plug	
US and CA models	NGK DP8EA-9 or ND X24EP-U9
Canadian models	NGK DPR8EA-9 or ND X24EPR-U9
European models (1990-on)	NGK DPR8EA-9 or ND X24EPR-U9
Spark plug gap	0.8-0.9 mm (0.031-0.035 in.)
Ignition timing	10° BTDC at 1300 rpm
Ignition advance	35° BTDC at 3000 rpm
Idle Speed	Slowest smooth idle speed
Pilot air screw	1 3/4 turns out
Valve clearance	
Intake	0.20-0.24 mm (0.008-0.009 in.)
Exhaust	0.20-0.24 mm (0.008-0.009 in.)
Cylinder compression	480-785 kPa (70-114 psi)
Brake pad thickness	4.5 mm (0.177 in.)
Brake pad wear limit	1.0 mm (0.039 in.)
Brake pedal height	To suit rider preference
Throttle lever free play	2-3 mm (0.08-0.12 in.)
Choke cable free play	2-3 mm (0.08-0.12 in.)
Clutch lever free play	2-3 mm (0.08-0.12 in.)
Reverse cable free play	2-3 mm (0.08-0.12 in.)
Parking brake cable free length	42-44 mm (1.65-1.73 in.)
Drive chain 20-link length	
Standard	317.5-318.2 mm (12.50-12.52 in.)
Service limit	324 mm (12.76 in.)
Drive chain slack	40-50 mm (1.58-1.97 in.)
Cooling system test pressure	103 kPa (15 psi)
Radiator cap relief pressure	76-103 kPa (11-15 psi)

Table 5 MAINTENANCE AND TUNE UP TIGHTENING TORQUES

Item	N•m	in.-lb.	ft.-lb.
Coolant drain bolt	7.8	69	−
Engine	−	−	−
Oil drain bolt	15	−	11
Oil passage bolt	15	−	11
Oil pipe banjo bolt	20	−	15
Spark plug	14	−	10
Brake bleed valve	7.8	69	−
Brake hose banjo bolt	23	−	17
Brake caliper mounting bolts	25	−	18
Parking brake adjuster locknut			
(1987 models)	18	−	13
Rear master-cylinder-pushrod			
locknut	18	−	13
Spark plugs	14	−	10
Valve adjusting screw locknut	25	−	18
Wheels	−	−	−
Wheel nut	34	−	25
Rear hub nut	145	−	107
Front hub nut	34	−	25
Rear axle locknut	160	−	118
Swing-arm clamp bolt	37	−	27

ENGINE TOP END

4

The engine in the Mojave is a liquid-cooled, dual overhead camshaft, four-valve single. The valves are operated by the two camshafts, which are driven by a single cam chain.

This chapter provides complete service and overhaul procedures, including information for disassembly, removal, inspection, service and assembly of the engine top end components. These include the camshaft, valves, cylinder head, piston, piston rings and cylinder block.

Before starting any work, read the service hints in Chapter One.

Table 1 lists general engine specifications, **Table 2** lists top end specifications, and **Table 3** lists top end torque specification. **Tables 1-3** are at the end of the chapter.

ENGINE PRINCIPLES

Figure 1 explains basic four-stroke engine operation. This will be helpful when troubleshooting or repairing the engine.

CYLINDER HEAD COVER

The cylinder head cover can be removed with the engine installed in the frame. Refer to **Figure 2** when servicing the cylinder head.

Removal/Installation

1. Remove the front and rear fenders as described in Chapter Fourteen.

2. Remove the fuel tank, snorkel duct and air filter housing as described in Chapter Eight.

3. Remove the six cylinder head cover bolts, and remove the cylinder head cover from the left side of the ATV. Do not lose the two dowels (**Figure 3**) beneath the cover.

4. Carefully remove the cylinder head cover gasket. The gasket may come out with the cover or it may remain on the cylinder head.

5. Inspect the cylinder head gasket. Replace it if necessary.

6. Inspect the cam chain guide (A, **Figure 4**) inside the head cover. Replace the guide as necessary.

FOUR-STROKE ENGINE PRINCIPLES

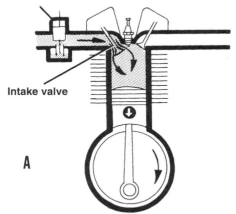

Carburetor

Intake valve

A

As the piston travels downward, the exhaust valve is closed and the intake valve opens, allowing the new air/fuel mixture from the carburetor to be drawn into the cylinder. When the piston reaches the bottom of its travel (BDC) the intake valve closes and remains closed for the next 1 1/2 revolutions of the crankshaft.

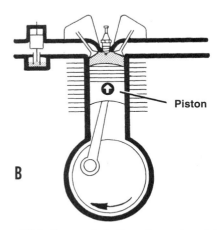

Piston

B

While the crankshaft continues to rotate, the piston moves upward, compressing the air/fuel mixture.

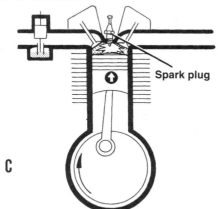

Spark plug

C

As the piston almost reaches the top of its travel, the spark plug fires, igniting the compressed air/fuel mixture. The piston continues to top dead center (TDC) and is pushed downward by the expanding gases.

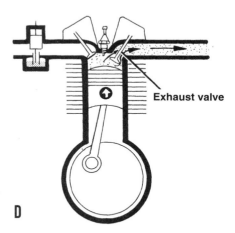

Exhaust valve

D

When the piston almost reaches BDC, the exhaust valve opens and remains open until the piston is near TDC. The upward travel of the piston forces the exhaust gases out of the cylinder. After the piston has reached TDC, the exhaust valve closes and the cycle repeats.

②

CYLINDER HEAD COVER

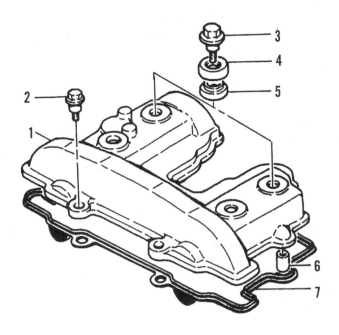

1. Cylinder head cover
2. Bolt
3. Bolt
4. Washer
5. O-ring
6. Dowel
7. Gasket

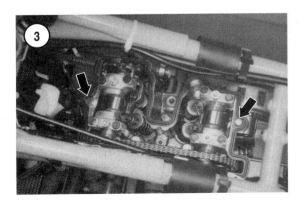

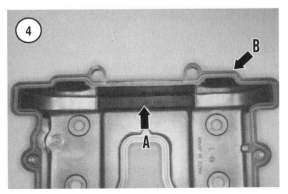

Installation

1. Apply silicone sealant to the two cutouts (**Figure 5**) on the side of the cylinder head.

2. Install the head cover gasket onto the cylinder head so the half-round projections in the gasket fit into the cutouts in the cylinder head. See **Figure 6**.

3. If removed, install the two dowels (**Figure 3**) in place on the cylinder head.

4. Set the cylinder head cover into place on the head. Make sure the gasket is seated in the groove (B, **Figure 4**) on the cover.

5. Make sure the washer and seal are in place on each of the four inner cylinder-head-cover bolts (**Figure 7**).

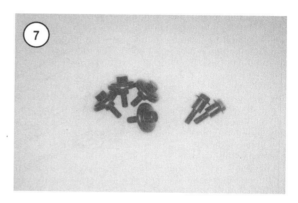

6. Install the four inner bolts (**Figure 8**) finger-tight. Check the gasket while tightening the bolts. Make sure the head cover groove remains seated around the gasket.

7. Install the two outer cylinder head cover bolts (**Figure 9**) finger-tight. Continue to check the cover and the gasket.

8. Torque the bolts to the specification in **Table 3**. Torque the four inner bolts first. Then torque the two outer bolts. Check the cover and gasket until all the bolts are tightened to the torque specification. If the gasket is not properly seated at any place around the cover, remove the cover and reinstall it.

CAM CHAIN TENSIONER

Removal/Inspection

> *CAUTION*
> *The cam chain tensioner is a non-return type tensioner. The internal pushrod will not return to its original position once it moves out.*

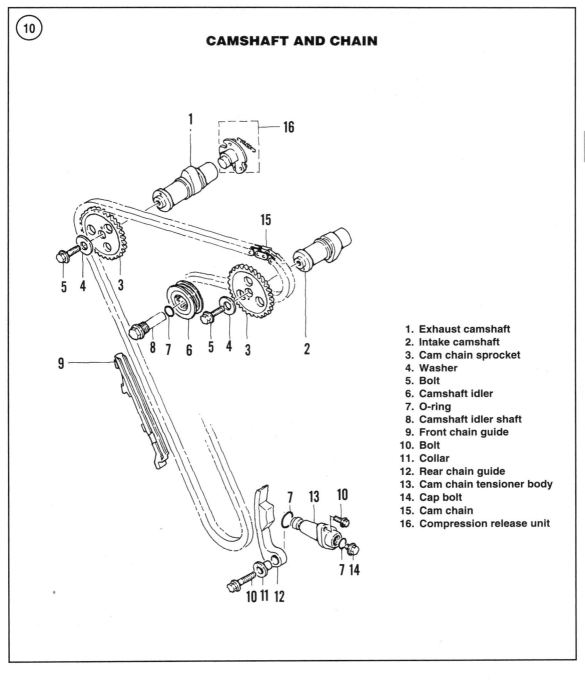

⑩

CAMSHAFT AND CHAIN

1. Exhaust camshaft
2. Intake camshaft
3. Cam chain sprocket
4. Washer
5. Bolt
6. Camshaft idler
7. O-ring
8. Camshaft idler shaft
9. Front chain guide
10. Bolt
11. Collar
12. Rear chain guide
13. Cam chain tensioner body
14. Cap bolt
15. Cam chain
16. Compression release unit

4

Whenever the tensioner mounting bolts are loosened, even by just a small amount, the tensioner assembly must be **completely removed** and the pushrod manually reset. Anytime the tensioner mounting bolts are loosened, remove the tensioner and reset the pushrod. Do not simply retighten the mounting bolts. If the mounting bolts are retightened without the pushrod being reset, the rod will be in its extended position. It will exert too much pressure on the chain and lead to engine damage.

Refer to **Figure 10** for this procedure

1. Remove the front and rear fenders as described in Chapter Fourteen.

2. Remove the air filter housing as described in Chapter Eight.

3. Check that the engine is at top dead center (TDC) on the compression stroke. If it is not, perform the following:

   a. Remove the cylinder head cover.

   b. Using the magneto rotor bolt, rotate the crankshaft counterclockwise and observe the intake valves. Once the intake valves open and close, continue turning the crankshaft until the T mark on the magneto rotor aligns with the slot in the timing window as shown in **Figure 11**.

   c. The engine should now be at TDC on the compression stroke.

   d. When the engine is at TDC on the compression stroke, the center of the timing mark on the exhaust camshaft sprocket should align with the top of the cylinder head. The bottom of the timing mark on the intake camshaft sprocket should also align with the top of the cylinder head. See **Figure 12**.

4. Remove the cap bolt (A, **Figure 13**) from the cam chain tensioner. Do not lose the O-ring behind the cap bolt.

5. Completely remove each mounting bolt (B, **Figure 13**). Remove the cam chain tensioner and its O-ring from the cylinder.

6. Inspect the body (A, **Figure 14**) for cracks or other damage. Replace the tensioner if necessary.

Installation

1. Make sure the O-ring (B, **Figure 14**) is installed on the tensioner body.

> *CAUTION*
> *A direction arrow is cast onto the tensioner body. Turn the rod in this direction (clockwise) only. Do not turn the rod counterclockwise when performing the next step. This could detach the rod from the tensioner, and it cannot be reinstalled.*

2. While pressing the pushrod into the tensioner body, turn the rod clockwise (in the direction indicated by the arrow) until the rod stops turning. See **Figure 15**.

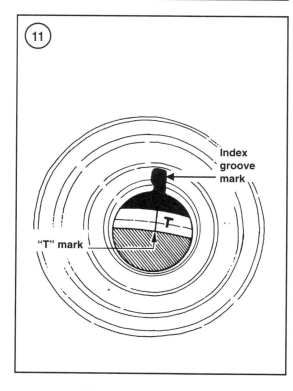

Index groove mark

"T" mark

3. Hold the rod in position with the screwdriver, and insert the tensioner body into place in the cylinder. See **Figure 16**.

4. While pressing the tensioner against the cylinder, install the mounting bolts finger-tight.

5. Torque the mounting bolts to the specification in **Table 3**.

6. Install the O-ring (C, **Figure 14**) onto the cap bolt, and install the bolt (A, **Figure 13**) onto the tensioner body. Tighten the cap bolt securely.

CAMSHAFT

Two camshafts are mounted in the cylinder head. Each camshaft is held in place by a pair of cam caps. Each cam cap is mated to the cylinder head, and must be installed in its proper location. The camshafts are driven by a chain from the timing sprocket, which is mounted onto the crankshaft. The camshafts can be removed with the engine in the frame.

Refer to **Figure 10** when servicing the camshafts.

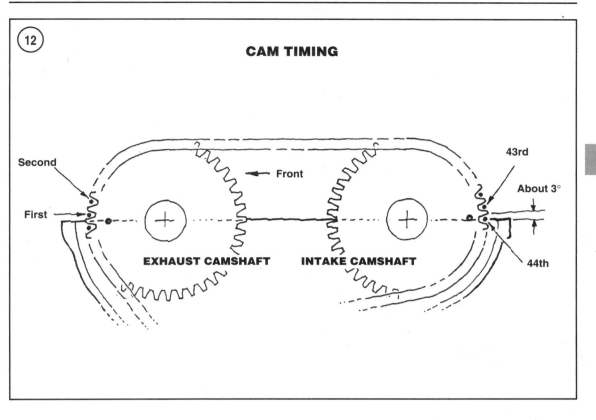

CAM TIMING

Second

First

Front

EXHAUST CAMSHAFT

INTAKE CAMSHAFT

43rd

About 3°

44th

12

4

13

B

A

B

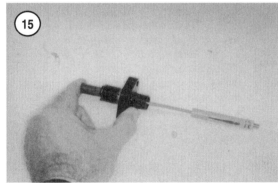

15

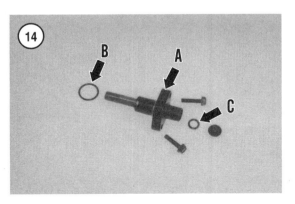

14

B

A

C

16

Removal

1. Remove the cylinder head cover and the cam chain tensioner as described in this chapter.

> *NOTE*
> *Take a moment to examine the timing marks (**Figure 17** and **Figure 12**) before disassembling the cylinder head. This makes cam timing easier. Be sure the engine is at top dead center on the compression stroke.*

2. Remove the camshaft caps from the intake camshaft (A, **Figure 18**) and then from the exhaust camshaft (B, **Figure 18**) by performing the following:
   a. Evenly loosen the four camshaft cap bolts on the intake or exhaust side of the head.
   b. Remove the bolts and the camshaft caps.
   c. Remove the two dowels beneath each cap.
   d. Repeat for the other side.
3. Disengage the cam chain from the camshaft sprockets. Remove the intake camshaft, then the exhaust camshaft.

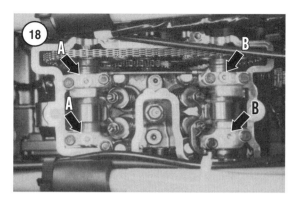

> *CAUTION*
> *If the crankshaft must be rotated while the camshafts are removed, pull up on the cam chain to make sure it is properly engaged with the timing sprocket on the crankshaft. Be sure the chain is correctly positioned on the crankshaft timing sprocket. If this is not done, the cam chain can become kinked and may damage the chain, the timing sprocket, and the surrounding crankcase area.*

4. Tie a piece of wire to the cam chain, and secure the other end to the exterior of the engine so the chain does not fall into the cam chain tunnel.
5. Inspect the camshaft as described in this chapter.

Installation

1. Pull the cam chain taut to ensure that the chain still engages the crankshaft timing sprocket.
2. Check the timing window on the magneto cover. Make sure the crankshaft is still at top dead center on the compression stroke. If necessary, rotate the rotor bolt until the T mark aligns with the cutout in the timing window. See **Figure 11**.

b. Set the cam cap (**Figure 21**) in place so its arrow points to the front of the engine.

c. Install and finger-tighten the two cam cap bolts.

8. Check the timing mark on the exhaust camshaft sprocket. The center of the mark must align with the top of the cylinder head (**Figure 12**).

9. Use Liquid Paper (or a wax marker) to mark the pin on the cam chain that sits directly above the tooth that is opposite the timing mark on the exhaust camshaft sprocket. See **Figure 12**. This is the first pin.

10. Counting the first pin as one, move clockwise along the cam chain until the 43rd and 44th pins on the chain are identified. Mark these pins as well.

11. Install the intake camshaft through the cam chain. Mesh the camshaft sprocket with the chain so the sprocket's timing mark sits between the 43rd and 44th pins on the chain as shown in **Figure 22**.

12. Lower the intake camshaft into place, and check the timing mark. The bottom of the mark on the intake sprocket should align with the top of the cylinder head (**Figure 12**).

13. Check the timing marks on both camshaft sprockets. Each should align with the top of the cylinder head as shown in **Figure 12**.

14. Install each of the remaining cam caps into its proper location in the cylinder head. Follow the procedure described in Step 7 for each cap.

15. Once all cam caps are in place, torque the cam cap bolts to the specification in **Table 3**.

16. Reinstall the cam chain tensioner and cylinder head cover as described in this chapter.

3. Lubricate the cam lobes and camshaft journals with engine oil. If a new camshaft(s) or cylinder head is installed, apply molybdenum disulfide grease to the new parts.

4. Fill the oil passages in the camshaft bearings with engine oil.

5. Install the exhaust camshaft through the cam chain and into place in the bearing surfaces in the cylinder head.

6. Lift the cam chain and rotate the camshaft so the center of the timing mark on the sprocket aligns with the top of the cylinder head (**Figure 19**).

NOTE
Each cam cap is identified by a stamping that locates its position in the cylinder head-intake left, intake right, exhaust left and exhaust right. Be sure each cap is installed in its proper location.

7. Install the left exhaust cam cap (EX L) to help hold the camshaft stationary. Perform the following:

a. Fit the two dowels (**Figure 20**) in place in the cylinder head.

Camshaft Sprocket Removal/Installation

1. Remove the camshaft as described in this chapter.

2. Secure the camshaft sprocket in a vise with soft jaws as shown in **Figure 24**.

3. Remove the sprocket bolt (A, **Figure 24**) and washer, and then remove the camshaft from the sprocket.

4. Install the new sprocket onto the camshaft. Make sure the indexing hole in the sprocket engages the pin on the end of the camshaft.

5. Apply Loctite 242 (blue) to the threads of the sprocket bolt and install the bolt along with its washer.

6. Secure the sprocket into a vise with soft jaws (**Figure 24**), and torque the sprocket bolt to the specification in **Table 3**.

Camshaft Inspection

1. Visually inspect the cam lobes (A, **Figure 25**) for wear. The lobes should not be scored, and the edges should be square.

2. Measure the height of each cam lobe with a micrometer (**Figure 26**). Replace the camshaft if a lobe height is less than the service limit specified in **Table 2**.

3. Inspect the camshaft bearing journals (B, **Figure 25**) for wear or scoring.

> *NOTE*
> *The cam caps and the cylinder head on the Mojave are mated. All cam caps and the cylinder head must be replaced as a set.*

4. If the journal is excessively worn or damaged, check the journal bearing surfaces in the cylinder head (A, **Figure 27**) and cam caps (**Figure 28**) for wear. If any bearing surface is scored or worn, replace the cylinder head and the four cam caps as a set.

5. Measure the camshaft bearing clearance as described in this chapter.

> *NOTE*
> *If the camshaft and crankshaft timing sprockets are worn, check the cam chain, chain guides and chain tensioner for damage.*

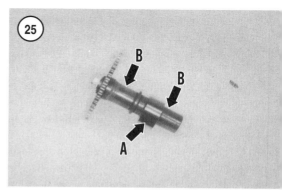

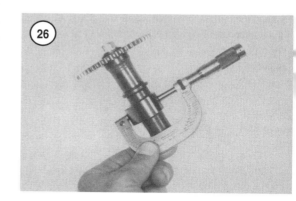

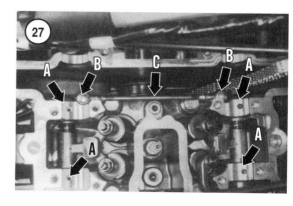

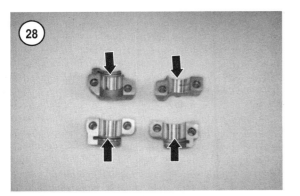

6. Inspect the camshaft sprockets (**Figure 29**) for worn, broken or chipped teeth. Also check the teeth for cracking or rounding. If a camshaft sprocket is damaged or severely worn, replace the sprocket as described in this chapter. Also inspect the timing sprocket mounted on the crankshaft as described in Chapter Five.

7. Inspect the compression release unit as described in this chapter.

Compression Release Inspection

The compression release eases starting by automatically opening the exhaust valve to release compression pressure. During starting, the compression release spring holds the weights at rest. As the unit rotates, the stopper presses against the follower on the exhaust rocker arm and opens the exhaust valve. Once the engine is running, however, oil pressure overcomes spring pressure. The weights (A, **Figure 30**) move away from the center of the release unit, and the stopper (B, **Figure 30**) is retracted inside the release unit so it cannot act on the rocker arm follower.

1. Visually inspect the compression release spring. Replace the spring if it is worn or damaged.

2. Manually move the weights back and forth. If they do not move smoothly, replace the compression release unit.

3A. On 1987 and 1988 models, the compression release unit, the exhaust camshaft and the exhaust rocker arm must be replaced as a set.

3B. On 1989-on models, the compression release unit and the exhaust camshaft must be replaced as a set.

Camshaft Bearing Clearance

Use Plastigage to measure the camshaft bearing clearance as described in the following procedure.

1. If removed, set each camshaft into place in the cylinder head.

CAUTION
Do not rotate the crankshaft while Plastigage is in the engine.

2. Place a strip of Plastigage across each camshaft journal. Be sure the strips run parallel to the camshaft.

3. Install the cam caps by performing the following:

  a. Identify the cap's location by the stamping on the cap (intake left, intake right, exhaust left, exhaust right). Install each cap in its proper location in the cylinder head.

  b. Install the two dowels (**Figure 20**) into place in the cylinder head.

  c. Fit the cap (**Figure 21**) in place so its arrow points toward the front of the engine, and install the cam cap bolts finger-tight.

d. Repeat this procedure for the camshaft's remaining cam cap.

e. Once both cam caps have been installed, torque the cam cap bolts to the specification in **Table 3**.

4. Repeat Steps 1-3 for the other camshaft.

5. Remove the cam caps, and measure each piece of Plastigage at its widest point (**Figure 31**).

6. If any clearance exceeds the service limit listed in **Table 2**, measure the diameter of each camshaft journal (B, **Figure 25**) with a micrometer.

> *NOTE*
> *On 1987 and 1988 models, the exhaust camshaft, the compression release unit and the exhaust rocker arm must be replaced as a set. On 1989-on, the exhaust camshaft and the compression release unit must be replaced as a set.*

7. If the camshaft journal is less than the service limit specified in **Table 2**, replace the camshaft.

8. Measure the bearing clearance of the new camshaft.

9. If the clearance is still outside the service limit, replace the cylinder head.

CYLINDER HEAD OIL PIPE

Removal/Installation

1. Remove both camshafts as described in this chapter.

2. Remove the two banjo bolts (B, **Figure 27**) and remove the oil pipe (C, **Figure 27**) from the cylinder head.

3. Flush the oil pipe with solvent and blow it clear with compressed air.

4. Fit the oil pipe in place by simultaneously pressing both ends of the pipe into position in the cylinder head.

5. Install the oil pipe banjo bolts, and torque the bolts to the specification in **Table 3**.

ROCKER ARMS

The rocker arms can be removed with the cylinder head installed in the frame. The head is shown removed in the photographs for clarity.

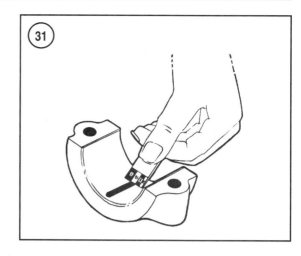

Refer to **Figure 32** when servicing the rocker arms.

1. Remove the cylinder head cover and the camshafts as described in this chapter.

2. Remove the rocker shaft plug (A, **Figure 33**) from the exhaust side of the cylinder head.

3. Remove the rocker shaft from the cylinder head (intake: A, **Figure 34**, exhaust: B, **Figure 33**). Make sure to remove the gasket (B, **Figure 34**) with the intake rocker shaft.

4. Remove the rocker arm spring (C, **Figure 34**), and remove the rocker arm from the cylinder head.

5. Inspect the rocker arms and rocker shafts as described in this chapter.

Assembly

1. Apply engine oil to the rocker arm bore before installation.

> *NOTE*
> *On 1987 and 1988 models, the exhaust rocker arm has a stamping (A-D) that matches the stamping on the compression release unit. When installing a new exhaust rocker arm, be sure the stamping on the new arm is the same as the stamping on the old arm or on the compression release unit. Compression release operation will be adversely affected if an incorrect exhaust rocker arm is installed.*

2. Set the rocker arm and the rocker arm spring into place in the cylinder head. Make sure the spring is

VALVES AND ROCKER ARMS

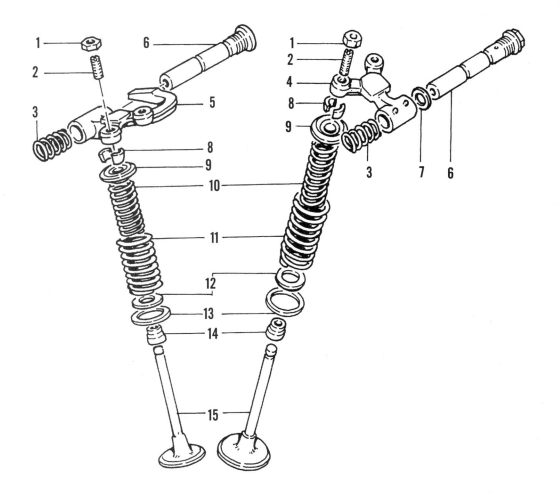

4

1. Adjuster locknut
2. Valve adjuster
3. Rocker arm spring
4. Intake rocker arm
5. Exhaust rocker arm
6. Rocker shaft
7. Gasket
8. Valve keepers

9. Valve spring retainer
10. Inner spring
11. Outer spring
12. Inner spring seat
13. Outer spring seat
14. Oil seal
15. Valve

on the cam-chain side of the rocker arm. See **Figure 34**.

3. When installing the intake rocker arm, install the gasket (B, **Figure 34**) onto the intake rocker shaft.

4. Apply engine oil to the rocker shaft, and install the shaft (intake: A, **Figure 34**, exhaust: B, **Figure 33**). Make sure the shaft passes through the cylinder head, rocker arm bore, and the rocker spring.

5. Torque the rocker shaft to the specification in **Table 3**.

6. When servicing the exhaust rocker arm, install the rocker shaft plug (A, **Figure 33**) and torque the plug to the specification in **Table 3**.

Inspection

1. Clean all parts in solvent. Dry them with compressed air.

> *NOTE*
> *If the rocker arm pad is worn, also check the mating camshaft lobe for wear or damage.*

2. Inspect the rocker arm pad (A, **Figure 35**) where it contacts the camshaft lobe, and where the adjuster contacts the valve stem. Check for scratches, flat spots, uneven wear and scoring.

3. Inspect the oil passage (B, **Figure 35**). Blow it clear with compressed air.

4. Inspect the rocker shaft for wear or scoring.

5. Insert each rocker shaft into its respective rocker arm. Slowly rotate the shaft and check for binding or looseness.

6. Measure the diameter of the rocker arm bore with a small hole gauge, then measure the small hole gauge with a micrometer (**Figure 36**). Replace the rocker arm if it is worn beyond the service limit specified in **Table 2**.

7. Measure the outside diameter of the rocker shaft with a micrometer (**Figure 37**). Replace the rocker shaft if it is worn beyond the service limit specified in **Table 2**.

> *NOTE*
> *If either the rocker arm or rocker shaft is worn to the service limit, consider replacing both the rocker arm and rocker shaft. Replacing a rocker arm and rocker shaft as a set is highly recommended.*

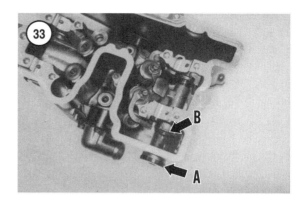

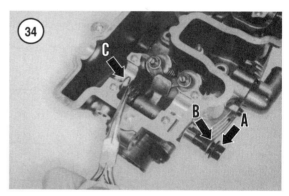

8. Replace the rocker arm and its rocker shaft if either is worn beyond the service limit listed in **Table 2**.

CAM CHAIN

A continuous cam chain is used on all models. Do not cut the chain; replacement link components are not available. Refer to **Figure 38** when servicing the cam chain.

Removal/Installation

1. Remove the camshaft as described in this chapter.

2. Remove the following components as described in Chapter Five.

   a. The magneto rotor.

   b. The balancer gear.

   c. The left balancer.

3. If still installed, lift the front cam chain guide (A, **Figure 39**) from its slot in the crankcase, and remove the guide from the top of the cylinder head.

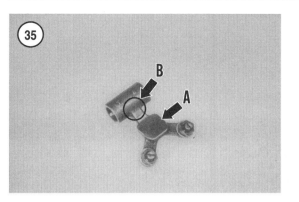

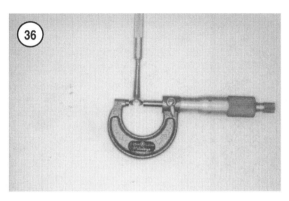

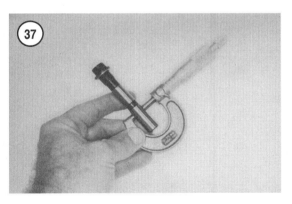

4. Remove the cam chain guide plate (A, **Figure 40**) from the crankcase.

5. Slip the cam chain (B, **Figure 40**) off the timing sprocket and remove it from around the crankshaft.

6. Inspect the cam chain as described in this chapter.

7. Install the cam chain over the crankshaft and pull it up through the chain tunnel with a piece of wire. Secure the chain with a piece of wire.

8. Mesh the chain with the timing sprocket on the crankshaft.

9. Install the cam chain guide plate (A, **Figure 40**) so its arm fits against the crankcase boss. Install the plate screw and tighten it securely.

10. Lower the front chain guide down the chain tunnel and seat the guide into its slot in the crankcase. See **Figure 39**.

11. Install the left balancer, the balancer gear and the magneto rotor as described in Chapter Five.

12. Install the camshafts as described in this chapter.

Inspection

If the following procedure shows that the cam chain is excessively worn or damaged, the automatic chain tensioner may not be operating properly. Inspect the cam chain tensioner and the chain guides as described in this chapter.

1. Clean the cam chain in solvent. Dry it with compressed air.

2. Check the cam chain (**Figure 41**) for:

    a. Worn or damaged pins and rollers.

    b. Cracked or damaged side plates.

3. Place the chain on a flat surface and pull the chain tight (no slack between pins). Then measure the length of any 20 links (21 pins) with a vernier caliper (**Figure 42**), and check the measurement against the specification in **Table 2**. Replace the chain if it is stretched to the service limit or greater. Do not attempt to repair the chain.

4. If the cam chain is excessively worn or damaged, inspect the camshaft sprockets and the crankshaft timing sprocket for the same wear conditions. If the sprockets show wear or damage, replace them at the same time.

> *CAUTION*
> *Do not run a new chain over worn or damaged sprockets. Doing so causes rapid and excessive chain wear.*

CHAIN GUIDES

Front and rear chain guides are used in the Mojave. Refer to **Figure 38** when servicing the chain guides.

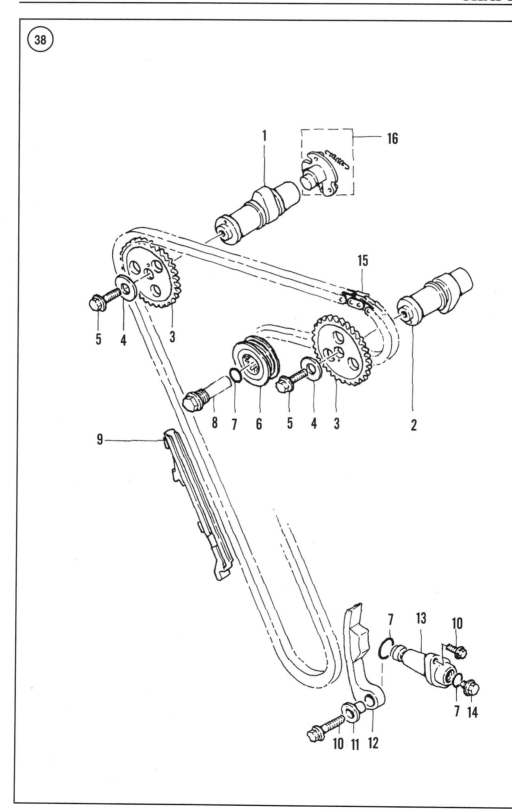

4

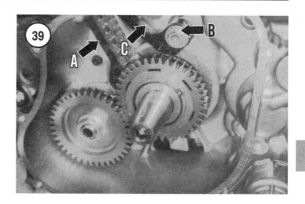

CAMSHAFT AND CHAIN

1. Exhaust camshaft
2. Intake camshaft
3. Cam chain sprocket
4. Washer
5. Bolt
6. Camshaft idler
7. O-ring
8. Camshaft idler shaft
9. Front chain guide
10. Bolt
11. Collar
12. Rear chain guide
13. Cam chain tensioner body
14. Cap bolt
15. Cam chain
16. Compression release unit

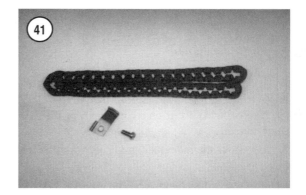

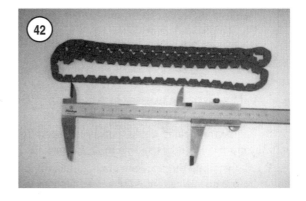

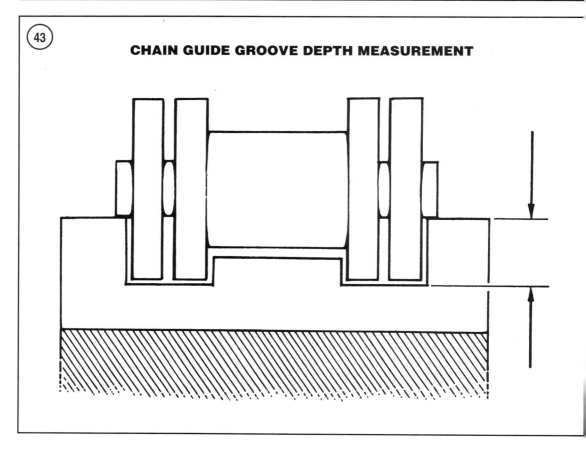

(43)

CHAIN GUIDE GROOVE DEPTH MEASUREMENT

Removal/Installation

1. To remove the front chain guide (A, **Figure 39**), remove the cylinder head as described in this chapter. Then lift the front chain guide from the cam chain tunnel.

2. To remove the rear chain guide, perform the following:

    a. Remove the magneto rotor as described in Chapter Five.

    b. Remove the rear chain guide pivot bolt (B, **Figure 39**) and remove the rear chain guide (C, **Figure 39**) and its collar.

3. Inspect the chain guides as described in this section.

4. Install by reversing these steps while noting the following:

5. Install the front chain guide so its bottom end fits into the crankcase slot as shown in A, **Figure 39**.

6. When installing the rear cam chain guide, oil the collar before installing it into the guide. Tighten the

rear chain guide pivot bolt to the torque specification in **Table 3**.

Inspection

1. Visually inspect the chain guides for excessive wear, cuts or other damage.

2. Measure the depth of the chain groove in each chain guide (**Figure 43**), and compare the measurement to the dimension in **Table 2**. Replace if worn to the service limit or greater.

> *NOTE*
> *New chain guides do not have chain grooves. The grooves are caused from normal wear.*

CYLINDER HEAD

The cylinder head can be removed with the engine installed in the frame. Refer to **Figure 44** when servicing the cylinder head.

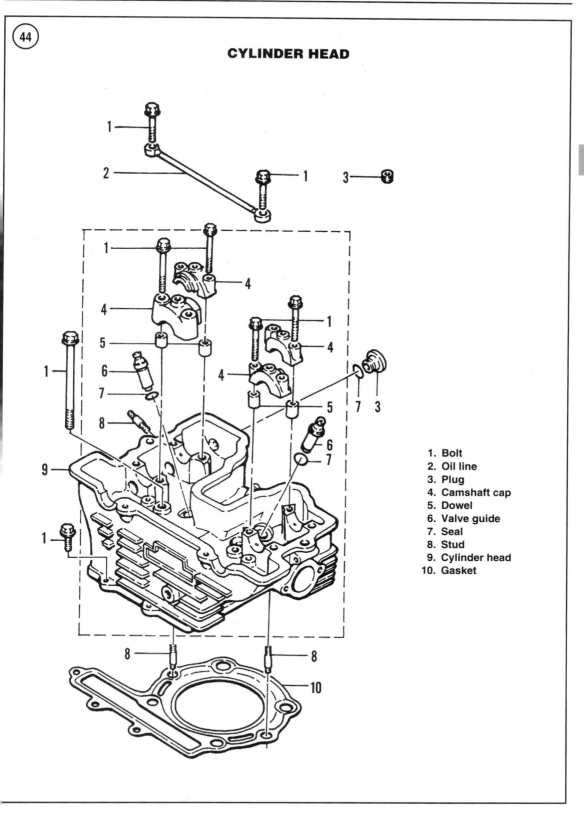

CYLINDER HEAD

1. Bolt
2. Oil line
3. Plug
4. Camshaft cap
5. Dowel
6. Valve guide
7. Seal
8. Stud
9. Cylinder head
10. Gasket

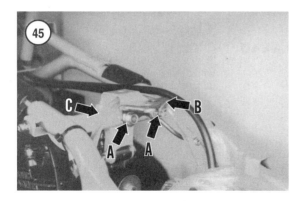

Cylinder Head Removal

1. Remove the front and rear fenders as described in Chapter Fourteen.
2. Drain the coolant as described in Chapter Three.
3. Remove the spark plug cap and remove the spark plug.
4. Remove the following components as described in Chapter Eight:
    a. Fuel tank.
    b. Carburetor.
    c. Exhaust system.
5. Remove the following components as described in this chapter:
    a. Cylinder head cover.
    b. Cam chain tensioner.
    c. Camshafts.
    d. Cylinder head oil pipe.
6. Remove the cylinder head bracket by performing the following:
    a. Remove the two cylinder head bracket bolts (A, **Figure 45**) and remove the fuel tank bracket (B, **Figure 45**) from the cylinder head bracket.
    b. Note how the carburetor vent hose (C, **Figure 45**) is routed between the cylinder head bracket and the frame. Reroute the hose in the same manner during assembly.
    c. Remove the 8 mm engine mounting bolt from the cylinder head bracket (A, **Figure 46**), and lift the bracket (B, **Figure 46**) from the frame.
7. Remove the banjo bolt from the crankcase (A, **Figure 47**) and from the cylinder head (B, **Figure 47**), and then remove the upper main oil line (C, **Figure 47**).
8. Remove the coolant hose (**Figure 48**) from the thermostat housing on the right side of the cylinder head.

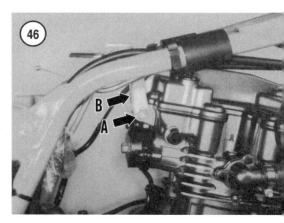

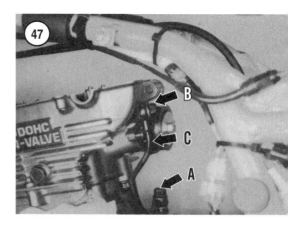

9. Loosen and remove the three cylinder head bolts (6 mm) shown in **Figure 49**.

10. Loosen and remove the two 8 mm cylinder head cap nuts (**Figure 50**).

11. Using a crisscross pattern, loosen the 10 mm cylinder head bolts (**Figure 51**) in equal amounts until all four bolts are loose. Remove the bolts.

12. Tap the cylinder head with a rubber mallet to free it from the head gasket.

13. Lift the cylinder head from the cylinder.

14. Remove the head gasket (A, **Figure 52**) and the two dowels (B, **Figure 52**) from the top of the cylinder block.

15. If necessary, remove the front cam chain guide.

16. Cover the cylinder block with a clean shop rag or paper towels.

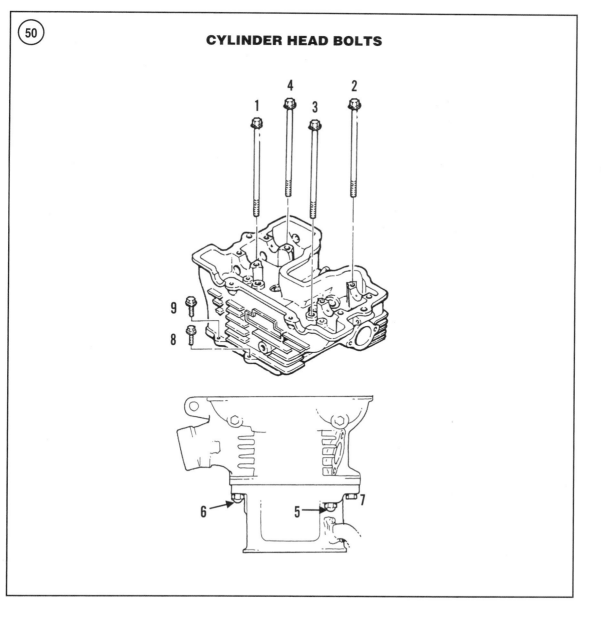

CYLINDER HEAD BOLTS

Cylinder Head Inspection

1. Remove all traces of gasket material from the cylinder head and cylinder mating surfaces. Do not scratch the gasket surfaces.

> *CAUTION*
> *Cleaning the combustion chamber with the valves removed can damage the valve seat surfaces. A damaged or even slightly scratched valve seat causes poor valve seating.*

2. Without removing the valves, remove all carbon deposits from the combustion chamber (**Figure 53**). Use a fine wire brush dipped in solvent or make a scraper from hardwood. Take care not to damage the head, valves or spark plug threads.

> *NOTE*
> *When using a tap to clean spark plug threads, coat the tap with an aluminum tap cutting fluid or kerosene.*

3. Examine the spark plug threads in the cylinder head for damage. If damage is minor or if the threads are dirty or clogged with carbon, use a spark plug thread tap to clean the threads following the manufacturer's instructions. If thread damage is excessive, the threads can be restored by installing a steel thread insert. Thread insert kits can be purchased at automotive supply stores or the inserts can be installed by a Kawasaki dealership or machine shop.

> *NOTE*
> *Aluminum spark plug threads are commonly damaged due to galling, cross-threading and overtightening. To prevent galling, apply an antiseize compound to the plug threads before installation and do not overtighten the plug.*

4. After all carbon is removed from combustion chambers and valve ports, and the spark plug thread hole is repaired, clean the entire head in solvent.

> *NOTE*
> *If the cylinder head is bead-blasted, make sure to clean the head thoroughly with solvent and then with hot soapy water. After bead blasting, gritty residue can seat in small crev-*

ices and other areas and can be hard to get out. Also, chase each exposed thread with a tap to remove grit between the threads or a thread may become damaged later. Grit residue remaining in the engine contaminates the oil and causes premature piston, ring and bearing wear.

5. Examine the piston crown. The crown should show no signs of wear or damage. If the crown appears pecked or spongy-looking, also check the

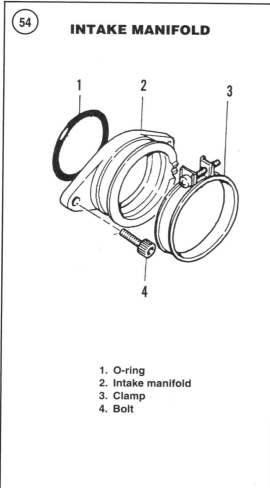

54

INTAKE MANIFOLD

1. O-ring
2. Intake manifold
3. Clamp
4. Bolt

56

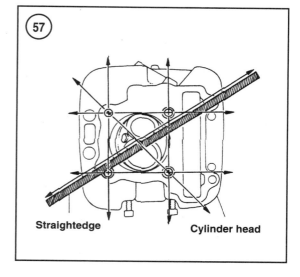

57

Straightedge   Cylinder head

55

spark plug, valves and combustion chamber for aluminum deposits. If these deposits are found, the cylinder is overheating caused by a lean fuel mixture or preignition.

6. Inspect the intake manifold for cracks or other damage that would allow unfiltered air to enter the engine. If necessary, remove the intake manifold and replace the O-ring. See **Figure 54**. When reinstalling the intake manifold, make sure the indexing marks are on the right side of the cylinder head as shown in **Figure 55**.

NOTE
The cam caps and the cylinder head on the Mojave are mated. When replacing the cylinder head, also replace all four cam caps.

7. Check for cracks in the combustion chamber and exhaust port (**Figure 56**). Replace a cracked head if it cannot be repaired by welding.

8. After the head has been thoroughly cleaned, place a straightedge across the gasket surface at several points (**Figure 57**). Measure warpage by attempting to insert a feeler gauge between the straightedge and cylinder head at each location

(**Figure 58**). Maximum allowable warpage is listed in **Table 2**. A warped or nicked cylinder head gasket surface could cause an air leak and result in overheating. If warpage exceeds the specified limit, replace or resurface the cylinder head. Consult a Kawasaki dealership or machine shop experienced in this type of work.

9. Check the cylinder head bolts (**Figure 59**) for thread damage, cracks and twisting.

10. Clear the oil passages with compressed air, and then fill the passages with clean engine oil.

Cylinder Head Installation

1. Clean all gasket residue from the cylinder head and cylinder mating surfaces.

2. If removed, install the following components as described in this chapter:
   a. Valves.
   b. Rocker arms and shafts.

3. If removed, install the front cam chain guide (A, **Figure 39**) into the guide slot in the crankcase. Make sure the chain guide's sliding surface faces toward the cam chain and that the cam chain is positioned between both chain guides.

4. Install a new head gasket (A, **Figure 52**) and the two dowels (B, **Figure 52**) onto the cylinder.

5. If the crankshaft is not positioned at TDC, perform the following:
   a. Lift the cam chain and make sure it properly engages the crankshaft timing sprocket. Hold the chain in this position when turning the crankshaft.

> *CAUTION*
> *The cam chain must be kept tight against the timing sprocket when turning the crankshaft; otherwise, the chain can roll off the sprocket and bind in the lower end, causing chain damage.*

   b. Turn the crankshaft counterclockwise and align the T mark on the magneto rotor with the index groove in the magneto cover (**Figure 60**).

6. Position the cylinder head between the frame and cylinder block. Run the cam chain and its wire through the chain tunnel in the cylinder head. Tie the wire to the frame.

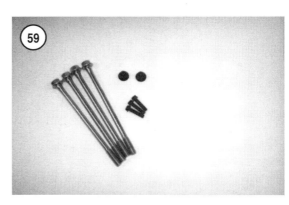

7. Seat the cylinder head on the cylinder block (**Figure 61**). Make sure the dowel pins engage the cylinder.

8. Pull up on the chain and make sure it properly engages the crankshaft timing sprocket before continuing.

9. Apply molybdenum disulfide grease to the threads and bearing surfaces of the four 10 mm cylinder head bolts. Install and finger-tighten these four bolts. See **Figure 51**.

10. Install and finger-tighten the two 8 mm cylinder head cap nuts, indicated by the arrows in **Figure 50**.

11. Install and finger-tighten the three 6 mm cylinder head bolts (**Figure 49**).

12. Tighten the cylinder head mounting bolts and nuts in 2-3 stages following the tightening sequence shown in **Figure 50**. Tighten them to the final torque specifications in **Table 3**.

13. Install the coolant hose (**Figure 48**) onto the thermostat housing.

14. Install the upper main oil pipe by performing the following:
   a. Set the upper main oil pipe in place on the engine. The upper main oil line (A, **Figure 62**)

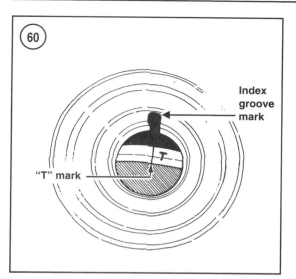

Index groove mark

"T" mark

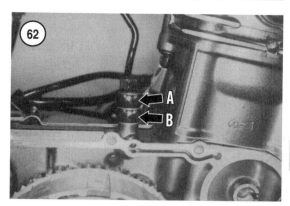

A
B

should sit atop the lower main oil (B, **Figure 62**) on the right side of the crankcase.

b. Install a new sealing washer on each side of the oil pipe fittings as shown in **Figure 62**. Install and finger-tighten the banjo bolt.

c. Install the oil pipe onto the cylinder head with a banjo bolt and two new sealing washers (B, **Figure 47**). Make sure a sealing washer is on each side of the oil pipe fitting.

d. Torque each banjo bolt to the specification in **Table 3**.

15. Install the cylinder head bracket by performing the following:

a. Lower the cylinder head bracket (B, **Figure 46**) in place on the frame. Make sure the carburetor vent hose (C, **Figure 45**) is routed between the bracket and the frame.

b. Install and finger-tighten the 8 mm engine mounting bolt (A, **Figure 46**). Make sure the bolt passes through the cylinder head and

threads into the weld nut on the left side of the bracket.

c. Set the fuel tank bracket (B, **Figure 45**) in place on the cylinder head bracket, and install the two cylinder head bracket bolts (A, **Figure 45**).

d. Torque the 8 mm engine mounting bolt and the cylinder head bracket bolts to the specifications in **Table 3**.

16. Install the following components as described in this chapter:

a. Cylinder head oil pipe.

b. Camshafts

c. Cam chain tensioner

d. Cylinder head cover

17. Install the following components as described in Chapter Eight:

a. Fuel tank.

b. Carburetor.

c. Exhaust system.

18. Install the spark plug and the spark plug cap.

19. Add coolant as described in Chapter Three.

20. Install the front and rear fenders as described in Chapter Fourteen.

21. If new parts were installed, the engine should be broken in just as though it were new. Follow the break-in procedure described in Chapter Five.

VALVES AND VALVE COMPONENTS

Complete valve service requires a number of special tools. The following procedures describe how to check for valve component wear and to determine what type of service is required. In most cases, valve troubles are caused by poor valve seating, worn valve guides and burned valves. A valve

VALVES AND ROCKER ARMS

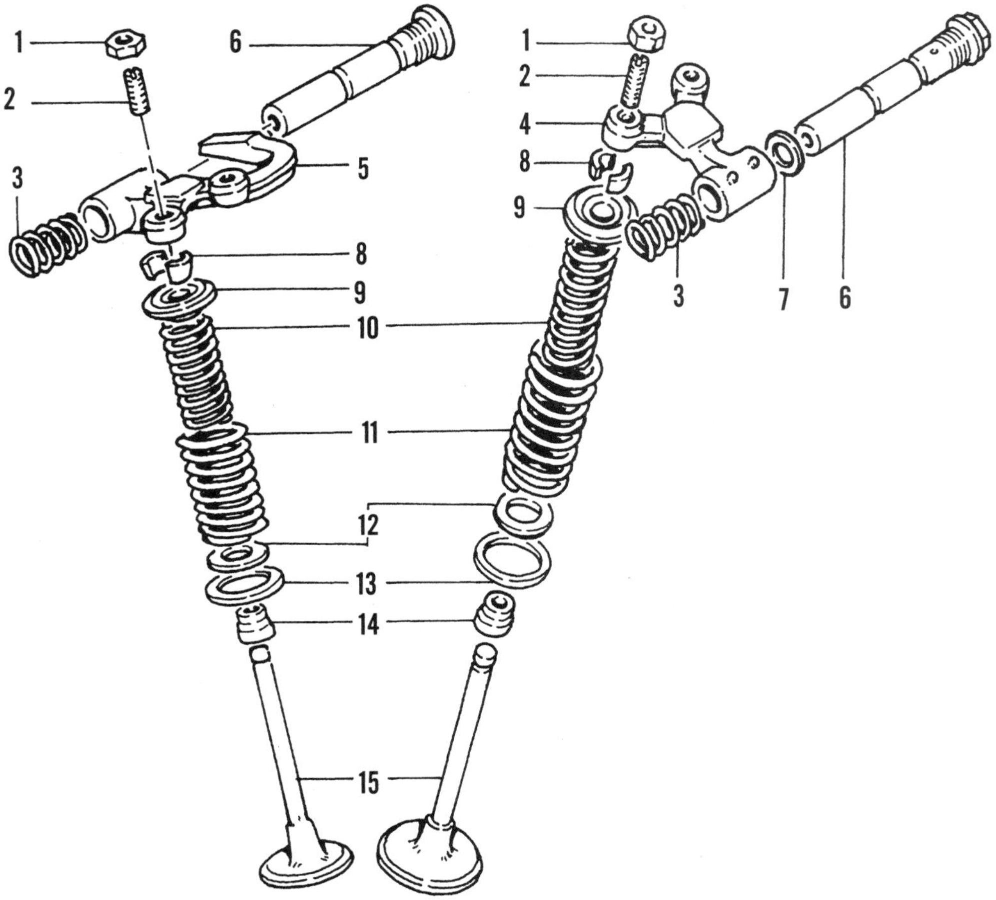

1. Adjuster locknut
2. Valve adjuster
3. Rocker arm spring
4. Intake rocker arm
5. Exhaust rocker arm
6. Rocker shaft
7. Gasket
8. Valve keepers
9. Valve spring retainer
10. Inner spring
11. Outer spring
12. Inner spring seat
13. Outer spring seat
14. Oil seal
15. Valve

4

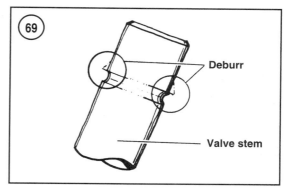

Deburr

Valve stem

spring compressor is required to remove and install the valves.

Refer to **Figure 63** when servicing the valves.

1. Remove the cylinder head as described in this chapter.

2. Remove the rocker arms as described in this chapter.

3. Install a valve spring compressor squarely over the valve spring seat with the other end of the tool placed against the valve head (**Figure 64**).

4. Tighten the valve spring compressor until the valve keepers separate. Lift the valve keepers out through the valve spring compressor with a magnet or needlenose pliers (**Figure 65**).

5. Gradually loosen the valve spring compressor and remove it from the head.

6. Remove the spring retainer (**Figure 66**) and both valve springs (**Figure 67**).

7. Remove both spring seats (**Figure 68**).

CAUTION
*Remove any burrs from the valve stem groove before removing the valve (**Figure 69**); otherwise, the valve guide will be damaged as the valve stem passes through it.*

8. Remove the valve.

9. Pull the oil seal (**Figure 70**) off of the valve guide. Discard the oil seal.

> *CAUTION*
> *All component parts of each valve assembly must be kept together. Do not intermix components from the two valve assemblies or excessive wear may result.*

10. Repeat Steps 3-10 and remove the remaining valves.

Inspection

Refer to the troubleshooting chart in **Figure 71** when performing valve inspection procedures in this section. Valve service specifications are listed in **Table 2**.

1. Clean valves in solvent. Do not gouge or damage the valve seating surface.

2. Inspect the valve face (**Figure 72**). Remove minor roughness and pitting by lapping the valve as described in this chapter. Excessive unevenness to the contact surface is an indication that the valve is not serviceable.

3. Inspect the valve stem for wear and roughness. Then measure the valve stem outside diameter with a micrometer (**Figure 73**). Check the measurement against the dimension in **Table 2**. Replace the valve if the stem is excessively worn.

4. Remove all carbon and varnish from the valve guides with a stiff spiral wire brush before measuring wear.

> *NOTE*
> *If the required measuring tools are not available, proceed to Step 6.*

5. Measure the valve guide inner diameter with a small hole gauge. Measure at the top, center and bottom positions. Then measure the small hole gauge with a micrometer, and check the measurement against the specification in **Table 2**. Replace the guide if it is worn to the service limit.

6. If a small hole gauge is not available, check the guide wear with the wobble method by performing the following:

    a. Insert each valve in its guide.

    b. Attach a dial gauge to the valve stem next to the valve head (**Figure 74**).

    c. Hold the valve just slightly off its seat and rock it back and forth in two directions that are 90° to each other.

    d. Note the reading on the dial guide while rocking the valve. If the movement exceeds the specification in **Table 2**, the valve guide is probably worn. However, as a final check, take the cylinder head to a dealership or machine shop and have the valve guides measured.

7. Check the inner and outer valve springs as follows:

    a. Visually inspect each valve spring for damage.

    b. Use a square and check each spring for distortion or tilt (**Figure 75**).

    c. Measure the valve spring free length with a vernier caliper (**Figure 76**). Replace the spring if its free length is less than the service limit specified in **Table 2**.

    d. Repeat for each valve spring.

    e. Replace defective springs as a set (inner and outer).

8. Check the valve spring seats, spring retainer and valve keepers for cracks or other damage.

9. Inspect the valve seats (A, **Figure 77**) in the cylinder head. If worn or burned, they may be reconditioned as described in this chapter. Seats and valves in near-perfect condition can be reconditioned by lapping with fine carborundum paste. Check as follows:

    a. Clean the valve seat and corresponding valve mating areas with contact cleaner.

    b. Coat the valve seat with machinist's dye.

    c. Install the valve into its guide and rotate it against its seat with a valve lapping tool. See *Valve Lapping* in this chapter.

(71)

VALVE TROUBLESHOOTING

Valve deposits	Check: •Worn valve guide •Carbon buildup from incorrect engine tuning •Carbon buildup from incorrect carburetor adjustment •Dirty or gummed fuel •Dirty engine oil

Valve sticking	Check: •Worn valve guide •Bent valve stem •Deposits collected on valve stem •Valve burning or overheating

Valve burning	Check: •Valve sticking •Cylinder head warped •Valve seat distorted •Valve clearance incorrect •Incorrect valve spring •Valve spring worn •Worn valve seat •Carbon buildup in engine •Engine ignition and/or carburetor adjustments incorrect

Valve seat/face wear	Check: •Valve burning •Incorrect valve clearance •Abrasive material on valve face and seat

Valve damage	Check: •Valve burning •Incorrectly installed or serviced valve guides •Incorrect valve clearance •Incorrect valve, spring seat and retainer assmbly •Detonation caused by incorrect ignition timing and/or carburetor adjustments

4

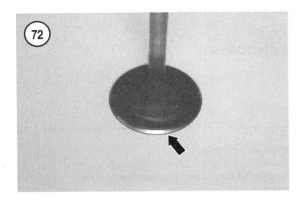

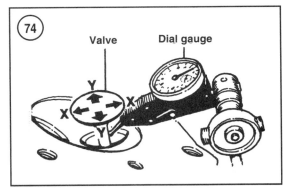

d. Lift the valve out of the guide, and measure the seat width with a vernier caliper.

e. The seat width for intake and exhaust valves should be within the specifications listed in **Table 2** all the way around the seat. If the seat width exceeds the service limit, regrind the seats as described in this chapter.

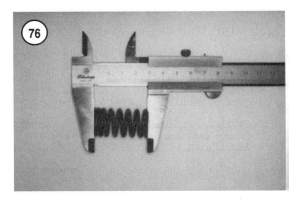

f. Remove all machinist's dye residue from the seats and valves.

10. Check the valve stem runout with a V-block and dial indicator as shown in **Figure 78**. Runout should not exceed the service limit listed in **Table 2**.

11. Measure the valve head thickness with a vernier caliper (**Figure 79**). Replace the valve if the thickness is less than the service limit listed in **Table 2**.

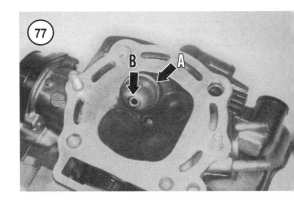

Valve Guide Replacement

If the valve guide-to-stem clearance is excessive, replace the guides. This should be entrusted to a Kawasaki dealership since the job requires considerable expertise. If the valve guide is replaced, the

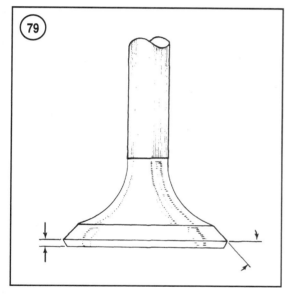

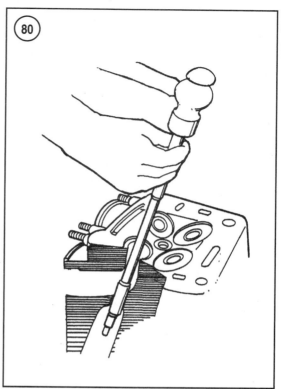

valve must also be refaced. The following procedure describes value guide replacement.

Use the following special tools to remove and in-
stall the shoulder-type valve guides used in the
Mojave. These tools can be ordered from a
Kawasaki dealership.

   a. Valve guide arbor (remover/installer),
      Kawasaki part No. 57001-1021.

   b. Valve guide reamer, Kawasaki part No.
      57001-1079.

NOTE
Freezing temperatures shrink the new
guides slightly and ease installation.

1. Place the new valve guides in a freezer.

CAUTION
Do not heat the cylinder head with a
torch—never bring a flame into con-
tact with the cylinder head. The direct
heat may warp the cylinder head.

WARNING
Wear heavy gloves when performing
this procedure—the cylinder head
will be very hot.

2. The valve guides (B, **Figure 77**) are installed
with a slight interference fit. Heat the cylinder head
to approximately 250-300° F (120-150° C) in a
shop oven or on a hot plate.

3. Remove the cylinder head from the oven or hot
plate and place it onto wooden blocks with the combustion chamber facing up.

4. Drive the old valve guide out from the combustion chamber side of the cylinder head with the
valve guide arbor (**Figure 80**). Note the position of
the O-ring on the valve guide for reference during
assembly.

5. After the cylinder head cools, check the guide
bore for carbon or other contamination. Clean the
bore thoroughly.

6. Reheat the cylinder head to approximately 250-300° F (120-150° C).

7. Remove the cylinder head from the oven or hot plate and place it on wooden blocks with the combustion chamber facing down.

8. Remove one valve guide from the freezer.

NOTE
Use the Kawasaki valve guide arbor (remover/installer tool) to install the valve guides.

9. Drive the new valve guide into the cylinder until the shoulder on the guide bottoms out in the guide recess.

10. If necessary, repeat Steps 2-9 to replace the other valve guides.

CAUTION
Always rotate the valve guide reamer in the same direction when installing and removing it from the guide. If the reamer is rotated in the opposite direction, the guide will be damaged and will require replacement.

11. After the cylinder head has cooled to room temperature, ream the new valve guides as follows:

 a. Coat the valve guide and valve guide reamer with cutting oil.

 b. Insert the reamer from the top side and rotate the reamer clockwise (**Figure 81**). Continue to rotate the reamer and work it down through the entire length of the new valve guide. Apply additional cutting oil during this procedure.

 c. While rotating the reamer clockwise, withdraw the reamer from the valve guide.

 d. Measure the valve guide inner diameter with a small hole gauge, and then measure the small hole gauge with a micrometer. Compare the reading to the dimension in **Table 2**.

12. Repeat for the other valve guide(s).

13. Thoroughly clean the cylinder head and valve guides with solvent to wash out all metal particles. Dry with compressed air.

14. Lightly oil the valve guides to prevent rust.

15. Recondition the valve seats as described in this chapter.

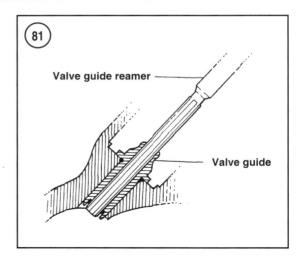

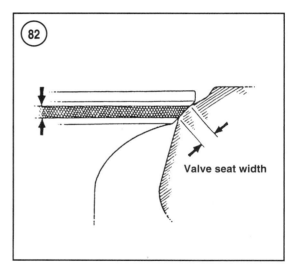

Valve Seat Inspection

The most accurate method for checking the valve seal is to use machinist's dye, available from auto parts and tool stores. Machinist's dye is used for locating high or irregular spots when checking or making close fits. Follow the manufacturer's directions.

NOTE
Because of the close operating tolerances within the valve assembly, the valve stem and guide must be in good condition (within tolerance); otherwise the inspection results will be inaccurate.

1. Remove the valves as described in this chapter.

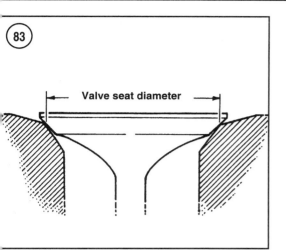

Valve seat diameter

2. Clean the valve seat and valve mating areas with contact cleaner.

3. Thoroughly clean all carbon deposits from the valve face with solvent or detergent, and then dry thoroughly.

4. Spread a thin layer of machinist's dye evenly on the valve face.

5. Attach the end of a suction-cup valve lapping tool to the valve. Insert the valve into the guide.

6. Using the valve lapping tool, press the valve against the valve seat with a light rotating motion in both directions. Turn the valve in the seat by spinning the lapping tool in both directions.

7. Remove the valve and examine the impression left by the machinist's dye. If the impression (on the valve or in the cylinder head) is not even and continuous and if the valve seat width (**Figure 82**) is not within the specified tolerance listed in **Table 2**, recondition the cylinder head valve seat.

8. Closely examine the valve seat in the cylinder head (A, **Figure 77**). It should be smooth and even, with a polished seating surface.

9. If the valve seat is in good condition, install the valve as described in this chapter.

10. If the valve seat is not correct, recondition the valve seat as described in this chapter.

11. Repeat for the other valves.

Valve Seat Reconditioning

Special valve cutting tools and considerable experience are required to recondition the valve seats in the cylinder head properly. If these tools are not available, considerable expense can be saved by re-moving the cylinder head and taking the cylinder head and valves to a dealership to have the valve seats reconditioned.

The following procedure describes valve seat reconditioning. The intake and exhaust valve seats are machined to 45°. The following tools are required:

   a. Valve seat cutters (32°, 45° and 60°. See a Kawasaki dealer for part numbers).

   b. Vernier caliper.

   c. Machinist's dye.

   d. Valve lapping tool.

NOTE
When using valve facing equipment, follow the manufacturer's instructions.

CAUTION
When grinding valve seats, work slowly to avoid overgrinding the seats. A valve will sink too far into the cylinder head if the seat is overground. Valve clearance may be reduced making it impossible to obtain the correct clearance. If this condition exists, it may be possible to gain additional clearance by grinding the end of the valve stem. However, since there is a maximum amount that can be ground from the end of the valve stem, refer this procedure to a dealership. If the valve clearance cannot be increased sufficiently by grinding the valve stems, replace the cylinder head since replacement valve seats are not available.

NOTE
Steps 1-5 cut the valve seat to its proper diameter. Steps 6-8 cut the valve seat to its proper width.

1. Install a 45° cutter onto the valve tool and lightly cut the seat to remove roughness.

2. Measure the valve seat diameter (**Figure 83**) with a vernier caliper, and compare it to the specification listed in **Table 2**. Note the following:

   a. If the diameter is too small, cut the seat once again with the 45° cutter as described in Step 1.

   b. If the diameter is too large, cut the seat with the 32° cutter as described in Step 3.

c. If the diameter is within specification, measure the seat width as described in Step 6.

> *CAUTION*
> *The 32° cutter removes material quickly. Work carefully and check the progress often.*

3. Install a 32° cutter (**Figure 84**) onto the valve tool. Press down very lightly and turn the 32° cutter one turn. Measure the seat diameter. Repeat until the seat diameter is within the specification in **Table 2**.

> *NOTE*
> *When the valve seat diameter is correct, proceed with Step 4.*

4. Measure the valve seat width (**Figure 82**) with a vernier caliper, and compare the reading to the dimension in **Table 2**. Measure at several places around the seat. Note the following:

   a. If the seat width is too narrow, cut the seat with the 45° cutter. Then remeasure the seat width and, if necessary, recut it to its proper width (see Steps 1-3).

   b. If the seat width is too wide, cut the seat with the 60° cutter as described in Step 5.

   c. If the seat width is correct, lap the valve to the seat as described in this chapter.

5. Install a 60° cutter (**Figure 84**) onto the valve tool. Press down very lightly and turn the 60° cutter one turn. Measure the seat width (Step 4). Repeat until the seat width is within the specification listed in **Table 2**.

6. After obtaining the desired valve seat diameter and width, use the 45° cutter and very lightly clean off any burrs that may have been caused by the previous cuts.

7. Lap the valve to the seat as described in this chapter.

8. Repeat Steps 1-7 for the other valves.

9. Clean the cylinder head and all valve components in solvent or detergent and hot water. Dry all parts thoroughly.

10. Once the components are completely dry, apply a light coat of engine oil to all bare metal surfaces to prevent rust.

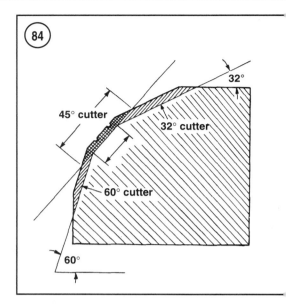

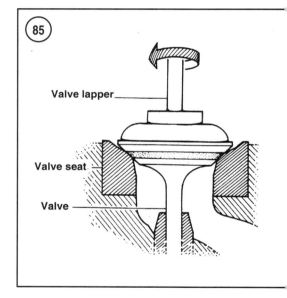

Valve Lapping

This procedure must only be performed after cutting the valve seats.

1. Smear a light coating of coarse grade valve lapping compound on the seating surface of the valve.

2. Insert the valve into the head.

3. Attach the suction cup of the lapping tool and onto the head of the valve. Lap the valve to the seat by spinning the lapping stick in both directions (**Figure 85**). Every 5 to 10 seconds, rotate the valve 180° in the valve seat. Continue this action until the

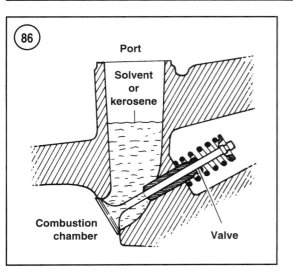

seating ring. The seating ring mark should be approximately in the middle of the valve face.

6. Thoroughly clean the valves and cylinder head in solvent to remove all grinding compound. Any compound left on the valves or the cylinder head causes excessive engine wear and damage.

7. After the lapping has been completed and the valves have been reinstalled into the head, test the valve seal. Check the seal of each valve by pouring solvent into the intake and exhaust ports (**Figure 86**). There should be no leakage past the seat in the combustion chamber. If leakage occurs, the combustion chamber will appear wet. If fluid leaks past any of the seats, disassemble that valve assembly and repeat the lapping procedure until there is no leakage.

4

Installation

1. Clean the end of the valve guide.

2. Oil the inside of the new oil seal and install it over the end of the valve guide (**Figure 70**).

3. Coat a valve stem with molybdenum disulfide paste. Install the valve partway into the guide. Then, slowly turn the valve as it enters the oil seal and continue turning it until the valve is installed all the way.

4. Install the outer spring seat and the inner spring seats (**Figure 68**). Center the spring seats in the spring recess.

5. Position the valve springs so their *closer* wound coils (**Figure 87**) face the cylinder head.

6. Install the outer- and inner-valve springs (**Figure 67**).

7. Install the valve spring retainer on top of the valve springs (**Figure 66**).

> *CAUTION*
> *To avoid loss of spring tension, do not compress the springs any more than necessary to install the valve keepers.*

8. Compress the valve springs with a valve spring compressor and install the valve keepers (**Figure 65**).

9. When both valve keepers are seated around the valve stem, slowly release tension from the compressor. Remove the compressor and inspect the valve keepers (**Figure 88**). Tap the end of the valve stem with a soft-faced hammer. This will ensure that the keepers are properly seated.

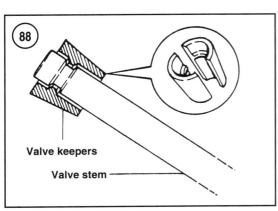

mating surfaces on the valve and seat are smooth and equal in size.

4. Repeat Step 3 with a fine grade lapping compound.

5. Closely examine the valve seat in the cylinder head. It should be smooth and even with a polished

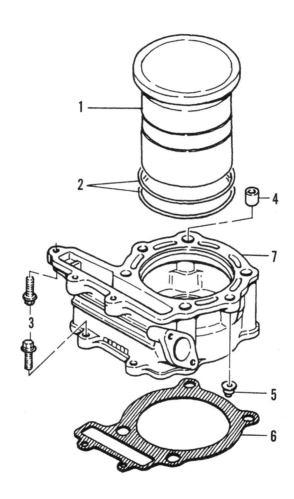

(89)

CYLINDER BLOCK

1
2
4
7
3
5
6

1. Cylinder liner
2. O-rings
3. Bolt
4. Dowel
5. Nut
6. Base gasket
7. Cylinder block

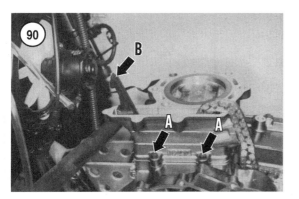

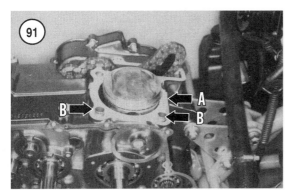

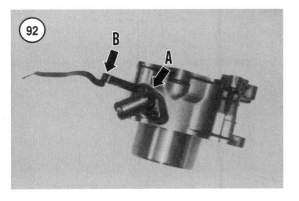

10. Repeat Steps 1-9 for other valves.

11. After installing the cylinder head, set the valve clearance as described in Chapter Three.

CYLINDER

The alloy cylinder has a pressed-in cast iron cylinder liner that can be bored to 0.50 mm (0.020 in.) or 1.0 mm (0.040 in.) oversize. Oversize pistons and rings are available through Kawasaki dealerships and aftermarket piston suppliers.

The cylinder can be removed with the engine installed in the frame. Refer to **Figure 89** when servicing the cylinder.

Removal

1. Remove the cylinder head as described in this chapter.
2. Disconnect the coolant hose from the fitting on the cylinder.
3. Remove the two cylinder base bolts (A, **Figure 90**).
4. If still installed, remove the front cam chain guide (B, **Figure 90**).
5. Loosen the cylinder by tapping around its perimeter with a soft-faced mallet.
6. Pull the cylinder block straight up and off the crankcase. Remove and discard the base gasket (A, **Figure 91**).
7. Remove the two cylinder dowels (B, **Figure 91**).
8. If necessary, remove the piston as described in this chapter.
9. Cover the crankcase opening to prevent objects and abrasive dust from falling into the crankcase.

Inspection

Use a bore gauge and micrometer to measure the cylinder bore accurately. If these tools are not available, take the cylinder to a Kawasaki dealership or machine shop.

1. Remove all gasket residue from the top and bottom cylinder block gasket surfaces.
2. If necessary, remove the bolts securing the coolant fitting to the cylinder. Remove the fitting (A, **Figure 92**) and its O-ring. Note the wire clamp (B, **Figure 92**) that is secured by the upper bolt. It must be reinstalled under the same bolt.
3. Wash the cylinder block in solvent. Dry it with compressed air.
4. Check the dowel pin holes for cracks or other damage.
5. Check the cylinder bore (**Figure 93**) for scoring, rust or other visible damage.

NOTE
*All cylinder bore measurements must be within the specifications in **Table 2**, and the difference between any two measurements must be less than 0.01*

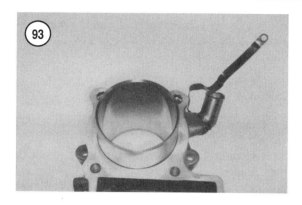

mm (0.0004 in.). The cylinder must be
rebored if it fails to meet either of
these requirements.

6. Measure the cylinder bore inner diameter, taper
and out-of-round with a bore gauge or inside micrometer (**Figure 94**). Measure the cylinder bore at
the three locations, measured from the top and bottom surfaces, as shown in **Figure 95**. Measure in
line with the piston pin and 90° to the pin at each location. Check all measurements against the specifications in **Table 2**. If any measurement is greater
than the service limit in **Table 2**, bore the cylinder to
the next oversize, and install oversize piston and
rings.

7. If the cylinder is not worn past the service limit,
check the bore carefully for scratches or gouges.
The bore may still require reconditioning.

8. If cylinder bore is within specification, determine piston-to-cylinder clearance as described in
this chapter.

> *CAUTION*
> *A combination of soap and water is
> the only solution that completely
> cleans the cylinder bore. Solvent and
> kerosene cannot wash fine grit out of
> cylinder crevices. Grit left in the cyl-
> inder bore acts as a grinding com-
> pound and causes premature wear to
> the new rings.*

9. After servicing the cylinder, wash the bore in hot
soapy water. After washing the cylinder wall, run a
clean white cloth through it. If the cloth is dirty, the
cylinder wall is not clean and must be rewashed.
When the cylinder bore is thoroughly cleaned, lubricate the cylinder bore with clean engine oil to
prevent the bore from rusting.

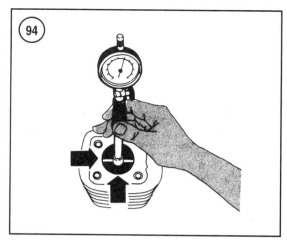

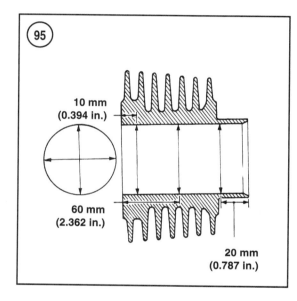

Installation

1. If removed, install the piston as described in this
chapter.

2. Clean the crankcase surface of all gasket residue.

3. Make sure the top and bottom cylinder surfaces
are clean of all gasket residue.

4. Install the two dowel pins (B, **Figure 91**) in the
crankcase.

5. Install a new base gasket (**Figure 91**). Make sure
all holes align.

6. Make sure the piston pin circlips are installed
and seated correctly.

7. Install a piston holding fixture (**Figure 96**) under
the piston.

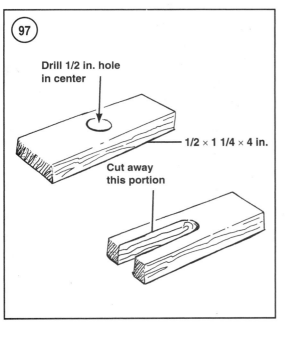

Drill 1/2 in. hole
in center

1/2 × 1 1/4 × 4 in.

Cut away
this portion

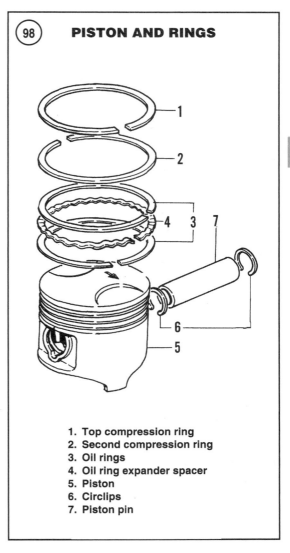

PISTON AND RINGS

1. Top compression ring
2. Second compression ring
3. Oil rings
4. Oil ring expander spacer
5. Piston
6. Circlips
7. Piston pin

NOTE
A piston holding fixture can be made
out of wood as shown in **Figure 97***.*

8. Stagger the piston ring end gaps around the piston as shown in **Figure 98**.

9. Lubricate the cylinder wall, piston and rings liberally with engine oil prior to installation.

10. Carefully align the cylinder with the piston and install the cylinder. Compress each ring as it enters the cylinder by hand.

11 Remove the piston holding fixture and slide the cylinder all the way down onto the crankcase.

12. While holding the cylinder down with one hand, turn the crankshaft with a wrench. The piston should move smoothly in the bore.

13. Run the cam chain up through the chain tunnel in the cylinder block.

14. Install the two cylinder base bolts (A, **Figure 90**). Tighten them to the torque specification in **Table 3**.

15. If removed, install the coolant fitting onto the cylinder. Use a new O-ring behind the fitting, and reinstall the cable clamp onto the upper bolt. See **Figure 92**. Torque the coolant fitting bolts to the specification in **Table 3**.

16. Install the cylinder head as described in this chapter.

PISTON AND PISTON RINGS

The piston is made of an aluminum alloy. The piston pin is made of steel and is a precision fit in the piston. The piston pin is held in place by a circlip at each end.

Refer to **Figure 98** when servicing the piston and rings in the following section.

Piston Removal/Installation

1. Remove the cylinder as described in this chapter.
2. Cover the crankcase below the piston with clean paper towels to prevent the piston pin circlips from falling into the crankcase.
3. Before removing the piston, hold the rod tightly and rock the piston (**Figure 99**). Any rocking motion (do not confuse with the normal sliding motion) indicates wear on the piston pin, rod bushing, pin bore, or a combination of all three.
4. Remove the circlips from the piston pin bore (**Figure 100**).

> *NOTE*
> *Discard the piston circlips. New circlips must be installed during assembly.*

5. Push the piston pin (**Figure 101**) out of the piston by hand. If the pin is tight, fabricate a tool (**Figure 102**) to remove it. Do not drive the piston pin out. Such action could damage the piston pin, connecting rod or piston.
6. Lift the piston off the connecting rod.
7. Inspect the piston as described in this chapter.

Piston Inspection

1. Remove the piston rings as described in this chapter.

> *CAUTION*
> *Be careful not to gouge or otherwise damage the piston or cylinder when removing carbon. Never use a wire brush to clean the piston skirt or ring grooves. Do not attempt to remove carbon from the sides of the piston above the top ring or from the cylinder bore near the top. Removal of carbon from these two areas may cause increased oil consumption.*

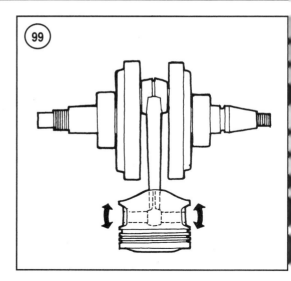

2. Carefully clean the carbon from the piston crown (**Figure 103**) with a soft scraper or wire wheel mounted in a drill. Large carbon accumulation reduces piston cooling and can result in detonation and piston damage.

3. After cleaning the piston, examine the crown. The crown should show no sign of wear or damage.

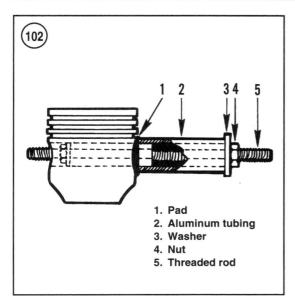

1. Pad
2. Aluminum tubing
3. Washer
4. Nut
5. Threaded rod

If the crown appears pecked or spongy-looking, also check the spark plug, valves and combustion chamber for aluminum deposits. If these deposits are found, the engine is overheating.

4. Examine each ring groove for burrs, dented edges or other damage. Pay particular attention to the top compression ring groove as it usually wears more than the others. Because the oil rings are constantly bathed in oil, these rings and grooves wear little compared to compression rings and their grooves. If there is evidence of oil ring groove wear or if the oil ring assembly is tight and difficult to remove, the piston skirt may have collapsed due to excessive heat. Replace the piston.

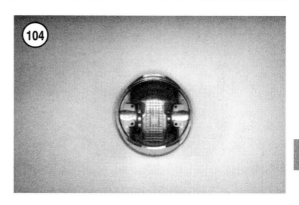

5. Check the oil control holes in the piston (**Figure 104**) for carbon or oil sludge buildup. Clean the holes with wire.

NOTE
If the piston skirt is worn or scuffed unevenly from side-to-side, the connecting rod may be bent or twisted.

6. Check the piston skirt for cracks or other damage. If the piston shows signs of partial seizure (bits of aluminum buildup on the piston skirt), replace the piston and bore the cylinder (if necessary) to reduce the possibility of engine noise and further piston seizure.

7. Check the circlip grooves in the piston for wear, cracks or other damage. If the grooves are questionable, check the circlip fit by installing a new circlip into each groove and then attempt to move the circlip from side-to-side. If the circlip has any side play, the groove is worn and the piston must be replaced.

8. Measure piston-to-cylinder clearance as described in *Piston Clearance* in this chapter.

9. If damage or wear indicates piston replacement is necessary, select a new piston as described in *Piston Clearance* in this chapter. If the piston, rings and cylinder are not damaged and are dimensionally correct, they can be reused.

Piston Pin Inspection

1. Clean the piston pin in solvent and dry it thoroughly.

2. Inspect the piston pin for flaking or cracks. Replace if necessary.

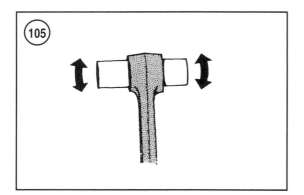

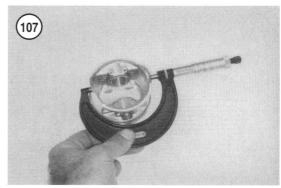

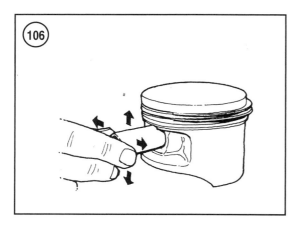

5 mm (0.20 in.)

3. Oil the piston pin and install it in the connecting rod. Slowly rotate the piston pin and check for excessive play (**Figure 105**).

4. Oil the piston pin and install it in the piston (**Figure 106**). Check the piston pin for excessive play.

5. Replace the piston pin and/or piston or connecting rod if necessary.

Piston Clearance

1. Make sure the piston skirt and cylinder wall are clean and dry.

2. Measure the cylinder bore inner diameter with a bore gauge or inside micrometer (**Figure 94**). Measure the cylinder bore at the three positions, measured from the top and bottom surfaces, as shown in **Figure 95**. Measure in line with the piston pin and 90° to the pin. Record the bore diameters.

3. Use a micrometer to measure the piston diameter at a right angle to the piston pin bore (**Figure 107**). Measure 5 mm (0.20 in.) up from the bottom edge of the piston skirt (**Figure 108**).

4. Subtract the piston diameter from the largest cylinder bore inside diameter; the difference is piston-to-cylinder clearance. If the clearance exceeds the specification in **Table 2**, the piston should be replaced and the cylinder bored oversize and then honed. Purchase the new piston first. Measure its diameter and add the specified clearance to determine the proper cylinder oversize diameter.

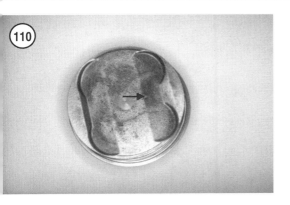

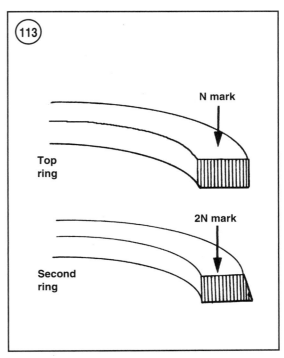

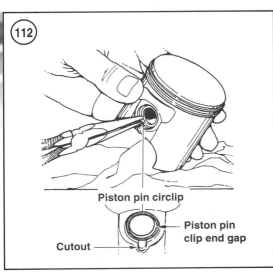

Piston pin circlip

Piston pin
clip end gap

Cutout

Piston Installation

1. Coat the connecting rod bushing, piston pin and piston with clean engine oil.

2. Slide the piston pin into the piston until its end is flush with the piston pin boss as shown in **Figure 109**.

3. Place the piston over the connecting rod so the arrow on the piston crown (**Figure 110**) faces forward.

4. Align the piston pin with the hole in the connecting rod. Push the piston pin (**Figure 111**) through the connecting rod and into the other side of the piston until it is centered in the piston.

5. Install new piston pin circlips in both ends of the piston pin boss. Make sure both clips are seated in the grooves in the piston. Position each circlip so its end gap does not align with the cutout in the piston. See **Figure 112**.

6. Install the piston rings as described in this chapter.

Piston Ring Inspection and Removal

A three piston ring assembly is used (**Figure 98**). The top and second rings are compression rings. The lower ring is an oil control ring assembly (consisting of two ring rails and an expander spacer). **Figure 113** identifies the top and second compression rings.

1. Measure the side clearance of each compression ring in its groove with a flat feeler gauge (**Figure 114**). If the clearance is greater than the specification in **Table 2**, replace the rings. If the clearance is

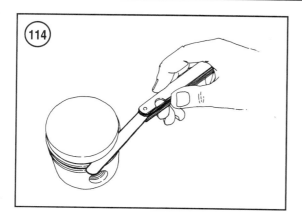

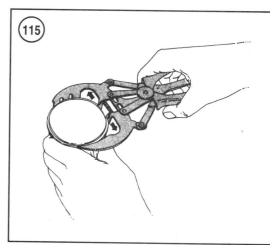

still excessive with the new rings, replace the piston.

> *WARNING*
> *The edges of all piston rings are very sharp. Be careful when handling them.*

> *NOTE*
> *Store the old rings in the order in which they are removed.*

2. Remove the compression rings with a ring expander tool (**Figure 115**) or by spreading the ring ends by hand and lifting the rings up evenly (**Figure 116**).

3. Remove the oil ring assembly (**Figure 117**) by first removing the upper and the lower ring rails. Then remove the expander spacer.

4. Using a broken piston ring, carefully remove carbon and oil residue from the piston ring grooves (**Figure 118**). Do not remove aluminum material from the ring grooves, as this will increase ring side clearance.

5. Measure each piston ring groove width with a vernier caliper and check the measurement against the dimensions in **Table 2**. Measure each groove at several points around the piston. Replace the piston if any groove is worn to the service limit or greater.

6. Inspect grooves carefully for burrs, nicks or broken or cracked lands. Replace the piston if necessary.

7. Measure the thickness of each compression ring with a micrometer (**Figure 119**). If the thickness is less than specified in **Table 2**, replace the ring.

8. Check the end gap of each compression ring. To check, insert the ring into the bottom of the cylinder bore and square it with the cylinder wall by tapping

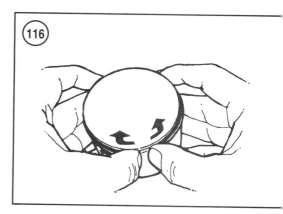

it with the piston. Measure the end gap with a feeler gauge (**Figure 120**), and check the measurement against the specification in **Table 2**. Replace the ring if the end gap is excessive. If the gap on a new compression ring is smaller than specified, hold a small file in a vise, then grip the ends of the ring by hand and enlarge the gap (**Figure 121**).

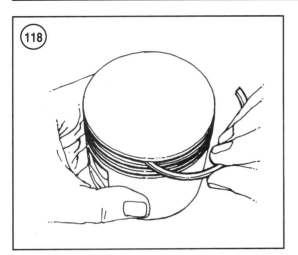

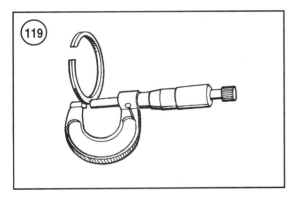

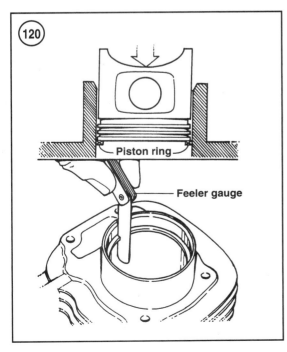

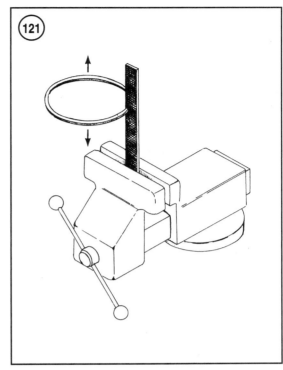

Piston Ring Installation

1. If new rings are installed, the cylinders must be deglazed or honed. This helps to seat the new rings. If necessary, refer honing service to a Kawasaki dealership or motorcycle repair shop. After honing, measure the end gap of each ring, and compare the measurement to the specification in **Table 2**.

NOTE
If the cylinder is deglazed or honed, thoroughly clean the cylinder as described in this chapter.

2. Clean the piston and rings. Dry with compressed air.

3. Install piston rings as follows:

NOTE
Install the piston rings, first the bottom, then the middle, then the top ring, by carefully spreading the ends by hand and slipping the rings over the top of the piston. Remember to install the piston rings with the marks on them facing toward the top of the piston. Incorrectly installed piston

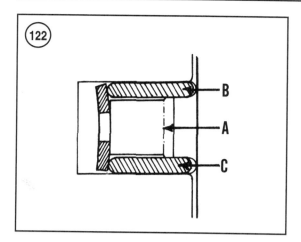

**OIL RING
EXPANDER SPACER**

Do not overlap

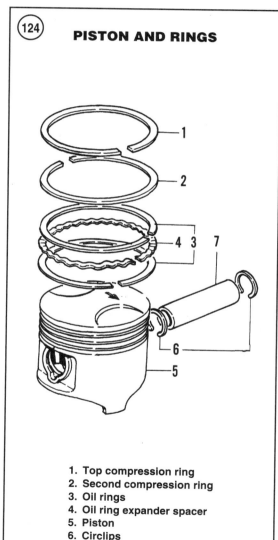

PISTON AND RINGS

1. Top compression ring
2. Second compression ring
3. Oil rings
4. Oil ring expander spacer
5. Piston
6. Circlips
7. Piston pin

rings can wear rapidly and/or allow oil to escape past them.

NOTE
The two ring rails are identical.

a. Install the oil ring assembly into the bottom ring groove. First, install the expander spacer (A, **Figure 122**) so its ends butt together (**Figure 123**). Do not overlap the ends. Then install the top (B, **Figure 122**) and bottom ring rails (C, **Figure 122**).

b. Install the compression rings with the manufacturer's mark facing up (**Figure 113**).

NOTE
When installing aftermarket piston rings, follow the manufacturer's directions.

c. Install the second or middle compression ring.

d. Install the top compression ring.

4. Make sure the rings are seated completely in their grooves all the way around the piston and the end gaps are distributed around the piston as shown in **Figure 124**. The ring gaps must not align with each other. If they do, compression pressure will escape past them.

5. If installing oversize compression rings, check the number to make sure the correct rings are being installed. The ring numbers should be the same as the piston oversize number.

6. If new parts are installed, the engine should be broken-in just as though it were new. Follow the break-in procedure described in Chapter Five.

4

Table 1 GENERAL ENGINE SPECIFICATIONS

	Specification
Type and number of cylinders	4-stroke, DOHC, liquid-cooled single cylinder
Bore x stroke	74.0 x 58.0 mm (2.91 x 2.28 in.)
Displacement	249 cc (15.19 cu. in.)
Compression ratio	11:1
Valve timing	
Intake	
Open	31° BTDC
Closed	53° ABDC
Duration	264°
Exhaust	
Open	57° BBDC
Close	27° ATDC
Duration	264°

Table 2 ENGINE TOP END SPECIFICATIONS

	Specification	Wear limit
Camshaft		
Cam lobe height	35.106-35.248 mm (1.3821-1.3877 in.)	35.01 (1.3783 in.)
Camshaft bearing oil		
clearance	0.045-0.073 mm (0.0018-0.0029 in.)	0.16 mm (0.0062 in.)
Camshaft journal diameter	22.940-22.955 mm (0.9031-0.9037 in.)	22.91 mm (0.9019 in.)
Camshaft bearing inside		
diameter	23.000-23.013 mm (0.9055-0.9060 in.)	23.07 mm (0.908 in.)
Cam chain 20-link length	127.00-127.36 mm (5.000-5.014 in.)	128.9 mm (5.075 in.)
Cam-chain-guide groove depth		
Front	No groove	2.0 mm (0.079 in.)
Rear	No groove	1.5 mm (0.059 in.)
Rocker arm inside diameter.	12.500-12.518mm (0.4921-0.4928 in.)	12.55 mm (0.4941 in.)
Rocker shaft diameter	12.466-12.484 mm (0.4907-0.4914 in.)	12.44 mm (0.4897 in.)
Cylinder head warp	–	0.05 mm (0.0019 in.)
Valves and valve springs		
Valve clearance		
Intake	0.20-0.24 mm (0.008-0.009 in.)	–
Exhaust	0.20-0.24 mm (0.008-0.009 in.)	–
Valve stem diameter.		
Intake	5.475-5.490 mm (0.2156-0.2161 in.)	5.46 mm (0.215 in.)
Exhaust	5.455-5.470 mm (0.2148-0.2154 in.)	5.44 mm (0.2142 in.)
Valve stem runout	0.01 mm (0.0004 in.) or less	0.05 mm (0.0020 in.)
Valve guide I.D.	5.500-5.512 mm (0.2165-0.2170 in.)	5.58 mm (0.2197 in.)
Valve/valve guide clearance		
(wobble method)		
Intake	0.02-0.09 mm (0.0007-0.0035 in.)	0.25 mm (0.0098 in.)
Exhaust	0.06-0.12 mm (0.0067-0.0047 in.)	0.26 mm (0.0102 in.)
Valve head thickness		
Intake	0.5 mm (0.020 in.)	0.25 mm (0.010 in.)
Exhaust	1 mm (0.039 in.)	0.7 mm (0.028 in.)
Valve seat surface		
Width	0.5-1.0 mm (0.020-0.039 in.)	
Outside diameter		
Intake	28.3-28.5 mm (1.114-1.122in.)	–
Exhaust	24.0-24.2 mm (0.945-0.953 in.)	–
Valve seat surface angle	45°	

(continued)

Table 2 ENGINE TOP END SPECIFICATIONS (continued)

	Specification	Wear limit
Valve seat cutting angle	32, 45, 60°	
Valve spring free length		
Inner	36.3 mm (1.429 in.)	34.5 mm (1.358 in.)
Outer	39.2 mm (1.543 in.)	37.5 mm (1.476 in.)
Cylinder		
Bore	74.000-74.012 mm (2.9134-2.9139 in.)	74.10 mm (2.9173 in.)
Oversize pistons and rings	+ 0.5 mm or + 1.0 mm	
Cylinder compression	480-785 kPa (70-114 psi)	
Pistons		
Outer diameter	73.950-73.965 mm (2.9114-2.9120 in.)	73.81 mm (2.9059 in.)
Piston/cylinder clearance	0.035-0.062 mm (0.00138-0.00244 in.)	–
Piston rings		
Ring/groove clearance		
Top	–	–
Second	–	–
Piston ring groove width		
Top	–	–
Second	–	–
Oil ring	2.51-2.53 mm (0.099-0.100 in.)	2.61 mm (0.103 in.)
Ring thickness		
Top	0.97-0.99 mm (0.038-0.039 in.)	0.9 mm (0.035 in.)
Second	0.97-0.99 mm (0.038-0.039 in.)	0.9 mm (0.035 in.)
Ring end gap		
Top and Second	0.20-0.35 mm (0.008-0.014 in.)	0.7 mm (0.028 in.)
Oil ring	0.2-0.7 mm (0.008-0.028 in.)	1.0 mm (0.039 in.)

Table 3 ENGINE TOP END TIGHTENING TORQUES

Item	N•m	in.-lb.	ft.-lb.
Valve adjuster locknut	25	–	18
Rocker shaft	39	–	29
Rocker shaft plug	15	–	11
Cylinder head cover bolt	7.8	69	–
Cylinder head bolts			–
10 mm	45	–	33
6 mm	9.8	87	–
Cylinder head nut	25	–	18
Cylinder head bracket bolt	25	–	18
Cylinder head oil pipe bolt	9.8	87	–
Oil pipe banjo bolt	20	–	15
Cylinder base bolt	9.8	87	–
Cylinder coolant fitting bolt	9.8	87	–
Camshaft cap bolt	12	106	–
Camshaft sprocket bolt	39	–	29
Camshaft idler shaft	39	–	29
Cam chain guide pivot bolt	25	–	18
Cam chain tensioner mounting bolt	9.8	87	–
Engine mounting bolts and nuts			–
8 mm	25	–	18
10 mm	34	–	25

CHAPTER FIVE

ENGINE LOWER END

This chapter describes service procedures for the following lower end components:
1. Crankcase.
2. Crankshaft.
3. Connecting rod.
4. Transmission and reverse shift assembly (removal and installation).
5. Internal shift mechanism (removal and installation).
6. Primary gear and oil pump spur gear.
7. Balancer drive gear.
8. Magneto.
9. Kickstarter.

Before removing and disassembling the crankcase, clean the entire engine and frame with a commercial degreaser, like Gunk or Bel-Ray engine degreaser. It is easier to work on a clean engine.

Make certain all the necessary hand and special tools are available. Also make sure there is a clean place to work.

One of the more important aspects of engine overhaul is preparation. Improper preparation and failure to identify and store parts during removal will make it difficult to reassemble the engine. Before removing the first bolt, get a number of boxes, plastic bags and containers to store the parts when removed (**Figure 1**). Also, have on hand a roll of

masking tape and a permanent, waterproof marking pen to label parts as required.

The text makes frequent references to the left and right side of the engine. This refers to the engine as it sits in the vehicle's frame, not as it sits on a workbench.

Table 1 lists engine lower end specifications, and **Table 2** lists lower end torque specifications. **Table 1** and **Table 2** are at the end of the chapter.

SERVICING ENGINE IN FRAME

Many components can be serviced with the engine mounted in the frame—(the vehicle's frame is a great holding fixture, especially for breaking loose stubborn bolts and nuts):
1. Cylinder head.
2. Cylinder and piston.
3. Gearshift mechanism.
4. Clutch.
5. Primary gear.
6. Left and right balancers.
7. Balancer gear.
8. Kickstarter.
9. Oil pump.
10. Carburetor.
11. Magneto.

ENGINE REMOVAL

This procedure describes engine removal. If service work requires only the removal of a top end component, leave the engine in the frame and service the top end as required to remove the desired sub-assembly. If the engine requires crankcase disassembly, it is easier to remove as many sub-assemblies as possible before removing the engine from the frame. By following this method, the frame can be used as a holding fixture when servicing the engine. Attempting to disassemble the complete engine while placed on a workbench is more time consuming. An assistant may be necessary to help hold the engine while you loosen many of the larger nuts and bolts.

1. Park the vehicle on a level surface. Set the parking brake.
2. Drain the engine oil.
3. Drain the coolant from the engine.
4. Remove the front and rear fenders as described in Chapter Fourteen.
5. Remove the fuel tank and exhaust system as described in Chapter Eight.
6. Remove the snorkel duct and the air cleaner housing as described in Chapter Eight.
7. Remove the carburetor as described in Chapter Eight.
8. Remove the left footpeg as described in Chapter Fourteen.
9. If necessary, use a punch to make indexing marks on the shift shaft and on the shift pedal. Loosen the pinch bolt and remove the shift pedal (**Figure 2**) from the shift shaft.
10. Remove the reverse mechanism cover as described in Chapter Seven.
11. On 1990-on models, remove the neutral/reverse switch as described in Chapter Seven, and free the cable from the clamp on the crankcase.
12. Remove the reverse cam and disconnect the reverse cable (**Figure 3**) from the reverse lever as described in *Reverse Mechanism* in Chapter Seven.
13. Disconnect the stator connector (A, **Figure 4**) and the pickup coil connector (B, **Figure 4**).
14. Disconnect the clutch cable from the clutch and from the clutch cover. Also release the clutch cable from the cable clamp on the right side of the cylinder head.
15. Disconnect the spark plug lead from the spark plug.

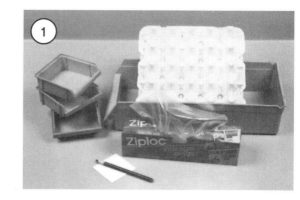

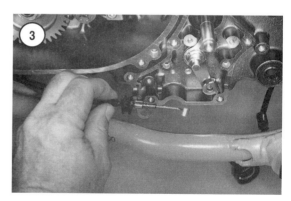

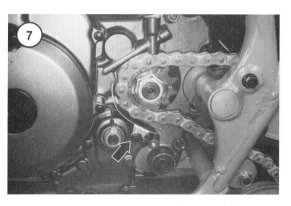

16. Disconnect the crankcase breather hose (C, **Figure 4**).

17. If the engine requires disassembly, remove the following sub-assemblies:

   a. Cylinder head (Chapter Four).

   b. Cylinder and piston (Chapter Four).

   c. Magneto rotor (this chapter).

   d. Clutch (Chapter Six).

   e. Primary gear, kick starter, balancer gear, and left and right balancers (this chapter).

   f. Oil pump (this chapter).

18. If removing the engine with the top end installed, remove the coolant hose from the cylinder and from the cylinder head.

19A. On 1987 models, remove the drive chain from the engine sprocket by performing the following:

   a. Loosen the clamp bolt on each side of the swing arm (A, **Figure 5**).

   b. Insert a drift or other suitable tool into the hole in the bearing housing (B, **Figure 5**). Use the tool to rotate the bearing housing and loosen the chain.

   c. Remove the two engine sprocket cover bolts and remove the engine sprocket cover (**Figure 6**).

   d. Remove the mounting bolt (**Figure 7**) and remove the chain guard from the crankcase.

   e. Lift the chain off the engine sprocket.

19B. On 1988-on models, remove the drive chain as described in Chapter Twelve.

20. Remove the engine mounting bolts and brackets by performing the following:

   a. Remove the engine skid plate from the frame.

   b. Place a jack underneath the engine. Place a block of wood on the jack pad to protect the engine case. Steady the engine by raising the jack so the wooden block just rests against the bottom of the engine.

   c. Remove the nut from the swing arm shaft (**Figure 8**) and remove the swing arm shaft. Pull the swing arm end from the frame.

   d. Remove the two 8 mm cylinder-head-bracket bolts (A, **Figure 9**) and remove the fuel tank bracket (B, **Figure 9**) from the cylinder head bracket.

e. Remove the 8 mm engine mounting bolt from the cylinder head bracket (A, **Figure 10**), and lift the cylinder head bracket (B, **Figure 10**) from the frame.

f. Remove the nut from the 10 mm front engine-mounting bolt (A, **Figure 11**), and remove the bolt.

g. Remove the nut from each 10 mm engine-mounting-bracket bolt (B, **Figure 11**), remove the two bolts, and remove the two front engine mounting brackets.

h. Remove the nut (**Figure 12**) from the 10 mm lower engine mounting bolt (C, **Figure 11**) and remove the bolt.

21. Move all cables, wires and harnesses out of the way.

NOTE
A minimum of two people are required to remove an assembled engine.

22. Check that all wires and hoses are free of the engine. Lift the engine and remove it from the left side of the frame.

ENGINE INSTALLATION

1. Clean all engine mounting bolts and nuts in solvent. Dry with compressed air. Remove corrosion from bolts with a wire wheel.

2. Prior to installation, spray the engine mounting bolts with a commercial rust inhibitor.

NOTE
A minimum of two people are required to install an assembled engine.

3. Set the engine into the frame. Use the jack to support and steady the engine in the frame.

4. Install the engine mounting hardware by performing the following:

a. Install a 10 mm lower engine mounting bolt (C, **Figure 11**), and loosely install the nut (**Figure 12**).

b. Fit the two front engine mounting brackets into place. Install the two 10 mm engine-mounting-bracket bolts (B, **Figure 11**), and loosely install the nut onto each bolt.

c. Install the 10 mm front engine mounting bolt (A, **Figure 11**). Be sure the bolt passes

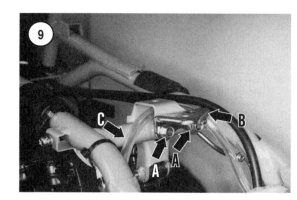

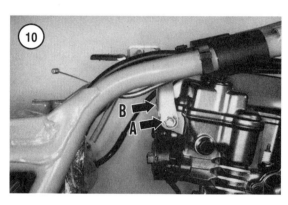

through the engine and both brackets, and loosely install the nut.

d. Raise the swing arm into place between the frame and the engine. Install the swing arm shaft (**Figure 8**), and the swing arm shaft nut.

e. Torque the swing arm nut to the specification in **Table 2**. Reinstall the swing arm plug on either side of the frame.

5. Torque the remaining mounting hardware to the specifications in **Table 2**.

6. If the top end is installed on the engine,

a. Place the cylinder head bracket (B, **Figure 10**) on the frame, and loosely install the 8 mm engine mounting bolt (A, **Figure 10**). Make sure the bolt passes through the bracket and the engine.

b. Fit the fuel tank bracket (B, **Figure 9**) onto the cylinder head bracket, and loosely install the two 8 mm cylinder head bracket bolts (A, **Figure 9**).

c. Torque the bolts to the specification in **Table 2**.

7. If removed, install the engine skid plate. Tighten the bolts securely.

8. If the engine is partially assembled, install the following sub-assemblies:
 a. Oil pump (this chapter).
 b. Kick starter, balancer gear, and left and right balancers (this chapter).
 c. Clutch and primary gear (Chapter Six).
 d. Magneto rotor (this chapter).
 e. Piston and cylinder (Chapter Four).
 f. Cylinder head (Chapter Four).
9. Reconnect the coolant hoses to the cylinder and cylinder head.
10. Reconnect the spark plug lead to the spark plug.
11. Clean the electrical connectors with contact cleaner.
12. Reconnect the following electrical connectors:
 a. Stator connector (A, **Figure 4**).
 b. Pickup coil connector (B, **Figure 4**).
 c. On 1990-on models, the neutral/reverse switch bullet connectors.
13. Reconnect the reverse cable (**Figure 3**) to the reverse lever and reinstall the reverse cam onto the shift drum shaft as described in *Reverse Mechanism* in Chapter Seven.
14. Reconnect the crankcase breather hose (C, **Figure 4**) to the crankcase.

15A. On 1987 models, install the drive chain onto the engine sprocket by performing the following:
 a. Set the chain onto the engine sprocket.
 b. Fit the chain guard onto the crankcase, and secure it in place with the mounting bolt (**Figure 7**).
 c. Install the engine sprocket cover (**Figure 6**). Secure it in place with the two engine sprocket cover bolts.
15B. On 1988-on models, install the drive chain as described in Chapter Twelve.
16. Align the indexing mark on the shift pedal with the mark on the shift shaft, and install the shift pedal. Tighten the pinch bolt securely.
17. Install the left footpeg as described in Chapter Fourteen.
18. Install the carburetor as described in Chapter Eight.
19. Install the air cleaner housing and the snorkel duct as described in Chapter Eight.
20. Install the exhaust system as described in Chapter Eight.
21. Install the fuel tank as described in Chapter Eight.
22. Refill the engine with new oil and new coolant as described in Chapter Three.
23. Be sure all cables and wires are properly routed and secured to the frame.
24. Adjust the following cables as described in Chapter Three.
 a. Choke cable.
 b. Throttle cable.
 c. Reverse cable.
 d. Parking brake cable.
25. Adjust the drive chain tension as described in Chapter Three
26. Adjust the carburetor idle as described in Chapter Three.
27. Install the front and rear fenders as described in Chapter Fourteen.

OIL SCREEN

An oil screen is mounted in the crankcase behind the clutch cover; see **Figure 13**. Removal and cleaning of the oil screen is not part of the engines periodic maintenance schedule described in Chapter Three. However, inspect and service the oil screen when removing the clutch cover, when troubleshooting a lubrication system problem, or when servicing the engine after it has overheated or seized.

Removal/Cleaning/Installation

1. Drain the engine oil as described in Chapter Three.
2. Remove the clutch cover as described in Chapter Six.
3. Pull the oil screen out of the crankcase (**Figure 13**).
4. Inspect the oil screen (A, **Figure 14**) for contamination or sludge buildup.

> *NOTE*
> *Any metal particles detected in the screen indicates internal engine damage.*

5. Clean the oil screen in solvent and dry with compressed air.
6. Check the oil screen for broken wires, tears, a loose or damaged gasket (B, **Figure 14**), or other damage.
7. Replace the oil screen if it is damaged.
8. Replace the gasket if it is damaged.
9. Before installing the oil screen, check that the gasket seats squarely around the oil screen.
10. Apply new engine oil to the oil screen gasket and install the screen into the crankcase.
11. Install the clutch cover as described in Chapter Six.
12. Refill the engine oil as described in Chapter Three. Check the clutch cover and drain plug for leaks.

OIL PUMP

The oil pump is mounted behind the clutch cover on the right side of the engine. The oil pump can be removed with the engine mounted in the frame.

Refer to **Figure 15** when servicing the oil pump cover.

Removal

1. Remove the clutch cover as described in Chapter Six.

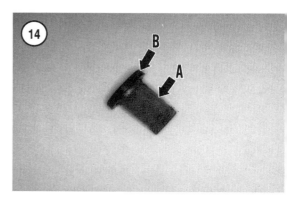

> *CAUTION*
> *Use an impact driver with a No. 3 Phillips bit to loosen the screws in Step 2 and Step 3. Loosening the screws with a Phillips screwdriver may damage the screw heads.*

2. If the oil pump is going to be disassembled, loosen the oil pump cover screw (A, **Figure 16**) while the pump is still installed in the engine. This is the screw just above the left oil pump mounting screw.
3. Remove the three oil pump mounting screws (B, **Figure 16**), and remove the oil pump from the crankcase. Do not lose the two dowels (B, **Figure 17**) that sit behind the oil pump.
4. Remove and discard the oil pump gasket.
5. Store the oil pump in a sealed plastic bag to prevent dirt and other abrasives from contaminating the pump rotors.

Oil Pump Disassembly/Inspection

Kawasaki does not provide service specifications for the oil pump rotors.

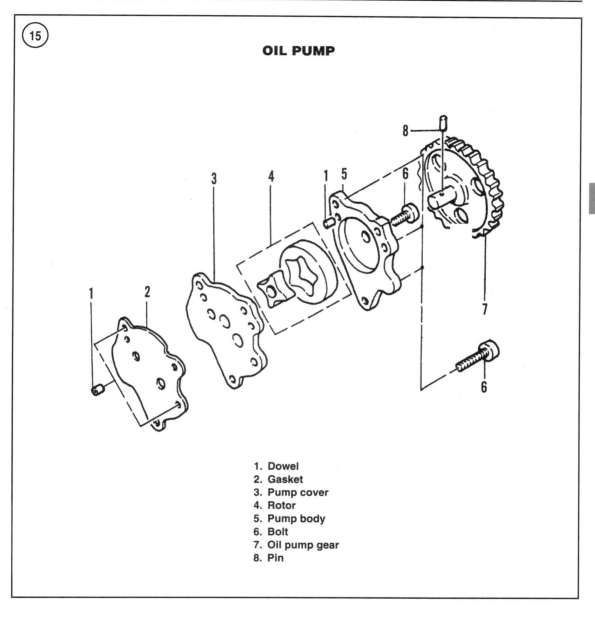

OIL PUMP

1. Dowel
2. Gasket
3. Pump cover
4. Rotor
5. Pump body
6. Bolt
7. Oil pump gear
8. Pin

1. Remove the oil pump cover screw (**Figure 18**), and separate the pump cover from the pump body. Do not lose the dowel (B, **Figure 19**) from the pump body.

2. Disassemble the oil pump assembly. See **Figure 20**.

3. Remove all gasket residue from the oil pump cover and crankcase mating surfaces.

4. Clean all parts in solvent, and dry them with compressed air. Place the parts on a clean lint-free cloth.

5. Inspect the oil pump body and cover for excessive wear, cracks or uneven wear.

6. Inspect the inner and outer rotors (**Figure 21**) for cracks, scoring or other damage.

7. Inspect the oil pump driven gear for broken or chipped teeth. Inspect the driven gear shaft for scoring, excessive wear or other damage.

8. Replace any part of the oil pump that is excessively worn or damaged.

Oil Pump Assembly

1. Coat all parts with clean engine oil prior to assembly.

2. Insert the shaft (A, **Figure 22**) of the oil pump driven gear through the pump body.

3. Install the pin (B, **Figure 22**) through the oil pump shaft hole.

4. Align the slot in the inner rotor with the pin and install the inner rotor (**Figure 23**).

5. Install the outer rotor around the inner rotor (A, **Figure 19**).

6. Be sure the dowel (B, **Figure 19**) is in place on the pump body, and install the pump cover. Secure the cover in place with the oil pump cover screw. (**Figure 18**). Tighten the screw securely.

7. Turn the driven gear by hand; making sure it turns smoothly.

Installation

1. Install the two dowel pins (B, **Figure 17**) and a new oil pump gasket onto the oil pump cover.

2. Fill the oil pump with new engine oil (**Figure 24**).

3. Be sure the two plugs (**Figure 25**) are in place in the crankcase, and set the oil pump in place.

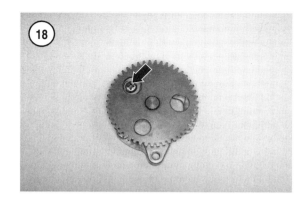

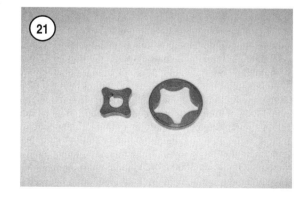

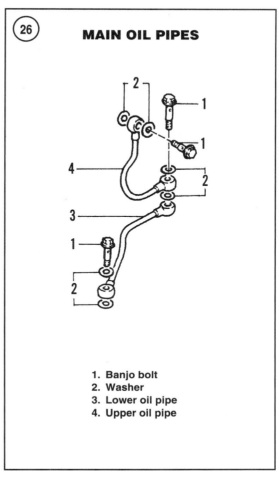

MAIN OIL PIPES

1. Banjo bolt
2. Washer
3. Lower oil pipe
4. Upper oil pipe

4. Secure the pump with the oil pump mounting screws (B, **Figure 16**), and tighten them securely.

5. Turn the driven gear by hand. The oil pump should turn smoothly.

6. Install the clutch cover as described in Chapter Six.

OIL PIPE

Two external oil pipes are used on the Mojave. Banjo bolts and washers are used at each pipe fitting. Refer to **Figure 26**.

Removal/Inspection/Installation

1. Remove the front and rear fenders as described in Chapter Fourteen.

2. Remove the air filter housing and carburetor as described in Chapter Eight.

3. Remove the banjo bolt (A, **Figure 27**) from the oil-pipe union on the right side of the crankcase.

4. Remove the banjo bolt (B, **Figure 27**) and two washers that secures the upper oil pipe (C, **Figure 27**) to the cylinder head. Remove the oil pipe.

5. Remove the banjo bolt (A, **Figure 28**) that secures the lower oil pipe (B, **Figure 28**) to the left side of the crankcase. Pull the oil pipe from under the wires, and remove the pipe.

6. Clean the oil pipes and banjo bolts (**Figure 29**) in solvent and dry them thoroughly.

7. Discard the sealing washers. Use new washers during installation.

8. Check the oil pipes for cracks or other damage. Replace if necessary.

9. Install the oil pipes by reversing these steps, while noting the following:

   a. Install a new sealing washer on each side of the oil pipe fittings as shown in **Figure 29**.

   b. When assembling the oil-pipe union, install the upper oil pipe (A **Figure 30**) on top of the lower pipe (B, **Figure 30**). Again, place a new sealing washer on each side of the oil pipe fittings. A total of three sealing washers should be used when assembling this union. See **Figure 30**.

   c. Tighten the oil pipe banjo bolts to the torque specification in **Table 2**.

Oil Pressure Relief Valve
Removal/Inspection/Installation

The oil pressure relief valve is installed on the inside of the clutch cover. When servicing the lubrication system, inspect and service the oil pressure relief valve as described in Chapter Six.

MAGNETO COVER

Removal/Installation

Refer to **Figure 31** for this procedure.

1. Place a drain pan underneath the left side cover.

2. Disconnect the stator (A, **Figure 32**) and pickup coil connectors (B, **Figure 32**).

3. Remove the nine magneto cover (A, **Figure 33**) mounting screws.

4. Remove the wire cap (B, **Figure 33**) from the top of the magneto cover.

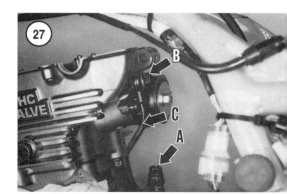

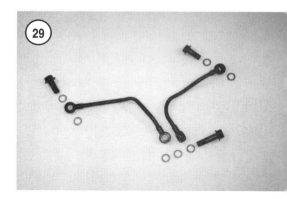

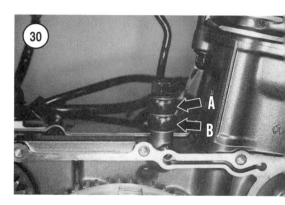

5

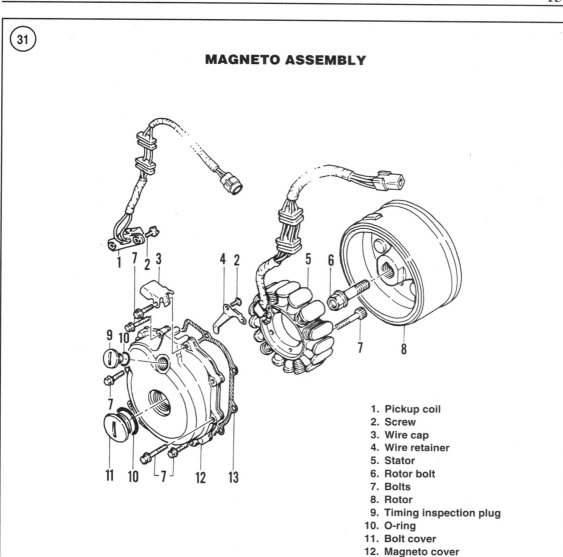

(31)

MAGNETO ASSEMBLY

1. Pickup coil
2. Screw
3. Wire cap
4. Wire retainer
5. Stator
6. Rotor bolt
7. Bolts
8. Rotor
9. Timing inspection plug
10. O-ring
11. Bolt cover
12. Magneto cover
13. Gasket

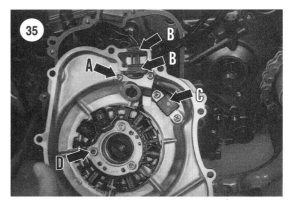

5. Depress the shifter, and remove the magneto cover from the crankcase. If necessary, tap the cover with a rubber mallet to free it from the gasket.

6. Remove the gasket and two dowels (**Figure 34**).

7. Installation is the reverse of removal. Pay attention to the following:

    a. Install a new magneto cover gasket.

    b. Fit the two dowels (**Figure 34**) into place in the crankcase.

    c. Make sure the wire cap (B, **Figure 33**) is in place and secured by the magneto mounting bolt.

STATOR AND PICKUP COILS

Removal/Installation

The stator and pickup coils are mounted inside the magneto cover. Each coil can be replaced separately. Do not cut any wires when removing the coil(s). Refer to **Figure 31** when servicing either coil.

1. Remove the magneto cover as described in this chapter.

2. Remove the two wire retainer screws and the retainer (A, **Figure 35**).

> *NOTE*
> *The pickup coil grommets sit on top of the grommets for the stator.*

3. Remove the pickup coil and the stator grommets (B, **Figure 35**) from the magneto cover.

4. Note how the pickup coil and stator wires are routed through the cover. Reroute these wires along the same path during assembly.

5. Remove the two pickup coil mounting screws, and remove the pick up coil (C, **Figure 35**).

6. Remove the three stator mounting bolts, and remove the stator (D, **Figure 35**).

7. Fit the stator (D, **Figure 35**) into the magneto cover. Route the stator wiring harness along the path noted during removal, and push the two grommets (B, **Figure 35**) firmly into the magneto cover grooves.

8. Install the stator mounting bolts and tighten them to the torque specification in **Table 2**.

9. Set the pickup coil (C, **Figure 35**) in place in the magneto cover. Route the pickup coil harness along the path noted during removal, and fit the two grommets into place on top of the stator grommets.

10. Install the pickup coil screws, and tighten them securely.

11. Be sure the rubber grommets are flush with the top of the magneto cover.

12. Install the wire retainer (A, **Figure 35**). Tighten the two screws securely.

Stator and Pickup Coil Testing

Refer to testing procedures described in Chapter Nine.

MAGNETO ROTOR

The rotor is permanently magnetized and cannot be tested except by installing a known good rotor. The rotor can lose its magnetism if it is struck by a sharp blow. Refer to **Figure 31** when servicing the rotor.

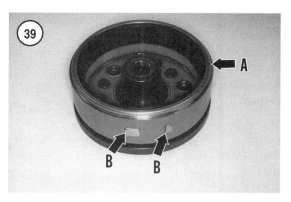

Removal

Use the Kawasaki flywheel holder (part No. 57001-1313) and a Motion Pro flywheel puller (part No. 08-116) or equivalent, to perform this procedure.

> *CAUTION*
> *Do not try to remove the rotor without the proper special tools. Any attempt to do so will ultimately lead to some form of damage to the crankshaft and rotor. If these tools are not available, have a dealership remove the rotor.*

1. Park the vehicle on level ground and set the parking brake.
2. Remove the magneto cover as described in this chapter.
3. Remove the shift pedal.

> *CAUTION*
> *If normal rotor removal attempts fail, do not force the puller. Excessive force strips the rotor threads, causing expensive damage. Take the engine to a dealership and have them remove the rotor.*

4. Hold the rotor with a flywheel holder, and remove the rotor bolt (**Figure 36**).
5. Thread the flywheel puller (**Figure 37**) into the rotor until it stops, and tighten it securely.
6. Hold the rotor with the flywheel holder, and gradually tighten the flywheel puller until the rotor disengages from the crankshaft.
7. Slide the rotor off the crankshaft and remove it.
8. Remove the Woodruff key (**Figure 38**) from the crankshaft groove.

Inspection

1. Clean the rotor in solvent and dry it with compressed air.
2. Check the rotor (A, **Figure 39**) for cracks or breaks.

> *WARNING*
> *Replace a cracked or chipped rotor. A damaged rotor can fly apart at high rpm, throwing metal fragments into the engine. Do not attempt to repair a damaged rotor.*

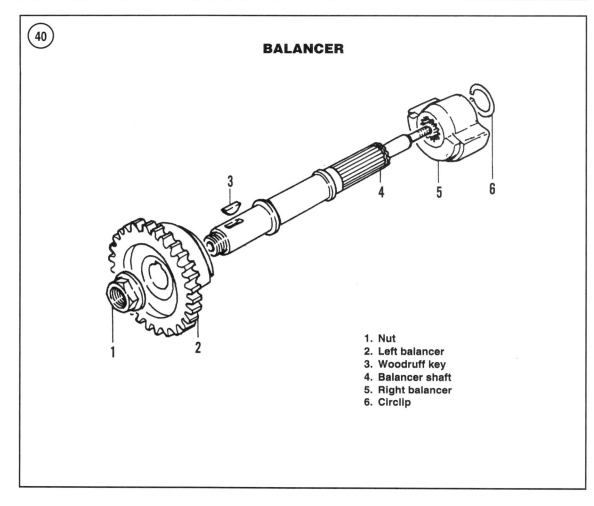

BALANCER

1. Nut
2. Left balancer
3. Woodruff key
4. Balancer shaft
5. Right balancer
6. Circlip

3. Inspect the timing projections (B, **Figure 39**) on the rotor for chipping, grooves or other signs of wear.

4. Check the rotor for loose or missing rivets.

5. Check the rotor tapered bore and the crankshaft taper for damage.

6. Check the crankshaft and rotor bolt threads for damage.

7. Replace damaged parts as required.

Installation

1. Install the Woodruff key (**Figure 38**) into the crankshaft keyway.

CAUTION
Do not install the rotor until the rotor magnets have been checked for small bolts, washers or other metal debris;

otherwise these parts can damage the stator coils.

2. Align the keyway in the rotor with the Woodruff key and slide the rotor onto the crankshaft.

3. Thread the rotor bolt (**Figure 36**) into the crankshaft threads.

4. Hold the rotor with a flywheel holder and tighten the magneto rotor bolt to draw the rotor onto the crankshaft taper. Torque the rotor bolt to the specification in **Table 2**.

5. Install the magneto cover as described in this chapter.

RIGHT BALANCER

Refer to **Figure 40** when servicing the right balancer.

Removal/Installation

1. Remove the clutch cover as described in Chapter Six.

2. Remove and discard the circlip (**Figure 41**).

3. Remove the right balancer from the balancer shaft. Inspect the balancer as described below.

4. Installation is the reverse of removal. Pay attention to the following:

   a. Install the right balancer so the timing mark on the weight aligns with the mark on the balancer shaft. See **Figure 42**.

   b. Install a new circlip. Make sure it is seated in the groove in the balancer shaft.

Inspection

1. Clean the right balancer (**Figure 43**) in solvent. Dry it with compressed air.

2. Check the right balancer for:

   a. Broken or chipped teeth.

   b. Heat discoloration and excessive wear.

   c. Worn or damaged center hole.

3. Replace the right balancer if it is worn or shows signs of damage.

LEFT BALANCER

Refer to **Figure 40** when servicing the left balancer.

Removal

1. Remove the magneto rotor as described in this chapter.

> *NOTE*
> *Use a discarded primary drive gear to hold the balancer gear while removing the nut in the next step. If an appropriate-sized gear is unavailable, a brass or aluminum washer will also work. However, do not use steel washers. These are too hard and could damage the gear teeth.*

2. Insert a holding gear (A, **Figure 44**) on the bottom of the left balancer and the balancer drive gear. Make sure the holding gear meshes with both the left balancer and the balancer drive gear.

3. Loosen and remove the left balancer nut (B, **Figure 44**).

4. Remove the left balancer from the balancer shaft, and then remove the Woodruff key (A, **Figure 45**).

Inspection

1. Clean all parts (**Figure 46**) in solvent. Dry them with compressed air.

2. Check the left balancer for:
   a. Broken or chipped teeth.
   b. Heat discoloration and excessive wear.
   c. Worn or damaged center hole.

3. Replace the left balancer if it is worn or shows signs of damage.

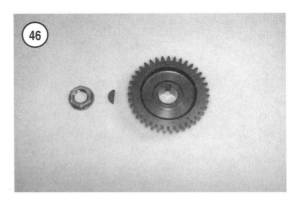

Installation

1. Install the Woodruff key (A, **Figure 45**) into the keyway in the balancer shaft.

2. Align the keyway in the left balancer with the Woodruff key, and slide the balancer onto the balancer shaft (A, **Figure 47**).

3. If the balancer drive gear is installed, be sure the timing mark on the left balancer aligns with the marks on the balancer gear as shown in B, **Figure 47**. Rotate the crankshaft and balancer shaft as necessary to align the marks.

4. Apply oil to the threads of the balancer shaft and the left balancer nut. Install the left balancer nut.

5. Hold the left balancer by inserting a holding gear (**Figure 48**) on top of the left balancer. Be sure the holding gear meshes with the left balancer and the balancer drive gear. Torque the left balancer nut to the specification in **Table 2**.

6. Install the magneto rotor as described in this chapter.

BALANCER DRIVE GEAR

Refer to **Figure 49** when servicing the balancer drive gear.

Removal

1. Remove the magneto rotor as described in this chapter.

CRANKSHAFT

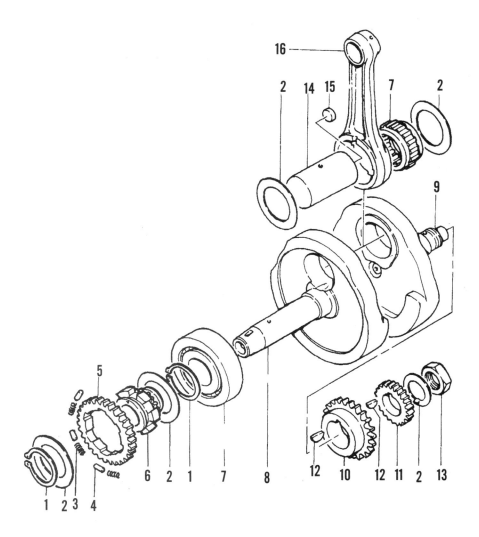

5

1. Circlip
2. Washer
3. Damper spring
4. Pin
5. Balancer drive gear
6. Timing sprocket
7. Bearing
8. Left crankwheel

9. Right crankwheel
10. Primary gear
11. Oil pump spur gear
12. Woodruff key
13. Primary gear nut
14. Crank pin
15. Plug (1988-on)
16. Connecting rod

2. Remove the circlip (B, **Figure 45**) and washer (C, **Figure 45**) from the balancer drive gear. Discard the circlip.

> *NOTE*
> *The damper springs and rollers may fall out when the balancer drive gear is pulled from the crankshaft. Place a cloth into the bottom of the case half so parts cannot fall into the crankcase.*

3. Remove the balancer drive gear (**Figure 50**) from the timing sprocket on the crankshaft. The damper springs and rollers should come out with the balancer drive gear.
4. Separate the springs and the rollers.

Inspection

1. Clean all parts (**Figure 51**) in solvent. Dry them with compressed air.
2. Check the balancer drive gear for:
   a. Broken or chipped teeth.
   b. Heat discoloration and excessive wear.
   c. Worn or damaged center hole.
3. Replace the balancer drive gear if it is worn or shows signs of damage.
4. Inspect the springs and rollers for cracks or other signs of wear. Replace worn components if necessary.

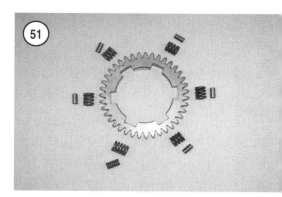

Installation

1. Five damper springs are installed with five rollers. The sixth spring, which is slightly longer than the other five, is installed with an inner spring. (**Figure 52**). Arrange the parts in an orderly fashion so it will be easy to quickly identify a spring and its related roller or spring.

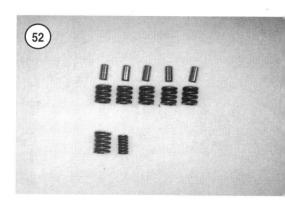

> *NOTE*
> *The inner spring mentioned in Step 1 was not used on some 1987 models (engine No. SF250AE000001-SF250AE008224). Each spring on these models was installed with a roller. If working on one of these models, install a roller into the damper spring when performing Step 2.*

2. Install the inner spring into the longer spring (**Figure 53**).

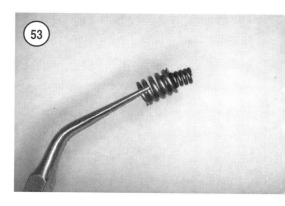

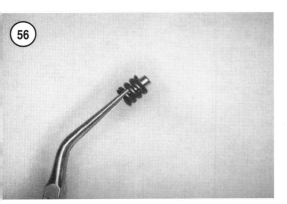

5. Slide a roller into a damper spring (**Figure 56**), and install the spring/roller assembly into another slot in the balancer drive gear (**Figure 57**). Repeat this process with the remaining spring/roller assemblies.

6. Slide the washer (C, **Figure 45**) into place against the balancer drive gear, and install a new circlip (B, **Figure 45**). Make sure the circlip is properly seated in the groove on the timing sprocket.

7. Install the magneto rotor as described in this chapter.

PRIMARY GEAR AND OIL PUMP SPUR GEAR

Refer to **Figure 49** when servicing the primary gear or the oil pump spur gear.

The primary gear and the oil pump spur gear are mounted on the right side of the engine.

The Kawasaki gear holder (part No. 57001-1015), or equivalent, is required to remove the primary gear nut.

Removal

1. Remove the clutch as described in Chapter Six.

2. Remove the oil pump as described in this chapter.

> *NOTE*
> *If the Kawasaki gear holder is not available, use a discarded primary gear as a gear holder. A brass or aluminum washer stuck between the primary gear and the clutch driven gear also works.*

3. Set this spring assembly into place in a slot in the balancer drive gear. See **Figure 54**.

4. Slide the balancer drive gear onto the timing sprocket on the crankshaft so the slots in the gear are opposite those on the timing sprocket. Make sure the timing mark on the balancer drive gear aligns with the mark on the timing sprocket (**Figure 55**). If the left balancer is installed on the balancer shaft, make sure these two timing marks also align with the timing mark on the left balancer as shown in B, **Figure 47**.

3. Bend the lock tab (**Figure 58**) away from the flat on the primary gear nut.

4. Use the gear holder to hold the crankshaft while loosening the primary gear nut.

   a. Install the gear holder (**Figure 59**) so it meshes with the primary gear and the clutch driven gear.

   b. With the gear holder in place, loosen the primary gear nut.

5. Remove the primary gear nut (A, **Figure 60**) from the crankshaft.

6. Remove and discard the lockwasher (B, **Figure 60**).

7. Remove the oil pump spur gear (**Figure 61**) from the crankshaft.

8. Remove the primary gear (A, **Figure 62**), and then remove the Woodruff key (B, **Figure 62**) from the crankshaft keyway.

9. Inspect the parts as described below.

Installation

1. Rotate the crankshaft so that its keyway faces up (12 o'clock). Install the Woodruff key (B, **Figure 62**) into the keyway.

2. Install the primary gear (A, **Figure 62**) onto the crankshaft so the shoulder faces in toward the crankcase.

3. Install the oil pump spur gear (**Figure 61**) so the side with the notch faces out.

4. Install a new lockwasher. Be sure the tooth in the lockwasher engages the notch in the oil pump spur gear.

5. Install the primary gear nut onto the crankshaft.

6. Using the same gear holder used during removal, install the gear holder beneath the primary gear. Be sure the holder meshes with the primary gear and with the clutch driven gear as shown in **Figure 63**.

7. Torque the primary gear nut to the specification in **Table 2**.

8. Bend over a portion of the lockwasher, and flatten it against a nut flat. See **Figure 58**.

Inspection

1. Clean all parts in solvent. Dry them with compressed air.

2. Check the primary gear and the oil pump spur gear for the following:

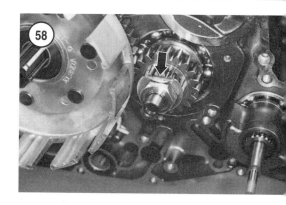

a. Broken or chipped teeth.

b. Heat discoloration and excessive wear

c. Worn or damaged center hole.

3. Replace an excessively worn or damaged nut or Woodruff key (**Figure 64**).

KICKSTARTER

See **Figure 65** for this procedure.

Removal

1. Place the vehicle on level ground, and set the parking brake.

2. Remove the clutch as described in Chapter Six.

3. Remove the spring's outer tang (A, **Figure 66**) from the hole in the crankcase.

4. Rotate the kick shaft clockwise until the ratchet arm clears the kick guide (A, **Figure 67**) in the crankcase, and remove the kickstarter mechanism.

Inspection

1. Remove the washer (**Figure 68**) from the kick shaft.

2. Remove the spring guide (A, **Figure 69**) and return spring (B, **Figure 69**).

3. Remove the washer (D, **Figure 70**) from the end of the kick shaft.

4. Remove the circlip (C, **Figure 70**), and then remove the washer (B, **Figure 70**).

5. Remove the spring (A, **Figure 70**) and ratchet (A, **Figure 71**).

6. Remove and discard the circlip (C, **Figure 72**) from the kick shaft.

7. Remove the washer (B, **Figure 72**) and kick gear (A, **Figure 72**) from the kick shaft.

8. Inspect the kick shaft splines for wear, cracks or other damage (**Figure 73**).

9. Inspect the kick gear for excessive wear, burrs, pitting or broken teeth.

10. Inspect the pawls on the kick gear (A, **Figure 74**) and ratchet (B, **Figure 74**) for excessive wear or damage.

11. Inspect the springs for fatigue or other signs of wear.

12. Replace any part as required.

Installation

1. Install the kick gear (A, **Figure 72**) onto the kick shaft.

2. Install the washer (B, **Figure 72**) and a new circlip (C, **Figure 72**). The flat side of the circlip must face in toward the kick gear, and the circlip

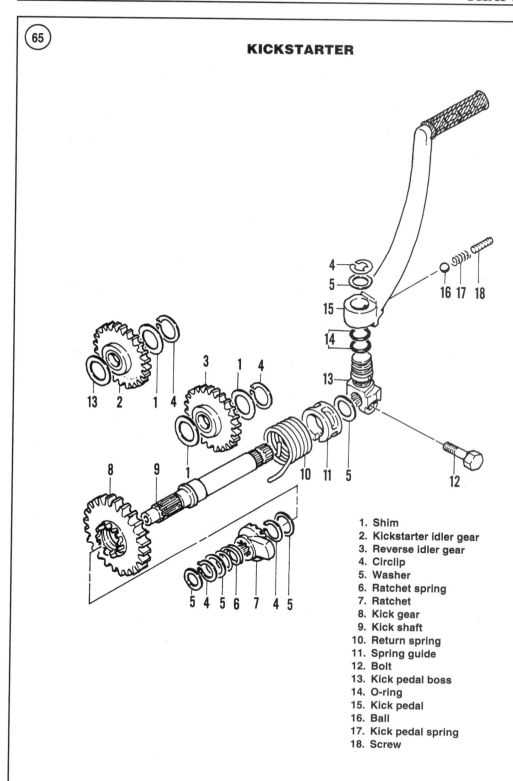

KICKSTARTER

1. Shim
2. Kickstarter idler gear
3. Reverse idler gear
4. Circlip
5. Washer
6. Ratchet spring
7. Ratchet
8. Kick gear
9. Kick shaft
10. Return spring
11. Spring guide
12. Bolt
13. Kick pedal boss
14. O-ring
15. Kick pedal
16. Ball
17. Kick pedal spring
18. Screw

5

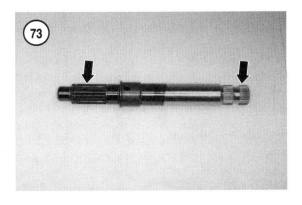

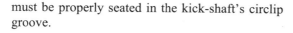

must be properly seated in the kick-shaft's circlip groove.

NOTE
The return spring will not be properly preloaded if the ratchet and kick shaft marks are not aligned.

3. Apply molybdenum disulfide grease to the pawls on the kick gear, and install the ratchet (A, **Figure 71**). Make sure the mark on the ratchet aligns with the mark on the kick shaft as shown in B, **Figure 71**.

4. Install the spring (A, **Figure 70**) on the kick shaft.

5. Install the washer (B, **Figure 70**) onto the kick shaft, and then install a new circlip (C, **Figure 70**). The flat side of the circlip must face in toward the washer, and the circlip must be properly seated in the kick shaft's circlip groove.

6. Install the second washer (D, **Figure 70**) onto the kick shaft.

7. Install the return spring so its inside tang (**Figure 75**) fits into the hole in the kick shaft.

8. Slide the spring guide against the kick gear. The slot in the guide should engage the spring tang. See **Figure 76**.

9. Install the washer (**Figure 68**) onto the kick shaft.

10. Apply a dab of molybdenum disulfide grease to the end of the kick shaft so the washer does not fall off during assembly. Also apply grease to the kickstarter bushing (B, **Figure 67**) in the crankcase.

11. Position the kick starter mechanism opposite the bushing in the crankcase. Be sure the ratchet arm is at 2 o'clock and the teeth of the kick gear align with the teeth of the kickstarter idler gear (B, **Figure 66**).

KICKSTARTER IDLER AND REVERSE IDLER GEARS

See **Figure 65** for this procedure.

Removal/Inspection

1. Remove the clutch as described in Chapter Six.

2. Remove the kickstarter as described in this chapter.

3. Remove the circlip and shim (**Figure 77**) from the reverse shaft.

4. Remove the reverse idler gear (A, **Figure 78**) from the reverse shaft.

5. Remove the shim (**Figure 79**) from the reverse shaft.

6. Remove the circlip and shim (**Figure 80**) from the countershaft.

7. Remove the kickstarter idler gear (A, **Figure 81**) from the countershaft, and then remove the collar (B, **Figure 81**).

8. Inspect the kickstarter idler gear, its collar, and shim (**Figure 82**). Also inspect the reverse idler gear and its two shims (**Figure 83**). Replace any part that is worn or shows signs of damage.

12. Slide the kick shaft into the bushing in the crankcase. Once the shaft is fully seated in the bushing, turn the shaft counterclockwise until it stops. The mechanism is properly installed when the ratchet arm is securely locked behind the kick guide (A, **Figure 67**) in the crankcase. See **Figure 66**.

13. Rotate the return spring counterclockwise, and insert the spring's outer tang (A, **Figure 66**) into the hole in the crankcase.

14. Fit the kick pedal onto the shaft, and test the movement of the kick starter mechanism.

15. Remove the kick pedal, and install the clutch as described in Chapter Six.

84

CRANKCASE

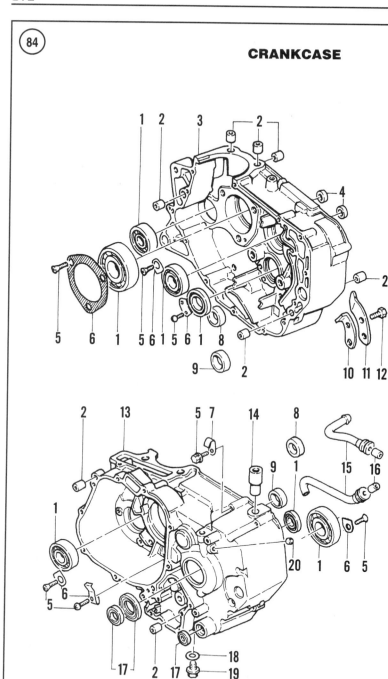

1. Bearings
2. Dowels
3. Right crankcase half
4. Plug
5. Screw
6. Retainers
7. Wire clamp
8. Bushings
9. Races
10. Stopper
11. Kick guide
12. Bolt
13. Left crankcase half
14. Breather fitting
15. Breather tube
16. Pin
17. Oil seals
18. Gasket
19. Oil drain bolt
20. Plug

Installation

1. Install the kickstarter idler gear (B, **Figure 78**) onto the countershaft by performing the following:
    a. Install the collar (B, **Figure 81**) onto the countershaft.
    b. Install the kickstarter idler gear (A, **Figure 81**) onto the countershaft.
    c. Install the shim and a new circlip (**Figure 80**). Make sure the circlip is properly seated in the groove on the countershaft.
2. Install the reverse idler gear (A, **Figure 78**) onto the reverse shaft by performing the following:
    a. Install the shim (**Figure 79**) onto the reverse shaft.
    b. Install the reverse idler gear (A, **Figure 78**). Make sure the reverse idler gear meshes with the kickstarter idler gear.
    c. Install the shim and a new circlip (**Figure 77**). Make sure the circlip is properly seated in the groove in the reverse shaft.
3. Install the kick starter as described in this chapter.
4. Install the clutch as described in Chapter Six.

CRANKCASE AND CRANKSHAFT

Disassembly of the crankcase—splitting the case halves—and removal of the crankshaft assembly requires engine removal from the frame. However, first remove the cylinder head, cylinder and all other attached assemblies with the engine installed in the frame.

The crankcase is made in two halves of thin-walled, precision diecast aluminum alloy. To avoid damaging them, do not hammer or pry on any of the interior or exterior projected walls—excessive force will damage these areas. They are assembled without a gasket; only gasket sealer is used. Dowels align the crankcase halves when they are bolted together. The crankcase halves are sold as a matched set only. If one crankcase half is damaged, both case halves must be replaced.

The crankshaft assembly consists of two full-circle flywheels pressed together on a crankpin. The connecting rod-to-crankpin bearing is a needle bearing assembly. Two ball bearings support the crankshaft in the crankcase.

The procedure that follows describes a complete, step-by-step major lower end overhaul. Remember that the right and left side of the engine refers to the engine as it sits in the frame, not as it sits on the workbench.

Crankcase Disassembly

This procedure describes disassembly of the crankcase halves and removal of the crankshaft, transmission, reverse assembly and internal shift mechanism. Service procedures for the transmission, reverse assembly and internal shift mechanism are covered in Chapter Seven.

Refer to **Figure 84** when disassembling the crankcase.

1. Remove all exterior engine assemblies as described in this chapter and other related chapters:
    a. Oil filter and oil pipes.
    b. Cylinder head.
    c. Cylinder and piston.
    d. Clutch.
    e. Oil pump.
    f. Primary gear and oil pump spur gear.
    g. Kickstarter, kickstarter idler gear and reverse idler gear.
    h. External shift mechanism.
    i. Left and right balancer.
    j. Balancer drive gear.
    k. Magneto rotor.
    l. Engine sprocket.
    m. Reverse cam and reverse lever.
    n. Neutral indicator and the neutral/reverse switch assembly (where applicable).
2. Place the engine assembly on wooden blocks with the left side facing up (**Figure 85**).

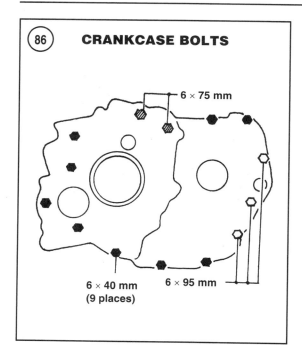

CRANKCASE BOLTS

6 × 75 mm

6 × 40 mm
(9 places)

6 × 95 mm

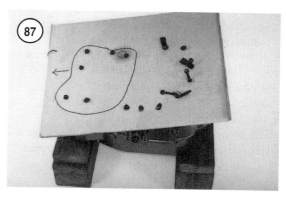

3. Loosen all crankcase bolts by a quarter turn.
Figure 86 shows the crankcase bolts and their individual sizes.

NOTE
*To keep track of the crankcase bolts, draw the crankcase outline on a piece of cardboard (**Figure 87**), then number and punch holes to correspond with each bolt location. Insert the bolts in their appropriate locations.*

4. Remove *all* bolts loosened in Step 3.

CAUTION
The crankcase halves may separate easily in the following procedure.

Therefore, work over a workbench. Do not allow either half to fall to the floor.

CAUTION
Do not pry between the crankcase mating surfaces when separating the crankcase halves. Doing so will damage the mating surfaces and result in oil leaks, requiring replacement of both case halves.

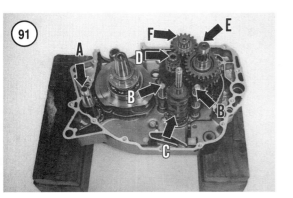

5. If necessary, using a wide-blade screwdriver, pry the crankcase halves apart at the two pry points located on the outside of the case halves. If necessary, lightly tap the end of the countershaft to prevent the left case from hanging up while removing it.

6. Lift the left crankcase off the engine.

7. If it is still installed, remove the collar from the left end of the countershaft.

8. Remove the two crankcase dowels (**Figure 88**).

9. Remove the upper oil breather tube (**Figure 89**) and the lower oil breather tube (**Figure 90**).

10. Refer to **Figure 91** and the following list to identify the individual transmission components before removing them:

   a. Balancer shaft (A).
   b. Shift shafts and forks (B).
   c. Shift drum (C).
   d. Mainshaft (D).
   e. Countershaft (E).
   f. Reverse shaft (F).

11. Lift the balancer shaft (**Figure 92**) from the crankcase.

12. Remove the shift fork shafts and shift forks as follows:

NOTE
The two countershaft shift forks are identical. Therefore, if the crankcase is being separated because of a shifting problem, mark the operating position of each shift fork while removing it.

   a. Remove the countershaft shift-fork shaft (A, **Figure 93**) and its two shift forks.

   b. Remove the mainshaft shift-fork shaft (B, **Figure 93**) and its shift fork.

13. Remove the shift drum (C, **Figure 93**).

14. Remove the mainshaft (A, **Figure 94**), the countershaft (B, **Figure 94**) and then the reverse shaft (C, **Figure 94**).

15. Store each individual shaft assembly. (**Figure 95**) in a sealed and labeled plastic bag until it is serviced.

16. Lift the crankshaft (**Figure 96**) out of the right crankcase and remove it.

Crankcase Inspection

1. Using a scraper, remove all sealer and gasket residue from all crankcase gasket surfaces.

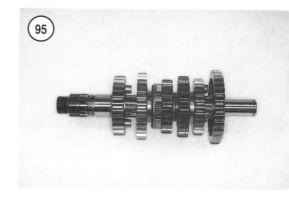

> *WARNING*
> *When drying the crankcase bearings in Step 2, do not allow the bearing to spin. When drying the bearings, hold the inner race by hand. The air jet will force the bearings to turn at speeds that exceed their designed limit. The bearing will be damaged and possibly disintegrate causing serious injury.*

2. Clean both crankcase halves and all crankcase bearings with cleaning solvent. Thoroughly dry them with compressed air.

3. Clean all crankcase oil passages with compressed air.

4. Lightly oil the crankcase bearings (**Figure 97**) with engine oil before checking the bearings in Step 5.

5. Check the bearings for roughness, pitting, galling and play by rotating them slowly by hand. Replace bearings that turn roughly or show excessive play.

> *NOTE*
> *Always replace the opposite bearing at the same time.*

6. Replace any worn or damaged bearings as described in *Crankcase Bearing and Bushing Replacement* in this chapter.

7. Inspect the crankcase bushings for roughness, pitting or galling. Replace any worn or damaged bushings as described in *Crankcase Bearing and Bushing Replacement* in this chapter.

8. Inspect the cases for cracks and fractures, especially in the lower areas where they are vulnerable to rock damage.

9. Check the areas around the stiffening ribs, around bearing bosses and threaded holes for damage. Repair or replace damaged cases.

10. Check the threaded holes in both crankcase halves for thread damage, dirt or oil buildup. If necessary, clean or repair the threads with a suitable size metric tap. Coat the tap threads with kerosene or an aluminum tap fluid before using.

11. Check the shift-shaft return spring stud to see if it is loose or damaged (A, **Figure 98**) on the outside

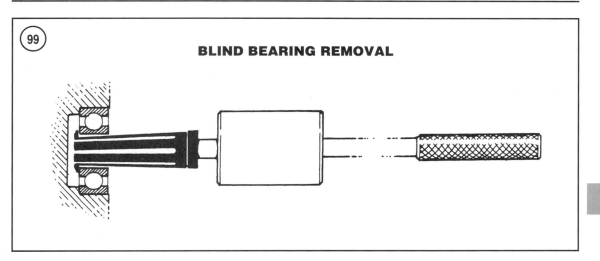

BLIND BEARING REMOVAL

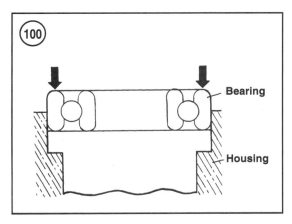

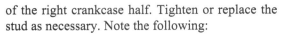

Bearing

Housing

of the right crankcase half. Tighten or replace the stud as necessary. Note the following:

   a. Apply Loctite 242 (blue) to the stud threads prior to installation.

   b. Tighten the shift-shaft return spring stud to the torque specification in **Table 2**.

Crankcase Bearing and Bushing Replacement

Prior to replacing a crankcase bearing or bushing, note the following:

1. Because of the number of bearings used in the left and right crankcase halves, make sure to identify a bearing before removing it. Identify each bearing by its size code markings.

2. Refer to *Bearing Replacement* in Chapter One for general information on bearing removal and installation.

3. After removing bearings and bushings, clean the crankcase in solvent and dry it thoroughly.

4. Use a blind bearing remover (**Figure 99**) to remove some of the blind bearings and bushings in the following procedures.

5. When installing new bearings in a crankcase half, press on the outer bearing race only (**Figure 100**).

Balancer shaft bearing replacement

1. To replace the left balancer-shaft bearing (A, **Figure 101**):

   a. Remove the retainer from the bearing.

   b. Press the bearing from the crankcase.

   c. Press in the new bearing until it bottoms in the crankcase.

   d. Position the bearing retainer onto the crankcase.

e. Apply Loctite 242 (blue) to the bearing retainer screw. Then install and tighten the screw securely.

2. To replace the right balancer-shaft bearing (B, **Figure 98**):

a. Use a pilot bearing remover and remove the bearing from crankcase.

b. Press in the new bearing until it bottoms in the crankcase.

Transmission bushing replacement

The bushings are identified as follows:

a. Left reverse-shaft bushing (B, **Figure 102**).

b. Right reverse-shaft bushing (C, **Figure 97**).

c. Left mainshaft bushing (A, **Figure 102**).

d. Right countershaft bushing (D, **Figure 97**).

1. Remove blind bushings with a blind bearing remover.

2. Remove the right reverse shaft and right countershaft bushings by pressing each out of the crankcase.

3. Align the new bushing with the crankcase and press it in place until its shoulder bottoms on the inside of the crankcase.

Right mainshaft bearing replacement

Refer to B, **Figure 97**.

1. Remove the bearing retainer screw and remove the retainer.

2. Press the bearing out of the crankcase.

3. Press the new bearing into the crankcase until it bottoms out.

4. Position the bearing retainer onto the crankcase.

5. Apply Loctite 242 (blue) to the bearing retainer screw. Then install and tighten the screw securely.

Right shift drum bearing replacement

Refer to E, **Figure 97**.

1. Remove the bearing retainer screws and remove the retainer.

2. Press the bearing out of the crankcase.

3. Press the new bearing into the crankcase until it bottoms out.

4. Position the bearing retainer plate onto the crankcase.

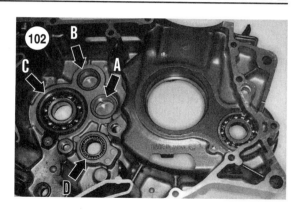

5. Apply Loctite 242 (blue) to the bearing plate retaining screws. Then install and tighten the screws securely.

Right main bearing replacement

> *NOTE*
> *To replace the left main bearing, refer to **Crankshaft Timing Sprocket and Main Bearing Replacement** in this chapter.*

Refer to A, **Figure 97**.

1. Remove the bearing retainer screws and remove the bearing plate.

2. Press the bearing out of the crankcase.

3. Press in the new bearing until it bottoms in the crankcase.

4. Position the bearing retainer in the crankcase.

5. Apply Loctite 242 (blue) to the bearing retainer screws. Then install and tighten the screws securely.

Left countershaft bearing and seal replacement

1. Pry the seal from the crankcase with a wide-blade screwdriver. Place a rag under the screwdriver to protect the crankcase. See **Figure 103**.

2. Remove the screw from the bearing retainer and remove the retainer.

3. Press the countershaft bearing (C, **Figure 102**) from the crankcase.

4. Press in a new bearing until it bottoms in the crankcase. Be sure the sealed side of the bearing faces the outside of the case half.

5. Position the bearing retainer in the crankcase.

6. Apply Loctite 242 (blue) to the bearing retainer screw. Then install and tighten the screw securely.

7. Apply a high-temperature grease to the lips of a new seal, and press the seal into place. Be sure the manufacturer's marks face out.

Crankshaft Inspection

Refer to **Figure 104**.
1. Clean the crankshaft thoroughly with solvent. Dry the crankshaft with compressed air. Also clear the crankshaft oil passageway with compressed air. Then lubricate all bearing surfaces with a light coat of engine oil.
2. Check the crankshaft journals (**Figure 105** and **Figure 106**) for scratches, heat discoloration or other defects.
3. Check the taper, threads, and keyway for damage. Have damaged crankshaft components replaced as described in *Crankshaft Overhaul* in this chapter.
4. Check the crankshaft bearing surfaces for chatter marks and excessive or uneven wear. Repair minor chatter marks with 320-grit carborundum cloth. Then, clean the crankshaft in solvent and recheck the surfaces. If they do not clean up properly, the crankshaft must be repaired or replaced.
5. Check the connecting rod crankpin end (A, **Figure 106**) for signs of seizure, bearing or thrust washer damage or connecting rod damage.
6. Check the connecting rod piston pin end (B, **Figure 106**) for signs of excessive heat (blue coloration) or other damage.
7. Slide the connecting rod to one side. Then measure the connecting rod-to-crankpin side clearance with a flat feeler gauge as shown in **Figure 107**. Compare the reading to the specification given in **Table 1**. Excessive clearance requires crankshaft overhaul.

8. Measure the connecting rod-to-crankpin radial clearance by performing the following procedure.
   a. Support the crankshaft journals on two V-blocks as shown in **Figure 108**.
   b. Support the connecting rod piston pin end as shown in **Figure 108**.
   c. Position a dial indicator so its stem rests against the connecting rod crankpin end, and then zero the dial gauge.
   d. Move the connecting rod toward the dial indicator and then away from it in the opposite direction.
   e. The difference between the two gauge readings is the connecting rod-to-crankpin radial clearance. Compare the readings to the specification in **Table 1**. Replace the connecting rod assembly if the radial clearance exceeds the service limit. See *Crankshaft Overhaul* in this chapter.
9. Measure crankshaft runout as follows:
   a. Support the crankshaft journals on two V-blocks as shown in **Figure 109**.
   b. Position a dial indicator so its stem rests against the left crank at the position indicated in **Figure 109**. Then zero the dial gauge.
   c. Slowly turn the crankshaft while reading the dial gauge. Record the runout limit.
   d. Repeat with the dial indicator placed at the position indicated in **Figure 109**.
   e. If the runout at either location exceeds the service limit in **Table 1**, retrue the crankshaft. See *Crankshaft Overhaul* in this chapter.

Crankshaft Timing Sprocket and Main Bearing Replacement

The crankshaft timing sprocket (C, **Figure 106**) and the left main bearing (D, **Figure 106**) are pressed onto the left crankwheel. Use a press and suitable adapters to replace the sprocket and/or bearing.

Although the timing sprocket and left main bearing are available separately, Kawasaki recommends replacing the entire crankshaft rather than replacing these parts. Be sure the timing sprocket is properly aligned with the center of the crankpin. If the sprocket timing mark is not precisely aligned with the crank pin as shown in **Figure 110**, cam timing will be incorrect. For this reason, replacing these parts should be left to a Kawasaki dealership or mo-

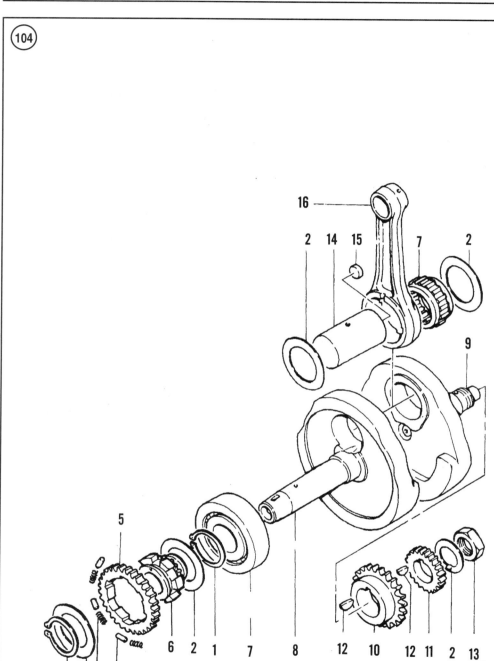

CRANKSHAFT

1. Circlip
2. Washer
3. Damper spring
4. Pin
5. Balancer drive gear
6. Timing sprocket
7. Bearing
8. Left crankwheel
9. Right crankwheel
10. Primary gear
11. Oil pump spur gear
12. Woodruff key
13. Primary gear nut
14. Crank pin
15. Plug (1988-on)
16. Connecting rod

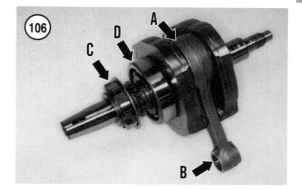

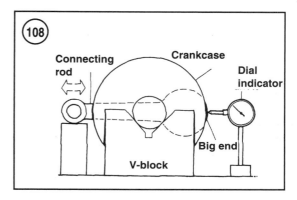

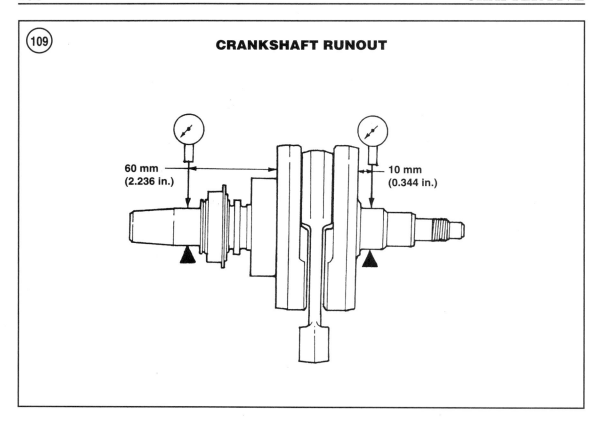

CRANKSHAFT RUNOUT

60 mm
(2.236 in.)

10 mm
(0.344 in.)

torcycle repair shop familiar with crankshaft re-building. Refer to crankshaft overhaul below.

Crankshaft Overhaul

Crankshaft overhaul requires a number of special tools: a 20-ton hydraulic press (minimum), holding jigs, crankshaft alignment jig, dial indicators and a micrometer or vernier caliper. For this reason, refer crankshaft overhaul to a Kawasaki dealership or motorcycle repair shop familiar with crankshaft re-building. When having the crankshaft rebuilt, make sure the mechanic aligns the crankshaft and crankpin oil passages and properly installs the crankshaft timing sprocket. See **Figure 110**

Balancer Shaft Inspection

1. Check the balancer shaft bearing journals (**Figure 111**) for deep scoring, excessive wear, heat dis-coloration or cracks.
2. Check the keyway in the end of the balancer shaft for cracks or excessive wear.

3. Replace the balancer shaft if necessary.

Transmission and Reverse Shaft Inspection

Refer to Chapter Seven for all disassembly, in-spection and assembly procedures.

Crankcase Assembly

This procedure describes crankcase assembly, in-cluding the installation of the crankshaft and trans-mission.

1. Refer to Chapter Seven for transmission, reverse assembly and internal shift mechanism reassembly.
2. Clean all the components in solvent, and dry them thoroughly with compressed air. Oil the bear-ings with new engine oil.

CAUTION
Do not assemble the engine with sol-vent left on parts or in the oil pas-sages; otherwise, the solvent will contaminate the new engine oil.

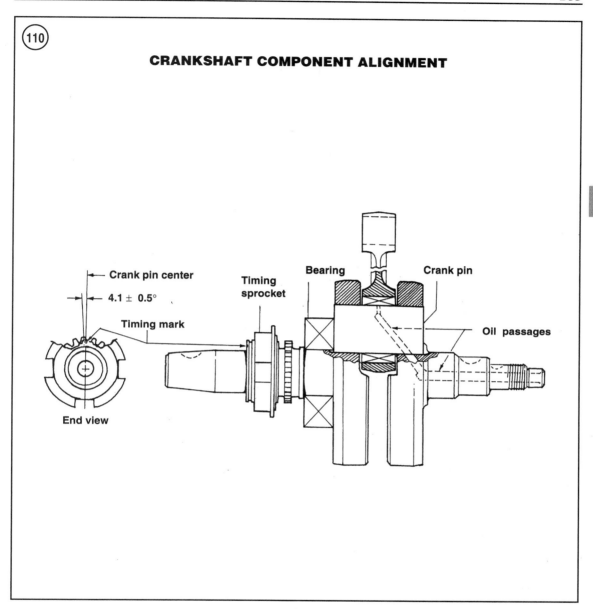

CRANKSHAFT COMPONENT ALIGNMENT

Crank pin center

4.1 ± 0.5°

Timing mark

End view

Timing sprocket

Bearing

Crank pin

Oil passages

5

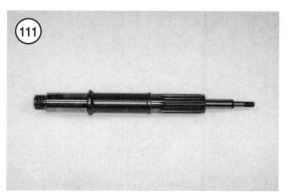

3. Place the right crankcase assembly (**Figure 112**) on wooden blocks.

NOTE
Step 5 describes two methods of installing the crankshaft. If a press is required, the use of the Kawasaki crankshaft jig (part No. 57001-1174) is also necessary.

4A. Apply a light coat of engine oil to the right crankshaft bearing journal. Then install the crankshaft into the right main bearing as shown in **Figure 113**. Make sure the crankshaft bottoms out in the bearing.

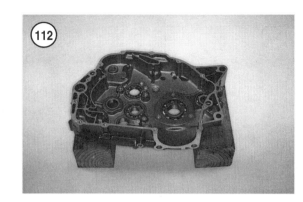

> *NOTE*
> *If the crankshaft cannot be installed by hand, install it with a press as described in Step 4B.*

4B. Install the crankshaft with a press as follows:

> *CAUTION*
> *If the crankshaft installation tools are not available, refer this service to a dealership or machine shop. Do not drive the crankshaft and bearing into the crankcase with a hammer.*

a. Position the right crankcase in a press. Support the right main bearing housing on a suitable press fixture and center the bearing under the press ram.

b. Apply a light coat of engine oil to the right crankshaft bearing journal.

c. Install the crankshaft into the main bearing so the crankshaft assembly is square with the crankcase mating surface.

d. Measure the distance from the left crank shoulder (bottom side) to the press bed or press fixture. Adequate clearance must be maintained so the crankshaft cannot bottom out as it is being installed.

e. Position the connecting rod at bottom dead center (BDC).

> *NOTE*
> *Use the crankshaft jig to prevent crankshaft distortion when pressing the crankshaft into the bearing.*

f. Center the Kawasaki crankshaft jig (part No. 57001-1174) around the connecting rod. Then adjust the crankshaft jig so its arms contact both crankshaft wheels as shown in **Figure 114**.

g. Press the crankshaft into the right main bearing until the crankshaft shoulder bottoms out against the main bearing inner race.

h. Release pressure from the press ram.

i. Remove the crankshaft jig from the crankshaft. Then turn the crankshaft slowly by hand. It should turn freely with no sign of roughness or noise.

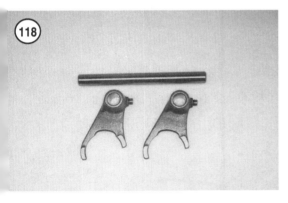

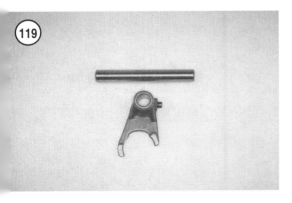

5

    j. Remove the crankcase/crankshaft from the press and place it onto wooden blocks.

5. Install the transmission (the mainshaft, countershaft and reverse shaft) as follows:

    a. Mesh the mainshaft and countershaft assemblies together as shown in **Figure 115**.

    b. Partially lower the two assemblies into the crankcase, but do not completely install them. See **Figure 116**.

NOTE
The needle bearing on the end of the countershaft may fall out of the crankcase after installation. This is not a problem. The bearing can be easily reinstalled once the crankcase halves are bolted together.

    c. While holding the partially installed mainshaft and countershaft assemblies, install the reverse shaft into the crankcase half, and lower the mainshaft and countershaft into place. See **Figure 117**.

NOTE
*The two countershaft shift forks (**Figure 118**) are identical. The mainshaft shift fork (**Figure 119**) rides on the shorter shift fork shaft.*

6. Install the shift forks and shift drum by performing the following:

    a. Insert the mainshaft shift fork into the groove in the mainshaft fifth/third combo gear. The guide pin should face in toward the shift drum bearing; see A, **Figure 120**.

    b. Insert the first countershaft shift fork (B, **Figure 120**) into the groove in the countershaft second gear. The guide pin should face in toward the shift drum bearing.

c. Insert the second countershaft shift fork (C, **Figure 120**) into the groove in the countershaft fourth gear. The guide pin should face in toward the shift drum bearing.

d. Set the shift drum into the bearing in the right crankcase (**Figure 121**).

e. Seat the guide pin of the mainshaft shift fork into the center shift drum groove.

f. Install the short shift shaft through the mainshaft shift fork and into the bushing in the crankcase. See **Figure 122**.

g. Seat the guide pin of each countershaft shift fork into the right (lower) and into the left (upper) shift drum groove respectively. See **Figure 123**.

h. Insert the long shift fork shaft (**Figure 124**) through the two countershaft shift forks and into the bushing in the crankcase half.

i. Make sure both shift fork shafts bottom out in their respective bushings.

NOTE
Perform Step 7 with an assistant because the assemblies do not rotate easily. Have an assistant rotate the transmission shaft while you turn the shift drum through all the gears.

7. Spin the transmission shafts and shift through the gears using the shift drum. Make sure to shift into all the gears, including reverse. This is the time to find a problem with the shifting—not after assembling and installing the crankcase.

8. After confirming that the transmission shifts into all the gears correctly, shift the transmission assembly into neutral.

9. Install the balancer shaft (**Figure 125**) into the right crankcase. Make sure the threaded end faces up, out of the right crankcase half.

10. Apply a light coat of nonhardening liquid gasket sealer, such as Kawasaki Bond (part No. 92104-002) or equivalent, to the groove at the end of each oil breather tube as shown in **Figure 126**.

11. Install the upper oil breather tube (**Figure 127**) and the lower oil breather tube (**Figure 128**) into place in the crankcase. Make sure the groove in each tube is properly seated in the crankcase.

12. Install the two locating dowels (**Figure 129**).

13. Check the left and right crankcase surfaces for old sealant material or other residue.

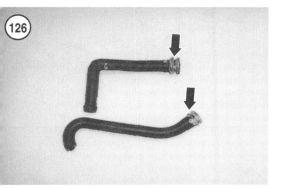

14. Apply a light coat of nonhardening liquid gasket sealer, such as Kawasaki Bond (part No. 92104-002) or equivalent, onto the right crankcase mating surface.

15. Align the left crankcase with the transmissions shafts, the crankshaft and balancer shaft and then install the left crankcase half. Push it down squarely into place until it engages the dowel, and then seat it completely against the right case half.

CAUTION
When properly aligned, the left case will slide over the shafts and seat against the opposite case half. If the crankcase halves do not fit together completely, do not attempt to pull them together with the crankcase bolts. Separate the crankcase halves and investigate the cause of the interference. Check the gears for proper installation. Crankcase halves are matched and must be replaced as a set. They are very expensive. Do not risk damage by trying to force them together.

16. Turn all the exposed transmission shafts, the crankshaft, balancer shaft and shift drum. Each shaft should turn smoothly. If not, determine the cause before continuing with Step 17.

NOTE
Kawasaki does not provide a torque sequence or tightening torque for the crankcase bolts.

17. Install all the crankcase bolts finger-tight. See **Figure 130**.

18. Follow a crisscross pattern, and tighten the crankcase mounting bolts in 2-3 stages. Tighten

each bolt to the general torque specification listed in **Table 5** in Chapter One.

19. Rotate the transmission shafts, balancer shaft, crankshaft and shift drum. Each assembly should turn smoothly. If there is a problem, remove the crankcase mounting bolts and the left crankcase half. Locate and correct the problem.

20. If necessary, turn the engine over so the right side faces up and install the countershaft needle bearing (**Figure 131**).

21. Install all exterior engine assemblies as described in this chapter and other related chapters:
  a. Neutral indicator and the neutral/reverse switch assembly (where applicable).
  b. Reverse cam and reverse lever.
  c. Engine sprocket.
  d. Magneto rotor.
  e. Balancer drive gear.
  f. Left and right balancer.
  g. External shift mechanism.
  h. Kickstarter, kickstarter idler gear and reverse idler gear.
  i. Primary gear and oil pump spur gear.
  j. Oil pump.
  k. Clutch.
  l. Cylinder and piston.
  m. Cylinder head.
  n. Oil filter and oil pipes.

ENGINE BREAK-IN

When replacing top end components or when performing major lower end work, break in the engine as though it were new. The performance and service life of the engine depends greatly on a careful and sensible break-in.

During break-in, oil consumption will be higher than normal. It is important to check and correct the oil level frequently (Chapter Three). Never allow the oil level to drop below the minimum level. If the oil level is low, the oil becomes overheated resulting in insufficient lubrication and increased wear.

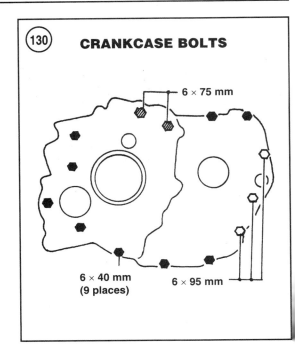

CRANKCASE BOLTS

6 × 75 mm

6 × 40 mm
(9 places)   6 × 95 mm

Kawasaki designates the first 10 hours of vehicle operation as the break-in period. During this period, do not exceed half throttle.

After the break-in period, change the engine oil and filter as described in Chapter Three. It is essential to perform this service to remove all the particles produced during break-in from the lubrication system. The small added expense is a smart investment that will pay off in increased engine life.

Table 1 ENGINE LOWER END SPECIFICATIONS

	Specification	Wear limit
Crankshaft runout		
Right	0.040 mm (0.0016 in.) or less	0.10 mm (0.004 in.)
Left	0.037 mm (0.0015 in.) or less	0.08 mm (0.003 in.)
Connecting rod		
Crankpin side clearance	0.25-0.35 mm (0.010-0.014 in.)	0.6 mm (0.024 in.)
Crankpin radial clearance	0.008-0.020 mm (0.00031-0.00079 in.)	0.07 mm (0.003 in.)
Crankpin-to-crankweb		
clearance (cold)	0.083-0.112 (0.0033-0.0044 in.)	–

5

Table 2 LOWER END TIGHTENING TORQUES

Item	N•m	in.-lb.	ft.-lb.
Engine mounting bolts			
8 mm	25	–	18
10 mm	34	–	25
Engine mounting-bracket bolts		–	
8 mm	25	–	18
10 mm	34	–	25
Swing arm shaft nut	74	–	55
Engine drain bolt	15	–	11
Primary gear nut	59	–	44
Balancer shaft nut	78	–	58
Oil pressure relief valve	15	–	11
Oil pipe banjo bolts	20	–	15
Magneto rotor bolt	93	–	69
Stator mounting bolt	12	106	–
Kick guide bolt	9.8	87	–
Shift-shaft return spring stud	39	–	29

CHAPTER SIX

CLUTCH

This chapter describes service procedures for the following components:

1. Clutch cover.

2. Oil pressure relief valve.

3. Clutch assembly.

4. External shift mechanism.

These components can be removed with the engine installed in the frame.

The clutch is a wet multi-plate type, which operates while immersed in the engine oil. It is mounted on the right end of the transmission mainshaft. The inner clutch hub is splined to the mainshaft, and the outer housing can rotate freely on the mainshaft. The outer housing is geared to the crankshaft. The clutch release mechanism is cable operated and requires routine adjustment that is covered in Chapter Three.

Clutch specifications are listed in **Table 1**, clutch torque specifications in **Table 2**. **Table 1** and **Table 2** are at the end of the chapter.

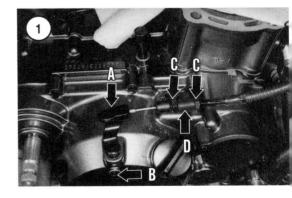

CLUTCH CABLE

Removal

1. Remove the front fender as described in Chapter Fourteen.

2. Loosen the locknuts (C, **Figure 1**) on the lower cable adjuster to create the maximum amount of slack in the cable.

3. At the handlebar, pull the boot back from the clutch lever housing.

4. Loosen the clutch cable locknut (A, **Figure 2**) and screw in the cable adjuster (B, **Figure 2**).

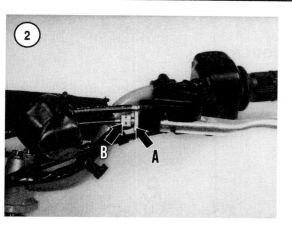

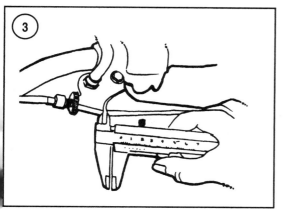

5. Align the slots in the locknut and adjuster with the slot in the lever housing.

6. Disconnect the inner cable end from the clutch lever and remove the cable from the housing.

7. Release the inner cable from the clutch release lever (A, **Figure 1**), and remove the cable from the bracket (D, **Figure 1**) on the clutch cover.

> *NOTE*
> *Attach a length of string to the lower end of the old cable before removing it in the next step. The string will make it easier to correctly install the new cable.*

8. Slowly pull the clutch cable from the motorcycle. Note how the cable is routed along the frame.

Installation

1. Following the path of the old cable, route the new cable along the frame.

2. Fit the cable through the bracket (D, **Figure 1**) on the clutch cover, and connect the inner cable to the clutch release lever (A, **Figure 1**).

3. At the handlebars, align the slots in the cable adjuster, the adjuster locknut and the cable lever housing. Fit the inner cable through the slot and connect it to the clutch lever.

4. Completely loosen the locknuts (C, **Figure 1**) at the clutch release lever.

5. Pull the outer cable until it is tight, and then tighten both locknuts against the bracket.

6. Loosen the locknut (A, **Figure 2**) at the clutch lever and turn the adjuster (B, **Figure 2**) until clutch lever free play is within the specification listed in **Table 1**. See **Figure 3**.

7. Tighten the clutch lever locknut.

8. Install the front fender as described in Chapter Fourteen.

9. Start the engine, and check the operation of the clutch. If further adjustment is required, refer to Chapter Three.

CLUTCH COVER

Removal/Installation

Refer to **Figure 4**

1. Park the vehicle on level ground and set the parking brake.

2. Drain the engine oil and the coolant as described in Chapter Three.

3. Remove the water pump cover (**Figure 5**) and the impeller (**Figure 6**) as described in Chapter Ten.

4. Remove the right footpeg as described in Chapter Fourteen.

5. Loosen the pinch bolt (A, **Figure 7**), and remove the kick pedal from the kick shaft.

6. Disconnect the clutch cable from the clutch release lever (A, **Figure 1**) as described in *Clutch Cable* above in this chapter.

7. Remove the clevis pin (**Figure 8**) that secures the brake pedal to the master cylinder. Separate the clevis from the brake pedal, and press the brake pedal down and out of the way.

8. Remove the twelve clutch cover mounting bolts (**Figure 9**).

9. Rotate the clutch release lever counterclockwise (rearward) approximately 90°, and remove the clutch cover from the crankcase.

6

CLUTCH COVER

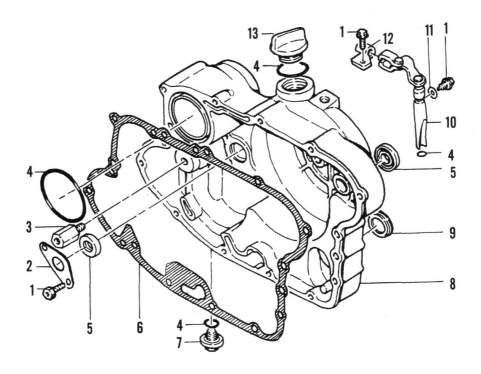

1. Bolt
2. Plate
3. Oil pressure relief valve
   (1988-on)
4. O-ring
5. Oil seal
6. Gasket
7. Oil passage plug
8. Clutch cover
9. Oil level gauge
10. Clutch release lever
11. Washer
12. Clutch cable bracket
13. Oil filler cap

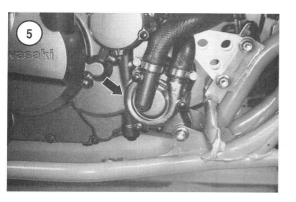

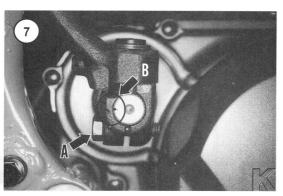

10. Remove the two dowel pins (A, **Figure 10**) and gasket.

11. Service the oil screen (B, **Figure 10**) as described in Chapter Five.

12. Remove all gasket residue from the cover and crankcase gasket surfaces.

13. Inspect the clutch cover as described in this chapter.

14. Installation is the reverse of removal. Pay attention to the following.

   a. Install the two dowels (A, **Figure 10**) and a new clutch cover gasket.

   b. Make sure the oil screen (B, **Figure 10**) is properly seated in the crankcase.

   c. Install the oil filter into its cavity in the clutch cover.

   d. Install the clutch cover and its twelve mounting bolts (**Figure 9**). Tighten the bolts securely.

   e. When installing the kick pedal, make sure the indexing mark on the pedal aligns with the mark on the kick shaft (B, **Figure 7**).

   f. Use a new cotter pin to secure the brake pedal clevis pin (**Figure 8**) in place.

g. Fill the engine with oil, and refill the cooling system as described in Chapter Three.

h. Start the engine and check for leaks.

Inspection

1. Remove and service the oil pressure relief valve (A, **Figure 11**) as described below in this chapter.
2. Inspect the O-ring (B, **Figure 11**) in the oil filter cavity. Replace the O-ring if it is cracked or brittle.
3. Remove the oil passage plug (**Figure 12**) from the bottom of the clutch cover. Blow the oil passage clear with compressed air. Reinstall the plug, and torque it to the specification in **Table 2**.

OIL PRESSURE RELIEF VAVLE

The 1987 Mojave was manufactured without an oil pressure relief valve. A new-style clutch cover-with an oil pressure relief valve-was introduced on 1988 models. The new-style clutch cover fits on 1987 models, and Kawasaki recommends its use on these models.

Consider installing the new-style cover and an oil pressure relief valve on 1987 models.

Removal/Inspection/Installation

1. Remove the clutch cover as described in this chapter.
2. Remove the oil pressure relieve valve (A, **Figure 11**) from the clutch cover.
3. Remove the circlip (**Figure 13**) and disassemble the relief valve. See **Figure 14**.
4. Clean the parts in solvent and dry them thoroughly. Place the parts on a clean, lint-free cloth.
5. Check the ball and the relief valve bore passage for scoring or other damage.
6. Check the washer for cupping or other damage.
7. Check the spring for bending, unequally spaced coils or other damage. If the spring shows any visible damage, the relief valve pressure will be altered.
8. If any parts show wear or damage, replace the oil pressure relief valve assembly.

> *CAUTION*
> *Do not replace any of the internal relief valve components with off-the-shelf items that may appear similar. Doing so may alter the relief*

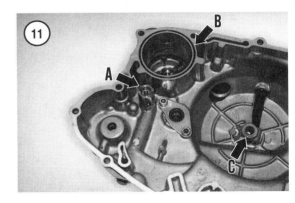

valve pressure and cause engine damage.

9. Coat the relief valve bore, ball, washer and spring with new engine oil. Then reassemble the relief valve in the order shown in **Figure 14**. Make sure the circlip is fully seated in the relief valve groove.

> *CAUTION*
> *Handle, clean and store the relief valve carefully to prevent dirt from entering the valve and scoring the relief valve bore and ball.*

10. Clear the oil passage with compressed air (**Figure 15**).

11. Hand thread the relief valve into the clutch cover (A, **Figure 11**). Then tighten the oil pressure relief valve to the torque specification in **Table 2**.

CLUTCH RELEASE MECHANISM

Refer to **Figure 4** when servicing the clutch release mechanism assembly.

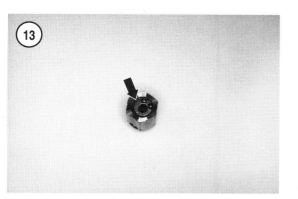

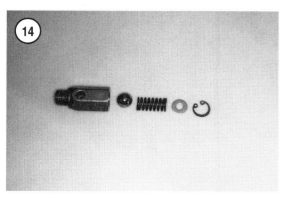

Removal/Installation

> *CAUTION*
> *The clutch release mechanism is located inside the clutch cover. Do not remove the release lever shaft unless absolutely necessary.*

1. Disconnect the clutch cable from the clutch release lever (A, **Figure 1**) as described in this chapter.

2. Remove the clutch-release-shaft bolt (B, **Figure 1**) and washer from the cover.

3. Rotate the release lever counterclockwise (rearward) approximately 90°, and carefully pull the release lever and shaft from the clutch cover.

4. Installation is the reverse of removal. Pay attention to the following:

   a. Apply engine oil to the O-ring and lever shaft.

   b. Carefully insert the release shaft into the clutch cover until the shaft is completely seated in the boss (C, **Figure 11**).

   c. Install the clutch-release-shaft bolt (B, **Figure 1**) and washer. Tighten the bolt securely.

CLUTCH

Removal/Disassembly

Refer to **Figure 16** for this procedure.

1. Remove the clutch cover as described in this chapter.

2. Shift the transmission into gear.

3. Using a crisscross pattern, loosen the five clutch spring bolts (**Figure 17**).

4. Remove the bolts.

5. Remove the clutch springs (A, **Figure 18**) and the pressure plate (B, **Figure 18**). Do not lose the clutch push rod (C, **Figure 18**). It may come out with the pressure plate.

6. If still installed, remove the clutch push rod (A, **Figure 19**), and then remove the friction discs (B, **Figure 19**) and clutch plates.

7. Remove the circlip from the mainshaft (**Figure 20**).

8. Remove the washer (A, **Figure 21**) and the clutch hub (B, **Figure 21**).

9. Remove the clutch housing (**Figure 22**) and the spacer (**Figure 23**) from the mainshaft.

Inspection

Refer to **Table 1** for clutch specifications.

1. Clean all clutch parts in a petroleum-based solvent such as kerosene. Thoroughly dry them with compressed air.

2. Measure the free length of each clutch spring as shown in **Figure 24**. Replace any spring that has sagged to or beyond the service limit in **Table 1**.

3. Measure the thickness of each friction disc at several places around the disc as shown in **Figure 25**. Replace any friction disc that is worn to or beyond the service limit in **Table 1**.

6

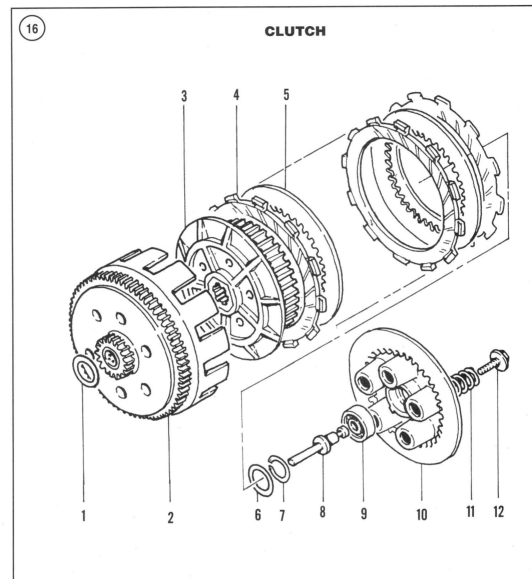

1. Spacer
2. Clutch housing
3. Clutch hub
4. Friction discs
5. Clutch plate
6. Washer
7. Circlip
8. Pushrod
9. Bearing
10. Pressure plate
11. Clutch spring
12. Clutch spring bolt

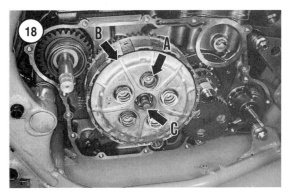

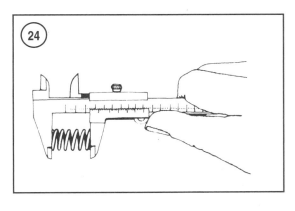

6

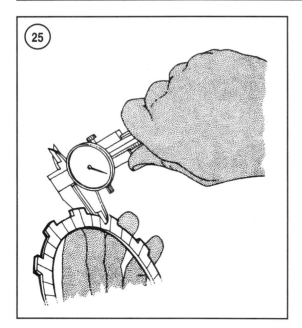

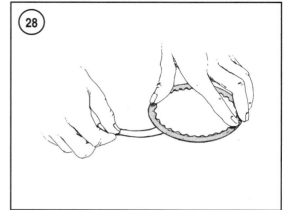

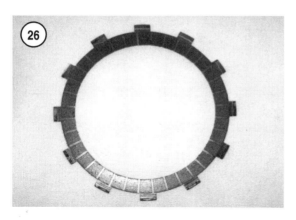

4. Check the friction discs (**Figure 26**) and clutch plates (**Figure 27**) for surface damage from heat or lack of oil. Replace any disc or plate that is damaged in any way.

5. Check each friction disc and the clutch plate for warpage. Use a flat feeler gauge on a surface plate such as a piece of plate glass (**Figure 28**). Replace any disc or plate that is warped to or beyond the service limit in **Table 1**.

> *CAUTION*
> *If any friction disc, clutch plate or clutch spring requires replacement, consider replacing all of them as a set to retain maximum clutch performance.*

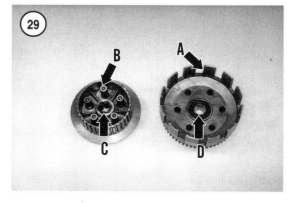

> *CAUTION*
> *When installing new friction discs and clutch plates, apply engine oil to the surfaces of each plate to avoid seizure.*

6. Inspect the slots (A, **Figure 29**) in the clutch housing for cracks, nicks or galling. Pay particular attention to the area where they contact the friction

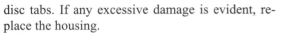

disc tabs. If any excessive damage is evident, re-place the housing.

7. Inspect the teeth (**Figure 30**) of both gears on the clutch housing. Remove any small nicks with an oilstone. If damage is excessive, replace the clutch housing.

8. Inspect the outer grooves (**Figure 31**) and studs (B, **Figure 29**) in the clutch hub. If either shows signs of wear or galling, replace the clutch hub.

9. Inspect the inner splines (C, **Figure 29**) in the clutch hub for damage. Remove any small nicks

with an oilstone. If damage is excessive, replace the clutch hub.

10. Inspect the spring receptacles (**Figure 32**) and inner grooves (A, **Figure 33**) in the clutch pressure plate for wear or damage. Replace the clutch pressure plate if necessary.

11. Check the inner bushing (D, **Figure 29**) of the clutch housing. Look for signs of wear or damage. Replace the clutch housing if necessary.

12. Check the clutch push rod (**Figure 34**) for wear or damage. Replace if necessary.

13. Check the clutch push rod bearing (B, **Figure 33**). Make sure it rotates smoothly with no signs of wear or damage. Replace if necessary.

Assembly/Installation

Refer to **Figure 16** for this procedure.

1. Install the spacer (**Figure 23**) onto the mainshaft.

2. Install the clutch outer housing (**Figure 22**) onto the mainshaft.

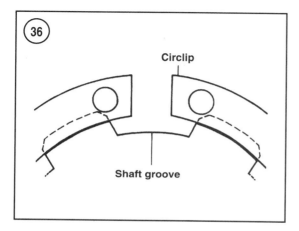

Circlip

Shaft groove

3. Install the clutch hub (B, **Figure 21**) and washer (A, **Figure 21**) onto the mainshaft.

4. Install a new circlip (**Figure 35**). Be sure the circlip is seated in the groove in the mainshaft. Position the circlip so its gap aligns with a groove (**Figure 36**) in the mainshaft.

> *NOTE*
> *The grooves cut into the friction discs radiate at an angle out from the center. Position the friction discs so the groove runs toward the center in the direction of the clutch hub rotation (counterclockwise as viewed from the right side).*

> *NOTE*
> *If installing new friction discs and clutch plates, apply new engine oil to all surfaces to avoid having the clutch lock up when used for the first time.*

5. First install a friction disc (**Figure 37**) onto the clutch hub with the friction disc tangs going into the slots in the clutch housing.

6. Install a clutch plate onto the clutch hub, and then install another friction disc.

7. Continue this process, alternately installing a clutch plate and then a friction disc, until all plates and discs are installed. A friction disc should be installed last (A, **Figure 38**).

8. Apply molybdenum disulfide grease to the clutch push rod, and install the push rod (B, **Figure 38**) into the clutch hub.

9. Install the clutch pressure plate so the arrow on the plate points to the alignment mark on the clutch hub. See **Figure 39**.

10. Install the springs (A, **Figure 18**) and bolts (**Figure 17**).

11. Using a crisscross pattern, tighten the clutch spring bolts to the torque specification listed in **Table 2**.

12. Reinstall clutch cover as described in this chapter.

13. Refill the engine with oil and coolant as described in Chapter Three.

14. Start the engine and warm it up to normal operating temperature. Shift the transmission into first gear and check clutch operation.

Table 1 CLUTCH SPECIFICATIONS

Item	Standard	Wear limit
Clutch type	Wet multi disc	–
Clutch lever free play	2-3 mm (0.08-0.12 in.)	–
Friction disc thickness	2.7-2.9 mm (0.106-0.114 in.)	2.5 mm (0.098in.)
Friction disc warp	0.15 mm (0.006 in.) or less	0.3 mm (0.012 in.)
Clutch plate warp	0.15 mm (0.006 in.) or less	0.3 mm (0.012 in.)
Clutch spring free length	33.6 mm (1.32 in.)	32.3 mm (1.27 in.)
Number of clutch plates		
Friction disc	7	–
Clutch plates	6	–

Table 2 CLUTCH TIGHTENING TORQUES

Item	N•m	in.-lb.	ft.-lb.
Clutch spring bolt	9.8	87	–
Oil pressure relief valve			
1988-on	15	–	11
Oil passage plug	15	–	11

CHAPTER SEVEN

TRANSMISSION AND GEARSHIFT MECHANISM

The transmission provides five forward speeds and one reverse speed. To gain access to the transmission and internal shift mechanism, it is necessary to remove the engine and split the crankcase (Chapter Five).

Drive train general specifications are listed in **Table 1** while drive train service specifications appear in **Table 2**. Transmission torque specifications are in **Table 3**. **Tables 1-3** are at the end of this chapter.

This chapter covers the transmission components; including the internal, external and reverse shift mechanisms.

EXTERNAL SHIFT MECHANISM

The external shift mechanism is located on the right side of the crankcase. It can be removed with the engine in the frame. It is necessary to remove the engine and split the crankcase to remove the shift drum and shift forks (see Chapter Five).

Removal

Refer to **Figure 1** for this procedure.

1. Remove the clutch assembly as described in Chapter Six.

2. If necessary, use a punch to make indexing marks on the shift shaft and on the shift pedal so the pedal can be installed in the same position.

3. Loosen the pinch bolt, and remove the shift pedal from the left side of the vehicle. See **Figure 2**.

4. Press the shift pawl (A, **Figure 3**) toward the shift shaft so the pawl clears the shift cam, and pull the shift shaft assembly from the crankcase.

5. Remove the stopper lever bolt (A, **Figure 4**), and then the stopper lever (B, **Figure 4**) and the spring.

6. If splitting the crankcase, remove the shift cam by perform the following:

   a. Remove the bolt (A, **Figure 5**) and remove the shift cam (B, **Figure 5**).

   b. Remove the pin (**Figure 6**) from the shift drum.

Inspection

Refer to **Figure 1** for this procedure.

1. Clean all parts in solvent and dry them thoroughly.

1

EXTERNAL SHIFT MECHANISM

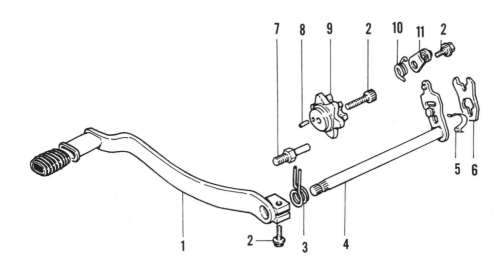

1. Shift pedal
2. Bolt
3. Shift shaft return spring
4. Shift shaft
5. Shift pawl spring
6. Shift pawl
7. Return spring stud
8. Pin
9. Shift cam
10. Stopper lever spring
11. Stopper lever

7

2

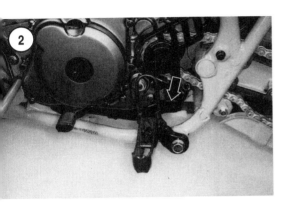

3

2. Check the shift shaft (A, **Figure 7**) for cracks or bending. Check the splines on the end of the shaft for damage.

3. Inspect the shift shaft return spring (B, **Figure 7**) and the shift pawl spring (C, **Figure 7**) for weakness or distortion. Replace either spring as necessary.

4. Check the shift pawl (D, **Figure 7**) for wear or signs of damage. Replace the shift pawl if necessary.

5. Check the stopper lever assembly for the following:

    a. Weak or damaged spring (A, **Figure 8**).

    b. Bent or damaged stopper lever and roller (B, **Figure 8**).

    c. Damaged bolt threads or shoulder.

    d. Replace damaged parts as necessary.

6. Inspect the shift cam (**Figure 9**) for excessive wear or other damage. Replace the shift cam if necessary.

7. Be sure the return spring stud (C, **Figure 5**) is secure in the crankcase. If it is loose, remove and reinstall the stud. Apply Loctite 242 (blue) to the stud threads, and torque the stud to the specification in **Table 3**.

Installation

1. If removed, install the shift cam by performing the following:

    a. Install the pin (A, **Figure 6**) into the shift drum.

    b. Fit the shift cam onto the shift drum so the hole in the shift cam engages the pin in the drum.

    c. Install the shift cam bolt (A, **Figure 5**). Apply Loctite 242 (blue) to the bolt threads, and tighten the shift cam bolt to the torque specification in **Table 3**.

2. Fit the stopper lever spring onto the stopper lever. Be sure the spring tang hooks over the lever as shown in **Figure 10**.

3. Fit the stopper lever/spring assembly into place in the crankcase. Make sure the long spring tang engages the boss (D, **Figure 5**) in the crankcase. Tighten the stopper lever bolt securely. Then move the stopper lever by hand, making sure it can move freely. The stopper lever roller should contact the shift cam as shown in B, **Figure 4**.

4. Slide the shift shaft into the crankcase. The shift pawl (A, **Figure 3**) should engage the shift cam and

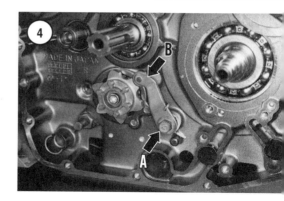

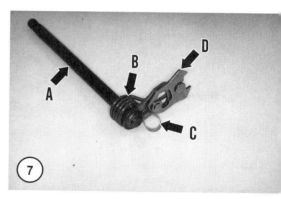

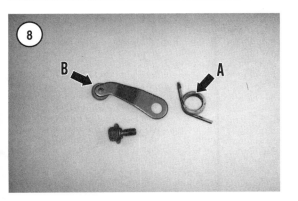

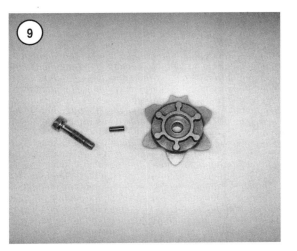

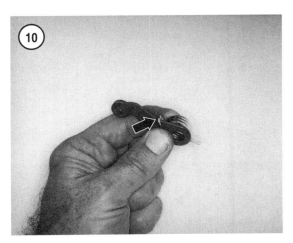

REVERSE MECHANISM COVER

Removal/Installation

1. Remove the left footpeg as described in Chapter Fourteen

2. If necessary, use a punch to make indexing marks on the shift shaft and on the shift pedal. That way the pedal can be reinstalled in the same position.

3. Loosen the pinch bolt and remove the shift pedal (**Figure 2**) from the shift shaft.

4. Remove the engine sprocket cover as described in Chapter Twelve.

5. Remove the mounting bolt (A, **Figure 11**) and the neutral indicator (B, **Figure 11**) from the end of the shift drum shaft.

6. Remove the five cover bolts (**Figure 12**), and remove the reverse mechanism cover. Do not lose the washer from the end of the reverse lever shaft (**Figure 13**). It may come out with the cover.

the arms of the shift-shaft return spring should straddle the return spring stud (B, **Figure 3**).

5. Install the shift pedal and secure it with its pinch bolt. Align the marks made prior to removal.

6. Install the clutch as described in Chapter Six.

7. Remove the two dowels (**Figure 14**) from the crankcase.

8. Remove the reverse-cover gasket.

9. Installation is the reverse of removal. Note the following:

   a. Inspect the seal in the cover (**Figure 15**). If necessary, replace the seal. Follow the procedure described in Chapter One.

   b. Make sure the two dowels (**Figure 14**) are in place in the crankcase.

   c. Apply silicon sealant to the outside face of the reverse cable grommet (C, **Figure 16**) and the neutral/reverse cable grommet (B, **Figure 16**; 1990-on), and then fit a new gasket in place.

   d. If removed, install the washer onto the end of the reverse lever shaft (**Figure 13**).

   e. Align the indexing marks when installing the shift pedal.

REVERSE MECHANISM

Refer to **Figure 17** when servicing the reverse mechanism.

Removal/Installation

1. Remove the reverse mechanism cover as described in this chapter.

2A. On 1987-1989 models, perform the following:

   a. Remove the circlip from the shift drum shaft.

   b. Slide the reverse cam (**Figure 18**) off the shift drum shaft.

   c. Remove the pin (**Figure 19**) from the shaft.

2B. On 1990-on models, perform the following:

   a. Remove the two mounting screws and the neutral/reverse switch (A, **Figure 16**) from the shift drum shaft.

   b. Remove the neutral/reverse switch grommet (B, **Figure 16**) from the crankcase, and tuck the switch safely out of the way.

   c. Slide the reverse cam (**Figure 18**) off the shift drum shaft.

   d. Remove the pin (**Figure 19**) from the shaft.

3. Remove the bolt and remove the reverse cable holder (A, **Figure 20**) from the crankcase.

4. Rotate the reverse lever forward to create some free play in the cable, and disconnect the reverse cable end (B, **Figure 20**) from the reverse lever.

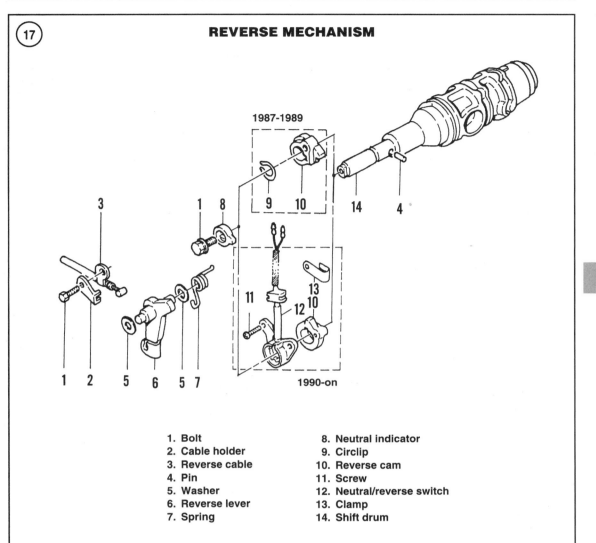

REVERSE MECHANISM

1987-1989

1990-on

1. Bolt
2. Cable holder
3. Reverse cable
4. Pin
5. Washer
6. Reverse lever
7. Spring
8. Neutral indicator
9. Circlip
10. Reverse cam
11. Screw
12. Neutral/reverse switch
13. Clamp
14. Shift drum

7

5. Pull the cable grommet from the crankcase, and remove the reverse cable. See **Figure 21**.

6. Remove the washer from the shift lever shaft (**Figure 13**).

7. Remove the reverse lever, spring and washer from the crankcase.

8. Inspect the parts as described below.

9. Installation is the reverse of removal. Note the following:

   a. Install the spring onto the reverse lever so the tang hooks over the lever as shown in **Figure 22**. Slide a washer against the spring, and apply molybdenum disulfide to the lever shaft.

   b. Fit the reverse lever (A, **Figure 23**) into the boss in the crankcase so the free spring tang fits into the hole (B, **Figure 23**) in the crankcase. Install the second washer onto the reverse lever shaft (**Figure 13**).

   c. Apply molybdenum disulfide grease to the end of the reverse cable, and connect the cable to the reverse lever.

   d. Make sure the reverse cam engages the pin in the shift drum shaft.

   e. On 1990-on models, apply Loctite 242 (blue) to the threads of the securing screws when reinstalling the neutral/reverse switch.

Inspection

1. Clean the parts in solvent, and thoroughly dry them with compressed air.

2. Inspect the reverse lever (A, **Figure 24**) for signs of damage. Replace the shaft if necessary.

3. Inspect the reverse lever spring (B, **Figure 24**) for fatigue or other signs of distortion. Replace the spring if necessary.

4. Inspect the reverse cam and its pin for signs of damage (**Figure 25**). Replace them as necessary.

REVERSE CABLE

All Mojaves are equipped with five forward gears and one reverse gear. Neutral is located between first and second gear. Reverse gear is adjacent to first gear. See the shift pattern decal on the vehicle or refer to **Figure 26**.

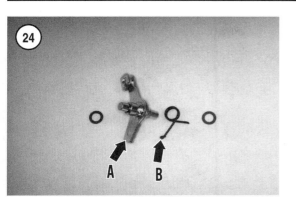

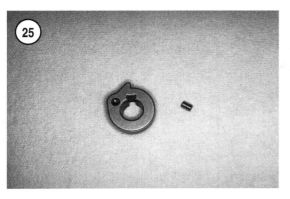

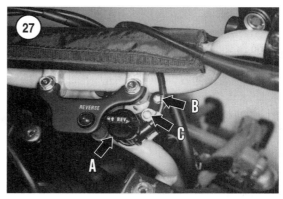

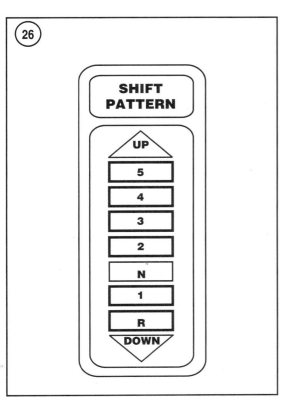

SHIFT
PATTERN

UP

5

4

3

2

N

1

R

DOWN

Reverse Operation

To shift the transmission in and out of reverse, perform the following.

1. Start the engine and let it idle. If the engine is cold, warm it up to normal operating temperature.

> *WARNING*
> *Improper use of the reverse system can cause an accident and possible injury to yourself and to people near the vehicle. Observe all of the WARNING labels affixed to the vehicle and to the information listed in the Owners Manual.*

2. To shift into reverse, perform the following:
   a. Shift transmission into NEUTRAL.
   b. Stop the vehicle and let the engine idle.
   c. Pull the clutch lever to the handlebar and press the shift pedal down and into first gear.
   d. Turn the reverse knob (A, **Figure 27**) clockwise while pressing the shift pedal down and into reverse. Then release the reverse knob and the shift pedal.
   e. The vehicle can now be operated in reverse gear.
3. To shift out of reverse, perform the following:
   a. Stop the vehicle and let the engine idle.
   b. Pull in the clutch lever, lift the shift pedal up and shift the transmission into first gear.
   c. The vehicle can now be operated in the forward gears.

Reverse Cable Replacement

1. Shift the transmission into NEUTRAL.

2. Remove the front fender as described in Chapter Fourteen. Note how the reverse cable is routed through the frame. The new cable must be routed along the same path.

3. Remove the reverse mechanism cover as described in this chapter.

4. Remove the bolt and the cable holder (A, **Figure 20**) from the crankcase.

5. Rotate the reverse lever forward to create some free play in the cable, and disconnect the reverse cable end (B, **Figure 20**) from the reverse lever.

6. Pull the cable grommet from the crankcase, and remove the reverse cable. See **Figure 21**.

7. At the handlebar, loosen the reverse cable mounting bolt (B, **Figure 27**) and the cable holder bolt (C, **Figure 27**). Remove the reverse knob assembly from the bracket on the steering head.

8. Remove the cover (**Figure 28**) from the bottom of the reverse knob housing.

9. Remove the screw from the pulley (**Figure 29**) in the housing and remove the reverse knob (**Figure 30**).

10. Push the pulley (A, **Figure 31**) from the housing. Do not lose the spring (B, **Figure 31**) from the housing.

11. Disconnect the cable end from the pulley, and pull the cable end from the reverse knob housing.

12. Check that the cable is free from the frame, and remove the cable.

13. Installation is the reverse of removal. Note the following:

    a. Lubricate the new cable as described in Chapter Three.

    b. Route the new cable along the same path as the old cable.

    c. Apply molybdenum disulfide grease to the lower cable end before connecting it to the reverse lever See **Figure 21**.

    d. Insert the upper cable end into the reverse knob housing and connect it to the reel. See **Figure 31**.

    e. When installing the pulley into the reverse knob housing, make sure the spring tang (B, **Figure 31**) engages the square notch in the pulley.

14. Adjust the reverse knob free play as described in Chapter Three.

15. Check reverse operation as described in this chapter.

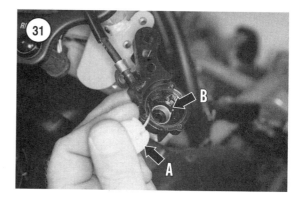

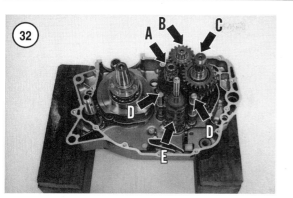

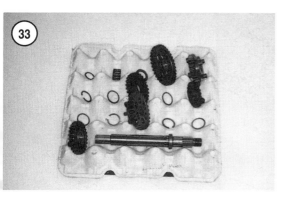

TRANSMISSION TROUBLESHOOTING

Refer to Chapter Two.

TRANSMISSION/INTERNAL SHIFT MECHANISM OVERHAUL

Removal/Installation

The transmission consists of the following three assemblies:

1. Mainshaft (A, **Figure 32**).
2. Reverse shaft (B).
3. Countershaft (C).

The internal shaft mechanism consists of these two assemblies:

1. Shift forks and shafts (D, **Figure 32**).
2. Shift drum (E).

Follow the *Crankcase Disassembly* and *Crankcase Assembly* procedure described in Chapter Five to remove and install the transmission and internal shift assemblies. The procedures for overhauling these assemblies are described in this chapter.

Transmission Service Notes

1. Use a divided container such as an egg carton to help maintain correct alignment and position of the parts while removing them from the transmission and reverse shafts. See **Figure 33**.
2. The circlips fit tightly on the transmission shafts. Remove and replace all circlips during disassembly.
3. Circlips will turn and fold over, making removal and installation difficult. To ease removal, open the circlip with a pair of circlip pliers while holding the back of the circlip with a pair of pliers. See **Figure 34**.

Mainshaft Disassembly/Assembly

Refer to **Figure 35** and **Figure 36** for this procedure.

1. Clean the assembled mainshaft in solvent. Dry it with compressed air or set it on rags to drip dry.
2. Remove the circlip, needle bearing and flat washer.
3. Remove the circlip and slotted washer.
4. Slide off second gear.
5. Remove the slotted washer and circlip.
6. Slide off the fifth/third combination gear.
7. Remove the circlip and flat washer.
8. Slide off fourth gear.

> *NOTE*
> *First gear (**Figure 37**) is an integral part of the mainshaft.*

9. Inspect the mainshaft assembly as described in this chapter.
10. Install fourth gear (**Figure 38**) with its gear dogs facing away from first gear.
11. Install the flat washer and new circlip (**Figure 39**). Install the circlip so its flat side faces away

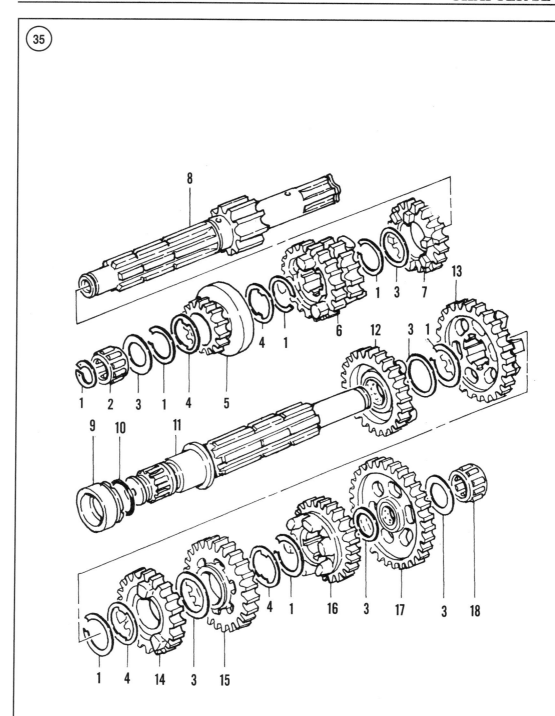

㉟

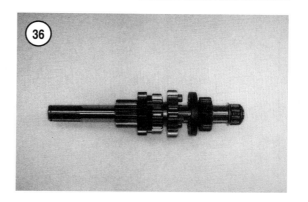

TRANSMISSION

1. Circlip
2. Needle bearing
3. Flat washer
4. Slotted washer
5. Mainshaft second gear
6. Mainshaft fifth/third combination gear
7. Mainshaft fourth gear
8. Mainshaft/first gear
9. Collar
10. O-ring
11. Countershaft
12. Reverse gear
13. Countershaft second gear
14. Countershaft fifth gear
15. Countershaft third gear
16. Countershaft fourth gear
17. Countershaft first gear
18. Needle bearing

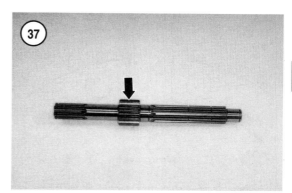

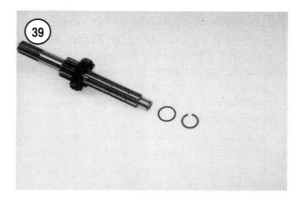

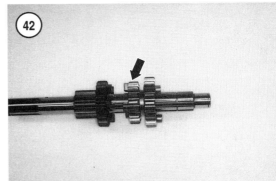

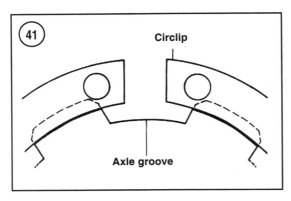

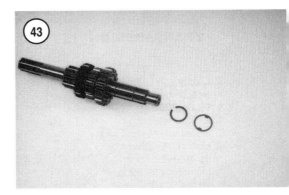

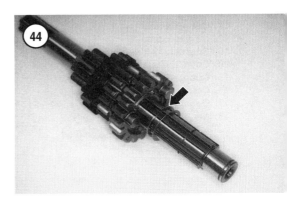

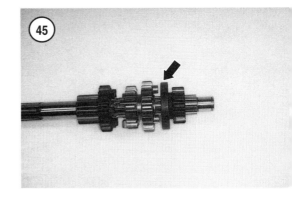

from fourth gear, and seat the circlip in the groove next to fourth gear (**Figure 40**). Position the circlip so that its gap aligns with a shaft groove (**Figure 41**).

12. Install the fifth/third combination gear with third gear (the smaller gear) facing fourth gear; see **Figure 42**.

13. Install a new circlip and slotted washer (**Figure 43**) with their flat sides facing out away from fifth/third combination gear. Seat the circlip in the groove shown in **Figure 44**. Position the circlip so its gap aligns with a shaft groove (**Figure 41**).

14. Install second gear (**Figure 45**) with its dog engagement slots facing fifth gear.

15. Install the slotted washer (A, **Figure 46**) and new circlip (B, **Figure 46**) so their flat sides face away from second gear. Seat the circlip in the groove next to second gear (A, **Figure 47**), and position the circlip so that its gap aligns with a shaft groove (**Figure 41**).

16. Install the flat washer (C, **Figure 46**) onto the mainshaft. See B, **Figure 47**.

17. Install the needle bearing and new circlip (**Figure 48**). Make sure the flat side of the circlip faces

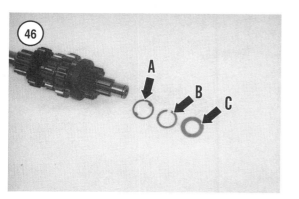

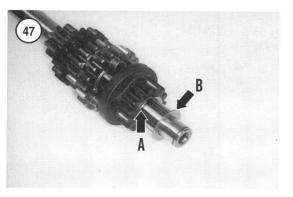

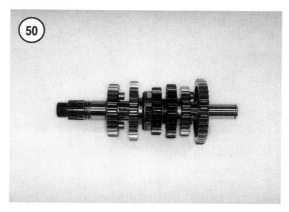

out away from the needle bearing, and seat the circlip (**Figure 49**) in the groove next to the bearing.

18. Refer to **Figure 36** for the correct placement of the mainshaft gears.

Countershaft Disassembly/Assembly

Refer to **Figure 35** and **Figure 50** for this procedure.

1. Clean the assembled countershaft in solvent. Dry it with compressed air or set it on rags to drip dry.
2. Remove the needle bearing (if still in place) and the flat washer.
3. Slide off first gear.
4. Remove the flat washer.
5. Slide off fourth gear.
6. Remove the circlip and slotted washer.
7. Slide off third gear.
8. Remove the flat washer.
9. Slide off fifth gear.
10. Remove the slotted washer and circlip.
11. Slide off second gear.
12. Remove the circlip and flat washer.
13. Slide off reverse gear.
14. Inspect the countershaft assembly as described in this chapter.
15. Install reverse gear (**Figure 51**) with its gear dogs facing away from the shoulder on the countershaft.

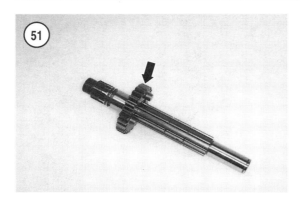

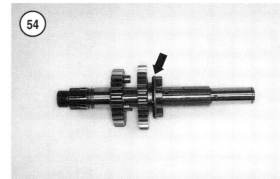

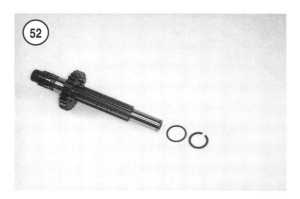

16. Install the flat washer and new circlip (**Figure 52**). Install the circlip so its flat side faces toward reverse gear. Seat the circlip in the groove next to reverse gear (**Figure 53**), and position the circlip so that its gap aligns with a shaft groove (**Figure 41**).

17. Install second gear (**Figure 54**) with its gear dogs facing away from reverse gear.

18. Install a new circlip and slotted washer (**Figure 55**) so their flat sides face in toward second gear. Seat the circlip in the groove as shown in **Figure 56**.

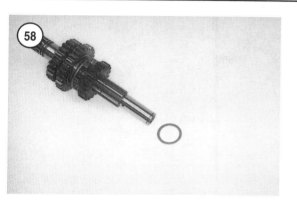

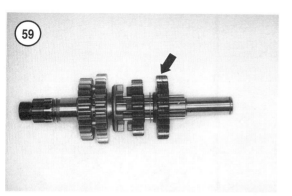

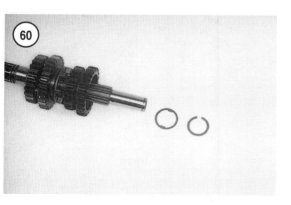

Position the circlip so its gap aligns with a shaft groove (**Figure 41**).

19. Install fifth gear (**Figure 57**) with its gear dogs facing in toward second gear.

20. Install the flat washer (**Figure 58**) and seat it next to fifth gear.

21. Install third gear (**Figure 59**) with its shoulder facing fifth gear.

22. Install the slotted washer and new circlip (**Figure 60**). Make sure the flat side of the circlip faces in toward third gear. Seat the circlip in the groove next to third gear (**Figure 61**), and position the circlip so its gap aligns with a shaft groove (**Figure 41**).

23. Install fourth gear (**Figure 62**) with its shift fork groove facing in toward third gear.

24. Install the flat washer (**Figure 63**).

25. Install first gear (**Figure 64**) so its chamfered side faces out away from fourth gear.

26. Install the flat washer (**Figure 65**). Be sure the flat side faces in toward first gear.

27. Refer to **Figure 50** for the correct placement of the countershaft gears.

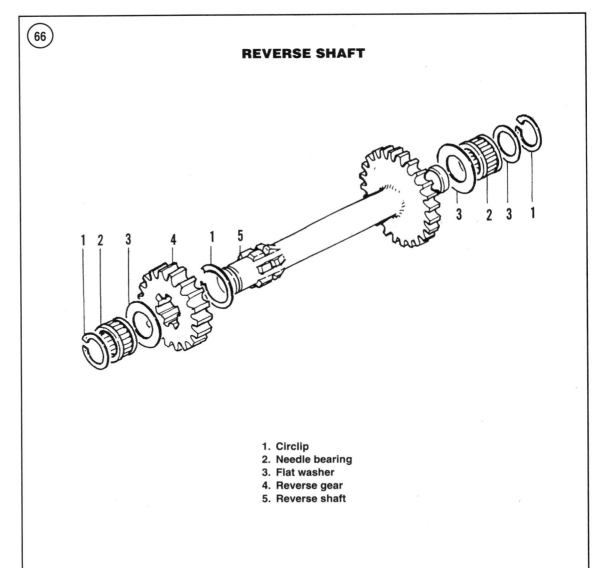

REVERSE SHAFT

1. Circlip
2. Needle bearing
3. Flat washer
4. Reverse gear
5. Reverse shaft

219

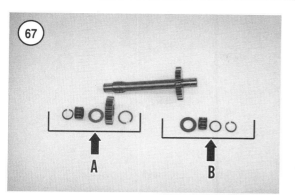

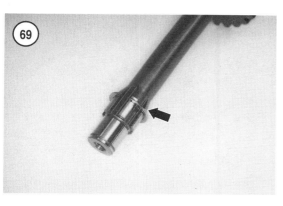

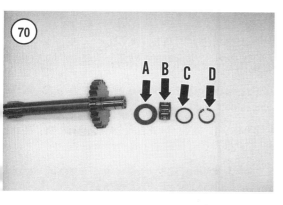

REVERSE SHAFT

The reverse shaft assembly is shown in **Figure 66**.

Removal/Installation

Remove and install the reverse shaft as described in *Crankcase Disassembly* and *Crankcase Assembly* in Chapter Five.

Disassembly/Reassembly

> *NOTE*
> *The parts in the outer left (A, **Figure 67**) and right needle bearing assemblies (B, **Figure 67**) are not interchangeable. The inner circlip on the left assembly is larger than the outer circlip. On the right assembly, the inner washer is larger than the outer washer. Keep the parts separate and properly ordered. They must be reinstalled in the reverse order in which they were removed.*

1. From the left side of the reverse shaft (A, **Figure 67**), remove the following parts in the stated order:
   a. Outer circlip (D, **Figure 68**), needle bearing (C, **Figure 68**) and flat washer (B, **Figure 68**).
   b. Reverse gear (A, **Figure 68**).
   c. The inner circlip (**Figure 69**).
2. From the right side of the reverse shaft, remove the following parts in the stated order:
   a. The circlip (D, **Figure 70**).
   b. The outer flat washer (C, **Figure 70**).
   c. The needle bearing (B, **Figure 70**).
   d. The inner washer (A, **Figure 70**).
3. Inspect the reverse shaft and gears as described in *Transmission Inspection* in this chapter.
4. To assemble the left side reverse shaft:
   a. Install a new inner circlip into the reverse shaft groove (**Figure 69**).
   b. Install the reverse gear (A, **Figure 68**).
   c. Install the flat washer (B, **Figure 68**, 17.3 × 28 × 1.0 mm).
   d. Install the needle bearing (C, **Figure 68**) and a new outer circlip (D, **Figure 68**).
5. To assemble the right side reverse shaft:

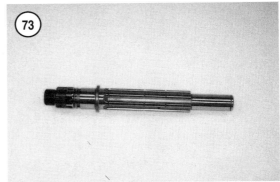

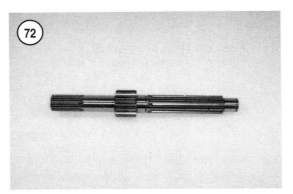

a. Install the inner washer (A, **Figure 70**, 17.3 × 30 × 0.5 mm).

b. Install the needle bearing (B, **Figure 70**) and outer washer (C, **Figure 70**, 17.3 × 22 × 0.5 mm).

c. Install a new circlip (D, **Figure 70**). Make sure the circlip is properly seated in the groove next to the needle bearing.

NOTE
Figure 71 shows a properly assembled reverse shaft.

TRANSMISSION INSPECTION

NOTE
Maintain the relative alignment of the various parts in each assembly while cleaning, drying and inspecting them. This will facilitate reassembly.

1. Clean all parts in solvent. Dry them with compressed air.

2. Check all shaft splines for wear, cracks or other damage. Identify the transmission shafts as follows:

a. Mainshaft (**Figure 72**).

b. Countershaft (**Figure 73**).

c. Reverse shaft (**Figure 74**).

3. Check the mainshaft first gear (**Figure 72**). If the gear is damaged, replace mainshaft.

4. Check the reverse shaft gear (**Figure 74**). If the gear is damaged, replace the reverse shaft.

5. Check each gear for excessive wear, burrs, pitting, or chipped or missing teeth.

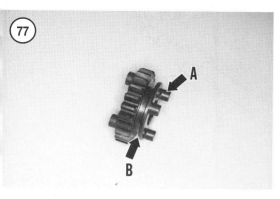

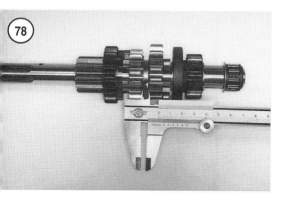

6. Check each stationary gear bore (**Figure 75**) and sliding gear splines (**Figure 76**) for scoring, cracks or other damage.

7. Check the gear dogs (A, **Figure 77**) for excessive wear or damage.

8. Check the shift fork groove (B, **Figure 77**) in each sliding gear for wear, cracks or other damage.

9. Measure the width of each shift fork groove (**Figure 78**) with a vernier caliper. Replace any gear that has a shift fork groove that is worn beyond the service limit in **Table 2**.

10. Make sure all gears slide or turn on their respective shafts smoothly.

NOTE
Replace defective gears. It is recommended to replace the mating gear even though it may not show as much wear or damage.

11. Check needle bearings (**Figure 79**) for excessive wear or damage.

12. Replace all circlips during assembly. In addition, check the washers for burn marks, scoring or cracks. Replace washers as necessary.

INTERNAL SHIFT MECHANISM

The internal shift mechanism consists of the shift drum, shift forks, and shift-fork shafts (**Figure 80**).

Removal/Installation

Remove and install these components as described in *Crankcase Disassembly and Crankcase Assembly* in Chapter Five.

Inspection

Refer to **Figure 80** for this procedure.

1. Clean all parts in solvent and dry them thoroughly.

2. Check the grooves in the shift drum (**Figure 81**) for wear or roughness.

3. Measure the width of each shift drum groove with a vernier caliper (**Figure 82**). Replace the shift drum if any groove is worn beyond the service limit in **Table 2**.

4. Inspect each shift fork (**Figure 83**) for excessive wear or damage. Examine the shift forks at the

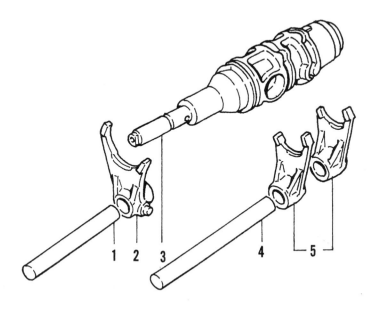

INTERNAL SHIFT MECHANISM

1. Mainshaft shift-fork shaft
2. Mainshaft shift fork
3. Shift drum
4. Countershaft shift-fork shaft
5. Countershaft shift fork

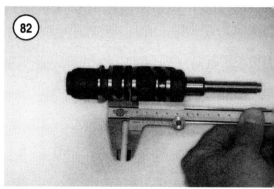

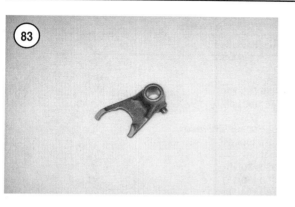

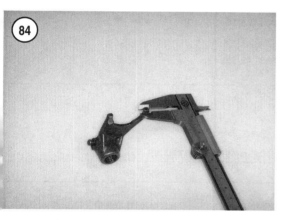

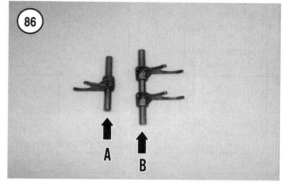

points where they contact the gear. This surface should be smooth with no signs of wear or damage.

5. Check for any arc-shaped wear or burn marks on the fingers of the shift fork. This indicates that the shift fork has excessive contact with the gear. If the shift fork fingers are excessively worn, replace the shift fork.

6. Measure the shift fork finger thickness at the gear contact point (**Figure 84**), and compare the measurement to the specification in **Table 2**. Replace the shift fork if a finger is excessively worn.

7. Measure the shift fork guide pin diameter (**Figure 85**). Replace the shift fork if the guide pin is worn beyond the service limit in **Table 2**.

NOTE
The countershaft shift forks are identical. They ride on the countershaft shift-fork shaft (B, Figure 86), which is the longer of the two shafts.

8. Visually inspect each shift fork shaft for bending or other damage. Check that each shift fork sits at a 90° angle on its respective shaft and that it slides smoothly along the shaft; see **Figure 86**.

9. Replace all worn or damaged parts.

Tables 1-3 are on the following pages.

Table 1 DRIVE TRAIN SPECIFICATIONS

Item	Specifications
Primary reduction system	
Type	Gea
Reduction ratio	3.050 (61/20)
Clutch type	Wet multi disc
Transmission	
Type	5-speed plus reverse,
	constant mesh, return shift
Gear ratios	
First gear	3.000 (30/10)
Second gear	2.000 (30/15)
Third gear	1.500 (24/16)
Fourth gear	1.250 (25/20)
Fifth gear	1.050 (21/20)
Reverse	2.933 (24/18 x 22/10)
Final drive system	
Type	Chain
Reduction ration	3.583 (43/12)
Overall drive ratio	11.475 in top gear

Table 2 DRIVE TRAIN SERVICE SPECIFICATIONS

Item	Specification	Wear limit
Reverse knob free play	2-3 mm (0.08-0.12 in.)	–
Shift fork finger thickness	4.4-4.5 mm (0.173-0.177 in.)	4.3 mm (0.169 in.)
Sliding gear shift fork		
groove width	4.55-4.65 mm (0.179-0.183 in.)	4.75 mm (0.187 in.)
Shift fork guide pin diameter	5.9-6.0 mm (0.232-0.236 in.)	5.8 mm (0.228 in.)
Shift drum groove width	6.05-6.20 mm (0.238-0.242 in.)	6.3 mm (0.248 in.)

Table 3 TRANSMISSION TIGHTENING TORQUE

Item	N•m	in.-lb.	ft.-lb.
Shift cam bolt	12	106	–
Return spring stud	39	–	29

FUEL AND EXHAUST SYSTEMS

8

This chapter includes service procedures for the fuel, intake and exhaust systems. The fuel system consists of the fuel tank, fuel valve, a single carburetor and air filter. The exhaust system consists of an exhaust pipe and muffler assembly. Air filter service is covered in Chapter Three.

Table 1 lists carburetor specifications while **Table 2** lists fuel system torque specifications. **Table 1** and **Table 2** are at the end of this chapter.

> *WARNING*
> *Gasoline is a known carcinogen as well as being extremely flammable. It must be handled carefully. Wear latex gloves when working on any part of the fuel system. If gasoline gets on the skin, rinse it off immediately, and thoroughly wash the area with soap and warm water.*

CARBURETOR OPERATION

The carburetor atomizes fuel and mixes it in correct proportions with air that is drawn in through the air intake. At the primary throttle opening (idle), a small amount of fuel is siphoned through the pilot jet by the incoming air. As the throttle is opened further, the air stream begins to siphon fuel through the main jet and needle jet. The tapered needle increases the effective flow capacity of the needle jet as it is lifted, in that it occupies progressively less area in the jet. At full throttle, the carburetor venturi is fully open and the needle is lifted far enough to permit the main jet to flow at full capacity.

The choke circuit is actually an enrichment system in which the choke lever opens a valve rather than closing the butterfly in the venturi area as on many carburetors. In the open position, the slow jet discharges a stream of fuel into the carburetor venturi, which richens the mixture.

CARBURETOR

Removal/Installation

1. Place the vehicle on level ground and set the parking brake.
2. Remove the front and rear fenders as described in Chapter Fourteen.
3. Remove the fuel tank as described in this chapter.

4. Remove the snorkel duct and air filter housing as described in this chapter.

5. Loosen the two throttle cable locknuts (**Figure 1**) at the carburetor bracket. Remove the cable from the bracket, and disconnect the cable end from the throttle lever. Position the throttle cable along the upper frame rail to prevent cable damage.

6. Remove the breather hose (A, **Figure 2**), and the overflow hose (B, **Figure 2**).

7. Loosen the screw (A, **Figure 3**) on the intake manifold clamp.

8. Slide the carburetor rearward to free it from the intake manifold, and then remove the carburetor from the surge tank duct (B, **Figure 3**).

9. Unscrew the starter plunger cap (**Figure 4**), and pull the starter plunger from the carburetor.

10. Cover the intake manifold and surge tank duct openings to prevent the entry of foreign matter.

11. Drain all gas from the carburetor float bowl before storing or working on the carburetor.

12. Install by reversing these removal steps. Adjust the idle speed and throttle lever free play as described in Chapter Three.

Disassembly

Refer to **Figure 5** when disassembling the carburetor.

1. Remove the carburetor as described in this chapter.

2. If still attached, disconnect the fuel hose and breather hose from the carburetor, noting their placement for assembly.

3. Remove the vacuum piston and jet needle by performing the following:

   a. Remove the cover screws and vacuum piston cover (A, **Figure 6**) from the top of the carburetor.

   b. Remove the spring (B, **Figure 6**) from the vacuum piston and remove the vacuum piston (**Figure 7**) from the carburetor body.

   c. Remove the spring seat (A, **Figure 8**) from the vacuum piston.

   d. Slide the jet needle (B, **Figure 8**) out of the vacuum piston.

4. Remove the pilot air screw by performing the following:

   a. Screw in the pilot air screw until it lightly seats, counting the number of turns so it can be reinstalled in the same position.

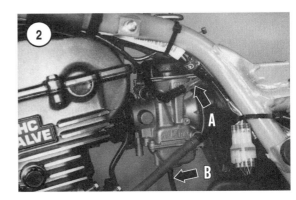

CARBURETOR

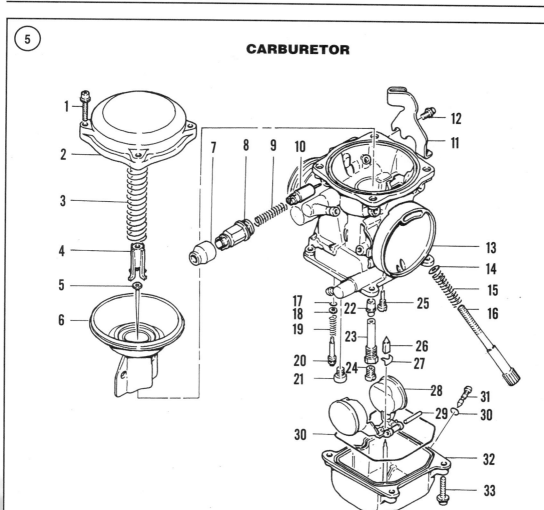

1. Screw
2. Cover
3. Spring
4. Spring seat
5. Jet needle
6. Vacuum piston
7. Boot
8. Cap
9. Spring
10. Starter plunger
11. Throttle cable bracket
12. Screw
13. Carburetor body
14. Washer
15. Spring
16. Idle speed screw
17. O-ring
18. Washer
19. Spring
20. Pilot air screw
21. Starter jet
22. Needle jet
23. Needle jet holder
24. Main jet
25. Pilot jet
26. Float valve
27. Clip
28. Float
29. Float pin
30. O-ring
31. Drain screw
32. Float bowl
33. Screw

8

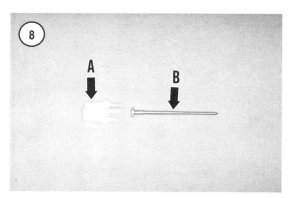

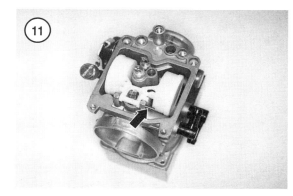

    b. Unscrew the pilot air screw (**Figure 9**), and
remove it.

5. Unscrew the four float bowl screws (**Figure 10**),
and lift the float bowl from the carburetor body.

6. Remove the float pin (**Figure 11**) from the posts
in the float bowl.

7. Lift the float (A, **Figure 12**) and needle valve (B,
Figure 12) from the carburetor.

8. Unscrew and remove the starter jet (**Figure 13**).

9. Unscrew and remove the pilot jet (**Figure 14**).

10. Unscrew and remove the main jet (**Figure 15**).

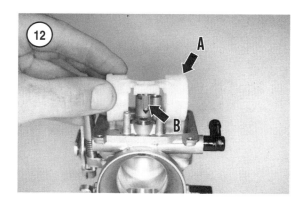

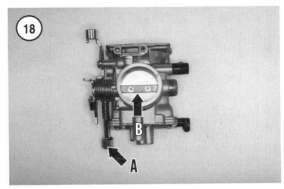

8

11. Unscrew and remove the needle jet holder (**Figure 16**).

12. From inside the carburetor bore, push the needle jet down, and remove it from the carburetor housing (**Figure 17**).

13. If necessary, unscrew and remove the idle speed screw (A, **Figure 18**).

NOTE
*Further disassembly is neither necessary nor recommended. Do not remove the throttle shaft and butterfly assembly (B, **Figure 18**). If these parts are damaged, the carburetor must be replaced because items are not available separately.*

14. Clean and inspect all parts as described in this chapter.

Cleaning and Inspection

CAUTION
The carburetor body is equipped with plastic parts that cannot be removed. Do not dip the carburetor body,

O-rings, float, needle valve or vacuum piston in carburetor cleaner or other harsh solutions that can damage these parts. Use a high flash-point cleaning solution that is safe for these parts.

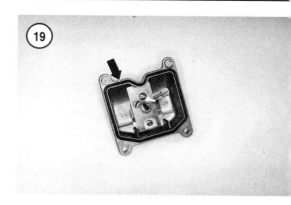

1. Clean all parts in a mild cleaning solution. Then clean in soap and hot water, rinse with cold water and dry with compressed air.

> *CAUTION*
> *If compressed air is not available, allow the parts to air dry or dry them with a clean, lint-free cloth. Do **not** use a paper towel to dry carburetor parts. Small paper particles may plug openings in the carburetor body or jets.*

> *CAUTION*
> *Do **not** use wire or drill bits to clean jets. They could cause minor gouges in the jet that alter flow rate and upset the air/fuel mixture.*

2. Make sure the float bowl overflow hose is clear. Blow it out with compressed air if necessary.

3. Inspect the float bowl O-ring (**Figure 19**). Replace the O-ring if it has become hard or is starting to deteriorate.

4. Inspect the vacuum piston diaphragm (**Figure 20**) for cracks, deterioration or other damage. Check the vacuum piston sides for excessive wear. Install the vacuum piston into the carburetor body. Move it up and down in the bore. The vacuum piston should move smoothly with no binding or excessive play. If there is excessive play, replace the vacuum piston and/or carburetor housing.

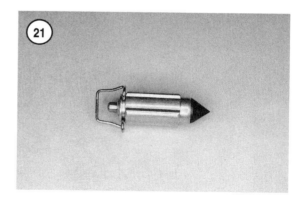

5. Inspect the needle valve (**Figure 21**) as follows:
   a. Inspect the tapered end for steps, uneven wear or other damage. Replace the needle valve if it is damaged.
   b. At the opposite end, push the needle in and release it. If the needle does not spring out, replace the needle valve.

6. Inspect the needle valve seat (**Figure 22**) for steps, uneven wear or other damage. The needle valve seat is an integral part of the carburetor body. If the seat is excessively worn or damaged, replace the carburetor body.

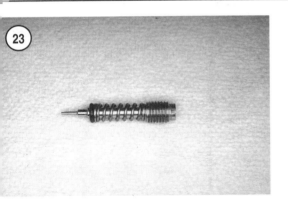

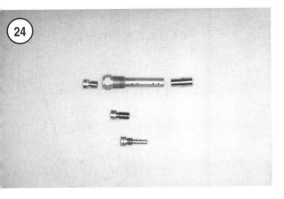

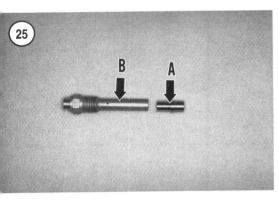

9. Inspect all the brass parts (**Figure 24**) for corrosion, excessive wear or other damage.

10. Inspect the float for deterioration or damage. Check for leaks. Place the float in a container of water and push it down. If the float sinks or if bubbles appear, replace the float.

11. Make sure the screws on the butterfly (B, **Figure 18**) are tight. Tighten them if necessary.

12. Move the throttle lever back and forth from stop-to-stop, and check the movement. The throttle lever should move smoothly and return under spring tension. Replace the carburetor housing if the throttle does not move freely or if it sticks in any position.

13. Make sure all openings in the carburetor housing are clear. Clean them out if they are plugged in any way.

Assembly

Refer to **Figure 5** when assembling the carburetor.

1. If removed, install the idle speed screw (A, **Figure 18**).

2. Install the needle jet (A, **Figure 25**) and the needle jet holder (B, **Figure 25**) by performing the following:

    a. Install the needle jet—small diameter end first—into the carburetor (**Figure 17**).

> *CAUTION*
> *Do not overtighten the needle jet holder. Doing so may damage the needle jet or the carburetor housing.*

    b. Install the needle jet holder (**Figure 16**), and seat it against the needle jet. Then carefully tighten the needle jet holder so it pushes the end of the needle jet into the carburetor bore.

3. Install the main jet (**Figure 15**), and tighten it securely.

4. Install the pilot jet (**Figure 14**), and tighten it securely.

5. Install the starter jet (**Figure 13**), and tighten it securely.

6. Install the float by performing the following:

    a. Hook the needle valve onto the float arm (**Figure 26**).

    b. Lower the float into the carburetor body so the needle valve (B, **Figure 12**) fits into its seat.

7. Inspect the pilot air screw (**Figure 23**) for damage. The tip must be straight without any visible damage. Replace if necessary.

> *NOTE*
> *A worn or damaged pilot air screw tip prevents the engine from idling smoothly.*

8. Inspect the pilot air screw O-ring. Replace the O-ring if it is hard or is deteriorating.

c. Secure the float in place with the float pin (**Figure 11**).

7. Make sure the O-ring is seated in the float bowl groove (**Figure 19**). Then install the float bowl onto the carburetor body. Tighten the four mounting screws securely (**Figure 10**).

8. Install the pilot air screw (**Figure 9**) and lightly seat it. Back it out the number of turns recorded during removal or to the pilot-air-screw setting listed in **Table 1**.

9. Check the float height. If necessary, adjust the float height as described in this chapter.

10. Install the vacuum piston and jet needle as follows:

   a. Drop the jet needle (B, **Figure 8**) into the vacuum piston.

   b. Install the vacuum piston (**Figure 7**) into the carburetor housing. Seat the diaphragm lip (C, **Figure 6**) into the carburetor body.

   c. Install the spring seat (A, **Figure 8**) onto the end of the spring.

   d. Install the spring (B, **Figure 6**)—spring seat facing down—into the vacuum piston.

   e. Install the cover (A, **Figure 6**) onto the carburetor housing. Make sure the vacuum piston spring is centered in the cover, and tighten the screws securely.

11. If removed during disassembly, install the fuel hose and breather hose onto the carburetor.

12. Install the carburetor as described in this chapter.

13. After assembly and installation are completed, adjust the carburetor as described in Chapter Three.

CARBURETOR ADJUSTMENTS

Idle speed and pilot air screw adjustments are covered in Chapter Three.

Float Height Check and Adjustment

The needle valve and float maintain a constant fuel level in the carburetor float bowl. Because the float height affects the fuel mixture throughout the engine's operating range, the height must be maintained within specification.

The carburetor assembly has to be removed and partially disassembled for this adjustment.

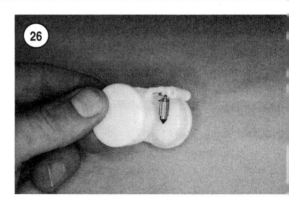

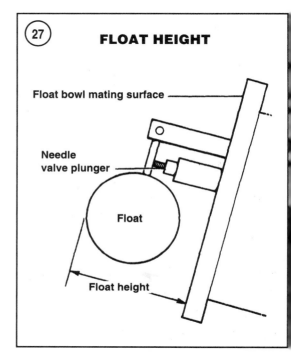

FLOAT HEIGHT

Float bowl mating surface

Needle valve plunger

Float

Float height

1. Remove the carburetor as described in this chapter.

2. Remove the mounting screws (**Figure 10**) and remove the float bowl from the carburetor body.

3. Hold the carburetor so the float arm tang is just touching the needle valve plunger—not pushing it down. Use a vernier caliper or small ruler to measure the distance from the float bowl mating surface to the top of the float (**Figure 27**). The float height specification is listed in **Table 1**.

4. If the float height is incorrect, adjust it by performing the following:

   a. Push the float pin out of the carburetor posts (**Figure 11**), and remove the float and needle

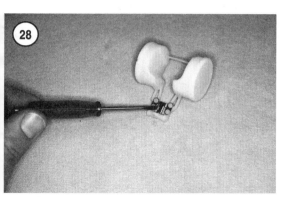

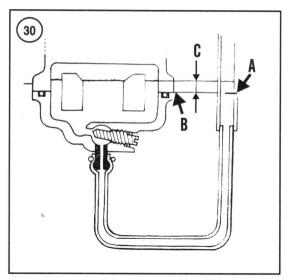

valve. Remove the needle valve from the float arm.

NOTE
Decreasing the float height raises the fuel level. Increasing the float height lowers the fuel level.

   b. Carefully bend the float arm tang (**Figure 28**) with a screwdriver to adjust the float height.

   c. Install the needle valve onto the float arm tang, and install the float and float pin.

   d. Recheck the float height as described in Step 3. Repeat this procedure until the float height is within specification.

5. Reassemble and install the carburetor.

Fuel Level Check and Adjustment

   Fuel level is measured from the bottom edge of the float bowl with the carburetor mounted on the engine. Use the Kawasaki fuel level gauge (part No. 57001-1017) for this procedure.

   The fuel level is adjusted by bending the float arm tang. Approximate the proper fuel level by setting the float height as described in this chapter.

WARNING
Some fuel may spill from the carburetor when performing this procedure. Because gasoline is extremely flammable, perform this procedure away from all open flames, including pilot lights and sparks. Do not smoke or allow someone who is smoking in the work area because an explosion and fire may occur. Always work in a well-ventilated area. Wipe up any spills immediately.

1. Park the vehicle on a level surface. Set the parking brake.

2. Turn the fuel valve to OFF.

3. Pull the carburetor overflow hose (A, **Figure 29**) out from underneath the engine. Do not disconnect the hose from the carburetor.

4. Check the end of the overflow hose for contamination. Clean the hose if required.

5. Insert the fuel level gauge into the open end of the overflow hose.

6. From the right side of the vehicle, hold the gauge vertically against the carburetor so that the 0 line (A, **Figure 30**) is slightly higher than the float bowl mating surface (B, **Figure 30**).

NOTE
Hold the fuel level gauge vertically against the carburetor housing when performing the following steps.

8

7. Turn the fuel valve to the ON position. Then open the carburetor drain plug (B, **Figure 29**) a few turns. Fuel will begin to run through the overflow hose and into the fuel level gauge.

NOTE
When performing Steps 8 and 9, be sure the 0 line on the fuel gauge does not drop below the mating surface of the float bowl. Lowering the gauge past this point and then raising it causes the gauge to show a higher than actual fuel level. If the gauge is lowered too far, turn the fuel valve off, and empty the fuel in the gauge into a gasoline storage container, then repeat the procedure.

8. Watch the fuel in the gauge. When the fuel level in the gauge settles, slowly lower the gauge (keeping it in a vertical position) until the 0 line on the gauge (A, **Figure 30**) is even with the edge of the float bowl mating surface (B, **Figure 30**).
9. Read the fuel level (C, **Figure 30**) on the gauge and note the reading.
10. Tighten the drain plug (B, **Figure 29**) and remove the fuel level gauge from the carburetor overflow hose.
11. Compare the reading to the specification in **Table 1**. Note the following:
  a. If the fuel level is correct, reroute the overflow hose underneath the engine.
  b. If the fuel level is incorrect, adjust the float height as described in this chapter.

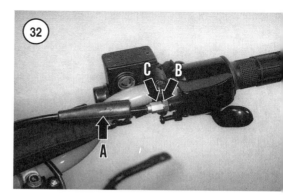

Jet Needle Adjustment

The jet needle is manufactured with a fixed height position. No adjustment is possible.

THROTTLE CABLE REPLACEMENT

A single throttle cable is used on all models.
1. Park the vehicle on level ground and set the parking brake.
2. Remove the front fender as described in Chapter Fourteen.
3. Remove the fuel tank as described in this chapter.
4. At the carburetor, loosen the throttle cable locknuts (**Figure 31**). Remove the throttle cable

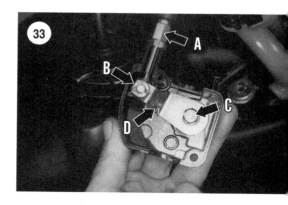

from the bracket, and disconnect the cable ball from the throttle lever on the carburetor.
5. At the handlebar, slide the rubber cover (A, **Figure 32**) away from the throttle cable adjuster.
6. Loosen the throttle cable adjuster locknut (B, **Figure 32**).
7. Remove the throttle case screws. Lift the upper case half from the lower case half, and then remove the lower case from the handlebar (**Figure 33**).
8. Unscrew the throttle cable adjuster (A, **Figure 33**), and disconnect the throttle cable from the throttle lever arm (B, **Figure 33**).

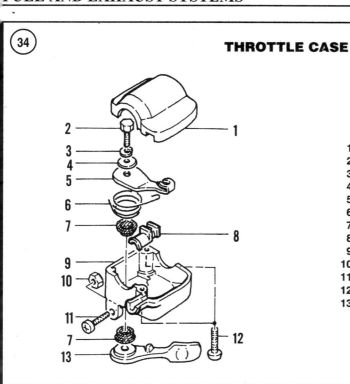

THROTTLE CASE

1. Upper case
2. Throttle lever bolt
3. Lockwasher
4. Flat washer
5. Throttle lever arm
6. Spring
7. Collar
8. Cap
9. Lower case
10. Nut
11. Limiter screw
12. Throttle case screw
13. Throttle lever

9. Disconnect the throttle cable from any clips holding the cable to the frame.

10. Note how the cable is routed through the frame, and remove the cable.

11. Installation is the reverse of removal. Note the following:

   a. Lubricate the new cable as described in Chapter Three.

   b. Route the new cable along the same path as the original cable.

   c. Apply a small amount of grease to the ball at each end of the cable.

   d. Place the lower housing half against the handlebar, and operate the throttle lever. Make sure the throttle lever arm in the housing moves smoothly and does not contact the handlebar.

NOTE
The upper and lower throttle case halves must fit flush against the handlebar. If they do not, check the throttle halves for a pin that fits into a hole in the handlebar.

   e. Operate the throttle lever and make sure the carburetor throttle linkage is operating cor-

rectly without binding. If operation is incorrect or there is binding, carefully check that the cable is attached correctly with no tight bends.

   f. Adjust the throttle cable free play as described in Chapter Three.

WARNING
An improperly adjusted or incorrectly routed throttle cable can cause the throttle to hang open. This could cause a crash. Do not ride the vehicle until the throttle cable is operating properly.

   g. Start the engine, and let it idle. Then turn the handlebar from side to side making sure the idle speed does not increase. If engine speed does increase, the throttle cable is adjusted incorrectly or it is improperly routed.

THROTTLE CASE

Refer to **Figure 34** when servicing the throttle case.

Disassembly/Assembly

1. Park the vehicle on level ground and set the parking brake.
2. Slide the rubber cover (A, **Figure 32**) away from the throttle cable adjuster, and loosen the adjuster locknut (B, **Figure 32**)
3. Remove the two throttle case screws and separate the case halves (**Figure 35**).
4. Loosen the cable adjuster (A, **Figure 33**).
5. Note how the spring tang (D, **Figure 33**) engages the throttle lever arm. It must be reinstalled on the arm in the same manner.
6. Remove the throttle lever bolt (C, **Figure 33**), lockwasher, and washer.
7. Lift the throttle lever arm (A, **Figure 36**) from the throttle case.
8. Remove the spring (B, **Figure 36**) and collar (C, **Figure 36**).
9. Loosen the throttle limiter nut, and unscrew the throttle limiter screw (**Figure 37**).
10. Remove the throttle lever from the throttle case. The collar should come out with the throttle lever. See **Figure 38**.
11. Installation is the reverse of removal. Note the following:
    a. Apply grease to the raised boss on the throttle lever, to both collars, and to the washer.
    b. Lubricate the throttle cable as described in Chapter Three.
    c. Make sure the spring tang (D, **Figure 33**) properly engages the throttle lever arm
    d. Torque the throttle lever bolt to the specification in **Table 2**.

CHOKE CABLE REPLACEMENT

Refer to **Figure 39** for this procedure.
1. Remove the front fender as described in Chapter Fourteen.
2. Unscrew the starter plunger cap (**Figure 40**) and pull the starter plunger from the carburetor.
3. Compress the starter plunger spring, and disconnect the choke cable end from the starter plunger.
4. Remove the left handlebar switch mounting screws, and separate the switch halves.
5. Unscrew the choke lever screw (A, **Figure 41**), and remove the flat and wave washers.
6. Remove the choke lever from the housing, and disconnect the choke cable end from the lever.

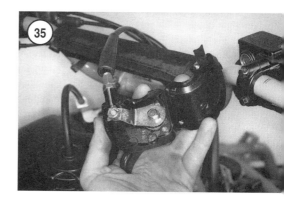

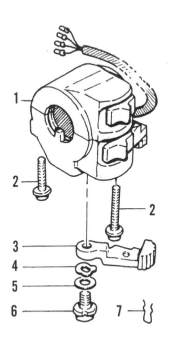

LEFT HANDLEBAR SWITCH

1. Housing
2. Mounting screws
3. Choke lever
4. Wave washer
5. Flat washer
6. Lever screw
7. Retaining clip

8

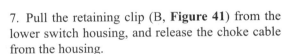

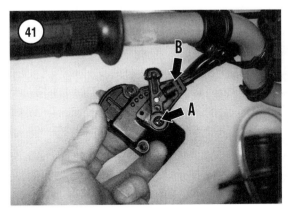

7. Pull the retaining clip (B, **Figure 41**) from the lower switch housing, and release the choke cable from the housing.

8. Note how the clutch cable is routed through the frame, and remove it.

9. Installation is the reverse of removal. Note the following:

    a. Lubricate the new choke cable before installation.

    b. Make sure the new cable follows the same path through the frame as the old cable.

    c. Connect the cable end to the choke lever, and fit the lever into place in the switch assembly.

    d. Install the wave washer, the flat washer, and then secure the lever in place with the screw.

    e. When installing the left handlebar switch assembly, insert the pin in the lower switch housing (**Figure 42**) into the hole in the handlebar.

   f. Adjust the choke cable free play as described in Chapter Three.

FUEL TANK

Removal/Installation

Refer to **Figure 43**.

> *WARNING*
> *Some fuel may spill when performing this procedure. Because gasoline is extremely flammable, perform this procedure away from all open flames, including pilot lights and sparks. Do not smoke or allow someone who is smoking in the work area because an explosion and fire may occur. Always work in a well-ventilated area. Wipe up any spills immediately.*

1. Park the vehicle on level ground, and set the parking brake.
2. Remove the front and rear fenders as described in Chapter Fourteen.
3. Turn the fuel valve to the OFF position (A, **Figure 44**), and disconnect the fuel line (B, **Figure 44**) from the valve. Plug the open end of the fuel line to prevent contamination.
4. If still installed, remove the rear fuel tank mounting bolt (**Figure 45**), and remove the fuel tank.
5. Inspect the fuel tank for signs of wear or leaks. Pay particular attention to tank seams. Replace the tank as necessary.
6. Inspect the damper and collar in each fuel tank mount for signs of wear or deterioration. Replace the dampers and collars as necessary.
7. Inspect the tank dampers (**Figure 46**) on each side of the frame rail. Replace both rubber dampers if either is damaged or deteriorating.
8. Install by reversing these removal steps. Tighten the fuel tank mounting bolts securely. Check for fuel leaks after installation is completed.

FUEL VALVE

The fuel valve is shown in **Figure 47**.

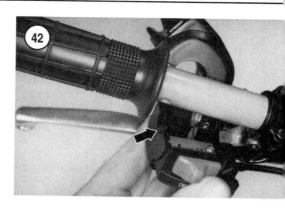

Removal/Installation

> *WARNING*
> *Some fuel may spill from the carburetor, fuel line and fuel tank when performing this procedure. Because gasoline is extremely flammable, perform this procedure away from all open flames, including pilot lights and sparks. Do not smoke or allow someone who is smoking in the work area because an explosion and fire may occur. Always work in a well-ventilated area. Wipe up any spills immediately.*

1. Remove the fuel tank as described in this chapter.
2. Drain all gas from the fuel tank. Store the fuel in a container approved for gasoline storage.
3. Remove the bolts (**Figure 48**) and nylon washers securing the fuel valve to the fuel tank, and remove the valve and O-ring.
4. To replace the fuel valve packing (4, **Figure 47**):
   a. Remove the two cover screws, and disassemble the valve in the order shown in **Figure 47**.
   b. Replace the packing, and its O-ring, and then reassemble the valve.
   c. Torque the cover screws to the specification in **Table 2**.

> *WARNING*
> *Use only nylon washers when installing the fuel valve. Steel washers do not seal properly, and could cause a leak.*

5. Install by reversing these steps. Note the following:
   a. Install a new fuel valve O-ring.

43

FUEL TANK

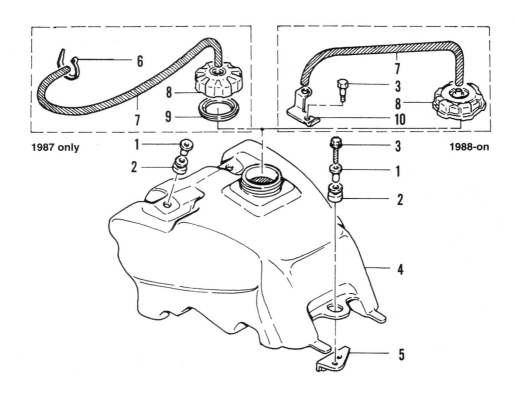

1987 only

1988-on

1. Collar
2. Damper
3. Bolt
4. Fuel tank
5. Tank bracket
6. Cable tie
7. Vent hose
8. Cap
9. Gasket
10. Vent bracket

8

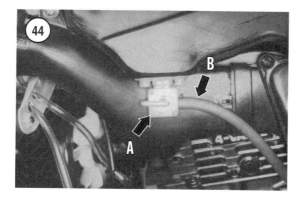

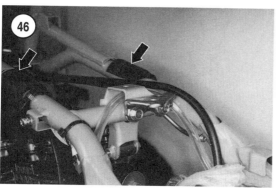

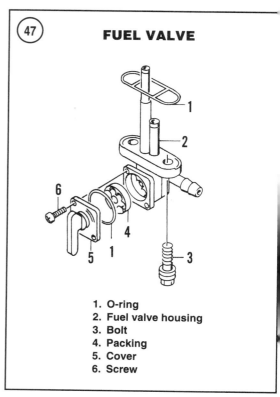

FUEL VALVE

1. O-ring
2. Fuel valve housing
3. Bolt
4. Packing
5. Cover
6. Screw

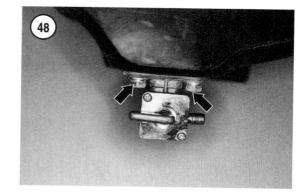

b. Make sure the nylon washers are in good condition. If necessary, replace them.

c. Torque the fuel valve mounting bolts to the specification in **Table 2**.

6. Check for fuel leaks after installation is completed.

AIR FILTER HOUSING

Refer to **Figure 49** when servicing the air filter housing.

Removal/Inspection

1. Place the vehicle on level ground, and set the parking brake.

2. Remove the front and rear renders as described in Chapter Fourteen.

3. Remove the snorkel duct by performing the following:

a. Remove the two snorkel-duct mounting screws (A, **Figure 50**).

49

AIR FILTER HOUSING

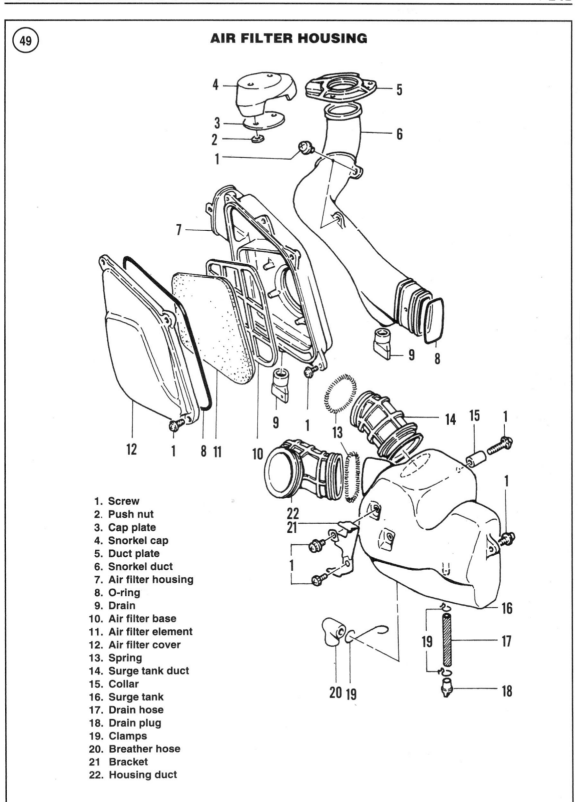

1. Screw
2. Push nut
3. Cap plate
4. Snorkel cap
5. Duct plate
6. Snorkel duct
7. Air filter housing
8. O-ring
9. Drain
10. Air filter base
11. Air filter element
12. Air filter cover
13. Spring
14. Surge tank duct
15. Collar
16. Surge tank
17. Drain hose
18. Drain plug
19. Clamps
20. Breather hose
21 Bracket
22. Housing duct

8

b. Gently pry open the tab on the air filter housing (B, **Figure 50**), and slide the snorkel duct from the housing.

c. The O-ring should come out with the snorkel duct (**Figure 51**). If it does not, remove it from the air filter housing.

4. Remove the mounting screws and remove the air filter cover (A, **Figure 52**).

5. Remove the air filter element (A, **Figure 53**) and the air filter base (A, **Figure 54**) from the housing.

6. Remove the air filter housing by performing the following:

a. Remove the housing mounting screws (B, **Figure 54**).

b. Slide the air filter housing forward, and disconnect the housing duct from the surge tank. Remove the housing.

c. Do not lose the spring from the end of the housing duct.

7. Cover the surge tank/housing duct opening to keep abrasives out of the carburetor.

8. Inspect all components of the air filter housing assembly. Replace any that are damaged or starting to deteriorate.

9. The air filter housing and snorkel duct each have a drain. Clean any water or oil that has accumulated in the air-filter-housing drain (B, **Figure 53**) or in the snorkel-duct drain (C, **Figure 53**).

10. Remove the plug from the surge tank drain hose, and clean any accumulated water or oil.

Installation

1. Make sure the crankcase breather hose (**Figure 55**) is still connected to the surge tank.

2. Install the air filter housing by performing the following.

a. If removed, install the housing duct into the opening in the air filter housing. Make sure the indexing notch on the duct aligns with the indexing tab on the back of the air filter housing.

b. Lubricate the housing duct with a soap solution.

c. Fit the housing duct over the surge tank, and slide the air filter housing into place.

d. If necessary, roll the duct spring into place so it secures the housing duct to the surge tank.

e. Install the air filter housing mounting screws (B, **Figure 54**).

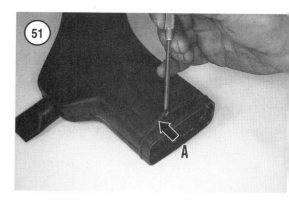

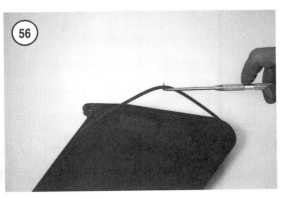

3. Set the air filter base (A, **Figure 54**) and the air filter element (A, **Figure 53**) into place in the air filter housing.

4. Check that the O-ring (**Figure 56**) is properly seated in the air filter cover.

5. Install the air filter cover (A, **Figure 52**), and secure it in place with the mounting screws.

6. Install the snorkel duct by performing the following:

   a. Make sure the O-ring (**Figure 51**) is in place on the snorkel duct.

   b. Lubricate the snorkel duct with soap solution.

   c. Slide the duct rearward and into the joint in the air filter housing. Make sure the tab (B, **Figure 50**) on the housing locks the snorkel duct in place.

   d. Install the snorkel duct mounting bolts (A, **Figure 50**).

7. Install the front and rear fenders as described in Chapter Fourteen.

SURGE TANK

Removal/Installation

Refer to **Figure 49** when performing this procedure.

1. Remove the front and rear fenders as described in Chapter Fourteen.

2. Remove the air filter housing as described in this chapter.

3. Slide the CDI unit (B, **Figure 52**) from the rubber mount.

4. Remove the bracket from the side of the surge tank.

5. Remove the upper chain roller mount (**Figure 57**) and remove the roller.

6. Disconnect the crankcase breather hose (**Figure 55**) from the surge tank.

7. Remove the rear shock absorber as described in Chapter Twelve.

8. Remove the two mounting bolts securing the surge tank to the frame tabs on the right (A, **Figure 58**) and left (B, **Figure 58**) upper frame rails. Do not lose the collar behind the bolt on the forward mount (A, **Figure 58**).

9. Slide the surge tank rearward and remove it from the frame.

10. Installation is the reverse of removal. Note the following:

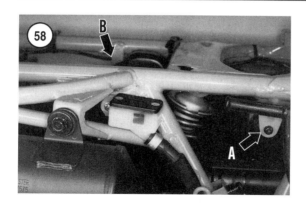

EXHAUST SYSTEM

1. Gasket
2. Header clamp
3. Nut
4. Exhaust pipe
5. Pipe cover
6. Screw
7. Washers
8. Bolt
9. Damper
10. Collar
11. Muffler
12. Muffler clamp

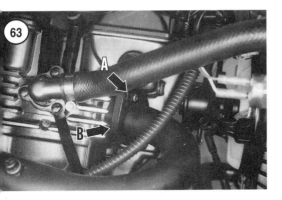

a. If reinstalling the surge tank duct to the surge tank, align the index mark on the duct with the mark on the surge tank.

b. Reinstall the crankcase breather hose (**Figure 55**) to the surge tank.

c. Make sure the surge tank duct properly engages the carburetor and that the securing spring (**Figure 59**) is in place.

EXHAUST SYSTEM

Check the exhaust system for deep dents and fractures. Repair or replace damaged parts immediately. Check the muffler mounting flanges on the frame for fractures and loose bolts. Check the cylinder head mounting flange for tightness. A loose exhaust pipe connection will cause excessive exhaust noise and reduce engine performance. Before removing the exhaust system, check for leaks at the exhaust port and at the muffler clamp.

The exhaust system is shown in **Figure 60**.

Removal/Installation

NOTE
The exhaust system can be removed with the front and rear fenders installed on the vehicle. The fenders have been removed in the following photographs for clarity.

1. Park the vehicle on level ground, and set the parking brake.

2. Loosen the muffler clamp bolt (**Figure 61**).

3. Remove the muffler hanger bolts (**Figure 62**).

4. Withdraw the muffler from the exhaust pipe, and remove the muffler.

5. Remove the exhaust pipe nuts (A, **Figure 63**), and slide the clamp (B, **Figure 63**) off the studs and down the exhaust pipe.

6. Pull the exhaust pipe fitting from the exhaust port, and remove the exhaust pipe.

7. Remove the exhaust pipe gasket (**Figure 64**) from the exhaust port, and discard the gasket. The exhaust pipe must be reinstalled with a new gasket.

8. If necessary, remove the pipe cover mounting screws, and the pipe covers from the exhaust pipe.

9. Inspect the gaskets for damage or signs of leaks. Replace as necessary.

8

10. Install the exhaust system by performing the following:

a. Install a new exhaust header gasket (**Figure 65**). Apply a small amount of grease to the gasket to hold it in place, and fit the gasket into the exhaust port (**Figure 64**).

b. Set the exhaust pipe in place so the pipe is on the inboard side of the frame member.

c. Fit the exhaust pipe into the exhaust port, and slide the clamp (B, **Figure 63**) over the header studs. Loosely install the exhaust pipe nuts (A, **Figure 63**).

d. Install a new exhaust pipe-to-muffler gasket. Fit the gasket into the muffler so the round side faces the front of the vehicle.

e. From the rear of the vehicle, slide the muffler forward and into the exhaust pipe. Make sure the muffler pipe is inboard of the frame member.

f. Slide the muffler clamp over the pipe joint, and loosely install the muffler hanger bolts (**Figure 62**).

11. To minimize the chances of an exhaust leak, tighten the bolts in the following order:

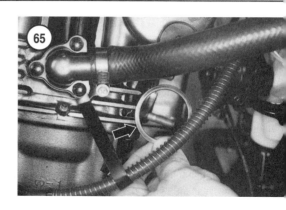

a. Exhaust pipe-to-cylinder head nuts (A, **Figure 63**).

b. Muffler clamp bolt (**Figure 61**).

c. Muffler hanger bolts (**Figure 62**).

12. After installation is complete, start the engine and make sure there are no exhaust leaks.

Spark Arrester Cleaning

Refer to the procedure in Chapter Three.

Table 1 CARBURETOR SPECIFICATIONS

Carburetor type	Keihin CVK34
Main jet	No. 132
Main air jet	No. 125
Needle jet	No. 6
Jet needle	N54C
Needle clip position	fixed
Pilot jet	No. 35
Pilot air jet	No. 135
Pilot air screw	1 3/4 turns out
Starter jet	No. 55
Fuel level	0.5 mm above the bottom edge of carburetor body.
Float height	15-19 mm (0.591 - 0.748 in.)
Idle speed	Slowest, smooth idle

Table 2 FUEL SYSTEM TIGHTENING TORQUES

Item	N•m	in.-lb.	ft.-lb.
Throttle lever bolt	6.9	61	–
Fuel valve cover screw	0.8	7	–
Fuel valve mounting bolt	0.8	7	–

CHAPTER NINE

ELECTRICAL SYSTEM

When working on the electrical system make sure that all electrical connections are secure. To prevent corrosion within the connector due to moisture, apply dielectric grease to the electrical terminals whenever they are disconnected. Information regarding the spark plugs and ignition timing is covered in Chapter Three.

The electrical system includes the following systems and components:
1. Ignition system.
2. Lighting system.
3. Cooling fan.
4. Electrical components.

Electrical specifications appear in **Table 1**, replacement bulb specifications in **Table 2**, and electrical system torque specifications appear in **Table 3**. **Tables 1-3** are at the end of this chapter.

MAGNETO

The magneto assembly consists of the magneto rotor, which is mounted to the crankshaft, and the stator and pickup coils, which are mounted inside the rotor cover. See **Figure 1**. The rotor is permanently magnetized and can only be tested by replacement with a known good rotor. Rotor removal and inspection procedures are described in Chapter Five.

Stator Testing

The stator in the Mojave includes three coils: the exciter coil, the lighting coil and the fan motor power coil. Each coil can be tested with the stator assembled and installed in the engine. To obtain accurate resistance measurements, the stator temperature must be approximately 20° C (68° F).

Stator removal and installation procedures appear in Chapter Five.

1. Remove the rear fender as described in Chapter Fourteen.

2. Disconnect the stator connector (B, **Figure 2**).

3. Test the exciter coil by performing the following:

    a. Set an ohmmeter to the R × 100 scale. Zero the meter if using an analog meter.

    b. Connect the ohmmeter probes to the black/white and the black/red terminals on the stator side of the connector.

    c. Note the ohmmeter reading and compare it to the specification in **Table 1**.

4. Test the lighting coil by performing the following:

    a. Set an ohmmeter to the R × 1 scale. Zero the meter if using an analog meter.

    b. Connect one ohmmeter probe to the black/yellow terminal in stator side of the

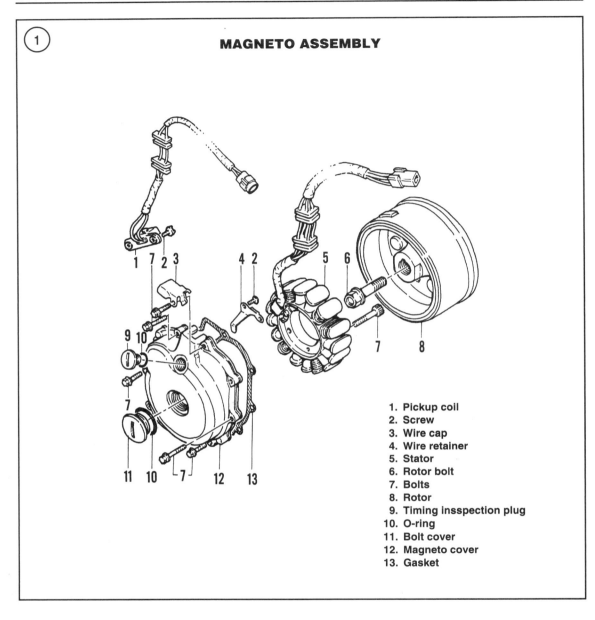

MAGNETO ASSEMBLY

1. Pickup coil
2. Screw
3. Wire cap
4. Wire retainer
5. Stator
6. Rotor bolt
7. Bolts
8. Rotor
9. Timing insspection plug
10. O-ring
11. Bolt cover
12. Magneto cover
13. Gasket

connector and connect the second probe to ground.

c. Note the ohmmeter reading and compare it to the specification in **Table 1**.

5. Test the fan motor power coil by performing the following:

a. Set an ohmmeter to the R × 1 scale. Zero the meter if using an analog meter.

b. Connect the ohmmeter probes to the two brown terminals on the stator side of the connector.

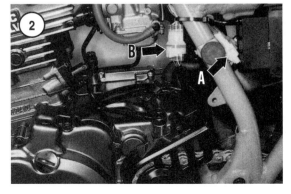

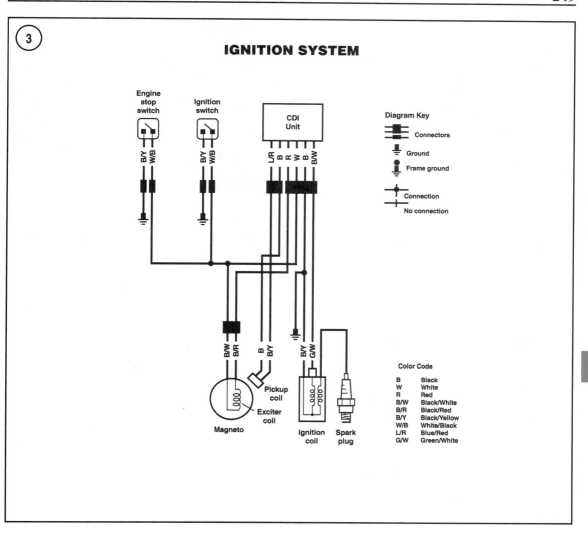

IGNITION SYSTEM

c. Note the ohmmeter reading and compare it to the specification in **Table 1**.

6A. If the resistance of any coil is zero (short circuit) or infinity (open circuit), inspect the connector pins and the wiring to the stator coils. If the wiring and connector are in good condition, the stator is damaged and must be replaced.

6B. If the resistance of any coil is outside the range specified in **Table 1**, replace the stator.

7. Reconnect the stator connector. Apply dielectric grease to the electrical connector to seal out moisture.

8. Install the rear fender as described in Chapter Fourteen.

IGNITION SYSTEM

All models are equipped with a capacitor discharge ignition system (CDI). The system consists of the exciter coil in the magneto, the pickup coil, CDI unit, ignition coil, ignition switch, engine stop switch and spark plug. **Figure 3** shows the circuit diagram for the ignition system. This solid-state system uses no contact breaker points or other moving parts so no periodic maintenance is required.

Precautions

Certain precautions must be taken to protect the solid-state ignition system.

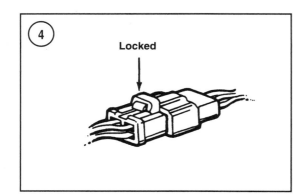

④ Locked

⑤

⑥   **CDI UNIT RESISTANCE**

Unit: kΩ

Range × 1kΩ		Tester Positive (+) Lead Connection					
		W	R	BL/R	R/G	BK/W	BK
Tester Negative (–) Lead Connections	W		∞	∞	∞	∞	∞
	R	10-40		10-50	3-15	∞	3-15
	BL/R	60-240	60-240		30-150	∞	30-150
	R/G	2-10	2-10	3-15		∞	0
	BK/W	∞	∞	∞	∞		∞
	BK	2-10	2-10	3-15	0	∞	

1. Never disconnect any electrical connections while the engine is running.

2. Apply dielectric grease to all electrical connectors to seal out moisture.

3. Make sure all electrical connectors are free of corrosion and are completely coupled to each other (**Figure 4**).

4. The CDI unit (C, **Figure 5**) is mounted within a rubber vibration isolator. Always make sure the isolator is in place when installing the unit.

Troubleshooting

Refer to Chapter Two.

CDI Unit Removal/Installation

1. Park the vehicle on level ground and set the parking brake.

2. Remove the rear fender as described in Chapter Fourteen.

3. Disconnect the two-pin connector (A, **Figure 5**) and the four-pin connector (B, **Figure 5**) from the CDI unit.

4. Slide the CDI unit (C, **Figure 5**) from the rubber holder and remove the CDI from the vehicle.

5. Install by reversing these removal steps, noting the following.

6. Apply dielectric grease to the terminals before connecting the connectors. This helps seal out moisture.

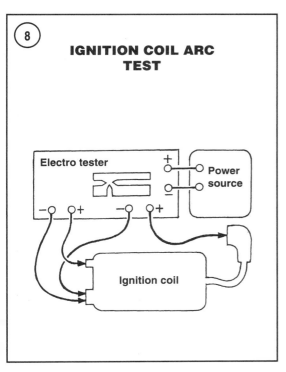

IGNITION COIL ARC TEST

Electro tester

Power source

Ignition coil

CDI Testing

The resistance values provided by Kawasaki are based on the use of its ohmmeter (part No. 57001-983). Tests made with another ohmmeter may yield different readings due to the different internal resistance of the individual ohmmeters.

1. Remove the CDI unit as described in this chapter.

2. Set the ohmmeter on the R × 1000 scale.

3. Refer to **Figure 6** for test connections and values. If any of the meter readings differ from the stated values, replace the CDI unit.

IGNITION COIL

The ignition coil is a form of transformer which develops the high voltage required to jump the spark plug gap. The only maintenance required is keeping the electrical connections clean and tight and occasionally checking to see that the coil is mounted securely.

The ignition coil is mounted underneath the front upper frame rail on the right side; see **Figure 7**.

Removal/Installation

1. Place the vehicle on level ground and set the parking brake.

2. Remove the front fender as described in Chapter Fourteen.

3. Disconnect the spark plug cap (A, **Figure 7**) from the spark plug.

4. Disconnect the green/white and black/yellow leads from the ignition coil primary terminals (B, **Figure 7**).

5. Remove the ignition coil mounting screw (C, **Figure 7**).

6. Remove the ignition coil bracket and the ignition coil.

7. Install by reversing these removal steps. Make sure all electrical connections are tight and free of corrosion.

Ignition Coil Arc Test

Use the Kawasaki Electro Tester (part No. 578001-980) or equivalent for this test.

1. Remove the ignition coil as described in this chapter.

WARNING
High voltage is produced during this test. Do not touch the ignition coil body or the leads when performing this test. Severe shock could result.

2. Connect the coil, with the spark plug cap still installed, to the Electro Tester as shown in **Figure 8**.

3. Follow the tester's instruction and measure the ignition coil spark gap.

4. Compare the test results to the specification in **Table 1**.

5. If the test results are less than specified, remove the spark plug cap from the secondary lead, and repeat the test.
   a. If the spark gap is still less than specified, replace the ignition coil.
   b. If the spark gap is within specification, replace the spark plug cap.

Ignition Coil Resistance Test

If an arc tester is not available, check the resistance of both windings in the ignition coil by performing the following.

NOTE
To obtain accurate resistance measurements, the coil temperature must be approximately 20° C (68° F).

1. If necessary, remove the front fender as described in Chapter Fourteen.
2. Disconnect the spark plug cap (A, **Figure 7**) from the spark plug.
3. Disconnect the green/white and black/yellow leads from the ignition coil's primary terminals (B, **Figure 7**).
4. Carefully remove the spark plug cap from the ignition coil secondary wire.

NOTE
If using an analog ohmmeter, recalibrate the meter after changing range scales.

5. Measure the coil primary resistance using an ohmmeter set to the R × 1 scale. Measure the resistance between the primary terminals shown in **Figure 9**. Compare the reading to the specification in **Table 1**.
6. Measure the secondary resistance by performing the following:
   a. Set the ohmmeter to the R × 1000 scale. Zero the meter if using an analog meter.
   b. Measure the resistance between the secondary lead (spark plug lead) and one of the ignition primary terminals as shown in **Figure 9**.
   c. Measure the resistance between the secondary lead and the other primary terminal.
   d. Compare the results of each test to the secondary winding resistance in **Table 1**.

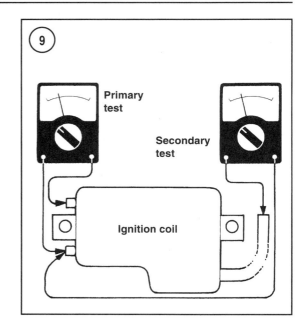

7. If the coil resistance in any test is outside the range specified in **Table 1**, replace the coil. If the coil exhibits visible damage, replace it.
8. Install the spark plug cap onto the ignition coil secondary wire.
9. Reconnect the ignition coil primary leads (B, **Figure 7**).

Pickup Coil Testing

The following test can be made with the pickup coil mounted on the engine. To get accurate resistance measurements, the pickup coil temperature must be approximately 20° C (68° F).
1. Remove the rear fender as described in Chapter Fourteen.
2. Disconnect the two-pin pickup coil electrical connector (A, **Figure 2**).
3. Set an ohmmeter to the R × 100 scale. Zero the meter if using an analog meter.
4. Connect the ohmmeter probes to the black and the black/yellow terminals on the pickup coil side of the connector.
5. Note the ohmmeter reading and compare it to the specification in **Table 1**. If the pickup coil resistance is not within specification, replace the pickup coil as described in Chapter Five.
6. Reconnect the pickup coil connector. Apply dielectric grease to the electrical connector to seal out moisture.

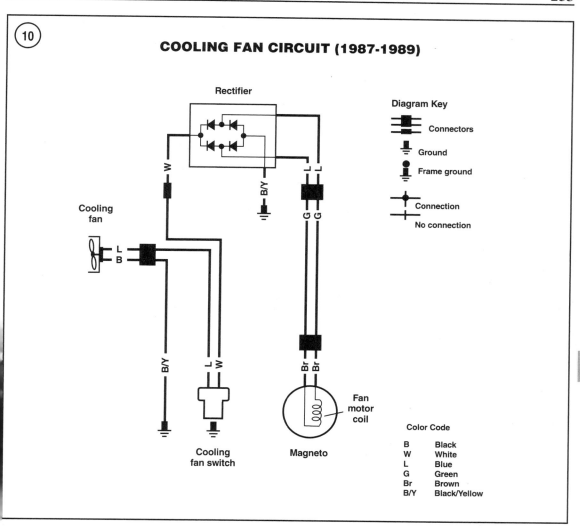

COOLING FAN CIRCUIT (1987-1989)

7. Install the rear fender as described in Chapter Fourteen.

COOLING FAN SYSTEM

The cooling system consists of the cooling fan, the fan switch, the fan motor coil in the magneto, the rectifier, and in 1990-on models the voltage regulator. The circuit diagram for 1987-1989 models is shown in **Figure 10**. The diagram for 1990-on models is shown in **Figure 11**.

Cooling Fan Circuit Testing

1. Visually inspect the radiator fan. Replace the fan assembly if the fan blades or shroud are damaged.

2. Disconnect the two electrical leads from the cooling fan switch (A, **Figure 12**).

NOTE
Clean any rust or corrosion from the electrical terminals on the fan switch.

3. Use a jumper wire to connect these two electrical leads together.

4. Turn the ignition switch on; the cooling fan should start running.

   a. If the cooling fan does not run, inspect the electrical wiring, the fan motor, rectifier, fan motor coil in the magneto and the voltage regulator (1990-on models only).

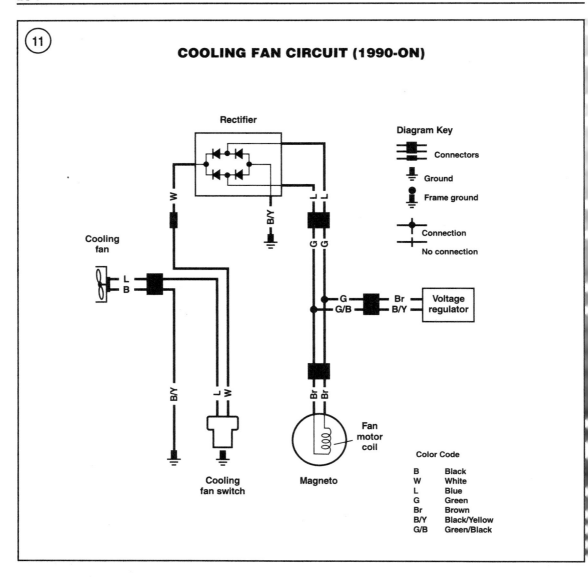

(11)

COOLING FAN CIRCUIT (1990-ON)

b. If the fan runs, the cooling fan switch may be defective. Test the switch as described in this chapter.

Cooling Fan Motor Test

1. Disconnect the fan motor two-pin connector (B, **Figure 12**).

2. Use two jumper wires to supply battery power directly to the motor. Connect the negative battery terminal to the black terminal in the motor connector. Connect the positive battery terminal to the blue terminal in the connector.

3. If the fan does not operate, replace the fan as described in Chapter Ten.

If the fan operates, check the cooling fan switch as described in this chapter. If the switch is working properly, check the rectifier as described in this chapter.

Cooling Fan Motor Coil Voltage Test (1990-On Only)

1. Remove the front fender cover.

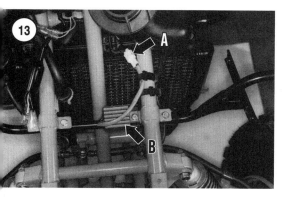

NOTE
Backprobing may involve piercing a sealed connector or wire with test probes to obtain contact with the wire(s) or terminals(s) to be tested. Be careful not to cause any excess damage to the insulation. Make sure to seal the wire or connection with a silicone sealant.

2. Backprobe the brown and black/yellow terminals at the voltage regulator connector (A, **Figure 13**), and connect a voltmeter to the probes.

3. Connect a tachometer to the engine following the manufacturer's instructions.

4. Start the engine and turn the headlight on.

5. Run the engine at 5,000 rpm and measure the voltage at the voltage regulator connector. It must be within the range specified in **Table 1**.

   a. If the voltage is lower than specified, check the fan motor power coil resistance as described in *Stator Testing* earlier in this chapter.

   b. If the voltage is much higher than specified, the voltage regulator is defective or the regu-

lator connection/wiring is faulty. Check the regulator connectors and wiring. If they are clean and in good working condition, replace the voltage regulator (B, **Figure 13**).

6. Disconnect the voltmeter probes and seal the connector with silicon sealant.

Cooling Fan Switch Test

The fan switch operates the cooling fan based on engine coolant temperature. When the coolant temperature is in the hot range, the cooling fan should operate. The cooling fan switch is mounted to the right side of the radiator (**Figure 12**).

NOTE
This test can be performed with the front fender installed on the ATV. The fender is shown removed for clarity.

1. Disconnect the two electrical leads from the cooling fan switch (A, **Figure 12**).

NOTE
Clean any corrosion from the electrical terminals on the fan switch.

2. Partially drain the cooling system as described in Chapter Three. Drain just enough coolant to lower the coolant level in the radiator below the fan switch. This will reduce the loss of coolant when the switch is removed.

3. Unscrew and remove the fan switch from the radiator.

WARNING
Wear safety glasses and gloves during this test. Protect yourself accordingly as the coolant is heated to a high temperature.

4. Place the cooling fan switch in a small pan full of a 50/50 mixture of distilled water and antifreeze. Position the cooling fan switch so all of its threads are submerged in the coolant.

5. Place a shop thermometer in the pan (use a thermometer that is rated higher than the test temperature).

NOTE
Suspend the switch and thermometer so neither touches the bottom or side

9

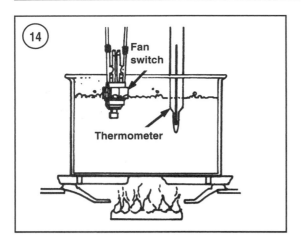

of the container as shown in **Figure 14**.

6. Use an ohmmeter and check the resistance between the terminals on the switch as shown in **Figure 14**. At room temperature there should be no continuity (infinite resistance).

7. Heat the coolant slowly until the temperature reaches 84-90° C (183-194° F). Watch the ohmmeter needle while the coolant is heating. The needle should move from infinity to 0.5 ohms. Maintain this temperature for at least three minutes before taking the final reading. A sudden change in temperature will cause a different ohmmeter reading. After this 3 minute interval is completed, check the ohmmeter; there should be continuity (0.5 ohms).

8. Turn the heat off and keep the ohmmeter test leads attached. When the coolant temperature falls to 71-77° C (160-170° F), check the ohmmeter; there should be no continuity (infinite resistance).

9. If the cooling fan switch fails either of these tests, replace the switch.

10. If the cooling fan switch tests good, allow it to cool down and remove it from the pan.

11. Apply a light coat of a silicon-based sealant to the threads of the cooling fan switch and install the switch in the radiator.

12. Tighten the cooling fan switch to the torque specification in **Table 1**.

13. Refill the cooling system with the recommended type and quantity of coolant. Refer to Chapter Three.

14. Attach the electrical wires to the cooling fan switch. Make sure the connections are tight and free from oil and corrosion.

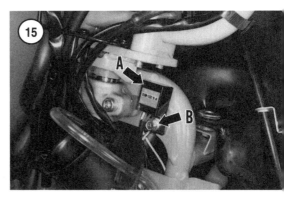

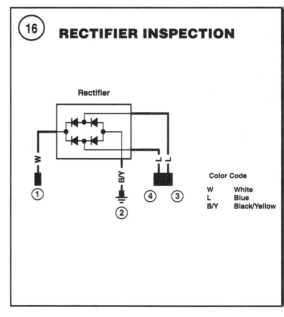

Rectifier

1. Remove the front fender cover as described in Chapter Fourteen.

2. Follow the rectifier's (A, **Figure 15**) electrical lead and disconnect the two connectors.

3. Refer to **Figure 16**, and use an ohmmeter to check the continuity between the following pairs of rectifier terminals: terminals 1 and 2, terminals 1 and 3, and terminals 1 and 4. Make sure to check the continuity in both directions at each pair of terminals.

4. Each pair should show continuity (zero ohms) in one direction and no continuity (infinity) in the other direction.

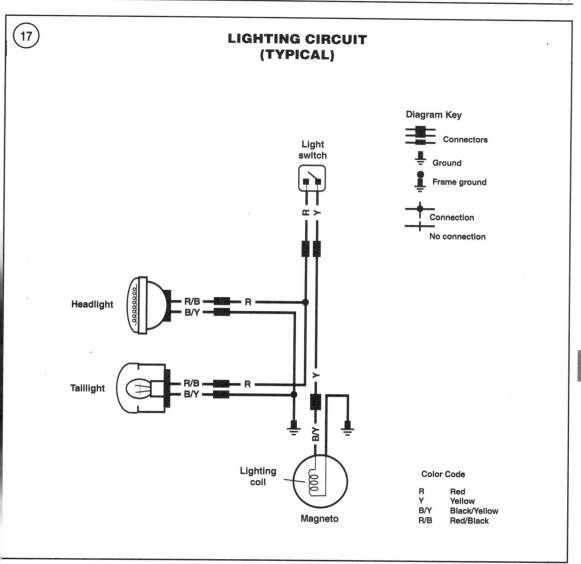

LIGHTING CIRCUIT (TYPICAL)

Diagram Key

■ Connectors

⊥ Ground

Frame ground

• Connection

No connection

Light switch

Headlight — R/B — R
— B/Y

Taillight — R/B — R
— B/Y

Lighting coil

Magneto

Color Code

R	Red
Y	Yellow
B/Y	Black/Yellow
R/B	Red/Black

5. The rectifier is defective if any test yields infinity or zero in both directions. Replace the rectifier by performing the following:

 a. Remove the rectifier mounting bolt (B, **Figure 15**) and the rectifier.

 b. Install a new rectifier and tighten the bolt securely.

 c. Connect the rectifier lead to the wiring harness.

LIGHTING SYSTEM

The lighting system consists of a headlight, taillight and reverse indicator light (1990-on models).

Table 2 lists replacement bulbs for these components. Always use the correct wattage bulb as indicated in this section. The use of a larger wattage bulb will give a dim light and a smaller wattage bulb will burn out prematurely.

Figure 17 shows a typical lighting circuit diagram.

Lighting Coil Voltage Test

Two test wires are required to perform this test. Fabricate each test wire from one male bullet connector, two female connectors, and two lengths of 18-gauge wire. Connect a male and female connec-

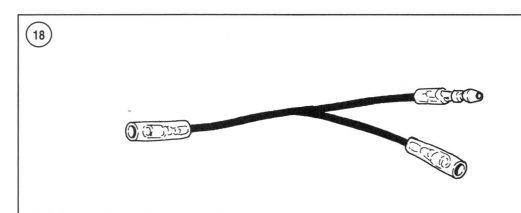

tor to each end of the wires, and splice the second female connector to the wire. See **Figure 18**.

1. Remove the front fender cover as described in Chapter Fourteen.

2. Connect a voltmeter in line between the headlight and (see A, **Figure 19**) the light switch by performing the following:

   a. Disconnect the black/yellow-to-black/yellow bullet connector from the headlight. Connect a test wire between the two bullet connectors.

   b. Disconnect the red-to-red bullet connector from the light switch. Connect a second test wire between the two bullet connectors.

   c. Connect the leads from a voltmeter to the test point on each of the test wires.

3. Install a tachometer following the manufacturer's instructions.

4. Turn the headlight switch on, and start the engine. Make sure the headlight and taillight operate. The results will not be accurate if these lights are not working.

5. Run the engine at 3000 rpm and check the voltage measured at the meter. If the measured output is less than the lighting voltage specified in **Table 1**, check the lighting coil resistance as described in *Stator Testing* earlier in this chapter.

Headlight Bulb Replacement

Refer to **Figure 20**.

WARNING
If the headlight has just burned out or has just been turned off, it will be hot! Do not touch the bulb until it cools off.

1. Remove the front fender cover as described in Chapter Fourteen.

2. Pull the dust cover (B, **Figure 19**) away from the lens assembly.

3. Turn the headlight socket counterclockwise, and remove the socket from the lens assembly.

4. Push the bulb into the socket, turn the bulb counterclockwise, and remove the bulb.

5. Installation is the reverse of removal.

6. Align the tangs on the new bulb with the notches in the socket and install the bulb.

7. Install the socket into the lens assembly, and slide the dust cover back in place (B, **Figure 19**).

8. Reinstall the fender cover, and check headlight operation.

9. Check headlight adjustment as described in this section.

Headlight Adjustment

1. Loosen the mounting screw (**Figure 21**) on each side of the front fender cover.

HEADLIGHT

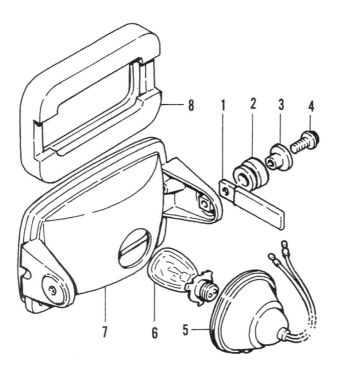

1. Wire clamp
2. Damper
3. Collar
4. Screw
5. Dust cover
6. Bulb
7. Lens assembly
8. Seal

9

2. Adjust the headlight vertically until the beam is at the desired height.

3. Tighten the mounting screws securely.

4. The headlight cannot be adjusted horizontally.

Taillight Bulb Replacement

Refer to **Figure 22** for this procedure.

1. Remove the Phillips screws and remove the taillight lens (**Figure 23**).

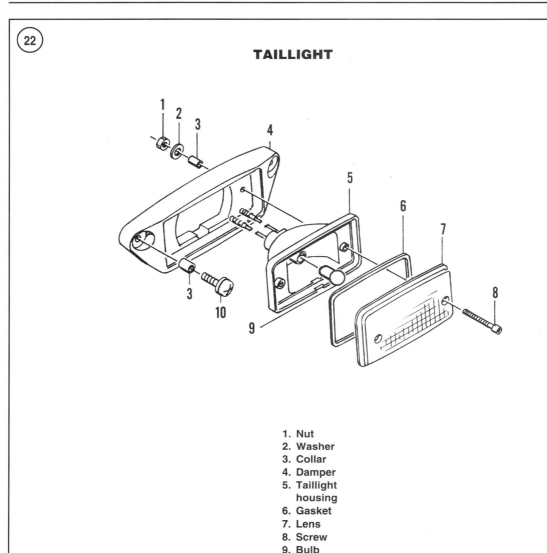

TAILLIGHT

1. Nut
2. Washer
3. Collar
4. Damper
5. Taillight
   housing
6. Gasket
7. Lens
8. Screw
9. Bulb
10. Screw

2. Push the bulb in (**Figure 24**), turn it counterclockwise, and remove it.

3. Align the bulb pins with the bulb socket grooves. Then push the bulb in, turn it clockwise, and release it. Make sure the bulb is locked in the bulb socket.

4. Replace the gasket if it is damaged or missing.

5. Clean the lens in a mild detergent and rinse with clear water.

6. Install the lens. Make sure the tab on the lens fits into the cutout in the taillight housing. Secure the lens with the two Phillips screws.

7. Check taillight operation.

ENGINE STOP SWITCH

	B/Y	W/B
RUN		
OFF	●————————————————●	

9

Reverse Indicator Lamp Replacement (1990-On Models)

1. Remove the lens (**Figure 25**) from the reverse indicator lamp.
2. Pull the bulb socket from the bracket. See **Figure 26**.
3. Pull the bulb (**Figure 27**) from the bulb socket.
4. Press a new bulb into the bulb socket.
5. Install the bulb socket into its mounting hole in the bracket, and install the lens.
6. Check each indicator light for proper operation.

SWITCHES

Testing

Test switches for continuity with an ohmmeter (see Chapter One) or a test light at the switch connector plug by operating the switch in each of its operating positions and comparing the results with its switch operating diagram. For example, **Figure 28** shows a continuity diagram for the engine stop switch. It shows which terminals should show continuity when the switch is in a given position.

When the engine stop switch is in the OFF position, there should be continuity between the black/yellow and white/black terminals. This is indicated by the line on the continuity diagram. An ohmmeter connected between these two terminals should indicate little or no resistance, or a test light should light. When the engine stop switch is in the RUN position, there should be no continuity (infinite resistance) between the same terminals.

When testing switches, note the following:
1. When separating two connector halves, pull on the connector housings and not the wires.

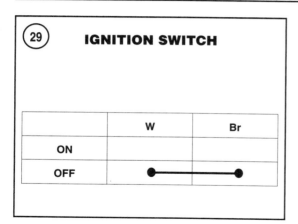

(29) IGNITION SWITCH

	W	Br
ON		
OFF	●———————●	

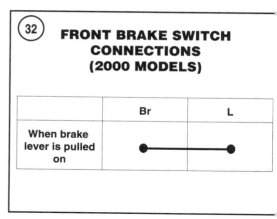

(32) FRONT BRAKE SWITCH CONNECTIONS (2000 MODELS)

	Br	L
When brake lever is pulled on	●———————●	

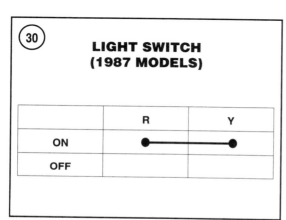

(30) LIGHT SWITCH (1987 MODELS)

	R	Y
ON	●———————●	
OFF		

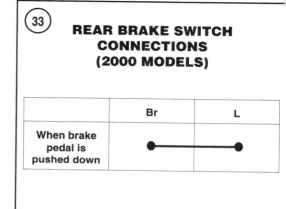

(33) REAR BRAKE SWITCH CONNECTIONS (2000 MODELS)

	Br	L
When brake pedal is pushed down	●———————●	

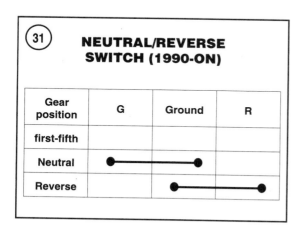

(31) NEUTRAL/REVERSE SWITCH (1990-ON)

Gear position	G	Ground	R
first-fifth			
Neutral	●———————●		
Reverse		●———————●	

2. After locating a defective circuit, check the connectors to make sure they are clean and properly connected. Check all wires going into a connector housing to make sure each wire is properly positioned and that the wire end is not loose.

3. When reconnecting connector halves, push them together until they click or snap into place.

If the switch or button does not perform properly, replace it. Refer to the following figures when testing the switch:

1. Engine stop switch: **Figure 28**.
2. Ignition switch: **Figure 29**.
3. Light switch (1987 models): **Figure 30**.
4. Neutral/reverse switch (1990-on): **Figure 31**.

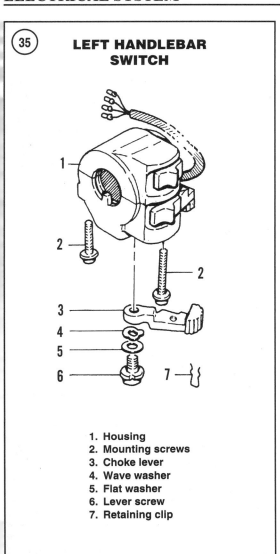

LEFT HANDLEBAR SWITCH

1. Housing
2. Mounting screws
3. Choke lever
4. Wave washer
5. Flat washer
6. Lever screw
7. Retaining clip

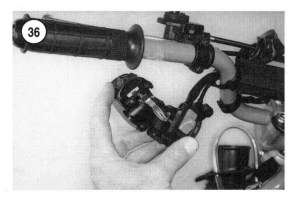

5. Front brake switch (2000 models): **Figure 32**.

6. Rear brake switch (2000 models): **Figure 33**.

Left Handlebar Switch Housing Replacement

The left handlebar switch housing is equipped with the following switches:

1. Light switch (A, **Figure 34**).

2. Engine stop switch (B, **Figure 34**).

Refer to **Figure 35**.

NOTE
The switches mounted in the left handlebar switch housing are not available separately. If one switch is
damaged, replace the housing assembly.

1. Remove the front fender cover as described in Chapter Fourteen.

2. Follow the switch harness and disconnect the connectors.

3. Remove or cut any clamps securing the switch wiring harness to the frame.

4. Remove the left handlebar switch mounting screws, and separate the switch halves. See **Figure 36**.

5. Unscrew the choke lever screw (A, **Figure 37**), and remove the flat and wave washers.

6. Remove the choke lever from the housing, and disconnect the choke cable end from the lever.

7. Pull the retaining clip (B, **Figure 37**) from the lower switch housing, and release the choke cable from the housing.

8. Pull the switch cable from the frame. Note how the cable is routed. The cable for the new switch must be routed along the same path.

9. Install by reversing these removal steps, noting the following:

a. Route the switch cable along the same path as the old cable.

b. When installing the left handlebar switch assembly, insert the round knob in the lower switch housing (**Figure 38**) into the hole in the handlebar.

c. Check the operation of each switch in the left switch housing.

Ignition Switch Replacement

The ignition switch (**Figure 39**) is mounted in the front fender cover.

1. Remove the front fender cover as described in this chapter.

2. Disconnect the ignition switch wires (A, **Figure 19**).

3. Pull the boot (C, **Figure 19**) off the switch, and slide the boot from the wiring.

4. Remove the ignition switch ring nut (**Figure 40**) and the damper.

5. Remove the switch from the cover.

6. Install a new ignition switch by reversing these removal steps.

7. Check the ignition switch in each of its operating positions.

Neutral/Reverse Switch Replacement (1990-On Models)

The combination neutral/reverse switch is mounted on the left side of the shift drum shaft, behind the reverse mechanism cover.

1. Remove the reverse mechanism cover as described in Chapter Seven.

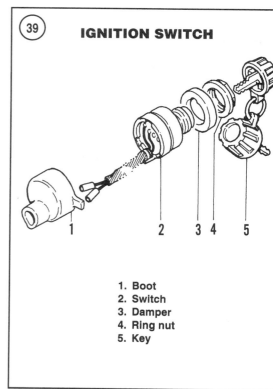

IGNITION SWITCH

1. Boot
2. Switch
3. Damper
4. Ring nut
5. Key

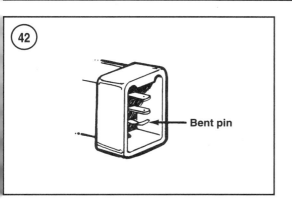

Bent pin

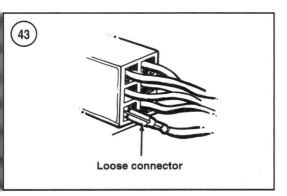

Loose connector

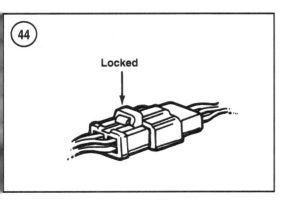

Locked

2. Remove the two mounting screws and the neutral/reverse switch (A, **Figure 41**) from the shift drum shaft.

3. Remove the neutral/reverse switch grommet (B, **Figure 41**) from the crankcase.

4. Follow the switch harness along the crankcase and disconnect the switch connectors. Note how the switch wiring harness is routed through the crankcase. It must be routed along the same path during assembly.

5. Installation is the reverse of these steps while noting the following.

a. Carefully route the switch wiring harness along the path as the original harness.

b. Apply Loctite 242 (blue) to the switch mounting screws. Install the screws and tighten them securely.

6. Start the engine and check switch operation.

WIRING AND CONNECTORS

Circuit and Wiring Check

Many electrical troubles can be traced to damaged wiring or to corroded or loose connectors.

1. Inspect all wiring for fraying, burning and any other visible damage.

2. Service the connectors by disconnecting them and cleaning the contacts with an aerosol electrical contact cleaner. After a thorough cleaning, pack the electrical connectors with dielectric grease to help seal out moisture.

3. Never pull on the wires when disconnecting an electrical connector. Only pull the connector plastic housing.

4. Disconnect each electrical connector in a suspect circuit, and inspect the male side of the connector. Make sure no pins are bent (**Figure 42**). A bent pin will not connect to its mate in the female side of the connector causing an open circuit.

5. Check the female side of each connector. Make sure the connector on the end of each wire (**Figure 43**) is pushed all the way into the plastic housing. If not, carefully push the connector into place with a narrow-blade screwdriver.

6. Once everything checks out, push the connector halves together. Make sure the male and female contacts are fully engaged and the connector halves are locked together (**Figure 44**).

WIRING DIAGRAMS

The wiring diagrams are located at the end of this book.

Table 1 ELECTRICAL SYSTEM SPECIFICATIONS

Magneto type	Single-phase AC
Magneto output voltage	12.8 VAC at 10,000 rpm
Exciter coil resistance	60-120 ohms, B/R - B/W
Lighting coil resistance	0.6-1.3 ohms, B/Y - ground
Lighting coil voltage	9.5 VAC at 3000 rpm, R - B/Y
Fan motor power coil resistance	0.6-1.3 ohms, Br - Br
Cooling fan motor voltage	
1987-1989	25 VAC at 3000 rpm
1990-on	12.3-13.7 VAC at 5000 rpm, G - B/Y
Cooling fan switch resistance	
Off to On	0.5 ohms at 183-194° F (84-90° C)
On to OFF	Infinity at 160-170° F (71-77° C)
Pickup coil resistance	100-150 ohms, B – B/Y
Pickup coil air gap (for reference)	0.7 mm (0.028 in.)
Ignition coil	
Ignition coil spark gap	7 mm (0.28 in.) or more
Primary winding resistance	0.4-0.22 ohms
Secondary winding resistance	3.3-4.9 k ohms
CDI unit resistance	See Figure 6
Spark plug	
US model	NGK DP8EA-9 or ND X24EP-U9
Canadian model	NGK DPR8EA-9 or ND X24EPR-U9
European models (1990-on)	NGK DPR8EA-9 or ND X24EPR-U9
Spark plug gap	0.8-0.9 mm (0.031-0.035 in.)
Spark plug cap resistance	3.75-6.25 k ohms
Ignition timing	
Static	10° at 1300 rpm
Advance	35° at 3000 rpm

Table 2 REPLACEMENT BULBS

Item	Voltage/wattage
Headlight (high/low beam)	12V 45/45W
Taillight	12V 8W
Reverse indicator (1990-on)	12V 3.4W

Table 3 ELECTRICAL SYSTEM TIGHTENING TORQUES

Item	N•m	in.-lb.	ft.-lb.
Magneto rotor bolt	93	–	69
Spark plugs	14	–	10
Cooling fan switch	25	–	18

CHAPTER TEN

COOLING SYSTEM

The pressurized cooling system consists of a radiator, radiator cap, thermostat, electric cooling fan and a coolant reservoir.

It is important to keep the coolant level between the LOW and FULL marks on the coolant reservoir (**Figure 1**) when the engine is cold. Always add coolant to the reservoir, not the radiator.

> *CAUTION*
> *Drain and flush the cooling system every 2 years. Refill it with a mixture of ethylene glycol antifreeze (formulated for aluminum engines) and purified water. **Do not** reuse old coolant because it deteriorates with use. **Never** operate the cooling system with only water (even in climates where anti-*

freeze protection is not required). The engine will oxidize internally and have to be replaced. When changing the coolant, follow the procedure described in Chapter Three.

> *WARNING*
> *Antifreeze (coolant) is a toxic waste material. Drain it into a suitable container and dispose of it according to local toxic waste regulations. Do not store coolant where it is accessible to children or animals.*

This chapter describes the repair and replacement of the cooling system components. **Table 1** at the end of this chapter lists the cooling system specifications. **Table 2** lists torque specifications. For routine maintenance of the system, refer to Chapter Three.

> *WARNING*
> *Do not remove the radiator cap (A, **Figure 2**) when the engine is hot. The coolant is very hot and under pressure. Severe scalding could result if the coolant touches the skin.*

The cooling system must be cool before any component of the system is removed.

HOSES AND HOSE CLAMPS

Hoses deteriorate with age and should be replaced periodically or whenever they show signs of cracking or leakage. To be safe, replace the hoses (A, B and C, **Figure 3**) every 2 years. The spray of hot coolant from a cracked hose can scald you. Loss of coolant can also overheat the engine causing damage.

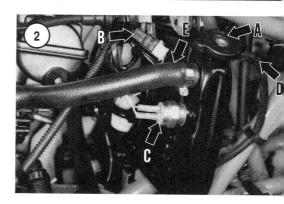

Whenever any component of the cooling system is removed, inspect the hoses and replace them if necessary.

The small diameter coolant hoses are very stiff and sometimes difficult to install onto their fittings. Before installing the hoses, soak the ends in hot water to make them pliable, and they will slide on much easier. *Do not* apply any type of lubricant to the inner surfaces of the hoses as the hose may slip off even with the hose clamp in place.

Always use the screw-adjusting type hose clamps. This type of clamp has superior holding ability, and it is easily released with a screwdriver.

1. Be sure the cooling system is cool before replacing the hoses.

2. Replace the hoses with Kawasaki replacement hoses. Each Kawasaki hose is formed to a specific shape and length, and its inner diameter properly fits a respective fitting.

3. Drain the cooling system as described in Chapter Three.

4. Loosen the hose clamp on the hose that is to be replaced. Slide the clamp back off the fitting.

> *CAUTION*
> *When removing a stubborn hose from the fittings, especially the fragile aluminum radiator inlet and outlet fittings, do not twist too hard. The fittings may be damaged, which could lead to expensive radiator repair.*

5. Twist the hose to release it from the fitting. If the hose has been on for some time, it may be difficult to break loose. If so, carefully cut the hose parallel to the fitting with a knife. Carefully pry the hose from the fitting with a broad-tipped screwdriver.

6. Examine the fitting for cracks or other damage. Repair or replace a fitting as necessary. If the fitting is good, use a wire brush and clean off any hose residue that may have transferred to the fitting. Wipe it clean with a cloth.

7. Inspect the hose clamps; replace if necessary. The hose clamps are as important as the hoses. If they do not hold the hose tightly in place, there will be a coolant leak. For best results, always use the screw-adjusting type hose clamps.

8. With the hose installed correctly on the fitting, position the hose clamp approximately one-half inch back from the end of the hose. Make sure the hose clamp is still positioned over the fitting, and tighten the clamps securely but not so tight that it damages the hose.

9. Install all removed components.

10. Refill the cooling system with the recommended type and quantity of coolant. Refer to Chapter Three.

11. Start the engine, and check for leaks.

COOLING SYSTEM INSPECTION

Two checks should be made before disassembly if a cooling system fault is suspected.

1. Run the engine until it reaches operating temperature. A pressure surge should be felt when the outlet hose (A, **Figure 3**) is squeezed while the engine is running.

2. If a substantial coolant loss is noted, the head gasket may be blown. In extreme cases sufficient coolant will leak into a cylinder(s) when the ATV is left standing for several hours so that the engine cannot be turned over with the kickstarter. White smoke (steam) might also be observed at the muffler when the engine is running. Coolant may also find its way into the oil. Check the dipstick; if the oil is foamy or milky looking, there is coolant in the oil system. If so, correct the cooling system immediately.

CAUTION
After correcting the cooling system problem, change the engine oil to remove all coolant residue. Refill with fresh engine oil; refer to Chapter Three. It may be necessary to change the oil more than once, to remove all traces of coolant.

3. Check the radiator for clogged or damaged fins. If more than 20 percent of the radiator fin area is damaged, repair or replace the radiator.
4. Check all coolant hoses for cracks or damage. Replace all questionable parts. Make sure all hose clamps are secure but not so tight that they cut into the hoses.
5. Pressure test the cooling system as described in Chapter Three.

COOLANT RESERVOIR

Removal/Installation

Refer to **Figure 4** for this procedure.
1. Remove the left front mud flap as described in Chapter Fourteen.
2. Disconnect the vent hose (A, **Figure 5**) from the top of the reservoir, and disconnect the reservoir hose from the bottom of the reservoir.
3. Remove the rubber strap (B, **Figure 5**), and remove the forward half of the reservoir cover.
4. Remove the mounting bolt (C, **Figure 5**) and lower the reservoir and the rear half of the cover from the mounting bracket.
5. Remove the filler cap, and drain the coolant from the reservoir. Dispose of the coolant properly.
6. If necessary, clean the inside of the reservoir with a detergent, and thoroughly rinse the reservoir

with clean water. Remove all detergent residue from the tank.
7. Install by reversing these removal steps.

RADIATOR AND COOLING FAN

Removal/Installation

Refer to **Figure 4** for this procedure.
1. Remove the front fender as described in Chapter Fourteen.
2. Drain the coolant as described in Chapter Three.
3. Disconnect the fan motor connector (B, **Figure 2**) and the two leads from the cooling fan switch (C, **Figure 2**).
4. Disconnect the reservoir hose (D, **Figure 2**) from the fitting on the radiator filler neck.
5. Loosen the hose clamp securing the upper radiator hose (E, **Figure 2**) to the inlet fitting, but do not disconnect the hose at this time.
6. Remove the vent hose from the fan (A, **Figure 6**). Bend open the clamp (B, **Figure 6**) on the fan and release the hose from the fan.
7. Loosen the hose clamp securing the lower radiator hose (C, **Figure 6**) to the outlet fitting, but do not disconnect the hose.
8. Remove the two bolts and collars (**Figure 7**) securing the radiator to the frame.
9. Pull the radiator slightly forward and disengage the upper radiator hose (E, **Figure 2**) from the radiator fitting.
10. Pull the radiator up to disengage the lower radiator hose (C, **Figure 6**) from the radiator fitting.
11. Carefully remove the radiator from the frame.
12. Inspect the radiator as described in this chapter.
13. Install by reversing these removal steps while noting the following:
   a. Replace all radiator hoses if they are starting to deteriorate or are damaged in any way.
   b. Make sure the connectors for the cooling fan and cooling fan switch are free of corrosion and are tight.
   c. Refill the cooling system with the recommended type and quantity of coolant as described in Chapter Three.

10

④

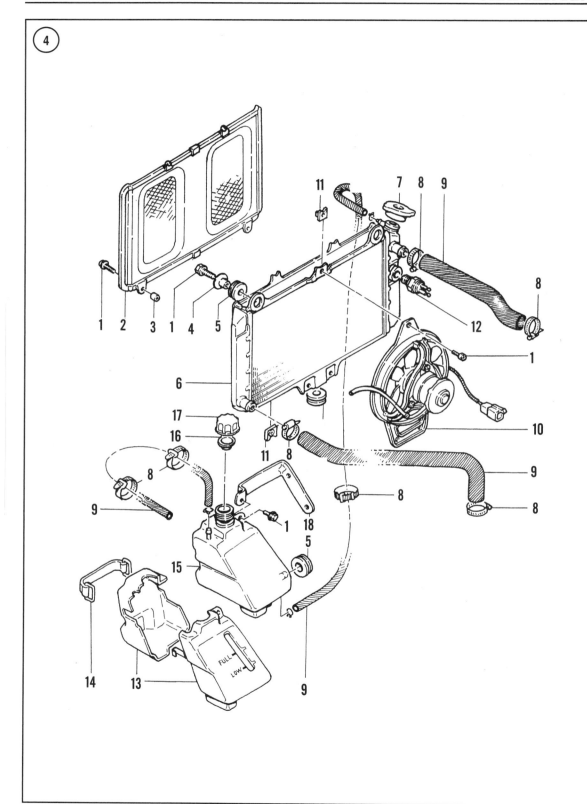

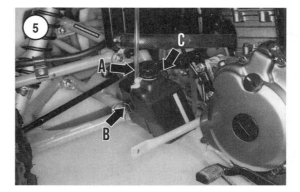

10

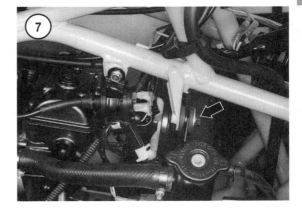

COOLING SYSTEM

1. Bolt
2. Radiator screen
3. Spacer
4. Collar
5. Damper
6. Radiator
7. Radiator cap
8. Clamp
9. Hose
10. Radiator fan
11. Nut
12. Fan switch
13. Reservoir cover
14. Strap
15. Reservoir
16. Gasket
17. Cap
18. Bracket

Radiator Inspection

1. Remove the cooling fan assembly as described in this chapter. This allows access to the back portion of the radiator for inspection.

2. Remove the two mounting screws (**Figure 8**) and lift the protective screen from the front of the radiator

3. If compressed air is available, use short spurts of air directed from the *backside* of the radiator core, and blow out dirt and bugs.

4. Flush off the exterior of the radiator with a garden hose on low pressure. Spray both the front and the back to remove all debris. Carefully use a whisk broom or stiff paint brush to remove any stubborn dirt from the cooling fins.

CAUTION
Do not press too hard when cleaning the cooling fins. The fins and tubes may be damaged causing a leak.

5. Carefully straighten out any bent cooling fins with a broad tipped screwdriver or putty knife.
6. If more than 20 percent of the air passages in the radiator are obstructed and cannot be cleared, replace the radiator.
7. Check for cracks or leakage (usually a moss-green colored residue) at the inlet hose fitting (A, **Figure 9**), outlet hose fitting and the seams (B, **Figure 9**) of both end tanks.
8. To prevent oxidation to the radiator, touch up any area where the paint is worn. Use quality spray paint and apply several *light* coats of paint. Do not apply heavy coats. Heavy coats will cut down on the cooling efficiency of the radiator.
9. Inspect the rubber dampers at the radiator mounts on the frame. Replace either damper if it is damaged or starting to deteriorate.
10. Check the cooling fan switch (C, **Figure 9**) for signs of leakage. Make sure the switch is tight. If necessary, torque the switch to the specification in **Table 2**.
11. Inspect the radiator cap as described in Chapter Three.

COOLING FAN

Removal/Installation

Replacement parts for the fan assembly are not available. If the fan motor is defective, replace the entire fan assembly.
Refer to **Figure 4** for this procedure.
1. Remove the radiator as described in this chapter.
2. Remove the three screws (**Figure 10**) securing the fan, and carefully detach the fan assembly from the radiator.
3. Testing the cooling fan is described in Chapter Nine.
4. Install by reversing these removal steps.

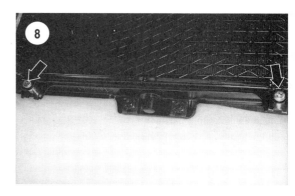
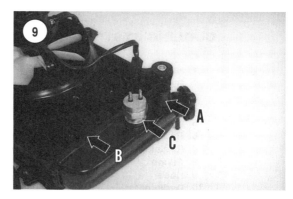

THERMOSTAT

Removal/Installation

The thermostat housing (B, **Figure 11**) is on the right side of the cylinder head.
1. Drain the coolant from the system as described in Chapter Three.
2. Remove the front fender as described in Chapter Fourteen.
3. Loosen the clamp (A, **Figure 11**) on the radiator hose.

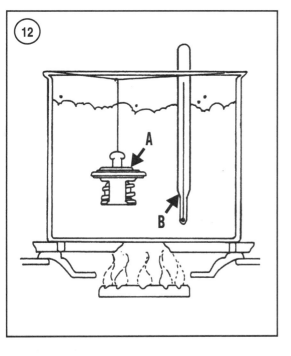

b. Install a new O-ring seal in the thermostat housing cover. Apply a light coat of multipurpose grease to hold the O-ring in place during installation.

c. Make sure the lower thermostat-housing bolt secures the clutch cable clamp (C, **Figure 11**).

d. Refill the cooling system with the recommended type and quantity of coolant as described in Chapter Three.

Testing

Test the thermostat to ensure proper operation. Replace the thermostat if it remains open at normal room temperature or stays closed after the specified temperature has been reached during the test procedure.

NOTE
Submerge the thermostat completely during the following test. Also, the thermostat and the thermometer must not touch the container sides or bottom because it will result in a false reading.

Suspend the thermostat (A, **Figure 12**) and a thermometer (B, **Figure 12**) in a beaker or pan of water. Use a cooking thermometer that is rated higher than the test temperature. Gradually heat the water and gently stir it until the water temperature reaches the opening temperature listed in **Table 1**. The thermostat valve should open at this temperature.

NOTE
Valve operation may be sluggish; it may require 3-5 minutes for the valve to open completely. If the valve fails to open, replace the thermostat (it cannot be serviced). The replacement thermostat should have the same temperature rating as the old thermostat.

WATER PUMP

Impeller Removal/Installation

Refer to **Figure 13** for this procedure.

1. Park the ATV on a level spot, set the parking brake and shift the transmission into gear.

2. Drain the cooling system as described in Chapter Three.

4. Remove the three bolts securing the thermostat housing to the cylinder head. Note that the clutch cable clamp (C, **Figure 11**) is mounted beneath the lower thermostat-housing bolt. Reinstall the clamp beneath this bolt during installation.

5. Remove the thermostat housing, and disconnect it from the radiator hose.

6. If necessary, test the thermostat as described in this chapter.

7. Install by reversing these removal steps while noting the following:

a. Inspect the O-ring seal on the housing cover. Replace the O-ring if it is damaged, deteriorated or starting to harden.

10

⑬

WATER PUMP

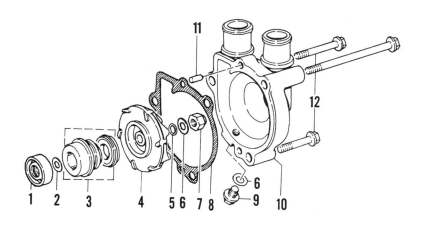

1. Oil seal
2. Shim
3. Mechanical seal
4. Impeller
5. O-ring
6. Washer
7. Impeller nut
8. Gasket
9. Drain bolt
10. Water pump cover
11. Dowel
12. Bolt

3. Remove the inlet and outlet hoses from the water pump cover.

4. Remove the water pump cover bolts and the water pump cover (**Figure 14**) and the gasket (A, **Figure 15**). Do not lose the two dowels (B, **Figure 15**) behind the cover.

5. Remove the impeller nut (C, **Figure 15**) and washer from the balancer shaft.

NOTE
The impeller O-ring sits inside the impeller. To prevent O-ring damage, turn the impeller counterclockwise to remove it from the balancer shaft.

6. Turn the impeller counterclockwise, and remove it from the balancer shaft.

7. Remove the shim (**Figure 16**) from the balancer shaft.

8. Installation is the reverse of removal. Note the following:

a. Lubricate the sealing surface of the ceramic seat in the impeller as well as the sealing surface of the mechanical seal in the water pump housing with fresh coolant.

b. When installing the impeller, turn it clockwise to prevent damage to the O-ring.

c. Torque the impeller nut to the specification in **Table 2**.

d. Make sure the dowels (B, **Figure 15**) are in place in the water pump housing, and install a new water pump cover gasket (A, **Figure 15**).

e. Refill the cooling system as described in Chapter Three.

Water Pump Inspection

1. Inspect the drainage outlet (**Figure 17**) beneath the water pump housing on the clutch cover.

2. If there are signs of leakage, coolant is leaking past the mechanical seal and out through the drain-

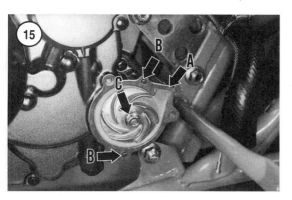

age outlet. Replace the mechanical seal and the oil seal as described in this chapter.

3. Inspect the water pump cover for wear or damage. Replace the cover if necessary.

4. Check the impeller for corrosion or damage. Replace the impeller if it is excessively corroded or cracked.

5. Inspect the ceramic seal in the impeller for roughness or other signs of damage. Replace the ceramic seal if necessary. Refer to *Mechanical Seal Removal/Installation* in this chapter.

6. Turn the balancer shaft, and check the bearing for excessive noise or roughness. If the bearing operation is rough, replace the bearings as described in Chapter Five.

Mechanical Seal Removal/Installation

1. Remove the water pump impeller as described in this chapter.

2. Remove the clutch cover as described in Chapter Six.

CAUTION
Do not damage the inner surface of the clutch cover receptacle while removing the mechanical seal.

3. Use a drift or other suitable tool to tap around the circumference of the seal, and drive the mechanical seal from the water pump housing in the clutch cover (**Figure 18**).

NOTE
The oil seal must be replaced whenever the mechanical seal is removed.

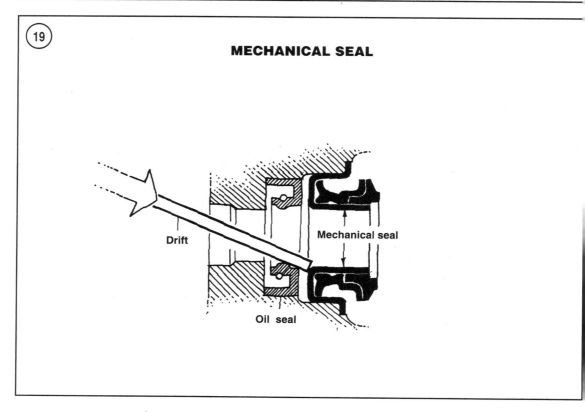

MECHANICAL SEAL

Drift

Mechanical seal

Oil seal

4. Remove the oil seal (**Figure 19**) from the housing. Note that the sealed side of the oil seal faces the outboard side of the clutch cover. The new seal will have to be installed in the same manner.

5. Apply a high-temperature grease to the lips of a new oil seal. Use the appropriate-sized bearing driver or socket and press the oil seal into place in the water pump housing. Install the oil seal with the manufacturer's marks facing the outboard side of the cover.

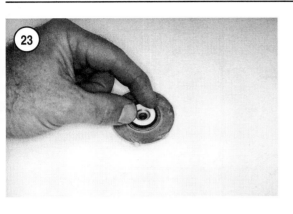

7. Use an appropriate tool to remove the old ceramic seal from the impeller (**Figure 21**).

8. From the outside of the impeller, pry out the O-ring (**Figure 22**) and then install a new O-ring (**Figure 22**). Lubricate the new O-ring with fresh coolant prior to installation.

CAUTION
Take care not to damage the mechanical seal during the next step.

9. Clean the sealing surface of the new mechanical seal with solvent and lubricate it with coolant.

10. Apply coolant to the rubber surface of a new ceramic seal and set the seal into the impeller. Press the seal into the impeller by hand until it bottoms. See **Figure 23**.

11. Install the clutch cover as described in Chapter Six.

12. Install the water pump impeller as described in this chapter.

NOTE
The mechanical seal has an adhesive coating on its body. Do not apply liquid gasket or other similar materials to the mechanical seal during installation.

6. Fit a new mechanical seal (**Figure 20**) into the water pump housing. Use an appropriate size bearing driver or socket to press the seal's flange seats against the top of the housing.

10

Table 1 COOLING SYSTEM SPECIFICATIONS

Total system capacity (engine, radiator, reservoir)	1.45 L (1.53 U.S. qt. [1.28 Imp. qt.])
Coolant ratio	50% distilled water, 50% coolant
Radiator cap relief pressure	76-103 kPa (11-15 psi)
Thermostat	
Opening temperature	69.5-72.5° C (157-162° F)
Minimum valve lift	3 mm (0.118 in.) at 85° C (185 ° F)

Table 2 COOLING SYSTEM TIGHTENING TORQUES

Item	N•m	in.-lb.	ft.-lb.
Thermostat housing bolt	9.8	87	–
Cooling fan switch	25	–	18
Water pump impeller nut	9.8	87	–
Water pump drain bolt	7.8	69	–
Coolant drain bolt	7.8	69	–
Hose fitting mounting bolt	9.8	87	–

CHAPTER ELEVEN

FRONT SUSPENSION AND STEERING

This chapter describes the repair and maintenance of the front wheels, hubs, front suspension arms, steering components and tires.

Tables 1-3 are located at the end of this chapter. **Table 1** lists front suspension and steering specifications. **Table 2** lists original equipment tire specifications. **Table 3** lists torque specifications

WHEEL ALIGNMENT

Toe-in is a condition where the front of the tires are closer together than the back. See **Figure 1**. Toe-in is adjusted by changing the length of the tie rods.

Steering Inspection

Before the toe-in can be adjusted, the steering centering adjustment must be checked and adjusted.

Test ride the vehicle on a smooth, level road. Hold the handlebar so that it points straight ahead. Note the following:

1. If the vehicle travels in a straight line with the handlebar pointed straight ahead, the steering centering position is correct. Adjust toe-in as described in this chapter.

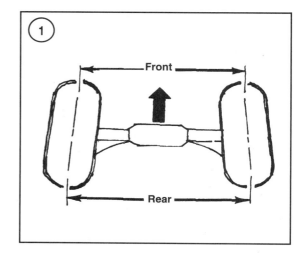

2. If the vehicle does not travel in a straight line, adjust the steering centering position as described in this chapter.

Steering Centering Adjustment

1. Inflate all four tires to the inflation pressure specified in **Table 2**.

2. Park the vehicle on level ground and set the parking brake. Support the vehicle so both front wheels are off the ground. In addition, position the

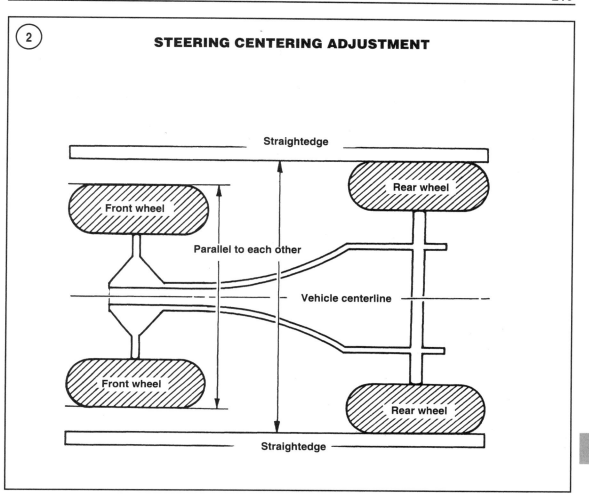

STEERING CENTERING ADJUSTMENT

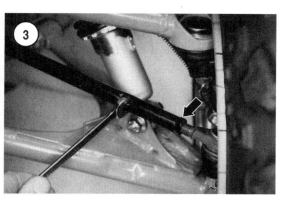

5. Check the position of the front wheel relative to the straightedge. The front wheel should be parallel to the straightedge. If not, perform Step 6.

6. Adjust the tie rod length by performing the following:

NOTE
*The adjusting sleeve end **without** the tie-rod adjusting flats has left-hand threads. Turn the locknut on this end clockwise to loosen it.*

a. Loosen the tie-rod adjusting sleeve locknut (**Figure 3**) at each end of the tie rod.

CAUTION
Adjust the tie-rod adjusting sleeve so the amount of visible thread on one end of the tie rod equals the amount of

vehicle so that the front spindles are at about the same height from the ground as the rear axle.

3. Turn the handlebar so it is pointing straight ahead.

4. Hold a straightedge across the rear wheel rim, at axle height, as shown in **Figure 2**.

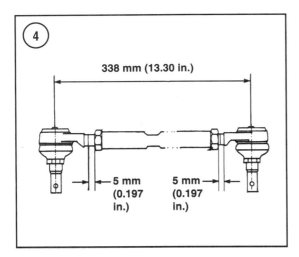

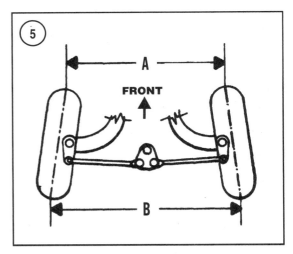

visible thread on the other end. See
Figure 4.

  b. Turn the tie-rod adjusting sleeve until the front wheel for the side being checked is parallel to the straightedge as shown in **Figure 2**.

  c. Tighten the tie-rod adjusting sleeve locknut to the torque specification in **Table 3**.

7. Repeat this procedure on the other side.

8. Adjust the toe-in as described in this chapter.

Toe-In Adjustment

1. Inflate all four tires to the tire pressure specified in **Table 2**.

2. Park the vehicle on level ground and set the parking brake. Raise and support the front end so that the front tires just clear the ground.

3. Turn the handlebar so the wheels are at the straight-ahead position.

4. Using a ruler, carefully measure the distance between the center of both front tires as shown in A, **Figure 5**. Mark the tires with a piece of chalk at these points. Record the measurement.

5. Rotate each tire exactly 180° and measure the distance between the center of both front tires at the points marked B in **Figure 5**. Record the measurement.

6. Subtract the measurement in Step 4 from Step 5. Compare the difference to the toe-in specification listed in **Table 1**. If the toe-in is outside the specified range, proceed to Step 7.

NOTE
When performing Step 7, turn both tie rods the same number of turns. This ensures that both tie rods are the same length.

WARNING
If the tie rods are not adjusted to equal lengths, the vehicle will not steer correctly. This may cause loss of vehicle control and an accident. If unable to adjust the toe-in to specification, have a dealership inspect the front suspension and steering system.

7. Adjust toe-in by performing the following:

NOTE
*The adjusting sleeve end **without** the tie-rod adjusting flats has left-hand threads. Turn the locknut on this end clockwise to loosen it.*

  a. Loosen the tie-rod adjusting sleeve locknuts (**Figure 3**) at each end of both tie rods.

CAUTION
*Adjust the tie-rod adjusting sleeve so the amount of visible thread on one end of the tie rod equals the amount of the visible thread on the other end. See **Figure 4**.*

  b. Use a wrench on the flat portion of the adjusting sleeve and slowly turn both tie-rod adjusting sleeves the same amount until the tie rod measurement is correct. The toe-in adjust-

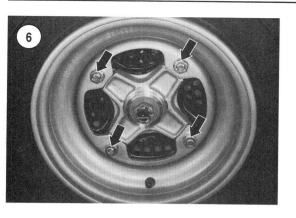

ment should be approximately correct if the tie rod length, measured between the tie rod ends, equals the length specified in **Table 1** or if there is 5 mm (0.197 in) of visible thread (**Figure 4**) at each end of the tie rod.

   c. Tighten the tie-rod adjusting sleeve locknuts to the torque specification in **Table 3**.

8. Measure the toe-in again. Repeat the adjustment procedure if necessary.

9. Test ride the vehicle slowly, checking the steering and handling.

FRONT WHEEL

Removal/Installation

> *NOTE*
> *All models are equipped with directional-type tires on the front and rear of the vehicle. Therefore, the wheels must be reinstalled on the same side of the ATV from which they were removed. Before removing the wheels, mark them for reference during installation.*

1. Park the vehicle on level ground and set the parking brake. Block the rear wheels to prevent the vehicle from rolling in either direction.

2. Loosen but do not remove the wheel nuts (**Figure 6**).

3. Raise the front of the vehicle with a small jack. Place the jack under the frame with a piece of wood between the jack and frame.

4. Place wooden blocks under the frame to support the vehicle with the front wheels off the ground.

5. Remove the wheel nuts loosened in Step 2 and remove the front wheel.

6. Install the tire and wheel onto the same side of the vehicle from which it was removed.

7. Install and finger-tighten the wheel nuts until the wheel is positioned correctly on all four wheel studs.

> *WARNING*
> *Always tighten the wheel nuts to the correct torque specification or the wheel nuts may work loose and the wheel could fall off.*

8. Tighten the wheel nuts in a crisscross pattern, and torque them to the specification in **Table 3**.

9. After the wheel is installed completely, rotate it. Apply the brake several times to make sure the wheel rotates freely and the brake is operating correctly.

10. Raise the front of the vehicle slightly and remove the wooden block(s).

11. Let the jack down, and remove the jack and wooden block.

FRONT HUB

Refer to **Figure 7** when servicing the front hub.

Inspection

Inspect each wheel bearing prior to removing it from the wheel hub.

> *CAUTION*
> *Do not remove the wheel bearings for inspection purposes. The bearings are damaged during the removal process. Remove the wheel bearings only if replacement is necessary.*

1. Perform Steps 1-9 of *Front Hub Removal/Disassembly* in this section.

2. Turn each bearing by hand. Make sure each bearing turns smoothly.

> *NOTE*
> *Some axial play is normal, but radial play should be negligible. The bearing should turn smoothly.*

3. Inspect the seals. Replace them if they are deteriorating or starting to harden.

11

⑦

FRONT HUB

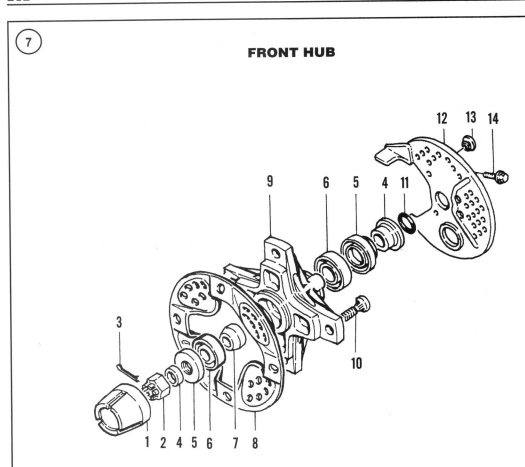

1. Cap
2. Hub nut
3. Cotter pin
4. Collar
5. Seal
6. Bearing
7. Distance collar
8. Outer guard
9. Hub
10. Wheel stud
11. O-ring
12. Disc guard
13. Damper
14. Bolt

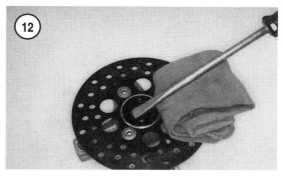

Front Hub Removal/Disassembly

Refer to **Figure 7** for this procedure.

1. Remove the front wheel as described in this chapter.

2. Remove the outer guard (**Figure 8**) from the hub.

> *WARNING*
> *Do not inhale brake dust. It may contain asbestos, which can cause lung injury and cancer.*

3. Remove the front brake caliper as described in Chapter Thirteen.

4. Remove the wheel cap.

5. Remove the cotter pin (A, **Figure 9**) and hub nut (B, **Figure 9**).

6. Remove the front hub assembly (**Figure 10**) from the steering-knuckle spindle.

7. Remove the inboard collar (A, **Figure 11**) from the seal (B, **Figure 11**) in the front hub.

8. Use a wide-blade screwdriver to pry the inboard seal from the front hub. Place a rag beneath the screwdriver to protect the brake disc. See **Figure 12**.

9. Pull the outboard collar (**Figure 13**) from the seal.

10. Pry the outboard seal (**Figure 14**) from the hub. Place a rag beneath the screwdriver to protect the hub.

11. Before proceeding any further, inspect the wheel bearings (**Figure 15**) as described in this chapter.

12. To remove the inner and outer bearings and distance collar, insert a soft aluminum or brass drift into one side of the hub. Push the distance collar over to one side and place the drift on the inner race of the outer bearing. Tap the bearing out of the hub with a hammer working around the perimeter of the inner race (**Figure 16**).

13. Remove the distance collar and tap out the inner bearing.

14. Thoroughly clean the inside of the hub with solvent, and dry it with compressed air or a shop cloth.

Front Hub Assembly/Installation

NOTE
The front hub bearings are sealed.
They cannot be lubricated.

1. Wipe the distance collar with bearing grease.

CAUTION
Install the wheel bearings with the manufacturer's marks facing out. During installation, drive the bearings squarely into place by tapping on the outer race only. Use a socket that matches the outer race diameter. Do not tap on the inner race or the bearing may be damaged. Make sure the bearings are completely seated in the hub.

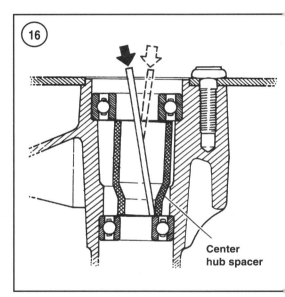

Center
hub spacer

2. Install the outer bearing into the hub.

3. Install the distance collar and the inner bearing.

4. Apply a light coat of multipurpose grease to the inboard seal at the points shown in **Figure 17**.

5. Install the inboard seal (B, **Figure 11**).

6. Install the inboard collar (A, **Figure 11**) into the inboard seal.

7. Apply a light coat of multipurpose grease to the outboard seal at the points shown in **Figure 17**.

8. Install the outboard seal (**Figure 14**) and seat it into the front hub.

9. Install the outboard collar (**Figure 13**) and seat it inside the outboard seal.

10. If removed, apply grease onto the O-ring (**Figure 18**) and install it into the groove in the steering-knuckle spindle.

11. Slide the front hub (**Figure 10**) onto the knuckle spindle.

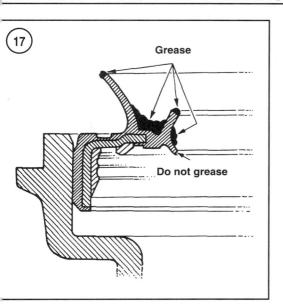

17

Grease

Do not grease

18

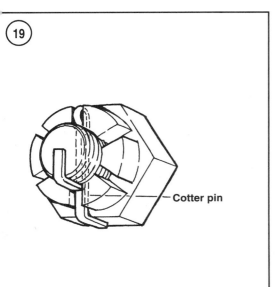

19

Cotter pin

12. Install the front hub nut (B, **Figure 9**) and tighten it to the torque specification in **Table 3**.

NOTE
Install a new cotter pin. Never reuse an old one as it may break and fall out.

13. Install a new cotter pin (A, **Figure 9**) through the spindle and hub nut. Bend the ends over completely (**Figure 19**).
14. Install the front brake caliper as described in Chapter Thirteen.
15. Install the outer guard (**Figure 8**) onto the wheel studs.
16. Install the front wheel as described in this chapter.

HANDLEBAR

Removal

Refer to **Figure 20** for this procedure.

CAUTION
Brake fluid destroys the finish on painted or plated surfaces. Cover the seat, fuel tank and front fender with a heavy cloth or plastic tarp to protect it from the accidental spilling of brake fluid. Wash any spilled brake fluid off any painted or plated surface immediately. Use soapy water and rinse the area thoroughly.

1. Remove the bolts securing the front master cylinder (A, **Figure 21**) to the handlebar. Remove the master cylinder and lay it over the front fender. Secure the reservoir upright to prevent the loss of brake fluid and to prevent air from entering the brake system. It is not necessary to remove the hydraulic brake line from the master cylinder.
2. Remove the screws and clamp securing the throttle assembly (B, **Figure 21**) to the handlebar and remove the assembly. Lay the assembly over the front fender. Make sure that the cable does not get kinked or damaged.
3. Remove the screws securing the left switch assembly (A, **Figure 22**) to the handlebar and set the switch assembly aside.
4. Remove the screws and clamp (B, **Figure 22**) securing the clutch lever assembly to the handlebar.

11

HANDLEBAR

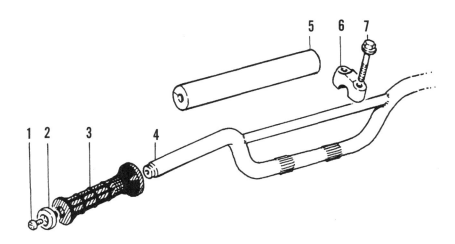

1. Screw
2. Plug
3. Grip
4. Handlebar
5. Pad
6. Handlebar holder
7. Handlebar holder bolt

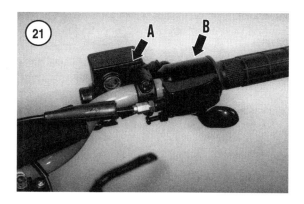

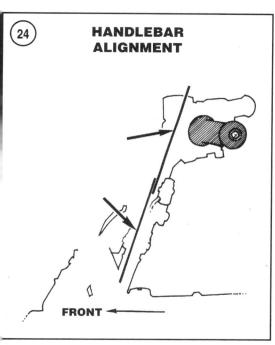

HANDLEBAR ALIGNMENT

FRONT ←

9. To maintain a good grip on the handlebar and to prevent it from slipping down, clean the knurled section of the handlebar with a wire brush. Keep it rough so it will be held securely by the holders. The holders should also be clean and free of any metal that may have been gouged loose by handlebar slippage.

Installation

1. Install the handlebar onto the lower holders.

2A. On 1987-1989 models, fit the handlebar holders in place. Install and finger-tighten the handlebar holder bolts.

2B. On 1990-on models, perform the following:

   a. Fit the handlebar holders in place. Install and finger-tighten the two front handlebar holder bolts.

   b. Set the reverse indicator bracket (B, **Figure 23**) in place on the handlebar holders. Install and finger-tighten the two rear handlebar holder bolts (A, **Figure 23**).

   c. Route the reverse indicator lamp lead through the handlebar and connect its mate on the harness.

3. Position the handlebar so the vertical axis of the handlebar parallels the steering stem as shown in **Figure 24**.

4. Tighten the two front handlebar holder bolts first, then tighten the two rear bolts. On 1990-on models, tighten all four bolts to the torque specification in **Table 3**. On 1987-1989 models, there must be an even gap at the rear of the handlebar holders and no gap at the front of the handlebar holders after the bolts are tightened.

5. Install the reverse knob bracket (C, **Figure 23**) and secure it with the mounting screw.

6. Install the clutch lever assembly (B, **Figure 22**) onto the handlebar. Tighten the clamp bolts securely.

7. Install the left switch assembly (A, **Figure 22**). Insert the round indexing pin in the lower switch housing (**Figure 25**) into the hole in the handlebar.

8. Position the front master cylinder (A, **Figure 21**) onto the handlebar. Then install its clamp—up mark facing up—and install the two clamp bolts. Tighten the upper bolt first, and then tighten the lower bolt. Torque the bolts to the specification in **Table 3**.

9. Install the throttle assembly (B, **Figure 21**) onto the handlebar.

Remove the assembly and lay it over the front fender. Make sure that the clutch and parking-brake cables do not get kinked or damaged.

5. Remove the reverse knob (C, **Figure 23**) and lay t over the front fender.

6. Remove any cable clamps that secure the wires and cables to the handlebar.

7. On 1990-on models, perform the following:

   a. Disconnect the reverse indicator lamp connector.

   b. Remove the two rear handlebar holder bolts (A, **Figure 23**) and the reverse indicator bracket (B, **Figure 23**).

8. Remove the handlebar holders and lift the handlebar from the lower holders.

11

STEERING

1. Bolt
2. Wire clamp
3. Seal
4. Bearing clamp
5. Nut
6. Plug
7. Steering shaft
8. Right tie rod
9. Washer
10. Cotter pin
11. Steering shaft bearing
12. Left tie rod

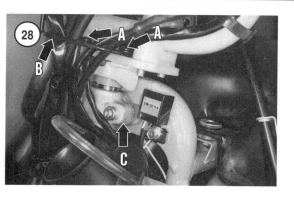

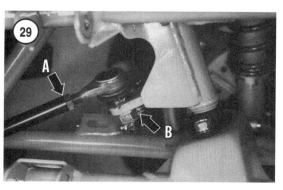

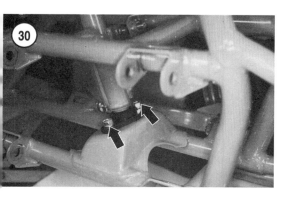

10. After all assemblies have been installed, test each one to make sure it operates properly with no binding. Correct any problem at this time.

Handlebar Grip Replacement

Refer to **Figure 20**.

1. Remove the screw and the plug (**Figure 26**) from the end of the handlebar.

2. Slide a thin screwdriver between the grip and handlebar. Then spray electrical contact cleaner into the opening under the grip.

3. Pull the screwdriver out and quickly twist the grip to break its bond against the handlebar. Then slide the grip off.

4. Clean the handlebar of all rubber or sealer residue.

5. Install the new grip following its manufacturer's directions. Apply an adhesive, such as ThreeBond Griplock, between the grip and handlebar. Follow the adhesive manufacturer's directions for drying time before operating the vehicle.

STEERING SHAFT

Refer to **Figure 27** when servicing the steering shaft:

Removal

1. Park the vehicle on level ground and set the parking brake. Block the rear wheels so the vehicle will not roll in either direction.

2. Remove the front fender as described in Chapter Fourteen.

3. Remove both front wheels as described in this chapter.

4. Remove the handlebar as described in this chapter.

5. Remove the two mounting screws (A, **Figure 28**) and cable/hose clamp (B, **Figure 28**) from the steering stem head.

> *NOTE*
> *Do not loosen the tie rod adjusting sleeve locknuts (A, **Figure 29**). Toe-in will require adjustment if a locknut is loosened.*

6. Each inboard tie-rod end is installed with an interference fit. Separate each tie rod end from the steering shaft by performing the following:

    a. Remove the cotter pin from the tie-rod end nut (B, **Figure 29**). Discard the cotter pin.

    b. Loosen the tie-rod end nut, but leave the nut on the tie-rod end to chase the threads.

    c. Use a drift to tap the tie rod end from the steering shaft.

    d. Remove the nut and washer, and then disconnect the tie rod from the steering shaft.

7. Remove the bolts (**Figure 30**) securing the bottom of the steering shaft to the frame.

11

8. Remove the bolts and nuts securing the upper steering shaft bearing clamp (C, **Figure 28**) to the frame. Then remove the bearing clamp halves.
9. Remove the steering shaft from the frame.

Inspection

1. Carefully inspect the entire steering shaft assembly, especially if the vehicle has been involved in a collision or spill. If the shaft is bent or twisted in any way, replace it. If a damaged shaft is installed in the vehicle, it will cause rapid and excessive wear to the bearings and place undue stress on other components in the frame and steering system.
2. Inspect the tie-rod attachment holes in the lower section of the steering shaft. Check for hole elongation, cracks or wear. Replace the steering shaft if necessary.

NOTE
The steering shaft bearing clamps must be replaced as a set.

3. Inspect the steering shaft bearing clamps for wear or damage. Replace if necessary.
4. Replace the upper steering shaft seals if excessively worn or damaged.
5. Hold the steering shaft and turn the lower bearing (**Figure 31**) back and forth by hand. The bearing should turn freely. If necessary, replace the lower bearing as described in this chapter.

Steering Shaft Bearing Lubrication
and/or Replacement

The steering shaft bearing (**Figure 31**) is mounted on the bottom of the steering shaft.
1. Remove and discard the cotter pin.
2. Remove the nut, washer and bearing from the bottom of the steering shaft.
3. Remove the two seals from the bearing.
4. If lubricating the bearing, perform the following:
   a. Wipe all the old grease out of the seals and steering stem.
   b. Pack the seals with molybdenum disulfide grease and install the seals onto the bearing.
5. Turn the bearing by hand. It should turn smoothly. If the bearing or either seal is excessively worn or damaged, replace the steering-shaft bearing assembly.

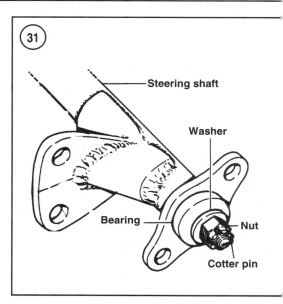

6. Install by reversing these removal steps, noting the following.
7. Tighten the steering shaft bottom end nut to the torque specification in **Table 3**.
8. Secure the nut with a new cotter pin. Bend the cotter pin ends over to lock it.

Installation

1. Install the steering shaft onto the frame.
2. Install the upper steering shaft seals. Position the seals with their open ends facing toward the front.
3. Apply molybdenum disulfide grease to the seal grooves.
4. Apply molybdenum disulfide grease to the steering-shaft bearing clamp halves.
5. Install the steering-shaft bearing clamp halves by performing the following:
   a. Install the clamp halves (C, **Figure 28**) so the lips in the seals fit into the grooves in the clamp halves.
   b. On 1988-on models, align the marks on the sides of both clamps.
   c. Install the clamp bolts finger-tight.
6. Install the bolts securing the bottom of the steering shaft to the frame. See **Figure 30**.
7. Tighten the steering stem bearing clamp bolts and nuts to the torque specification in **Table 3**.
8. Tighten the steering shaft bottom bolts securely.
9. Reconnect the tie rod at the steering shaft, and install the washer and nut. Tighten the tie-rod end

nut (B, **Figure 29**) to the torque specification in **Table 3**. Install a new cotter pin through the nut and bend the ends over completely.

10. Repeat Step 9 for the other tie rod.
11. Install the reverse knob and cable onto the steering stem head.
12. Install the handlebar as described in this chapter.
13. Install the front wheels as described in this chapter.
14. Install the front fender as described in Chapter Fourteen.
15. If the tie rods were replaced, adjust the toe-in as described in this chapter.

TIE ROD

Refer to **Figure 27** when servicing the tie rods.

Removal

Both tie rod assemblies are the same.
1. Place the vehicle on level ground and set the parking brake. Block the rear wheels so the vehicle will not roll in either direction.
2. Remove both front wheels as described in this chapter.
3. Remove the front fender as described in Chapter Fourteen.

NOTE
*Do not loosen the tie-rod adjusting sleeve locknut (A, **Figure 32**). Toe-in will require adjustment if a locknut is loosened.*

4. Disconnect the tie rod end from the steering knuckle by performing the following:

a. Remove the cotter pin from the tie-rod end nut. Discard the cotter pin.
b. Remove the tie-rod end nut (B, **Figure 32**) and washer.
c. Disconnect the tie rod from the steering knuckle.

NOTE
*Do not loosen the tie-rod adjusting sleeve locknut (A, **Figure 29**). Toe-in will require adjustment if a locknut is loosened.*

5. The inboard tie-rod end is installed with an interference fit. Separate the tie rod from the steering shaft by performing the following:

a. Remove the cotter pin from the tie-rod end nut (B, **Figure 29**). Discard the cotter pin.
b. Loosen the tie-rod end nut, but leave the nut on the tie-rod end to chase the threads.
c. Use a drift to tap the tie rod end from the steering shaft.
d. Remove the nut and washer, and then disconnect the tie rod from the steering shaft.

6. Remove the tie rod.

Inspection

NOTE
When cleaning a tie rod with solvent, work carefully to prevent the solvent from contaminating the grease in the rubber boot.

1. Inspect the tie-rod adjusting sleeve for damage. There should be no creases or bends along the sleeve.
2. Inspect the rubber boot of the ball joint at each tie rod end. The ball joints are permanently packed with grease. If the rubber boot is damaged, dirt and moisture can enter the ball joint and damage it. If the boot is damaged in any way, disassemble the tie rod and replace the tie rod end(s) as described in the following procedure.
3. Pivot the ball joint stud back and forth by hand. If it moves roughly or with excessive play, replace it as described in the following procedure.

Tie Rod Disassembly/Assembly

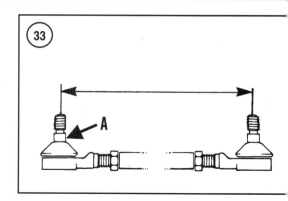

NOTE
*The adjusting sleeve end **without** the tie-rod adjusting flats has left-hand threads. Turn the locknut on this end clockwise to loosen it.*

1. Hold the tie rod with a wrench across the adjusting sleeve flats and loosen the adjusting sleeve locknut for the tie rod end being replaced.

2. Unscrew and remove the damaged tie rod end(s).

3. Clean the mating shaft and tie rod end threads with contact cleaner.

4. Thread the tie rod end (with locknut) into the tie rod shaft.

5. Adjust the tie rod length to the specification listed **Table 1**. Measure the length between the center of each stud as shown in **Figure 33**.

6. Install the tie rod and adjust the toe-in as described in this chapter.

Installation

1. Oil the ball joint stud at the point indicated in A, **Figure 33**.

2. Attach the tie rod end to the steering shaft.

3. Install the washer and nut onto each tie rod end. Torque each tie-rod end nut to the torque specification in **Table 3**.

4. Tighten the nut(s), if necessary, to align the cotter pin hole with the nut slot.

5. Install new cotter pins through all tie rod end nuts and studs. Open and bend the cotter pin ends to lock them in place.

6. Install the front fender as described in Chapter Fourteen.

7. Install the front wheels as described in this chapter.

8. Check the toe-in adjustment, and adjust if necessary, as described in this chapter.

STEERING KNUCKLE

Refer to **Figure 34** when servicing the steering knuckle.

Removal

1. Remove the front wheel and front hub as described in this chapter.

2. Remove the bolt (A, **Figure 35**) securing the brake hose to the upper control arm.

3. Remove the disc guard bolt (B, **Figure 35**) and the disc guard.

4. Remove the shock absorber as described in this chapter.

5. Disconnect the tie rod from the steering knuckle by performing the following:

    a. Remove the cotter pin from the tie-rod end nut. Discard the cotter pin.

    b. Remove the tie-rod end nut (B, **Figure 32**) and washer.

    c. Disconnect the tie rod from the steering knuckle.

NOTE
*The upper control-arm ball joint is installed in the steering knuckle with an interference fit. Use the Motion Pro ATV Ball Joint Separator (part No. 08-120, **Figure 36**) or equivalent to separate this ball joint from the steering knuckle. Follow the tool instructions.*

6. Separate the upper control arm from the steering knuckle with a ball joint separator (**Figure 37**) or by performing the following:

    a. Remove the cotter pin from the ball joint stud. Discard the cotter pin.

    b. Loosen the nut (A, **Figure 38**) on the ball joint stud but leave the nut on the stud to chase the threads.

    c. Use a drift to tap the ball joint stud from the upper control arm.

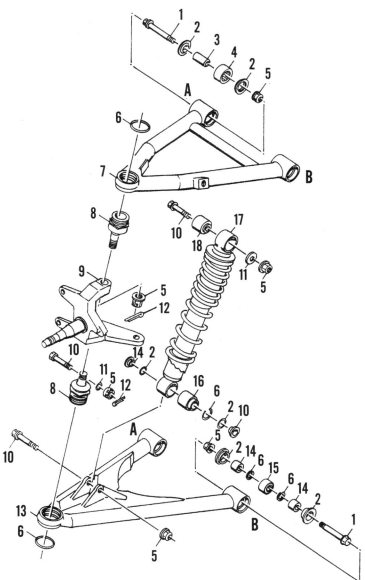

FRONT SUSPENSION

1. Pivot bolt	7. Upper control arm	13. Lower control arm
2. Seal	8. Ball joint	14. Collar
3. Sleeve	9. Steering knuckle	15. Spherical bearing
4. Needle bearing	10. Bolt	16. Spherical bearing
5. Nut	11. Washer	17. Shock absorber
6. Circlip	12. Cotter pin	18. Bushing

11

d. Remove the nut, and disconnect the upper-control-arm ball joint from the steering knuckle. See **Figure 39**).

7. Separate the lower control arm from the steering knuckle by performing the following:

   a. Remove the cotter pin from the steering-knuckle clamp nut (B, **Figure 38**).

   b. Remove the clamp nut and washer from the steering-knuckle clamp bolt.

   c. If necessary, use a drift to tap the clamp bolt from the steering knuckle.

   d. Lift and remove the steering knuckle from the lower-control-arm ball joint.

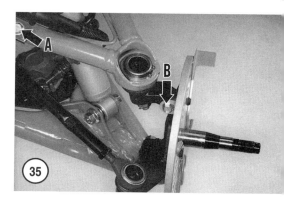

Inspection

1. Clean the steering knuckle in solvent, and dry it with compressed air.

2. Inspect the steering knuckle (**Figure 40**) for bending, thread damage, cracks or other damage.

3. Inspect the portion of the spindle where the front wheel bearings make contact for wear or damage. A hard spill or collision may cause the spindle to bend or fracture. If the spindle is damaged in any way, replace the steering knuckle.

4. Check the hole at the end of the spindle where the cotter pin fits. Make sure there are no fractures or cracks leading out toward the end of the steering knuckle. If any are present, replace the steering knuckle.

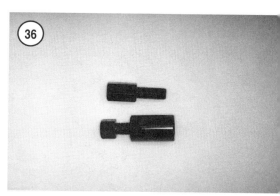

Installation

1. Make sure the O-ring (A, **Figure 40**) is in place on the steering knuckle spindle.

2. Apply molybdenum disulfide grease to the ball joint boot on each control arm.

3. Attach the steering knuckle to the lower control arm by performing the following:

   a. Lower the steering knuckle onto the ball joint stud in the lower control arm.

   b. Install the clamp bolt, the washer and finger-tighten the clamp nut (B, **Figure 38**).

4. Attach the upper control arm to the steering knuckle by performing the following:

   a. Fit the upper-control-arm ball joint into the steering knuckle upper joint.

   b. Install the nut onto the ball joint stud (A, **Figure 38**). Finger-tighten the nut at this time.

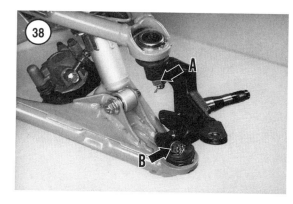

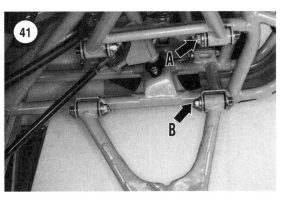

5. Attach the tie rod to the steering knuckle by performing the following:

a. Oil the tie rod stud at the point indicated in A, **Figure 33**.

b. Attach the tie-rod ball joint to the arm on the steering knuckle.

c. Install the tie-rod end nut (B, **Figure 32**). Finger-tighten the nut at this time.

6. Tighten the upper ball joint nut, the lower steering knuckle clamp nut, and the tie rod end nut to the torque specifications in **Table 3**. If necessary,

tighten a nut to align the cotter pin holes with the nut slots.

7. Install a new cotter pin through each nut. Open the cotter pins arms to lock them in place.

8. Install the shock absorber as described in this chapter.

9. Turn the handlebar from side to side. Check that the steering knuckle moves smoothly.

10. Install the disc guard and secure it in place with its mounting bolt (B, **Figure 35**).

11. Secure the brake hose to the upper control arm (A, **Figure 35**).

12. Install the brake caliper as described in Chapter Thirteen.

13. Install the front hub and wheel as described in this chapter.

CONTROL ARMS

Refer to **Figure 34** when servicing the control arms.

Removal/Installation

1. Remove the steering knuckle as described in this chapter.

NOTE
The front and rear pivots on each control arm have different bearing assemblies. Do not intermix the pivot bolts, nuts, seals, collars and other parts when removing the upper and lower control arms. Separate the parts so they can be installed in their original positions.

2. Before removing a control arm, check the bearings by performing the following:

a. Inspect the control arm bearings by moving each arm up and down. The arm should move smoothly. If abnormal friction is noted, the bearing(s) may be damaged.

b. Check the control arm bearing play by pushing and pulling the arm in and out. A small amount of play is normal. If play is excessive, check the bearing(s) for wear.

3. Remove the nut from each pivot bolt that secures the upper control arm to the frame. See A, **Figure 41**. Remove each pivot bolt and lower the control arm from the frame.

11

4. Remove the nut from each pivot bolt that secures the lower control arm to the frame. See B, **Figure 41**. Remove each pivot bolt and remove the lower control arm from the frame.

5. Install by reversing these removal steps, noting the following.

    a. Lubricate the bearings, seals and ball joints with molybdenum disulfide grease.

    b. Tighten the upper and lower control arm pivot nuts to the torque specification in **Table 3**.

    c. Raise and lower both control arms by hand. Each control arm should pivot smoothly.

Control Arm Cleaning and Inspection

> *NOTE*
> *The front and rear pivots on each control arm use different bearing assemblies. The front pivot uses a needle bearing. The rear pivot, however, uses a spherical bearing. Do not intermix the pivot bolts, nuts, seals, collars or other parts when disassembling and cleaning the bearing assemblies. Separate the parts so they can be installed in their original locations.*

1. Remove the sleeve (A, **Figure 42**) and remove each seal (B, **Figure 42**) from the front control arm pivot.

2. Remove the seal (A, **Figure 43**) and collar (B, **Figure 43**) from each side of the rear control arm pivot.

> *NOTE*
> *When cleaning the control arms, do not wash the ball joints (**Figure 44**) in solvent. Handle the ball joints carefully to avoid damaging them or contaminating the grease.*

3. Clean parts in solvent and dry them with compressed air.

4. Inspect the pivot bolts for bending or other damage. Replace damaged bolts.

5. Inspect each control arm (**Figure 45**) for cracks, fractures and dents. If there is damage, replace the control arm. Never attempt to straighten a damaged control arm as it cannot be straightened properly.

6. Inspect the needle bearing in the front pivot bore. If there is any abrasion, change in color, or other damage, replace the bearing and sleeve as a set. To

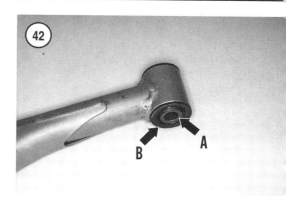

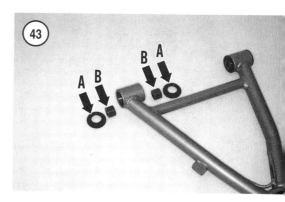

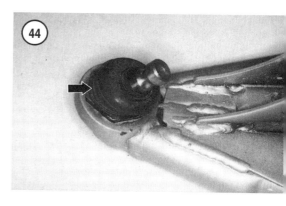

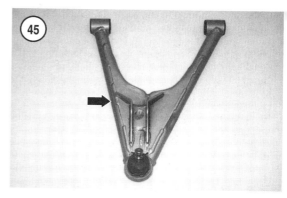

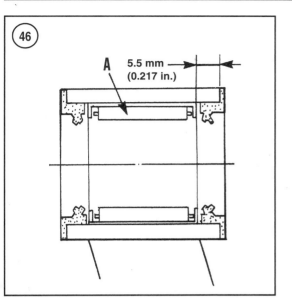

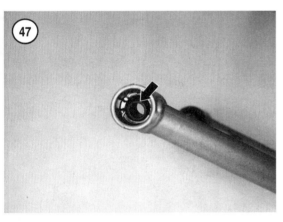

To replace the spherical bearing, perform the following:

  a. Remove the circlip from either side of the spherical bearing (**Figure 47**). Use the appropriate size bearing driver (Kawasaki part No. 57001-1129) or its equivalent, and press the bearing from the pivot bore.

  b. Clean the pivot bore in solvent and dry it thoroughly. Remove all rust and dirt residue.

  c. Lubricate the spherical bearing with molybdenum disulfide grease and press it into the pivot bore.

  d. Install a new circlip on either side of the spherical bearing. Make sure each circlip is seated in its groove in the pivot bore.

8. Inspect the seals for each pivot bore. If there is any abrasion, or if a seal is changing color or becoming hard, replace them both.

9. Inspect the ball joints (**Figure 44**) as described in this chapter.

Control Arm Pivot Assembly

1. If necessary, assemble the front pivot by performing the following:

  a. Pack the needle bearing with grease.

  b. Lubricate each seal (B, **Figure 42**) with molybdenum disulfide grease, and install a seal into each end of the pivot bore.

  c. Install the sleeve (A, **Figure 42**) into the bore. Use a new sleeve when installing a new needle bearing.

2. If necessary, assemble the rear pivot by performing the following:

  a. Pack the spherical bearing with grease.

  b. Install a collar (B, **Figure 43**) into each side of the bore.

  c. Lubricate each seal (A, **Figure 43**) with molybdenum disulfide grease, and install a seal into each end of the pivot bore. Install new seals when installing a new spherical bearing.

Ball Joint Inspection and Replacement

1. Inspect the ball joint rubber boot (**Figure 44**). The ball joint is packed with grease. If there is damage to the rubber boot or ball joint, replace the ball joint as follows.

replace the needle bearing, performing the following:

  a. Use the appropriate size bearing driver (Kawasaki part No. 57001-1129) or its equivalent, and press the needle bearing from the pivot bore.

  b. Clean the pivot bore in solvent and dry it thoroughly. Remove all rust and dirt residue.

  c. Pack the new bearing with molybdenum disulfide grease.

  d. Drive the bearing (A, **Figure 46**) into the pivot bore. Position the bearing 5.5 mm (0.217 in.) from the end of the pivot as shown in **Figure 46**.

7. Inspect the spherical bearing in the rear pivot. If there is any abrasion, color change or other damage, replace the spherical bearing and the seals as a set.

11

2. Secure the control arm in a vise, and remove the circlip (**Figure 48**).

3. Unscrew and remove the ball joint from the control arm.

4. Clean the control arm threads.

5. Hand thread the ball joint into the control arm. Then tighten the ball joint to the torque specification in **Table 3**.

6. Install a new circlip (**Figure 48**).

STEERING STOPPER ADJUSTMENT

1. Turn the handlebar to the left until the edge of the stop bracket at the top of the steering shaft (A, **Figure 49**) touches the top of the frame (B, **Figure 49**).

2. Loosen the locknut (**Figure 50**) and turn the steering shaft stopper bolt until its head just touches the lower bracket on the steering shaft. Tighten the locknut.

3. Turn the handlebar to the right and repeat Step 2.

SHOCK ABSORBER

Refer to **Figure 51** when servicing the shock absorbers.

Spring Preload Adjustment

The front shock absorber springs are provided with five preload positions. See **Figure 52**. The No. 1 position is the softest setting and the No. 5 position is the hardest. The spring preload can be changed by rotating the cam at the end of the spring. Set both front shock absorbers to the same preload position.

Removal/Installation

1. Remove the front wheel(s) as described in this chapter.

2. Remove the front fender as described in Chapter Fourteen.

3. Remove the upper and lower shock absorber mounting nuts and bolts and remove the shock absorber. See **Figure 53** and **Figure 54**.

> *WARNING*
> *If either shock absorber needs replacement, replace both front shock*

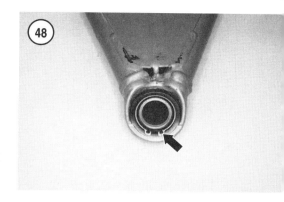

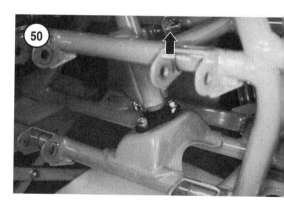

absorbers. The vehicle will be unstable if the shock absorbers are not balanced.

4. Inspect each damper unit (**Figure 55**) for fluid leakage, dents or other damage. Replace both shock absorbers if leakage is found.

> *WARNING*
> *Do not attempt to disassemble the damper unit. Disassembly can release high-pressure gas and cause injury.*

FRONT SUSPENSION

51

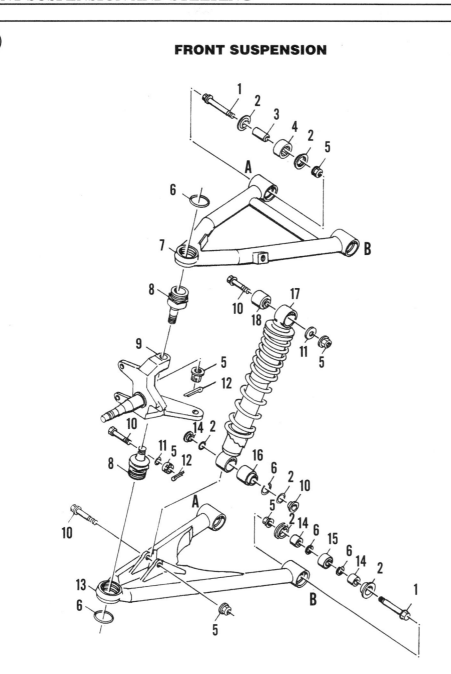

1. Pivot bolt
2. Seal
3. Sleeve
4. Needle bearing
5. Nut
6. Circlip
7. Upper control arm
8. Ball joint
9. Steering knuckle
10. Bolt
11. Washer
12. Cotter pin
13. Lower control arm
14. Collar
15. Spherical bearing
16. Spherical bearing
17. Shock absorber
18. Bushing

11

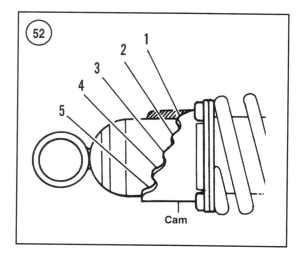

Cam

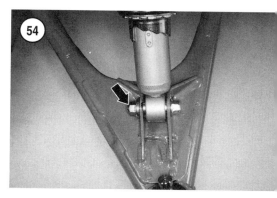

5. Inspect the spring for cracking or other signs of damage. Replace both shock absorbers if either spring is damaged.

6. Inspect the bushing and spherical bearing as described in this chapter.

7. Clean the upper and lower mounting bolts and nuts in solvent. Dry them thoroughly.

8. Install by reversing these removal steps, noting the following.

    a. Make sure the collar (**Figure 55**) is in place on each side of the lower shock absorber mount.

    b. Apply a molybdenum disulfide grease to the upper and lower mounting bolts prior to installation.

    c. Tighten the upper and lower shock mounting nuts to the torque specification in **Table 3**.

9. Repeat for the other side as required.

NOTE
The upper and lower shock mounts use different bearing assemblies. The upper mount uses a bushing. A spherical bearing is used in the lower mount.

Bushing Inspection/Replacement (Upper Mount)

1. Check the shock bushings (**Figure 56**) for deterioration, excessive wear or other damage. If necessary, replace bushings by performing the following:

    a. Support the damper unit in a press and press out the damaged bushing.

    b. Clean the shock-bushing bore of dirt, rust an' other debris.

    c. Press in the new bushing until its outer sur face is flush with the bushing bore inside sur face as shown in **Figure 56**.

Spherical Bearing Inspection/Replacement (Lower Mount)

1. Remove the collar (A, **Figure 57**) from the shock absorber lower mount.

2. Remove the seal (B, **Figure 57**) from each side of the lower mount.

3. Inspect the spherical bearing for roughness or excessive play. If necessary, replace the spherica' bearing by performing the following:

    a. Remove the circlip from the mount bore, and remove the spherical bearing.

4. Assembly is the reverse of disassembly.

    a. Lubricate the spherical bearing and the seals with molybdenum disulfide grease.

    b. Install new seals when installing a new spherical bearing.

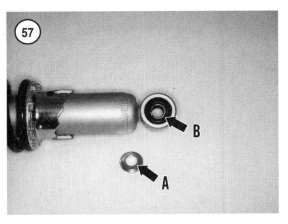

c. Make sure the circlip is seated in the groove inside the mount bore.

TIRES AND WHEELS

All models are equipped with tubeless, low pressure tires (**Figure 58**) designed specifically for off-road use only. Rapid tire wear occurs if the vehicle is ridden on paved surfaces.

> *CAUTION*
> *Do not over inflate the original equipment tires. Over inflation will cause the tire to distort in shape. The tire will not return to its original shape.*

Tire Changing

The front and rear wheels use one-piece rims. These have a deep built-in ridge to keep the tire bead seated on the rim under severe riding conditions. The tire and rim design can make tire removal difficult.

To change the tires on a Kawasaki, use the following tools:

    a. Bead breaker tool.

    b. Tire irons.

1. Remove the valve stem cap and core, and deflate the tire. Do not reinstall the core at this time.

> *CAUTION*
> *Do not use engine oil or petroleum distillates to lubricate the tire bead. These products damage the rubber in the tire.*

2. Lubricate the tire bead and rim flanges with a liquid dish detergent or a rubber lubricant. Press the tire sidewall/bead down to allow the liquid to run into and around the bead area. Also apply lubricant to the area where the bead breaker arm will make contact with the tire sidewall.

3. Position the wheel in the bead breaker tool (**Figure 59**).

4. Slowly work the bead breaker, making sure the tool is up against the inside of the rim, and force the tire bead away from the rim.

11

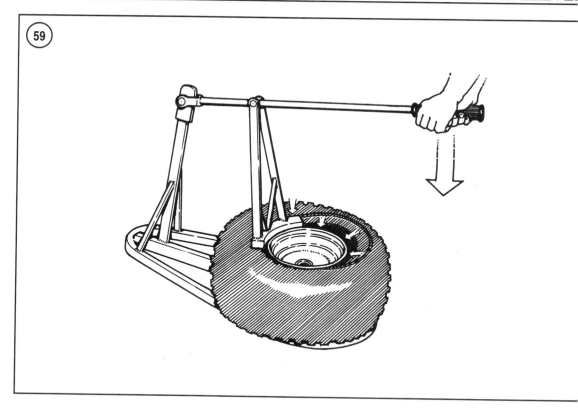

(59)

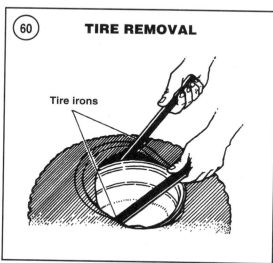

TIRE REMOVAL

(60)

Tire irons

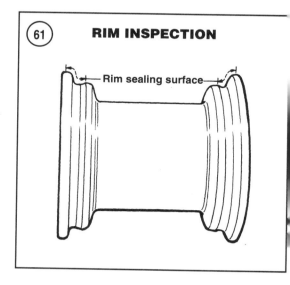

RIM INSPECTION

(61)

Rim sealing surface

5. By hand, press down on the tire on either side of the tool and try to break the rest of the bead free from the rim.

6. If the entire tire bead cannot be broken loose by hand, raise the tool, rotate the tire/rim assembly and repeat Steps 4 and 5 until the entire bead is broken loose from the rim.

7. Turn the wheel over and repeat steps 2-6 to break the opposite side loose.

CAUTION
When using tire irons in the following steps, work carefully to avoid damaging the tire or rim sealing surfaces.

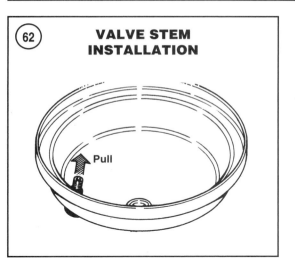

VALVE STEM INSTALLATION

Pull

Damage to these areas may cause an air leak.

8. Lubricate the tire bead and rim flanges as described in Step 2. Then pry the bead over the rim with two tire irons as shown in **Figure 60**. Take small bites with the tire irons.

9. When the top tire bead is free, lift the second bead up into the center rim well. Pry the second bead over the rim as described in Step 8, and lift the tire from the rim.

10. Inspect the sealing surface on both sides of the rim (**Figure 61**). If the rim has been damaged, it may leak air.

NOTE
Special tools are available for installing valve stems into the rims. See your dealer or an automotive parts store.

11. To replace the valve stem, perform the following:

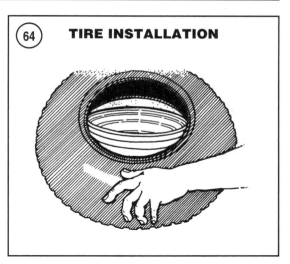

TIRE INSTALLATION

a. Support the rim and pull the valve stem out of the rim. Discard the valve stem.

CAUTION
Do not use engine oil or petroleum distillates to lubricate the valve stem. These products damage the rubber in the valve stem.

b. Lubricate the new valve stem with soap and water.

c. Pull the new valve stem into the rim, from the inside out, until it snaps in place (**Figure 62**).

12. Inspect the tire for cuts, tears, abrasions or any other defects.

13. Wipe any lubricating agent used in Step 2 from the tire beads and from the rim.

NOTE
Use only clean water and make sure the rim flange is clean. Wipe with a lint-free cloth prior to wetting down the tire.

14. Apply clean water to the rim flanges, tire rim beads and outer rim.

15. The original equipment tires are directional. Position the tire onto the rim with the rotation arrow on the side wall (**Figure 63**) pointing in the direction of forward wheel rotation.

16. Install the tire onto the rim starting with the side opposite the valve stem. Push the first bead over the rim flange. Force the bead into the center of the rim to help installation (**Figure 64**).

11

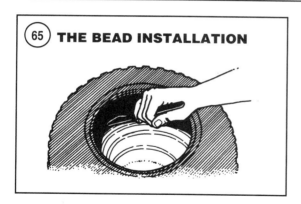

65 THE BEAD INSTALLATION

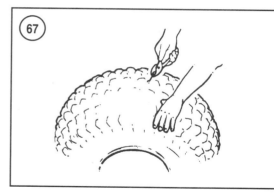

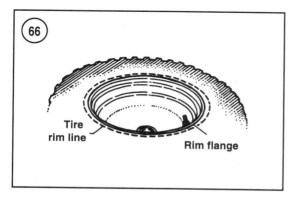

Tire
rim line

Rim flange

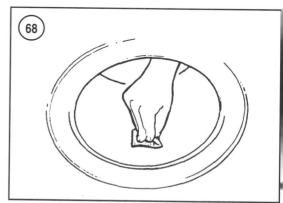

17. Install the rest of the bead with tire irons (**Figure 65**).

18. Repeat to install the second bead onto the rim.

19. Install the valve stem core.

> *WARNING*
> *Do not inflate the tire past the maximum inflation pressure (for seating tires) listed in **Table 2**. The tire can explode and cause injury.*

> *CAUTION*
> *Do not use engine oil or petroleum distillates to lubricate the tire bead. These products damage the rubber in the tire.*

20. Apply tire mounting lubricant or a liquid dish detergent to the tire bead and inflate the tire to the maximum tire pressure (for seating tires) listed in **Table 2**.

21. Make sure the rim lines on both sides of the tire are parallel with the rim flanges as shown in **Figure 66**. If the rim flanges are not parallel, deflate the tire and break the bead. Then lubricate the tire bead and reinflate the tire.

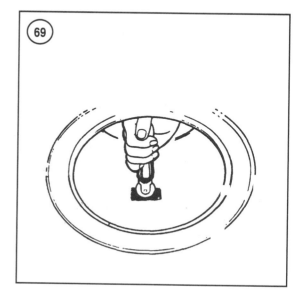

22. Deflate the tire to the cold inflation pressure listed in **Table 2**.

23. Inspect the tire bead-to-rim surface for air leaks.

24. Install the air valve cap.

Cold Patch Repair

The rubber plug type of repair is recommended only for an emergency repair, or until the tire can be patched correctly with the cold patch method.

Follow the manufacturer's instructions for the tire repair kit being used. If there are no instructions, use the following procedure.

1. Remove the tire as described in this chapter.

2. Before removing the object that punctured the tire, mark the location of the puncture with chalk or crayon on the outside of the tire. Remove the object (**Figure 67**).

3. On the inside of the tire, roughen an area around the hole slightly larger than the patch (**Figure 68**). Use the cap from the tire repair kit or pocket knife. Do not scrape too vigorously, as this may cause additional damage.

4. Clean the area with a nonflammable solvent. Do not use an oil base solvent as it leaves a residue rendering the patch useless.

5. Apply a small amount of special cement to the puncture and spread it by hand.

6. Allow the cement to dry until tacky—usually 30 seconds or so is sufficient.

7. Remove the backing from the patch.

CAUTION
Do not touch the newly exposed rubber or the patch will not stick firmly.

8. Center the patch over the hole. Hold the patch firmly in place for approximately 30 seconds to allow the cement to dry. If a roller is available, use it to help press the patch into place (**Figure 69**).

9. Dust the area with talcum powder.

Table 1 FRONT SUSPENSION AND STEERING SPECIFICATIONS

Front suspension type	Double wishbone
Wheel travel	175 mm (6.9 in.)
Caster	3.0°
Camber	0.5°
Trail	13 mm (0.512 in.)
Toe-in	20 mm (0.787 in.)
Tie-rod length	338 mm (13.30 in.)
Front shock absorber standard setting	No. 2

11

Table 2 TIRE SPECIFICATIONS

Front tire	
Type	Knobby/trail tubeless
Size	AT21 x 7.0–10
Manufacturer	Dunlop KT846
Rear tire	
Type	Knobby/trail tubeless
Size	
1987-1989	AT22 x 11.00–10
1990-on	AT22 x 10.00–10
Manufacturer	Dunlop KT847
Inflation pressure (cold)*	
Front	25 kPa (3.6 psi)
Rear	21 kPa (3.0 psi)
(continued)	

Table 2 TIRE SPECIFICATIONS (continued)

Maximum tire pressure	
cold, to seat beads when installing tire)	
Front	250 kPa (36 psi)
Rear	
1987	210 kPa (30 psi)
1988-on	250 kPa (36 psi)

*Tire inflation pressure for original equippment tires. Aftermarket tires may require different inflation pressures; refer to aftermarket manufacturer's specifications.

Table 3 FRONT SUSPENSION AND STEERING TIGHTENING TORQUES

Item	N•m	in.-lb.	ft.-lb.
Steering shaft clamp bolt and nut	20	–	15
Stem shaft bottom end nut	29	–	21
Tie rod end nut	41	–	30
Tie rod adjusting sleeve locknut	27	–	20
Ball joint	44	–	32.5
Upper ball joint nut			
(upper control arm stud nut)	41	–	30
Lower steering knuckle clamp nut	41	–	30
Control arm pivot nut	34	–	25
Front hub nut	34	–	25
Wheel nut	34	–	25
Front shock absorber mounting nut	34	–	25
Handlebar clamp bolts (1990-on)	27	–	20
Front master cylinder clamp bolt	8.8	78	–

CHAPTER TWELVE

REAR AXLE, SUSPENSION AND FINAL DRIVE

This chapter contains repair and replacement procedures for the rear wheels, swing arm, rear suspension, rear axle, drive chain, as well as the engine and rear sprockets. Rear-suspension maintenance consists of periodically checking bolt tightness, replacing suspension bushings/bearings and checking the condition of the rear shock absorbers. Tire removal and repair are covered in Chapter Eleven.

Tables 1-3 are at the end of this chapter. Rear suspension specifications are listed in **Table 1**. Final drive specifications are in **Table 2**. Rear suspension and final drive torque specifications are in **Table 3**.

REAR WHEEL

Removal/Installation

1. The tires and wheels are directional and must be installed on the correct side of the vehicle. Note the directional arrow mark on each tire (**Figure 1**).
2. Place the vehicle on level ground, and set the parking brake. Block the front wheels so the vehicle does not roll in either direction.
3. Raise the rear of the vehicle with a small jack. Place the jack under the frame with a piece of wood between the jack and the frame.

4. Place wooden block(s) under the frame to support the vehicle securely with the rear wheels off the ground.
5. Remove the rear wheel nuts (**Figure 2**) securing the rear wheel to the rear hub. Remove the tire and wheel assembly.
6. Install the rear wheel onto the same side of the vehicle from which it was removed.
7. Install the wheel nuts (**Figure 2**) finger-tight until the wheel is positioned correctly onto all four studs.
8. Tighten the wheel nuts in a crisscross pattern, and torque them to the specification in **Table 3**.
9. After installing the wheel, rotate it and apply the brake several times. Make sure the wheel rotates freely and the brake operates correctly.
10. Lower the vehicle so both rear tires are on the ground.

REAR HUB

Removal/Installation

Refer to **Figure 3** when servicing the rear hub.
1. Remove the rear wheel as described in this chapter.

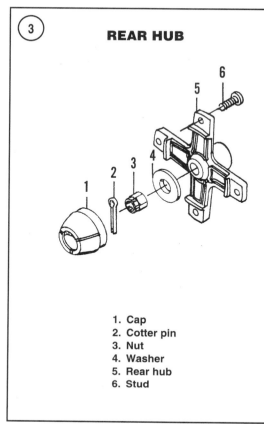

REAR HUB

1. Cap
2. Cotter pin
3. Nut
4. Washer
5. Rear hub
6. Stud

2. Remove the cap from the axle nut.

3. Remove the cotter pin and the rear hub nut. See **Figure 4**.

4. Remove the washer, and slide the hub off the rear axle.

5. Inspect the wheel studs on the hub. If there is damage on the studs, replace the hub assembly. Individual studs cannot be replaced.

6. Installation is the reverse of removal. Note the following:

    a. Apply grease to the axle splines.

    b. Tighten the hub nut (**Figure 4**) to the torque specification in **Table 3**.

> *NOTE*
> *Install a new cotter pin. Never reuse an old one as it may break and fall out.*

    c. Install a new cotter pin, and bend the ends over completely (**Figure 5**).

**DRIVE CHAIN
(1987 MODELS)**

Removal

1. Place the ATV on level ground and set the parking brake.

2. Remove the rear wheels as described in this chapter.

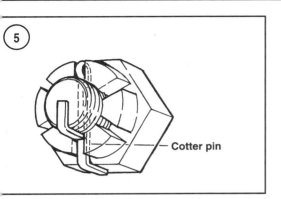

Cotter pin

8. Remove the rear brake caliper as described in Chapter Thirteen.

9. Open the cable holders (**Figure 9**) on the swing arm and release the rear brake hose and the parking brake cable from the swing arm.

NOTE
Do not let the chain touch the ground during removal. It will pick up excessive dirt that will make cleaning the chain more difficult.

10. Disconnect the lower shock mount from the swing arm by performing the following:

   a. Remove the lower shock absorber mounting nut, and pull the lower shock absorber mounting bolt (**Figure 10**) from the mount.

   b. Lower the swing arm from the shock absorber mount.

11. Remove the pivot cap from the swing-arm pivot on each side of the frame.

. Remove the left (**Figure 6**) and right mounting olts (A, **Figure 7**), and lower the chain/disc guard B, **Figure 7**) from the swing arm.

. Loosen the clamp bolt on each side of the swing rm (A, **Figure 8**).

. Insert a drift or other suitable tool into the hole in he bearing housing (B, **Figure 8**).

. Use the tool to rotate the bearing housing and oosen the chain.

. Lift the chain off the rear sprocket and let it rest n the left end of the axle.

12. Remove the swing-arm shaft nut from the right side, and pull the swing-arm shaft (A, **Figure 11**) from the left side of the ATV. Lower the swing arm from between the frame and the rear engine mount.

13. Remove the left footpeg (B, **Figure 11**) as described in Chapter Fourteen.

14. Remove the two engine sprocket cover bolts and the engine sprocket cover (C, **Figure 11**).

15. Remove the mounting bolt (**Figure 12**) and the chain guard from the crankcase.

16. Lift the chain from the engine sprocket, and remove the chain.

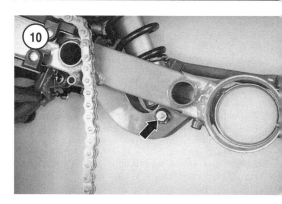

> *NOTE*
> *Always check both sprockets every time the drive chain is removed. If there is any wear on the teeth, replace both sprockets and the drive chain. Never install a new drive chain over worn sprockets or a worn drive chain over new sprockets.*

17. Clean and inspect the chain as described in Chapter Three.

Installation

1. Set the swing arm/axle assembly into place under the frame.

2. Slide the chain over the left end of the axle, and fit the chain onto the engine sprocket. Make sure the lower chain run rests on top of the chain roller on the left side of the frame. See D, **Figure 11**.

3. Lift the swing arm up into place between the frame pivots and the rear engine mount. Make sure the chain's lower run passes between the lower guard on the swing arm (A, **Figure 13**) and the chain roller (B, **Figure 13**) on the frame.

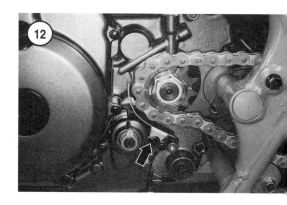

4. Install the swing-arm shaft (A, **Figure 11**) from the left side of the ATV. The shaft must pass through the frame pivot on each side of the ATV, through the bearing in each swing-arm pivot, and through the mount in the rear of the engine.

5. Install the swing-arm shaft nut and torque it to the specification in **Table 3**. Install a pivot cap into the swing-arm pivot on each side of the frame.

> *NOTE*
> *The engine sprocket cover is made of plastic. Tighten the cover bolts carefully so the cover does not break.*

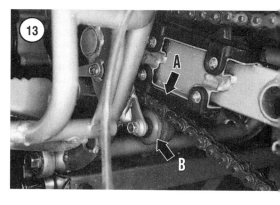

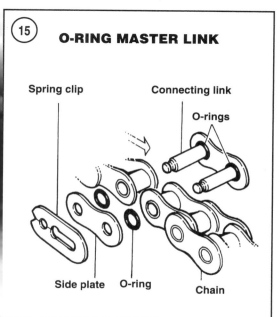

c. Install the mounting nut. Torque the nut to the specification in **Table 3**.

9. Install the rear brake caliper as described in Chapter Thirteen.

10. Secure the rear brake hose and the parking brake cable in the cable holders (**Figure 9**) on the swing arm.

11. Set the chain onto the rear sprocket, and adjust the chain tension as described in Chapter Three.

12. Install the chain/disc guard (B, **Figure 7**).

13. Check the operation of the rear brake and parking brake. Adjust the parking brake as described in Chapter Three if necessary.

DRIVE CHAIN
(1988-ON)

Removal

1. Place the ATV on level ground and set the parking brake.

2. Remove the two engine sprocket cover bolts and remove the engine sprocket cover (C, **Figure 11**).

3. Remove the mounting bolt (**Figure 12**) and remove the chain guard from the crankcase.

4. Remove the spring clip (A, **Figure 14**) from the master link.

5. Remove the side plate (**Figure 15**) from the master link. Do not lose the two O-rings behind the side plate.

12

NOTE
Do not let the chain touch the ground during removal. It will pick up excessive dirt that will make cleaning the chain more difficult.

6. Remove the connecting link (**Figure 15**), disengage the chain from the engine and rear sprockets and remove the chain. Make sure the two O-rings come off with the connecting link.

NOTE
Always check both sprockets every time the drive chain is removed. If there is any wear on the teeth, replace both sprockets and the drive chain. Never install a new drive chain over worn sprockets or a worn drive chain over new sprockets.

6. Secure the chain guard onto the crankcase (**Figure 12**) and reinstall the engine sprocket cover (C, **Figure 11**). Apply Loctite 242 (blue) to the threads of the engine sprocket cover bolts and tighten the bolts securely.

7. Install the left footpeg (B, **Figure 11**) as described in Chapter Fourteen.

8. Secure the swing arm to the shock absorber by performing the following:

a. Pivot the swing arm up to the lower shock mount.

b. From the left side of the swing arm, install the lower shock absorber mounting bolt (**Figure 10**) through the swing arm and through the lower shock mount.

7. Clean and inspect the chain as described in Chapter Three.

Installation

1. Install the chain so the ends meet at the rear sprocket (**Figure 16**). Make sure the chain's lower run passes between the lower guard on the swing arm (A, **Figure 13**) and the chain roller (B, **Figure 13**) on the frame.

2. Apply grease to the two O-rings on the connecting link (**Figure 15**), and install the link through each end of the chain.

3. Apply grease to the O-rings, and install an O-ring (**Figure 17**) onto each connecting link stud as it emerges from the chain.

4. Install the side plate onto the connecting link studs.

5. Install the spring clip so the closed end points in the direction of rotation. See **Figure 14**.

6. Fit the chain guide to the crankcase, and tighten its mounting bolt (**Figure 12**) securely.

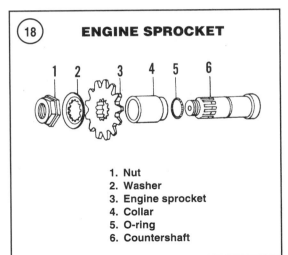

ENGINE SPROCKET

1. Nut
2. Washer
3. Engine sprocket
4. Collar
5. O-ring
6. Countershaft

NOTE
The engine sprocket cover is made of plastic. Tighten the cover bolts carefully so the cover does not break.

7. Install the engine sprocket cover (C, **Figure 11**). Apply Loctite 242 (blue) to the threads of the engine sprocket cover bolts, and tighten the bolts securely.

8. Lubricate and adjust the chain as described in Chapter Three.

ENGINE SPROCKET

Removal

Refer to **Figure 18**.

1. Park the vehicle on level ground, and set the parking brake.

2. Loosen the clamp bolt on each side of the swing arm (A, **Figure 19**).

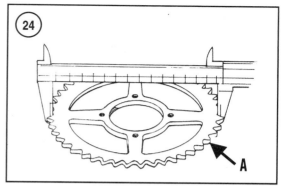

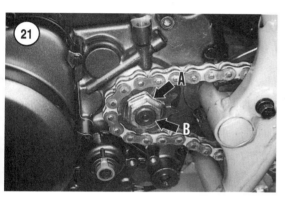

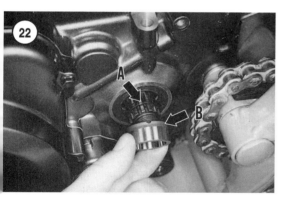

3. Insert a drift or other suitable tool into the hole in the bearing housing (B, **Figure 19**). Use the tool to rotate the bearing housing and loosen the chain.

4. Remove the two engine sprocket cover bolts and the engine sprocket cover (**Figure 20**).

5. Remove the mounting bolt (**Figure 12**) and the chain guard from the crankcase.

6. Push the lock tab (A, **Figure 21**) away from the flat of the engine sprocket nut (B, **Figure 21**).

7. Remove the engine sprocket nut and washer from the countershaft.

8. Lift the chain from the sprocket and then remove the sprocket from the countershaft.

9. Remove the collar (B, **Figure 22**) and the O-ring (A, **Figure 22**) from the countershaft.

> *NOTE*
> *Always check both sprockets every time the drive chain is removed. If there is any wear on the teeth, replace both sprockets and the drive chain. Never install a new drive chain over worn sprockets or a worn drive chain over new sprockets.*

10. Visually inspect the engine sprocket (**Figure 23**) and the rear sprocket for wear or missing teeth. If there is any wear on the teeth, replace the engine sprocket, the rear sprocket and the drive chain.

11. Use a vernier caliper to measure the diameter of each sprocket from the base of the teeth (**Figure 24**). If the diameter of either sprocket is worn beyond the service limit in **Table 2**, replace the engine sprocket, the rear sprocket, and the drive chain.

12

Installation

1. Apply molybdenum disulfide grease to a new O-ring (**Figure 25**) and install it into the groove in the countershaft.

2. Install the collar (B, **Figure 22**) onto the countershaft so the side with the oil groove faces in toward the crankcase. Make sure the collar does not pinch the O-ring (A, **Figure 22**).

3. Set the engine sprocket (**Figure 26**) onto the countershaft so the side with the shoulder faces in toward the crankcase.

4. Install a new washer (A, **Figure 21**) and the engine sprocket nut (B, **Figure 21**) onto the countershaft.

5. Torque the nut to the specification in **Table 3**.

6. Bend a portion of the washer (A, **Figure 21**) over a nut flat to lock the nut in place.

7. Fit the chain onto the engine sprocket.

8. Install the chain guard onto the crankcase, and tighten its mounting bolt (**Figure 12**) securely.

NOTE
The engine sprocket cover is made of plastic. Tighten the cover bolts carefully so the cover does not break.

9. Install the engine sprocket cover (**Figure 20**). Apply Loctite 242 (blue) to the threads of the engine sprocket cover bolts and tighten the bolts securely.

10. Adjust the chain tension as described in Chapter Three.

REAR SPROCKET

Removal/Installation

1. Remove the left rear hub as described in this chapter.

2. Loosen the clamp bolt on each side of the swing arm (A, **Figure 19**).

3. Insert a drift or other suitable tool into the hole in the bearing housing (B, **Figure 19**).

4. Use the tool to rotate the bearing housing and loosen the chain.

5. Remove the left (**Figure 6**) and right (A, **Figure 7**) mounting bolts, and lower the chain/disc guard (B, **Figure 7**) from the swing arm.

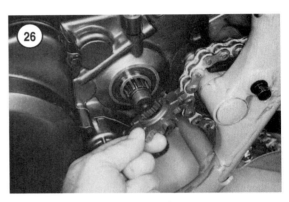

6. Lift the drive chain from the rear sprocket. Lay it over the bearing housing on the inboard side of the rear sprocket.

7. Remove the four rear sprocket nuts (**Figure 27**) and the rear sprocket from the axle.

NOTE
Always check both sprockets every time the drive chain is removed. If there is any wear on the teeth, replace both sprockets and the drive chain. Never install a new drive chain over worn sprockets or a worn drive chain over new sprockets.

8. Visually inspect the rear sprocket and the engine sprocket for wear or missing teeth. If there is any wear on the teeth, replace the engine sprocket, the rear sprocket and the drive chain.

9. Use a vernier caliper to measure the diameter of the sprocket from the base of the teeth (**Figure 24**). If the diameter is worn beyond the service limit in **Table 2**, replace the rear sprocket, the engine sprocket and the drive chain.

10. Installation is the reverse of removal. Note the following:

a. Install the rear sprocket so the side with the number-of-teeth stamp (**Figure 28**) faces out away from the swing arm.

b. Torque the rear sprocket nuts to the specification in **Table 3**.

c. Adjust the chain tension as described in Chapter Three.

REAR AXLE

Refer to **Figure 29** when servicing the rear axle.

Removal

1. Park the ATV on level ground and set the parking brake.

2. Raise the rear of the vehicle with a small jack. Place the jack under the frame with a piece of wood between the jack and frame.

3. Place wooden blocks under the frame to support the vehicle with the rear wheels off the ground.

4. Remove the left (A, **Figure 6**) and right mounting bolts (A, **Figure 7**), and lower the chain/disc guard (B, **Figure 7**) from the swing arm.

NOTE
Use the Motion Pro ATV Axle Nut Wrench (part No. 08-155) or equivalent to loosen and tighten the axle locknuts.

5. Hold the axle by shifting the transmission into gear and setting the parking brake, and then break loose the two axle locknuts (**Figure 30**). Do not remove them at this time.

6. Loosen the clamp bolt on each side of the swing arm (A, **Figure 19**).

7. Insert a drift or other suitable tool into the hole in the bearing housing (B, **Figure 19**).

8. Use the tool to rotate the bearing housing and loosen the chain.

9. Lift the drive chain from the rear sprocket. Lay it over the bearing housing on the inboard side of the rear sprocket.

NOTE
The axle can be removed with the rear sprocket on the sprocket flange and with the brake disc on the disc holder. However, the sprocket and disc must be removed to inspect the sprocket flange and disc holder. Removing them is easier if done now rather than after the flange and holder are removed.

10. Remove the rear sprocket as described in this chapter.

11. Remove the rear caliper as described in Chapter Thirteen. Use a wire or Bunjee cord to suspend the caliper from the frame. Do not suspend the caliper from the brake hose.

12. Remove the brake disc as described in Chapter Thirteen.

13. Remove the two rear axle locknuts (A, **Figure 31**) from the rear axle.

14. Remove the washer (B, **Figure 31**), and slide the disc holder (C, **Figure 31**) from the axle.

15. Remove the O-ring (**Figure 32**) from the right side of the bearing housing.

16. Slide the axle to the left in order to remove the sprocket-flange retaining ring (A, **Figure 33**).

17. Remove the sprocket flange (B, **Figure 33**) from the rear axle.

18. From the left side of the ATV, pull the axle from the bearing housing.

12

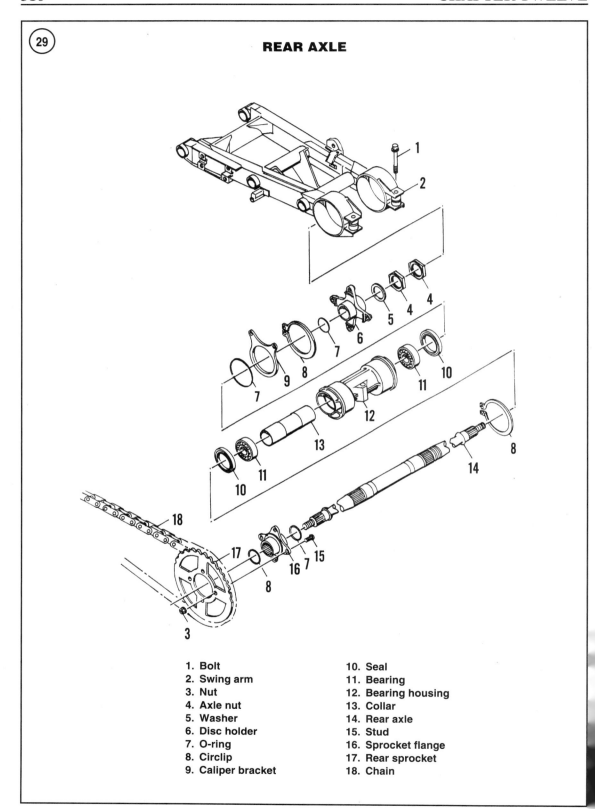

REAL AXLE

29

1. Bolt
2. Swing arm
3. Nut
4. Axle nut
5. Washer
6. Disc holder
7. O-ring
8. Circlip
9. Caliper bracket
10. Seal
11. Bearing
12. Bearing housing
13. Collar
14. Rear axle
15. Stud
16. Sprocket flange
17. Rear sprocket
18. Chain

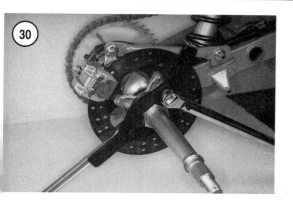

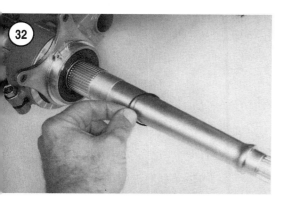

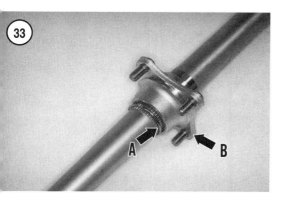

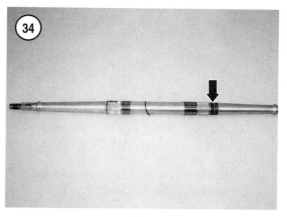

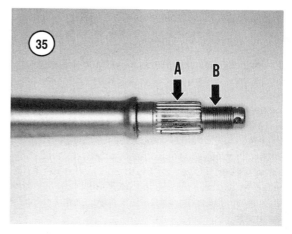

Inspection

12

1. Clean all parts in solvent. Dry them with compressed air.

2. Inspect the axle (**Figure 34**) by performing the following:

   a. Check the axle for wear, cracks or other signs of damage.

   b. Check all splines (A, **Figure 35**) and threads (B, **Figure 35**) for scoring, cracks or other damage. Dress the threads if necessary.

   c. Check the rear axle runout at the points shown in **Figure 36**. Turn the shaft slowly on the V-blocks and note the difference between the highest and lowest readings. This is the runout.

   d. If the runout exceeds the service limit in **Table 2** or if damage is excessive, replace the axle.

3. Inspect the sprocket flange (**Figure 37**) and the disc holder (**Figure 38**) by performing the following:

    a. Inspect the splines for scoring, cracks or other damage.

    b. Inspect each body for wear, cracks or other signs of damage.

    c. Inspect the studs for wear or cracks. If there is any, replace the sprocket flange or the disc holder. Individual studs cannot be replaced.

    d. If damage is excessive, install a new sprocket flange or new disc holder.

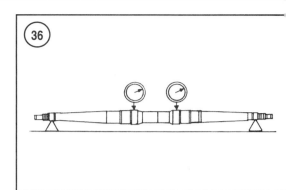

Installation

1. Apply grease to the lips of the seals in the bearing housing.

2. From the left side of the ATV, slide the axle into the bearing housing. Make sure the side of the axle with the threads (**Figure 34**) for the rear axle locknuts is on the right side.

3. Lubricate a new O-ring, and install it (A, **Figure 39**) onto the left side of the axle.

4. Apply grease to the splines of the axle, and slide the sprocket flange (B, **Figure 39**) onto the axle. Make sure the splines in the flange engage the splines on the axle. Press the flange until it rests against the bearing housing.

5. Install the retaining ring (A, **Figure 33**) into the groove on the left side of the axle. If necessary, pull the axle to the left to expose the retaining ring groove.

6. Tap the left side of the axle until the retaining ring bottoms inside the sprocket flange.

7. Lubricate a new O-ring, and install it (**Figure 32**) onto the right side of the axle. Roll the O-ring along the axle until it sits against the right bearing in the bearing housing.

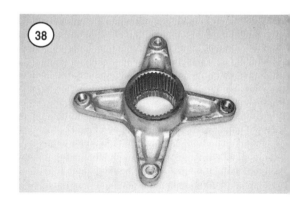

8. Apply grease to the splines of the axle. Slide the disc holder (C, **Figure 31**) onto the axle so the holder's splines engage the splines on the axle.

9. Install the washer (B, **Figure 31**) onto the axle and slide it against the disc holder.

> *NOTE*
> *Motion Pro provides ATV Axle Nut Wrench (part No. 08-155) to torque the 37 mm axle nuts.*

10. Install the inboard rear axle locknut, and snug it against the washer.

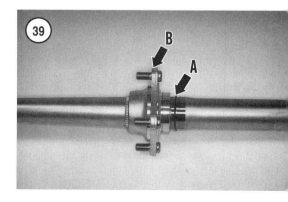

11. Install the outboard rear axle locknut and snug it against the inboard locknut. Torque both locknuts (A, **Figure 31**) to specification after the chain and brake have been reinstalled.

12. Install the rear sprocket as described in this chapter.

13. Install the brake disc as described in Chapter Thirteen.

14. Install the rear caliper as described in Chapter Thirteen.

15. Adjust the chain tension as described in Chapter Three

16. Hold the axle by shifting the transmission into gear and setting the parking brake. Torque the inboard axle locknut to the specification in **Table 3** and then torque the outboard locknut to specification. See **Figure 30**.

17. Position the chain/disc guard (B, **Figure 7**) into place on the swing arm, and secure it with the left (**Figure 6**) and right mounting bolts (A, **Figure 7**).

18. Install each rear hub and wheel as described in this chapter.

BEARING HOUSING

Removal/Installation

Refer to **Figure 29** when performing this procedure.

1. Remove the axle as described in this chapter.

2. Remove the circlip (A, **Figure 40**) and remove the caliper bracket (B, **Figure 40**) from the right side of the bearing housing.

3. Remove the O-ring (**Figure 41**) from the right side of the bearing housing.

4. Remove the circlip (A, **Figure 42**) from the left side of the bearing housing.

5. Loosen the swing-arm clamp bolts (B, **Figure 42**) and slide the bearing housing out from the right side of the swing arm.

6. Installation is the reverse of removal. Note the following:

    a. Install the housing from the right side.

    b. Position the bearing housing so the word TOP stamped into the housing faces up as shown in **Figure 43**.

    c. Install a new O-ring (**Figure 41**) onto the right side of the bearing housing.

    d. Torque the swing-arm clamp bolts (B, **Figure 42**) to the specification in **Table 3**.

12

Rear Axle Bearing Inspection

1. Remove the rear axle bearing housing as described in this chapter.

2. Examine each seal (A, **Figure 44**) for tears or leaks. If a seal is torn or leaking, replace the bearing.

3. Check each bearing (B, **Figure 44**) by turning it back and forth by hand. If there is any binding or roughness, replace the bearing.

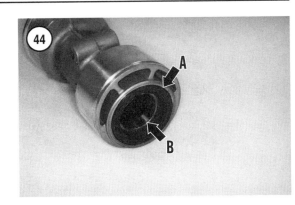

Rear Axle Bearing Replacement

Refer to **Figure 29** when performing this procedure.

1. Remove the rear axle bearing housing as described in this chapter.

2. Move the collar in the bearing housing to one side.

3. Use a drift to tap along the exposed portion of the collar and drive the bearing and seal from the housing. See **Figure 45**.

4. Use the collar and appropriate size bearing driver to drive out the remaining bearing and seal.

5. Deburr the collar as necessary.

6. Installation is the reverse of removal. Note the following:

    a. Install new bearings and seals. The side of the bearing with the manufacturer's marks should face out.

    b. When installing a bearing or a seal, use a driver (**Figure 46**) that matches the outside diameter of the bearing or seal.

    c. Drive a bearing into the housing until it bottoms and then install the seal.

SWING ARM

Refer to **Figure 47** when servicing the swing arm.

Removal

1. Remove the rear axle as described in this chapter.

2. If necessary, remove the bearing housing as described in this chapter.

3. Separate the lower shock mount from the swing arm by performing the following:

    a. Remove the lower shock absorber mounting nut, and pull the lower shock absorber mounting bolt (**Figure 48**) from the mount.

    b. Lower the swing arm from the shock absorber mount.

4. Check the swing arm bearings by performing the following:

    a. Grasp the bearing housing end of the swing arm, and lift the swing arm up and down. I

REAR SUSPENSION

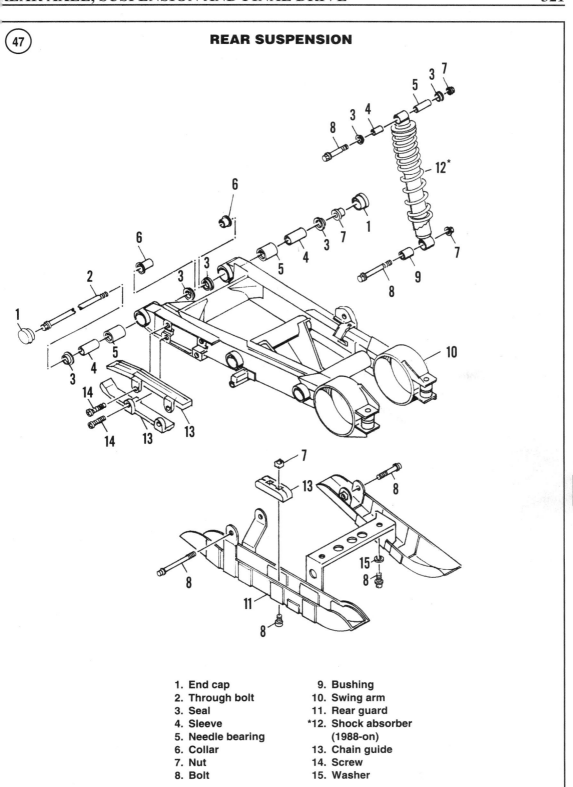

1. End cap
2. Through bolt
3. Seal
4. Sleeve
5. Needle bearing
6. Collar
7. Nut
8. Bolt
9. Bushing
10. Swing arm
11. Rear guard
*12. Shock absorber (1988-on)
13. Chain guide
14. Screw
15. Washer

12

there is any binding or roughness, replace the bearing and sleeve in both swing-arm pivots.

b. Move the swing arm end from side to side and check for axial play. If play is noticed, remove the swing arm and inspect the bearings as described in this chapter.

5. Remove the pivot cap from the pivot on each side of the frame.

6. Remove the swing arm shaft nut from the right side, and pull the swing arm shaft (A, **Figure 49**) from the left side of the frame.

7. Lower the swing arm from between the frame and the rear of the engine.

8. Inspect the swing arm as described in this chapter.

Installation

1. Lubricate the swing arm bearings with molybdenum disulfide grease.

2. Fit the swing arm between the frame and the rear of the engine. Make sure the upper chain run (B, **Figure 49**) sits atop the upper chain guard on the swing arm, while the lower run (C, **Figure 49**) is between the roller on the frame and the lower guard on the swing arm.

3. Install the swing arm shaft (A, **Figure 49**) from the left side of the ATV. Make sure the shaft passes through the frame pivot on each side of the ATV, through the bearing in each swing-arm pivot, and through the mount in the rear of the engine.

4. Install the swing-arm shaft nut and torque it to the specification in **Table 3**.

5. Install a pivot cap into each frame pivot.

6. Secure the swing arm to the shock absorber by performing the following:

a. Pivot the swing arm up to the lower shock mount.

b. From the right side of the ATV, install the lower shock absorber mounting bolt (**Figure 48**) through the swing arm and through the lower shock mount.

c. Install the mounting nut. Torque the nut to the specification in **Table 3**.

7. If removed, install the bearing housing as described in this chapter.

8. Install the rear axle as described in this chapter.

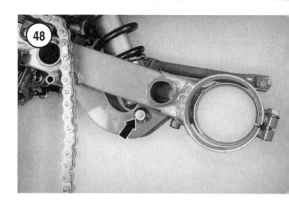

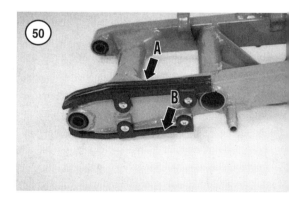

Swing Arm Inspection/Lubrication

1. Remove the upper (A, **Figure 50**) and lower (B, **Figure 50**) chain guards from the swing arm.

2. Remove both seals and the sleeve from each swing arm pivot. See **Figure 51**.

3. Inspect each pivot by performing the following:

a. Use a clean lint-free cloth and wipe excessive grease off from the needle bearing. Clean as much of the old grease as possible.

b. Turn the bearing (**Figure 52**) by hand. The bearing should turn smoothly without exces-

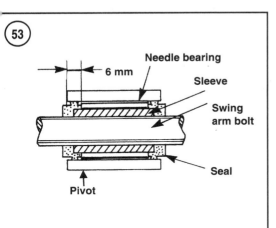

Needle bearing

6 mm

Sleeve

Swing arm bolt

Seal

Pivot

NOTE
Replace needle bearings and sleeves as a set. Install a new bearing and new sleeve in each pivot whenever any bearing or any sleeve is worn.

    e. If any needle bearing or any sleeve is worn or damaged, replace the needle bearing and sleeve in both pivots.

4. Check the welded sections of the swing arm for cracks or fractures.

5. Check the swing-arm shaft and its threads. Replace the shaft if it is bent, worn or damaged.

6. Lubricate each bearing by performing the following:

    a. Pack the needle bearing with molybdenum disulfide grease.

    b. Lubricate the sleeve with molybdenum disulfide grease and insert the sleeve in the needle bearing.

    c. Use a driver that matches the outer diameter of the seal, and install a new seal on each side of the pivot. Lubricate each seal with molybdenum disulfide grease, and tap the seal until it is seated as shown in **Figure 53**.

Bearing Removal/Installation

1. Pry the seal from each side of the swing arm pivot.

2. Remove the sleeve from the needle bearing.

3. Use the Kawasaki Seal and Bearing Remover (part No. 57001-1058) to remove the needle bearing. If the remover or its equivalent is not available, use a soft aluminum or brass drift to tap around the outer circumference of the needle bearing and drive it from the pivot.

4. Clean the inside of the swing arm pivot with solvent, and thoroughly dry it with compressed air.

5. Lubricate a new needle bearing and the inside of the swing arm pivot with molybdenum disulfide grease.

6. Use a driver that matches the diameter of the outer race, and drive the bearing into place in the swing arm pivot. Position the bearing as shown in **Figure 53**.

7. Make sure the bearing is properly seated within the pivot bore. Turn the bearing by hand. It should turn smoothly.

sive play. Visually inspect the rollers for signs of wear, pitting or rust.

  c. Reinstall the sleeve into its respective bearing and slowly rotate the sleeve in the bearing. It must turn freely without noise, tight spots or excessive looseness.

  d. Repeat this check for the other swing-arm pivot.

8. Lubricate a new sleeve and insert it through the needle bearing.

9. Use a driver that matches the outer diameter of the seal, and install a new seal on each side of the pivot. Lubricate each seal with molybdenum disulfide grease, and tap the seal until it is seated as shown in **Figure 53**.

> *NOTE*
> *Replace needle bearings and sleeves as a set. Install a new bearing and new sleeve in each pivot whenever any bearing or any sleeve is worn.*

10. Repeat this procedure for the other swing-arm pivot.

SHOCK ABSORBER

Refer to **Figure 47** when servicing the shock absorber.

Spring Preload Adjustment (1987)

The spring preload on 1987 models is adjusted by turning the ring-nut adjuster on the shock absorber. Raising the adjuster up the shock body shortens the spring length. This increases preload, which results in a harder setting. Lowering the adjuster, on the other hand, increases the spring length. This decreases preload and produces a softer setting. When adjusting the preload, make sure the spring length remains within the adjustable range specified in **Table 2**.

Use the ring-nut wrenches supplied in the tool kit (Kawasaki part No. 92110-1128 or 57001-1101) to adjust the spring preload.

> *NOTE*
> *Spring length (A, **Figure 54**) equals the distance between the inside edges of the upper and lower spring seats on the shock absorber.*

1. Measure the spring length (A, **Figure 54**).
2. Loosen the adjuster locknut (B, **Figure 54**).
3. Turn the adjuster nut (C, **Figure 54**) up the shock body to increase the spring preload. Turn the adjuster down the shock body to decrease preload.
4. Tighten the locknut securely.

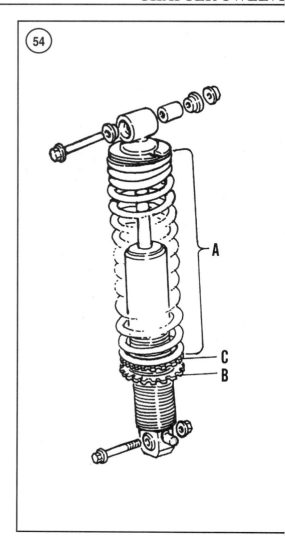

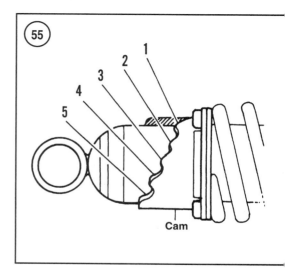

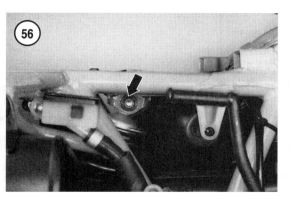

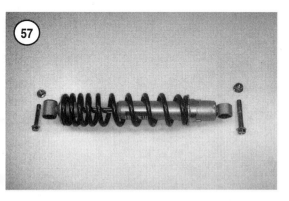

Spring Preload Adjustment (1988-on)

The rear shock absorber spring is provided with five preload positions. See **Figure 55**. The No. 1 position is the softest setting and the No. 5 position is the hardest. To change the spring preload, rotate the cam at the end of the spring.

Removal/Installation

1. Park the ATV on level ground and set the parking brake.
2. Remove the rear fender as described in Chapter Fourteen.
3. Raise the rear of the vehicle with a small jack. Place the jack under the frame with a piece of wood between the jack and frame.
4. Place wooden blocks under the frame to support the vehicle with the rear wheels off the ground.
5. Separate the lower shock mount from the swing arm by performing the following:
    a. Remove the lower shock absorber mounting nut, and pull the lower shock absorber mounting bolt (**Figure 48**) from the mount.

    b. Lower the swing arm from the shock absorber mount.
6. Remove the nut (**Figure 56**) from the upper shock absorber mount.
7. Remove the upper shock absorber mounting bolt, and lower the shock absorber from the frame.
8. Installation is the reverse of removal. Note the following:
    a. Use molybdenum disulfide grease to lubricate the upper shock pivot. Pack the needle bearing with grease and apply grease to the sleeve.
    b. Install the upper and lower shock absorber mounting bolts from the right side.
    c. Torque the shock absorber mounting nuts to the specification in **Table 3**.

Inspection

The needle bearing, sleeve, seals and bushings are available for original equipment shock absorbers. If any other part of the shock absorber is faulty, replace the shock absorber assembly.

WARNING
Do not attempt to disassemble the damper unit. Disassembly can release high-pressure gas and cause injury.

1. Inspect the damper unit (**Figure 57**) for fluid leakage or other damage. Replace the shock if leakage is found.
2. Inspect the damper rod. It must be straight.
3. Check the spring for cracks or other damage.
4. Inspect the needle bearing in the upper mount (**Figure 58**) by performing the following:

12

a. Remove the sleeve (A, **Figure 59**) from the upper shock mount.

b. Remove the seal (B, **Figure 59**) from each side of the mount.

c. Use a clean lint free cloth and wipe the old grease from the needle bearing. Clean as much of the old grease off as possible.

d. Turn the bearing (**Figure 58**) by hand. The bearing should turn smoothly without excessive play. Visually inspect the rollers for signs of wear, pitting or rust.

e. Reinstall the sleeve into the bearing and slowly rotate the sleeve in the bearing. It must turn freely without noise, tight spots or excessive looseness.

f. If the sleeve or bearing is damaged, replace both the bearing and sleeve.

5. Inspect the bushing in the lower mount (**Figure 60**) for wear or damage. Replace the bushing as necessary.

Bushing Replacement

1. Support the shock absorber lower mount in a press.

2. Use a suitable bearing driver or socket to press out the damaged bushing.

3. Clean the shock bushing bore to remove dirt, rust and other debris.

4. Lubricate a new bushing with a soapy water solution.

5. Press the new bushing into the shock bushing bore until its outer surface is flush with the bushing bore inside surface.

Needle Bearing Replacement

1. Remove the sleeve (A, **Figure 59**) from the upper shock mount.

2. Remove the seal (B, **Figure 59**) from each side of the mount.

3. Use a soft aluminum or brass drift to tap around the outer circumference of the needle bearing, and drive the bearing from the shock mount.

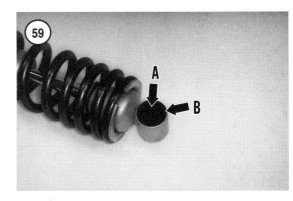

4. Clean the mount with solvent and dry it with compressed air.

5. Lubricate a new needle bearing and the inside of the shock mount with molybdenum disulfide grease.

6. Use a driver that matches the diameter of the outer race, and drive the bearing into place.

7. Make sure the bearing is properly seated within the mount. Turn the bearing by hand. It should turn smoothly.

8. Use a driver that matches the outer diameter of the seal, and drive a new seal on each side of the shock mount. Tap each seal (B, **Figure 59**) until it is flush with the outer surface of the mount.

9. Lubricate a new sleeve (A, **Figure 59**) with molybdenum disulfide grease, and insert it through the seals and needle bearing in the shock mount.

Table 1 REAR SUSPENSION SPECIFICATIONS

Rear shock absorber standard setting	No. 2
Rear suspension	
Type	Swing arm
Wheel travel	215 mm (8.5 in.)

Table 2 FINAL DRIVE SPECIFICATIONS

Drive chain	
Type	
1987	Daido DID520 VC5 endless chain, 90-link
1988-on	Euma EK520 SR-02 90-link w/master link
20-link length	
Standard	317.5-318.2 mm (12.50-12.53in.)
Service limit	324 mm (12.76 in.)
Chain slack service limit	40-50 mm (1.57-1.97 in.)
Rear axle runout	
Standard	0.02 mm (0.00079 in.) or less
Service limit	0.02 mm (0.00079 in.)
Engine sprocket diameter	
Standard	50.98-51.18 mm (2.007-2.015 in.)
Service limit	50.3 mm (1.98 in.)
Rear sprocket diameter	
Standard	207.23-207.73 mm (8.16-8.18 in.)
Service limit	207.0 mm (8.15 in.)
Rear shock absorber preload settings	
1987 models	
Spring length	267 mm (10.51 in.)
Spring length adjustable range	260-280 mm (10.24-11.02 in.)
1988-on	
Standard preload setting	No. 2

12

Table 3 REAR SUSPENSION AND FINAL DRIVE TIGHTENING TORQUES

Item	N•m	in.-lb.	ft.-lb.
Shock absorber mounting nut		–	
Upper	34	–	25
Lower	54	–	40
Engine sprocket nut	98	–	72
Rear sprocket nut	34	–	25
Rear brake disc nut	36	–	26.5
Rear hub nut	145	–	107
Rear axle locknuts, 37 mm	160	–	118
Swing arm clamp bolt	37	–	27
Swing arm shaft nut	74	–	55
Wheel nut	34	–	25

BRAKES

This chapter describes service procedures for the front and rear brakes. **Table 1** and **Table 2** are at the end of this chapter. Brake specifications are listed in **Table 1**. Brake torque specifications appear in **Table 2**.

DISC BRAKE

The front and rear disc brakes are actuated by hydraulic fluid. A hand lever on the front master cylinder controls the front brakes. The brake pedal controls the rear brake. As the brake pads wear, the pistons move out of the calipers, automatically compensating for wear. The fluid level in the reservoir will drop as the pads wear.

When working on a hydraulic brake system, it is essential that the work area and all tools be absolutely clean. Any tiny particles of foreign material or grit in the caliper assembly or master cylinder can damage the components.

Consider the following when servicing the disc brakes.

1. Use only DOT 3 or DOT 4 brake fluid from a sealed container. Do not mix the two types. Do not mix different brands of brake fluid. One manufacturer's brake fluid may not be compatible with another's. Always use the same grade and brand of brake fluid.

2. Brake fluid absorbs moisture from the air, which greatly reduces its ability to perform correctly. It is recommended that brake fluid be purchased in small containers and to discard any small leftover quantities. Do not store a container of brake fluid with less than a quarter of the fluid remaining. This small amount absorbs moisture very rapidly.

CAUTION
Do not use silicone based (DOT 5) brake fluid. It can cause brake system failure.

3. Do not allow disc brake fluid to contact any plastic parts or painted surfaces because damage will result.

4. Always keep the master cylinder reservoir and spare cans of brake fluid closed to keep out dust and moisture. Brake fluid contamination can result in brake system failure.

5. Use only disc brake fluid (DOT 3 or DOT 4) to wash parts. Never clean any internal brake components with solvent or any other petroleum-based cleaners.

6. Whenever any component is removed from the brake system, the system is considered *opened* and must be bled to remove air bubbles. Also, if the brakes feel *spongy*, this usually means air bubbles are in the system, and it must be bled. For safe brake

operation, bleed the brakes as described in this chapter.

> **CAUTION**
> *Disc brake components rarely require disassembly. Do not disassemble them unless absolutely necessary. Do not use solvents of any kind on the brake system's internal components. Solvents cause the seals to swell and distort. When disassembling and cleaning brake components (except brake pads) use new DOT 3 or DOT 4 brake fluid.*

> **CAUTION**
> *Never reuse brake fluid. Contaminated brake fluid can cause brake failure. Dispose of brake fluid according to local EPA regulations.*

FRONT BRAKE PADS

Refer to **Figure 1** when replacing the front brake pads or servicing the front brake caliper.

Brake Pad Inspection

Inspect the brake pads at the interval recommended in the maintenance schedule in Chapter Three. Measure brake pad wear with the brake caliper installed on the vehicle.

1. Remove the front wheels as described in Chapter Eleven.
2. Measure the distance from the disc surface to the back of the pad's friction material (**Figure 2**) with a small ruler. Replace the brake pads if the brake pad thickness is equal to or less than the service limit specification in **Table 1**.
3. Install the front wheels as described in Chapter Eleven, or replace the brake pads as described in the following section.

Front Brake Pad Replacement

There is no recommended time interval for changing the front brake pads. Pad wear depends greatly on riding habits and conditions.

To maintain even brake pressure on the disc, always replace both pads in both calipers at the same time.

1. Read the information listed under *Disc Brake* in this chapter.
2. Remove the front wheel as described in Chapter Eleven.
3. Loosen the brake caliper mounting bolts (A, **Figure 3**) and remove them from the caliper. Lift the caliper off the brake disc.
4. Push the caliper bracket (A, **Figure 4**) toward the piston side of the caliper, and remove the outer (B, **Figure 4**) and inner brake pads.
5. Check the pad spring (**Figure 5**) in the caliper. Replace the pad spring if it is corroded or damaged.
6. Support the brake caliper with a Bunjee cord or heavy wire hook.
7. Measure the thickness of each brake pad (**Figure 6**). Replace the brake pads if the thickness of any one pad is equal to or less than the service limit in **Table 1**. Replace all four front brake pads as a set.
8. Visually inspect the brake pads (**Figure 7**) for uneven wear, damage or grease contamination. Replace all four front brake pads as a set if one is damaged or contaminated.
9. Check the end of the piston (**Figure 8**) for fluid leakage. If the dust seal is damaged and/or if there is fluid leaking from the caliper, overhaul the brake caliper as described in this chapter.
10. Check the brake disc for wear as described in this chapter.
11. To prevent the reservoir from overflowing in the following steps, remove some brake fluid by performing the following:
   a. Clean all dirt from the top of the master cylinder.
   b. Remove the cap and diaphragm from the master cylinder.

> **WARNING**
> *Brake fluid is poisonous. Do not siphon with your mouth.*

   c. Siphon fluid, if necessary, from the reservoir. Constantly check the reservoir to make sure brake fluid does not overflow.
   d. Temporarily install the inner brake pad into the caliper and slowly push the piston back into the caliper.
   e. The caliper piston should move freely. If not, remove and overhaul the caliper as described in this chapter.
   f. Push the caliper piston in all the way to allow room for the new pads.

13

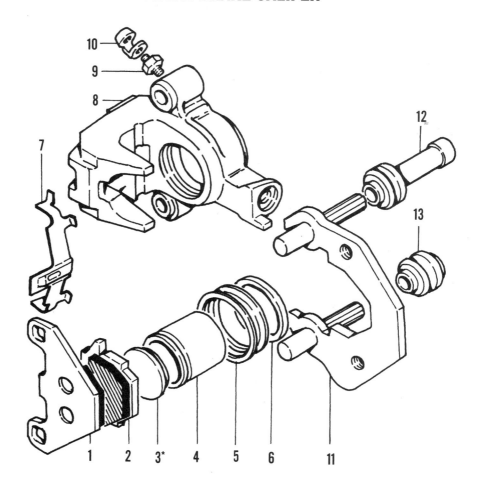

① **FRONT BRAKE CALIPER**

1. Brake pad
2. Brake pad
*3. Insulator
4. Piston
5. Dust seal
6. Piston seal
7. Pad spring
8. Caliper housing
9. Bleed screw
10. Cover
11. Caliper bracket
12. Friction boot
13. Friction boot

*A separate piston insulator was used on 1987-1990 models.
On 1991-on models, the insulator is an integral part of the piston.

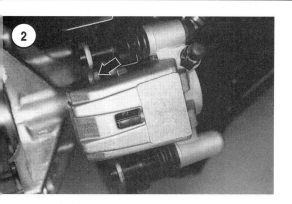

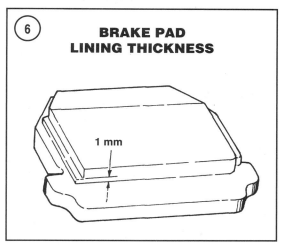

**BRAKE PAD
LINING THICKNESS**

1 mm

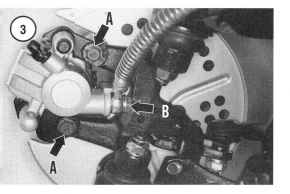

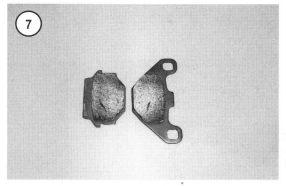

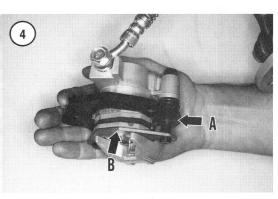

13

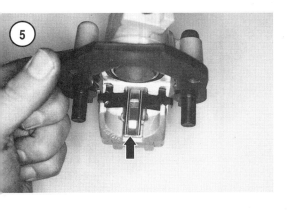

g. Remove the inner pad.

12. Install the pad spring into the caliper as shown in **Figure 5**.

13. Install the inner and outer brake pads as shown in **Figure 4**. The holes of the outer brake pad should contact the bracket arms (A, **Figure 4**).

14. Slide the brake caliper over the brake disc, and install the brake caliper mounting bolts (A, **Figure 3**). Torque the bolts to the specification in **Table 2**.

15. Repeat for the other brake caliper.

16. Install the master cylinder reservoir diaphragm and top cover. Tighten the cover screws securely.

> *WARNING*
> *Use new brake fluid clearly marked DOT 3 or DOT 4 from a sealed container.*

17. Pull and release the brake lever a few times to seat the pads against each disc, then recheck the brake fluid level in the reservoir. If necessary, add fresh DOT 3 or DOT 4 brake fluid.

18. Install the front wheels as described in Chapter Eleven.

> *WARNING*
> *Do not ride the vehicle until there is certainty that both front brakes are operating correctly with full hydraulic advantage. If necessary, bleed the front brakes as described in this chapter.*

FRONT CALIPER

Removal/Installation

1. Remove the front wheel(s) as described in Chapter Eleven.

2. Remove the bolts (A, **Figure 3**) that secure the brake caliper to the steering knuckle. Then lift the caliper off the brake disc.

> *NOTE*
> *The procedures in Steps 3b and 3c use hydraulic pressure to partially push the piston from the caliper bore. This eases piston removal during caliper disassembly.*

3. If the caliper will be disassembled for service perform the following:

    a. Remove the brake pads as described in this chapter.

    b. Reinstall the caliper onto the brake disc and steering knuckle. Tighten the caliper mounting bolts securely.

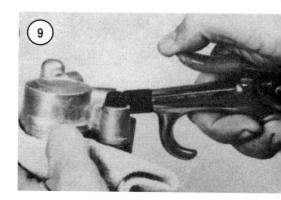

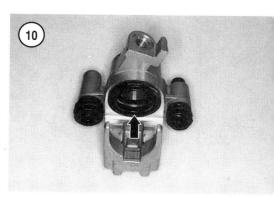

> *CAUTION*
> *Do not let the piston travel out far enough to contact the brake disc. If this occurs, the piston may scratch or gouge the disc during caliper removal.*

    c. Slowly apply the brake lever and partiall push the piston out of the caliper cylinder.

    d. Loosen the brake hose banjo bolt (B, **Figur 3**) at the caliper.

    e. Remove the caliper mounting bolts (A, **Fig ure 3**), and lift the caliper off the brake disc

> *CAUTION*
> *Do not allow brake fluid to contact the control arm or other parts of the ATV because damage will result. Use soapy water to wash off any spilled brake fluid immediately.*

4. Remove the banjo bolt and lift the brake hos from the caliper. Do not lose the sealing washer o either side of the brake hose fitting.

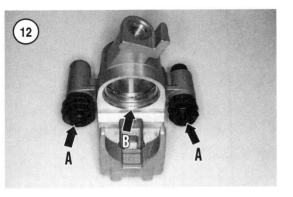

5. Place the loose end of the brake hose in a recloseable plastic bag to prevent brake fluid from dribbling out.

6. If necessary, disassemble the front caliper as described in this chapter.

7. Installation is the reverse of removal. Note the following.

   a. Spread the brake pads, and slide the front caliper over the brake disc so the leading edge of the pads is not damaged.

   b. Install the two caliper mounting bolts that secure the caliper to the steering knuckle, and torque them to the specification in **Table 2**.

   c. Install a new sealing washer on each side of the brake hose fitting, and torque the banjo bolt to the specification in **Table 2**.

   d. Bleed the brakes as described in this chapter.

WARNING
Do not ride the ATV until there is certainty that both front brakes are operating properly.

Disassembly

1. Remove the caliper as described in this chapter.

WARNING
The piston is forced out of the caliper with considerable force in Step 2. Do not try to cushion the piston by hand as injury could result.

2. Remove the piston from the cylinder. If the piston was not pushed from the cylinder during caliper removal, perform the following:

   a. Cushion the caliper piston with shop rags making sure to keep your hand away from the piston area.

   b. Apply compressed air through the brake line port (**Figure 9**) to remove the piston.

3. Remove the caliper bracket.

4. Remove the dust seal (**Figure 10**) and piston seal (**Figure 11**) from the cylinder bore grooves.

5. If necessary, remove the friction boots (A, **Figure 12**) from the caliper body.

6. Remove the bleed valve and its cover from the caliper.

Inspection

1. Clean the caliper housing in solvent. Remove stubborn dirt with a soft brush, but do not brush the cylinder bore. Clean the dust and piston seal grooves with a plastic-tipped tool so they and the cylinder bore do not become damaged. Clean the caliper in hot soapy water, and rinse it in clean, cold water. Dry the caliper with compressed air.

2. Clean the piston in new DOT 3 or DOT 4 brake fluid.

3. Check the piston and cylinder bore (B, **Figure 12**) for deep scratches or other obvious wear marks. Do not hone the cylinder. If the piston or cylinder is damaged, replace the caliper assembly.

4. Clean the bleed valve with compressed air. Check the valve threads for damage. Replace the dust cap if it is missing or damaged.

5. Clean the banjo bolt with compressed air. Check the threads for damage. Replace the sealing washers. Always use new sealing washers when installing the brake hose to the caliper.

6. Check the friction boots (A, **Figure 12**). Replace them both if either one is swollen, cracked or excessively worn.

13

7. Check the caliper bracket shafts for exessive wear, damage or uneven wear (steps). The shafts must be in good condition for the caliper to slide back and forth. Remove all grease residue from the bracket. If the caliper bracket is damaged, replace the entire caliper.

8. Measure the thickness of each brake pad (**Figure 6**) with a vernier caliper or ruler. If the pad thickness is equal to or less than the wear limit in **Table 1**, replace the front pads. Replace all four front pads as a set.

9. Visually inspect the brake pads (**Figure 7**) for uneven wear, damage or grease contamination. Replace the pads as a set, if necessary.

10. Replace the piston seal and dust seal as a set.

Assembly

NOTE
Use new DOT 3 or DOT 4 brake fluid in the following steps.

1. If removed, install the friction boots (A, **Figure 12**).

2. Soak the piston seal and dust seal in brake fluid for approximately five minutes.

3. Lightly coat the piston and cylinder bore with brake fluid.

4. Install a new piston seal into the second groove in the cylinder bore (**Figure 11**).

5. Install the piston as follows:

  a. Slide a new dust seal over the rear piston end (A, **Figure 13**).

NOTE
The piston ends can be identified by the insulator. The insulator is installed in the front side of the piston; see B, Figure 13.

  b. Place the piston between the caliper arms as shown in **Figure 14**. The front of the piston must be pointing out (away from the caliper bore).

  c. Slide the piston into the caliper bore (**Figure 15**). Stop before the groove in the front of the piston enters the dust seal.

  d. Pull the seal out and install its lip into the piston groove, then push the piston all the way into the caliper bore (**Figure 16**).

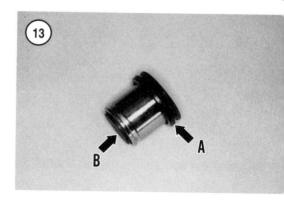

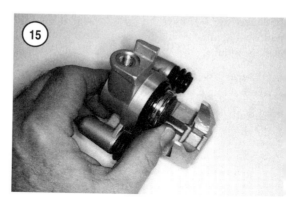

6. If the caliper bracket was removed, perform the following:

  a. Apply a thin coat of silicon grease to the caliper bracket shafts.

  b. Slide the support bracket shafts into the caliper (**Figure 17**). Slide the bracket back and forth, without removing it, to distribute the grease and to check the shafts for binding. The bracket must move smoothly. If there is any binding, remove the bracket and inspect the shafts for damage. Wipe off any excess

grease from the outside of the caliper or bracket.

7. If necessary, install the bleed screw and its dust cover. Tighten the screw securely.

8. Install the brake caliper assembly and brake pads as described in this chapter.

FRONT MASTER CYLINDER

The front master cylinder is attached to the handlebar with two bolts and a removable clamp.

Refer to **Figure 18** when servicing the master cylinder.

Read the information listed in *Disc Brake* earlier in this chapter before servicing the front master cylinder.

Removal/Installation

1. Park the vehicle on level ground and set the parking brake.

CAUTION
Brake fluid damages plastic, painted and plated surfaces. If brake fluid

should contact any surface, wash the area immediately with soapy water and rinse it completely.

2. Cover the area under the master cylinder to prevent damage from spilled brake fluid.

3. On 2000 models, disconnect the electrical connector (**Figure 19**) from the front brake switch.

4. To remove brake fluid from the reservoir:
   a. Remove the master cylinder cap and diaphragm.
   b. Use a clean syringe and remove the brake fluid from the reservoir. Discard the brake fluid.

5. Pull the rubber cover away from the brake hose at the master cylinder.

6. Remove the banjo bolt (**Figure 20**) and the washers securing the brake hose to the master cylinder. Place the brake hose in a recloseable plastic bag to prevent brake fluid from dripping on the ATV.

7. Remove the two clamp bolts and the clamp holding the master cylinder to the handlebar, and remove the master cylinder (A, **Figure 21**).

8. If necessary, service the master cylinder as described in this chapter.

9. Clean the handlebar, master cylinder and clamp mating surfaces.

10. Position the master cylinder onto the handlebar. Install its clamp—arrow mark facing up (B, **Figure 21**)—and install the two clamp bolts. Torque the upper clamp bolt to the torque specification in **Table 2** and then torque the lower clamp bolt to specification.

11. Install the brake hose onto the master cylinder, using the banjo bolt (**Figure 20**) and two new sealing washers, one on each side of the hose fitting. Tighten the banjo bolt to the torque specification listed in **Table 2**.

12. On 2000 models, connect the electrical connector (**Figure 19**) to the front brake switch.

13. Refill the master cylinder with DOT 3 or DOT 4 brake fluid, and bleed the brake as described in this chapter.

WARNING
Do not ride the vehicle until the front brakes are working properly. Make sure brake lever travel is not excessive and the lever does not feel spongy—both indicate that the bleeding operation needs to be repeated.

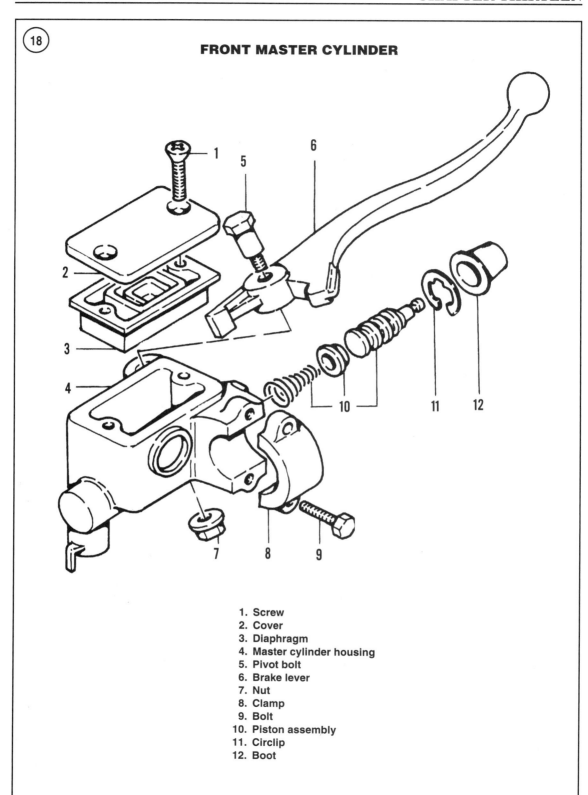

FRONT MASTER CYLINDER

1. Screw
2. Cover
3. Diaphragm
4. Master cylinder housing
5. Pivot bolt
6. Brake lever
7. Nut
8. Clamp
9. Bolt
10. Piston assembly
11. Circlip
12. Boot

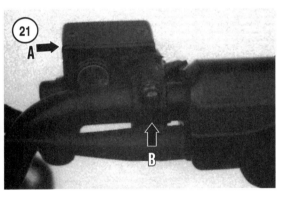

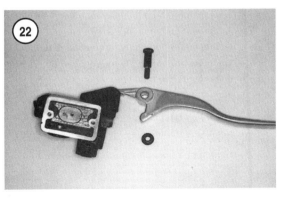

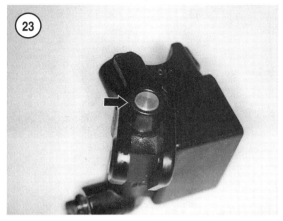

Disassembly

1. Remove the master cylinder as described in this chapter.

2. If still installed, remove the master cylinder cap screws, and remove the cap and diaphragm from the reservoir. Discard any brake fluid in the reservoir.

3. Remove the brake lever pivot bolt, nut and lever (**Figure 22**) from the master cylinder.

4. Carefully remove the dust cover (**Figure 23**) from the groove in the end of the piston.

NOTE
If brake fluid is leaking at the front of the piston bore, the piston cups are worn or damaged. Replace the piston assembly during assembly.

5. Compress the piston and remove the circlip (**Figure 24**) from the groove in the master cylinder.

13

Withdraw the circlip, washer and piston assembly (**Figure 25**) from the master cylinder.

Inspection

Worn or damaged master cylinder components prevent proper brake fluid pressure from building in the brake line. If pressure is reduced, the brakes will feel weak and will not hold properly.

1. Clean the piston and cylinder with clean DOT 3 or DOT 4 brake fluid.

CAUTION
*Do not remove the secondary cup (C, **Figure 26**) from the piston. Removal will damage the cup, requiring replacement of the piston assembly.*

2. Check the piston assembly (**Figure 26**) for the following defects:
   a. Broken, distorted or collapsed piston return spring (A, **Figure 26**).
   b. Worn, cracked, damaged or swollen primary (B, **Figure 26**) and secondary cups (C, **Figure 26**).
   c. Scratched, scored or damaged piston (D, **Figure 26**).
   d. Corroded, weak or damaged circlip (E, **Figure 26**).
   e. Worn or damaged boot.

If any of these parts are worn or damaged, replace the piston assembly.

3. Inspect the master cylinder bore (**Figure 27**). If the bore is corroded, scored or damaged in any way, replace the master cylinder assembly. Do not hone the master cylinder bore to remove scratches or other damage.

NOTE
A plugged relief port causes the pads to drag on the disc.

4. Check for plugged supply and relief ports in the master cylinder. Clean each port with compressed air.

5. Check the brake lever and pivot bolt for excessively worn or damaged parts.

6. Check the reservoir cap and diaphragm for damage. Check the diaphragm for cracks or deterioration. Replace damaged parts as required.

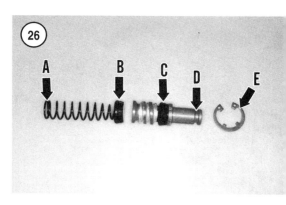

7. Check all the threaded holes in the master cylinder. Clean them with compressed air. The small Phillips screws used to secure the reservoir cap strip easily. Check the screw heads and threads for damage. Replace or repair a screw if necessary.

Assembly

Use new DOT 3 or DOT 4 brake fluid when assembling the master cylinder.

1. If installing a piston repair kit, note the following:
   a. Check the repair kit to make sure it contains all of the necessary new parts.
   b. Coat the new parts with new brake fluid.

2. Lightly coat the piston assembly and cylinder bore with brake fluid.

3. Assemble the piston assembly as shown in **Figure 26**. The primary cup fits onto the return spring.

CAUTION
When installing the piston assembly in Step 4, make sure the primary and secondary cups do not tear or turn in-

*side out. Both cups are slightly larger
than the bore.*

4. Insert the piston assembly into the master cylinder bore in the direction shown in **Figure 25**.

5. Compress the piston assembly and install the circlip. Make sure the circlip seats in the master cylinder groove (**Figure 24**). Push and release the piston a few times to make sure it moves smoothly within the cylinder bore.

6. Slide the boot (**Figure 23**) over the piston. Seat the cover into the cylinder bore groove.

7. Install the brake lever onto the master cylinder. Lightly grease the pivot bolt shoulder with silicon grease and install the bolt through the master cylinder and brake lever. Install the nut, and torque it to the specification in **Table 2**.

8. Operate the hand lever, making sure the lever moves freely.

9. Install the master cylinder as described in this chapter.

FRONT BRAKE DISC

The front brake discs are mounted onto the front hubs. See **Figure 28**.

Inspection

It is not necessary to remove the disc to inspect it. Small marks on the disc are not important, but radial scratches deep enough to snag a fingernail reduce braking effectiveness and increase brake pad wear. If these grooves are evident and the brake pads are wearing rapidly, replace the disc.

See **Table 1** for standard and wear limit specifications for the brake discs. When servicing the brake discs, do not have the discs reconditioned (ground) to compensate for warpage. The discs are thin and grinding only reduces their thickness, causing them to warp quite rapidly. If a disc is warped, the brake pads may be dragging on the disc, causing the disc to overheat. Overheating also happens if there is unequal brake pad pressure on each side of the disc. Four main causes of unequal pad pressure are:

a. The floating caliper binds on the caliper bracket shafts, thus preventing the caliper from floating (side-to-side) on the disc.

b. The brake caliper piston seal is worn or damaged.

c. The small master-cylinder relief port is plugged.

d. The primary cup on the master cylinder piston is worn or damaged.

1. Set the parking brake and block the rear wheels so that the vehicle cannot roll in either direction. Support the vehicle with both front wheels off the ground.

2. Remove the front wheels as described in Chapter Eleven.

3. Measure the disc thickness at several locations (**Figure 29**) and compare the measurements to the dimension in **Table 1**. Replace the disc if the thickness at any point is less than the specified service limit.

4. Make sure the disc bolts are tight before performing this check. Using a magnetic stand, install a dial indicator and position its stem against the brake disc. Then zero the dial gauge. Slowly turn the hub to measure runout. If the runout exceeds the service limit in **Table 1**, replace the disc.

13

5. Clean any rust or corrosion from the disc, and wipe it clean with brake parts cleaner. Never use an oil-based solvent. It may leave an oil residue on the disc.

Removal/Installation

1. Remove the front hub(s) as described in Chapter Eleven.
2. Remove the screws securing the disc to the hub and remove the disc. See **Figure 30**.
3. Install by reversing these removal steps.
   a. Install the brake disc so the marked side faces in toward the steering knuckle.
   b. Tighten the disc mounting bolts to the torque specification in **Table 2**.

> *CAUTION*
> *The disc mounting bolts are made of a hard material. When replacing these bolts, make sure to purchase the correct type.*

REAR BRAKE PADS

Refer to **Figure 31** when servicing the rear brake pads.

Pad Removal/Inspection

Inspect the brake pads at the interval recommended in the maintenance schedule in Chapter Three.

1. Remove the right rear wheel as described in Chapter Twelve.
2. Remove the two caliper mounting bolts (**Figure 32**), and lift the caliper from the brake disc.
3. Bend back the tabs on the lock plate (A, **Figure 33**) behind the pad holder bolts and remove the pad holder bolts (B, **Figure 33**) from the caliper.

> *NOTE*
> *Do not confuse the two pads. A wear shim (**Figure 34**) is used on the inner pad. If reusing the pads, install them in their original locations.*

4. Remove the outer pad (B, **Figure 35**) and the inner pad (A, **Figure 35**).

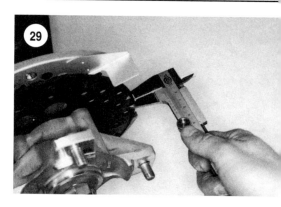

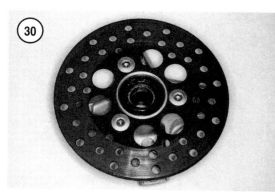

5. Visually inspect the pad spring (**Figure 36**) in the caliper. Replace the spring if it is corroded or damaged.
6. Use a Bunjee cord or wire to suspend the caliper from the frame.
7. Measure the thickness of each brake pad (**Figure 37**). Replace both pads if either one is worn beyond the service limit.
8. Inspect the brake pads for uneven wear, damage or grease contamination. Replace both pads if either one is worn, damaged or contaminated.
9. Check the piston (**Figure 38**) for signs of damage or fluid leak. If there is any, overhaul the rear brake caliper as described in this chapter.
10. Check the brake disc for wear as described in this chapter.

Pad Installation

1. To prevent the reservoir from overflowing in Step f, remove some brake fluid by performing the following:
   a. Clean all dirt from the top of the rear brake master cylinder.

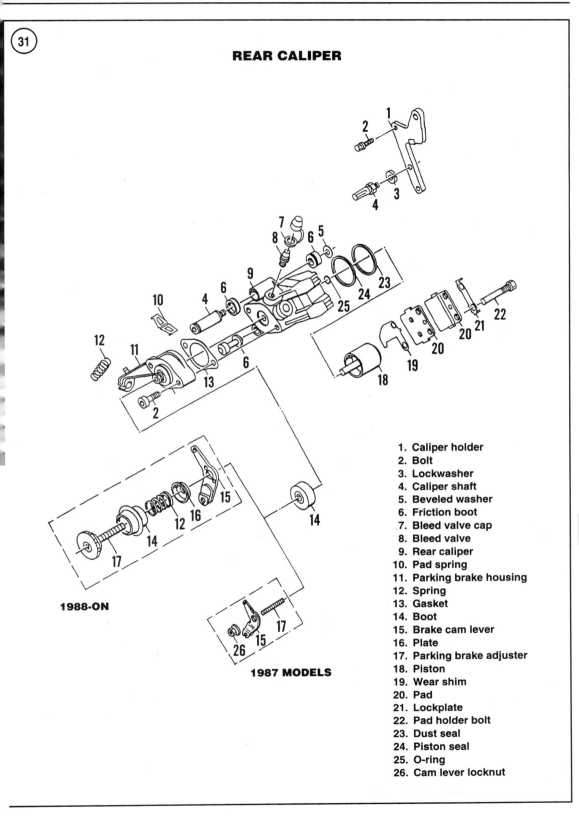

REAR CALIPER

31

1. Caliper holder
2. Bolt
3. Lockwasher
4. Caliper shaft
5. Beveled washer
6. Friction boot
7. Bleed valve cap
8. Bleed valve
9. Rear caliper
10. Pad spring
11. Parking brake housing
12. Spring
13. Gasket
14. Boot
15. Brake cam lever
16. Plate
17. Parking brake adjuster
18. Piston
19. Wear shim
20. Pad
21. Lockplate
22. Pad holder bolt
23. Dust seal
24. Piston seal
25. O-ring
26. Cam lever locknut

1988-ON

1987 MODELS

13

b. Remove the cap and diaphragm from the master cylinder.

> *WARNING*
> *Brake fluid is poisonous. Do not siphon with your mouth.*

c. Siphon fluid, if necessary, from the reservoir. Constantly check the reservoir to make sure brake fluid does not overflow

d. Temporarily install the inner brake pad into the caliper and slowly push the piston back into the caliper.

e. The caliper piston should move freely. If not, remove and overhaul the caliper as described in this chapter.

f. Push the caliper piston in all the way to allow room for the new pads.

g. Remove the inner pad.

2. Make sure the pad spring (**Figure 36**) is in place in the caliper.

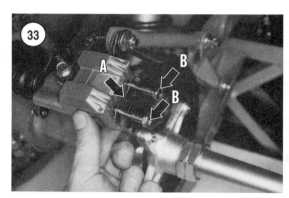

3. Install the inner pad (A, **Figure 35**) into the caliper. Make sure the end with the holes faces into the caliper. The pad with the wear shim (**Figure 34**) is the inner pad. If installing new brake pads, fit the wear shim onto one pad so the holes in the shim align with the holes in the pad. Install this pad next to the piston.

4. Install the outer pad (B, **Figure 35**).

5. Fit the lock plate (A, **Figure 33**) in place on the caliper, and install the pad holder bolts (B, **Figure 33**). Torque the bolts to the specification in **Table 2**.

6. Bend a lock tab over a flat of each pad holder bolt.

7. Spread the brake pads, and carefully slide the rear caliper over the brake disc so the leading edge of each pad is not damaged. Make sure the caliper holder (**Figure 39**) sits outside of the caliper bracket (**Figure 40**).

8. Install the two caliper mounting bolts (**Figure 32**), and torque them to the specification in **Table 2**. The mounting bolts must pass through the caliper bracket (**Figure 40**) and thread into the caliper holder.

9. Install the rear master cylinder reservoir diaphragm and top cover. Tighten the cover screws securely.

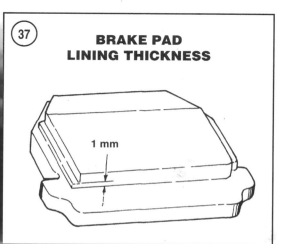

BRAKE PAD LINING THICKNESS

1 mm

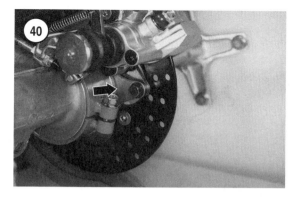

fluid level in the reservoir. If necessary, add fresh DOT 3 or DOT 4 brake fluid.

11. Install the rear wheel as described in Chapter Twelve.

> *WARNING*
> *Do not ride the vehicle until there is certainty that the rear brake operates correctly with full hydraulic advantage. If necessary, bleed the rear brake as described in this chapter.*

REAR BRAKE CALIPER

Removal/Installation

1. Remove the right rear wheel as described in Chapter Twelve.

2. Remove the torque arm by performing the following:

> *WARNING*
> *Use new brake fluid clearly marked DOT 3 or DOT 4 from a sealed container.*

10. Press and release the brake pedal a few times to seat the pads against the disc, then recheck the brake

    a. Remove the clip from each torque arm nut (A, **Figure 41**).

    b. Remove the torque arm nuts and bolts.

    c. Lift the torque arm from the caliper holder and from the swing arm.

13

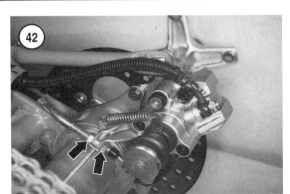

3. Loosen the parking brake cable adjuster nuts (**Figure 42**).

4. Slide the cable from the slot in the cam assembly and disconnect the cable end from the brake cam lever.

5. Loosen the brake hose banjo bolt (B, **Figure 41**).

6. Remove the caliper mounting bolts (**Figure 32**), and slide the caliper off the brake disc.

> *CAUTION*
> *Do not spill brake fluid on the rear axle or other part of the ATV. Brake fluid destroys the finish. Use soapy water to wash off any spilled brake fluid immediately.*

7. Remove the banjo bolt (B, **Figure 41**) and lift the brake hose from the caliper. Do not lose the sealing washer on either side of the brake hose fitting.

8. Place the loose end of the brake hose in a recloseable plastic bag to prevent brake fluid from dripping out.

9. If necessary, disassemble the rear caliper as described in this chapter.

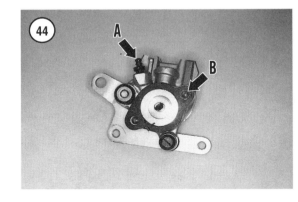

10. Installation is the reverse of removal. Note the following.

    a. Spread the brake pads, and carefully slide the rear caliper over the brake disc so the leading edge of either pad is not damaged. Be sure the caliper holder (**Figure 39**) sits outside the caliper bracket (**Figure 40**).

    b. Install the two caliper mounting bolts (**Figure 32**), and torque them to the specification in **Table 2**. The mounting bolts must pass through the caliper bracket and thread into the caliper holder.

    c. Install the torque arm so the end with the raised boss mounts to the caliper holder. Secure the arm to the caliper holder and swing

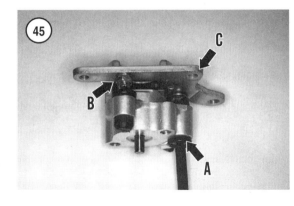

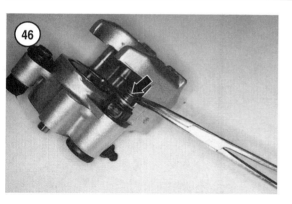

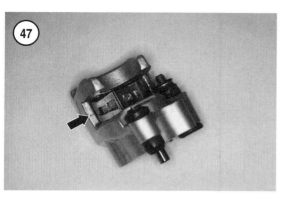

arm with the torque arm bolts and nuts (A, **Figure 41**). Torque the nuts to the specification in **Table 2** and install the securing clips.

d. Install a new sealing washer on each side of the brake hose fitting, and torque the banjo bolt (B, **Figure 41**) to the specification in **Table 2**.

e. Bleed the brake as described in this chapter.

f. Adjust the parking brake as described in Chapter Three.

> *WARNING*
> *Do not ride the ATV until there is certainty that the brakes are operating properly.*

REAR CALIPER

Disassembly

1. Remove the rear brake caliper as described in this chapter.
2. Remove the parking brake assembly bolts (**Figure 43**) and remove the assembly from the rear caliper. If necessary, disassemble the parking brake assembly as described in this chapter.
3. Remove the bleed valve (A, **Figure 44**) from the caliper.
4. Unthread the caliper shaft (A, **Figure 45**) from the caliper holder.
5. Pull the caliper holder shaft (B, **Figure 45**) from the friction boot in the caliper and remove the caliper holder (C, **Figure 45**).
6. Remove the beveled washer from the threads of the caliper shaft (**Figure 46**).
7. Remove the pad spring (**Figure 47**) from the caliper.
8. Press the piston stud from the caliper cylinder and remove the piston (A, **Figure 48**).
9. Remove the dust seal (B, **Figure 49**) and the piston seal (A, **Figure 49**) from their grooves in the caliper cylinder.
10. Remove the O-ring from the piston-stud bore in the caliper cylinder. See **Figure 50**.
11. Inspect the caliper as described in this chapter.

Inspection

1. Clean the caliper housing in solvent. Remove stubborn dirt with a soft brush, but do not brush the

cylinder bore. Clean the dust and piston seal grooves with a plastic-tipped tool so they and the cylinder bore do not become damaged. Clean the caliper in hot soapy water, and rinse it in clear, cold water. Dry with compressed air.

2. Clean the piston in new DOT 3 or DOT 4 brake fluid.

3. Check the piston and cylinder bore for deep scratches or other obvious wear marks. Do not hone the cylinder. If the piston or cylinder is damaged, replace the caliper assembly.

4. Clean the bleed valve with compressed air. Check the valve threads for damage. Replace the dust cap if it is missing or damaged.

5. Clean the banjo bolt with compressed air. Check the threads for damage. Replace worn or damaged washers.

6. Check the friction boots (B and C, **Figure 48**). Replace both if either one is swollen, cracked or excessively worn.

7. Check the caliper shaft and the caliper holder shaft for excessive wear, damage or uneven wear (steps). The shafts must be in good condition for the caliper to slide back and forth. If a shaft is damaged, replace the shaft along with its friction boot.

8. Remove all grease residue from the caliper holder. If the caliper holder is damaged, replace it.

9. Measure the thickness of each brake pad (**Figure 37**) with a vernier caliper or ruler and compare the measurement to the specification in **Table 1**. If either pad thickness is equal to or less than the wear limit, replace both rear brake pads.

10. Inspect each brake pad for uneven wear, damage or grease contamination. Replace the pads as a set, if necessary.

11. Inspect the piston and dust seal. If either one is cracked, swollen or damaged, replace the piston seal and the dust seal.

Assembly

Lubricate all parts, except the caliper shaft and the caliper holder shaft, with clean DOT 3 or DOT 4 brake fluid.

1. Install the small O-ring into the piston-stud bore in the rear-caliper cylinder (**Figure 50**). The O-ring must be installed from the inside of the caliper cylinder.

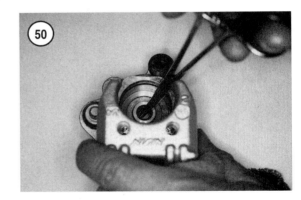

2. Install the piston seal (A, **Figure 49**) and dust seal (B, **Figure 49**) into their respective grooves in the caliper cylinder.

3. Install the piston, stud side first, into the caliper. See A, **Figure 48**.

4. If removed, apply silicon grease to the caliper shaft, and install the shaft through the friction boot (B, **Figure 48**) in the caliper.

5. Install the beveled washer (**Figure 46**) onto the threads of the caliper shaft.

6. Install the pad spring into the caliper so the tangs point outward. See **Figure 47**.

7. Fit the caliper holder onto the caliper by performing the following:

   a. Apply silicon grease to the caliper holder shaft (B, **Figure 45**).

   b. Slide the caliper holder shaft into the friction boot (C, **Figure 48**), and set the caliper holder in place on the caliper.

   c. Turn the caliper shaft (A, **Figure 45**) into the threaded hole in the caliper holder (C, **Figure 45**), and torque the caliper shaft to the specification in **Table 2**.

b. Apply Loctite 242 (blue) to the threads of the parking brake assembly bolts.

c. Torque the parking brake assembly bolts (**Figure 43**) to the specification in **Table 2**.

d. If the rear caliper is installed, adjust the parking brake as described in Chapter Three.

Disassembly

1. If still installed, remove the parking brake assembly as described in this chapter.

2. Disconnect the lever return spring (A, **Figure 51**) from the lever and from the boss on the housing.

NOTE
Note the position of the brake cam lever so it can be reinstalled in the same position on the parking brake housing.

3A. On 1987 models, perform the following:

a. Remove the locknut from the parking brake adjuster and remove the brake cam lever.

b. Unthread the adjuster from the parking brake housing.

3B. On 1988-on, perform the following:

a. Unthread the adjuster (B, **Figure 51**) from the parking brake housing.

b. Remove the spring (**Figure 52**) and the plate (**Figure 53**).

4. Remove the brake cam lever (**Figure 54**) from the parking brake housing, and then remove the boot (A, **Figure 55**).

NOTE
The parking brake housing can be disassembled for cleaning. However, individual parts are not available. If

8. Install the bleed valve (A, **Figure 44**) into the caliper. Torque the valve to the specification in **Table 2**.

9. Fit a new gasket (B, **Figure 44**) onto the caliper, and install the parking brake assembly. Apply Loctite 242 (blue) to the threads of the parking brake assembly bolts (**Figure 43**) and torque the bolts to the specification in **Table 2**.

PARKING BRAKE ASSEMBLY

Removal/Installation

1. Loosen the parking brake cable adjuster nuts (**Figure 42**).

2. Slide the cable from the slot in the cam assembly and disconnect the cable end from the brake cam lever.

3. Remove the parking brake assembly bolts (**Figure 43**) and the assembly from the rear caliper.

4. Installation is the reverse of removal. Note the following:

a. Fit a new gasket onto the parking brake housing (B, **Figure 44**), and install the parking brake assembly onto the rear caliper.

13

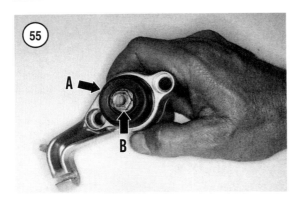

these parts are worn, replace the parking brake housing.

5. Push the spring (**Figure 56**) into the bore, release the spring coil from the groove in the housing and remove the spring from the housing.
6. Carefully remove the ramp (A, **Figure 57**) from the housing.
7. Remove the three ball bearings (**Figure 58**) from the housing, and then remove the bearing base (**Figure 59**).

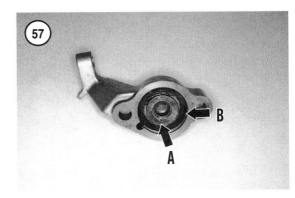

Inspection

1. Clean all parts in solvent, and dry them with compressed air.
2. Visually inspect the boot (A, **Figure 55**) for signs of cracks or swelling. Replace the boot if necessary.
3. Inspect the shaft (B, **Figure 55**) on the ramp. Replace the parking brake housing if the shaft is worn or damaged.

Reassembly

1. Install the bearing base (**Figure 59**) into the bore of the parking brake housing. Make sure the tang in the base engages the cutout in the housing.
2. Apply silicone grease to the three ball bearings, and install a bearing into each detent in the bearing base (**Figure 58**).
3. Install the ramp (A, **Figure 57**) into the housing. Make sure the indents in the ramp engage the bearings in the housing.
4. Lubricate the inside of the housing bore (B, **Figure 57**) with silicone grease, and install the spring so its narrow coils face into the bearing housing.

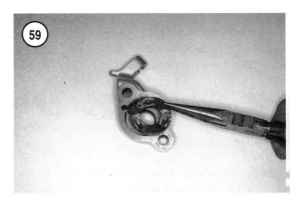

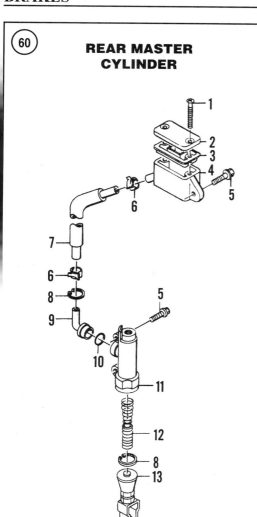

(60)

REAR MASTER CYLINDER

1. Cover screw
2. Cover
3. Diaphragm
4. Reservoir
5. Bolt
6. Clamp
7. Hose
8. Circlip
9. Elbow joint
10. O-ring
11. Master cylinder body
12. Piston
13. Plunger

Push the spring into the housing until the coil is seated in the groove. See **Figure 56**.

5. Apply silicon grease to the boot, and install the boot (A, **Figure 55**) onto the boss on the outside of the housing.

6A. On 1987 models, perform the following:

   a. Set the brake cam lever onto the nut on the housing. Set the lever in the same position noted during disassembly.

   b. Thread the adjuster into the housing so there is good thread engagement.

   c. Install the adjuster locknut. The parking brake will be adjusted after the rear caliper has been installed on the ATV.

6B. On 1988-on models, perform the following:

   a. Set the brake cam lever (**Figure 54**) onto the nut on the housing.

   b. Set the plate (**Figure 53**) in place on the lever so the dimples on the plate engages the holes in the lever.

   c. Set the spring (**Figure 52**) into the plate.

   d. Make sure the grommet is installed on the adjuster, and thread the adjuster (B, **Figure 51**) into the parking brake housing so there is good thread engagement. The parking brake will be adjusted after the caliper has been installed on the ATV.

7. Install the lever return spring (A, **Figure 51**) onto the lever and onto the boss on the housing. Make sure the spring hooks point toward the parking brake housing.

8. Install the parking brake housing onto the rear caliper as described above in this chapter.

13

REAR MASTER CYLINDER

The rear master cylinder is attached to the frame on the right side of the vehicle. Refer to **Figure 60** when servicing the rear master cylinder.

Removal

1. Remove the cap and diaphragm from the rear brake reservoir.

2. Use a clean syringe to remove the brake fluid from the reservoir. Discard the fluid.

CAUTION
Brake fluid damages plastic, painted and plated surfaces. Immediately

clean any spilled brake fluid with soapy water and rinse the area completely.

3. Remove the banjo bolt (A, **Figure 61**) and two sealing washers securing the brake hose to the master cylinder, and remove the hose fitting from the master cylinder. Insert the end of the brake hose into a recloseable plastic bag so brake fluid does not drip onto the ATV.

4. Remove the hose clamp and pull the reservoir hose (B, **Figure 61**) from the master cylinder inlet pipe.

5. If necessary, remove the reservoir mounting bolt (**Figure 62**) and remove the reservoir and hose.

6. Disconnect the push rod from the brake pedal by performing the following:

    a. Remove the cotter pin (A, **Figure 63**) from the clevis pin.

    b. Remove the washer that sits behind the cotter pin, and remove the clevis pin.

    c. Separate the pedal from the master cylinder and remove the shim. See *Brake Pedal* in this chapter.

7. Remove the lower and upper master cylinder mounting bolts (C, **Figure 61**) and remove the master cylinder.

Installation

1. Fit the master cylinder onto the bracket.

2. Secure the master cylinder to the bracket with the two mounting bolts (C, **Figure 61**), and tighten the bolts securely.

3. Press the reservoir hose (B, **Figure 61**) over the master cylinder inlet pipe, and secure the hose with the clamp.

4. If removed, secure the reservoir to the frame. Tighten the reservoir mounting bolt (**Figure 62**) securely.

5. Secure the push rod to the rear brake pedal as shown in **Figure 63** by performing the following:

    a. Fit the brake pedal between the arms of the push rod. Make sure the shim is in place on the brake pedal.

    b. Insert the clevis pin through the push rod arms and brake pedal.

    c. Install the washer onto the clevis pin and install a new cotter pin (A, **Figure 63**).

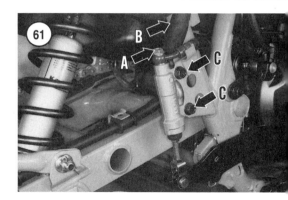

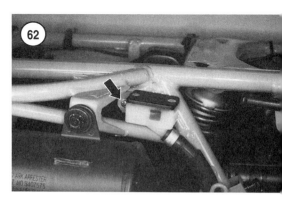

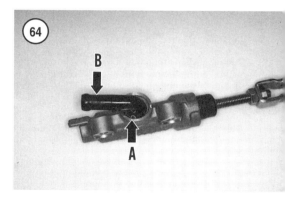

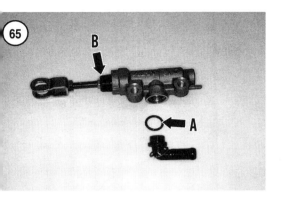

6. Set the brake hose in place on the master cylinder so the hose rests in the cradle on the bracket. See **Figure 61**.

7. Secure the brake hose onto the master cylinder with the banjo bolt (A, **Figure 61**) and two new sealing washers. Make sure a washer is on either side of the hose fitting, and torque the banjo bolt to the specification in **Table 2**.

Disassembly

1. Remove the circlip (A, **Figure 64**) from the master cylinder inlet port, and remove the inlet pipe (B, **Figure 64**).

2. Remove the O-ring (A, **Figure 65**) from the inlet port.

3. Roll the plunger boot (B, **Figure 65**) away from the master cylinder.

4. Free the circlip from its groove in the master cylinder (**Figure 66**), and remove the plunger assembly (**Figure 67**).

5. Remove the piston assembly (**Figure 68**) from the master cylinder. Remove the spring if it did not come out with the piston.

6. Inspect the master cylinder as described in this chapter.

7. Assembly is the reverse of disassembly. Note the following:

    a. Lubricate all parts with clean brake fluid.

    b. Install a new inlet-pipe O-ring.

    c. Install the piston assembly as shown in **Figure 68**.

    d. Make sure each circlip is properly seated in its groove within the master cylinder body.

Inspection

1. Clean all parts in solvent and dry them with compressed air.

2. Inspect the master cylinder for scratches, rust or pitting. If there is any damage, replace the master cylinder.

3. Inspect the supply and relief ports (**Figure 69**) in the master cylinder. Make sure they are not plugged.

4. Inspect the primary and secondary cups on the piston assembly (**Figure 68**). If either cup is worn, swollen or damaged, replace the piston assembly.

5. Check the piston return spring. If there is any damage, replace the piston assembly.

13

6. Inspect the dust boot on the plunger assembly (**Figure 67**) for cracks, swelling or damage. If there is any damage, replace the plunger assembly.

BRAKE PEDAL

Removal/Installation

Refer to **Figure 70**.

1. On 1989-on models, remove the footpeg assembly as described in Chapter Fourteen.

2. Disconnect the brake pedal from the master cylinder push rod by performing the following:

  a. Remove the cotter pin (A, **Figure 63**) from the clevis pin.

  b. Remove the washer that sits behind the cotter pin, and pull out the clevis pin.

  c. Separate the pedal from the master cylinder and remove the shim (10, **Figure 70**).

3. Remove the cotter pin (B, **Figure 63**) from the pedal shaft, and remove the nut.

4. On 2000 models, unhook the brake-pedal-switch spring (**Figure 71**) from the post on the brake pedal.

5. Pull the pedal shaft from the pivot boss in the frame and remove the pedal. Be prepared to catch the washer and cap that sit behind the cotter pin. The two O-rings should come off with the pedal.

6. If necessary, remove the brake-pedal spring (A, **Figure 72**) from the frame.

7. Installation is the reverse of removal. Note the following:

  a. Lubricate the two new O-rings and the pedal shaft with molybdenum disulfide grease.

  b. Install the small O-ring onto the pedal shaft. Install the large O-ring (B, **Figure 72**) into the pivot boss in the frame.

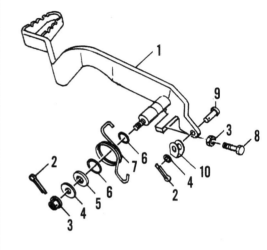

REAR BRAKE PEDAL

1. Brake pedal
2. Cotter pin
3. Nut
4. Washer
5. Cap
6. O-ring
7. Spring
8. Bolt
9. Clevis pin
10. Shim

  c. If removed, install the brake-pedal spring (A, **Figure 72**) so the large tang rests on the frame.

  d. Make sure the arm on the pedal passes through the spring tang as shown in **Figure 73**.

  e. Install new cotter pins.

  f. When connecting the brake pedal to the master cylinder, make sure the shim (10, **Figure 70**) is in place on the brake pedal.

  g. On 2000 models, hook the brake-pedal-switch spring (**Figure 71**) onto the brake pedal post.

  h. Adjust the brake pedal height as described in Chapter Three.

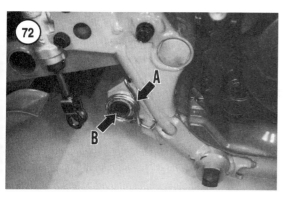

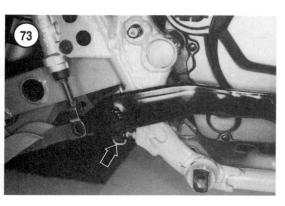

REAR BRAKE DISC

Removal/Installation

1. Place the vehicle on level ground, and set the parking brake. Block the front wheels so the vehicle does not roll in either direction.
2. Raise the rear of the vehicle with a small jack. Place the jack under the frame with a piece of wood between the jack and the frame.
3. Place wooden block(s) under the frame to support the vehicle securely with the rear wheels off the ground.
4. Remove the right rear wheel as described in Chapter Twelve.
5. Remove the rear caliper as described in this chapter.
6. Remove the disc mounting bolts (**Figure 74**).
7. Rotate the brake disc so its cutout aligns with the arms of the disc holder and slide the disc past the holder. See **Figure 75**.
8. Manipulate the brake disc so it clears the arms of the rear hub, and remove the brake disc. See **Figure 76**.
9. Installation is the reverse of removal. Note the following.

    a. Install the disc so the marked side faces in toward the swing arm.

    b. Make sure the disc sits against the inboard side of the disc holder.

    c. Torque the disc mounting bolts to the specification in **Table 2**.

Inspection

It is not necessary to remove the disc to inspect it. Small marks on the disc are not important, but radial scratches deep enough to snag a fingernail reduce

13

braking effectiveness and increase brake pad wear. If these grooves are evident and the brake pads are wearing rapidly, replace the disc.

See **Table 1** for standard and wear limit specifications for the brake discs. When servicing the brake discs, do not have the discs reconditioned (ground) to compensate for warpage. The discs are thin and grinding only reduces their thickness, causing them to warp quite rapidly. If a disc is warped, the brake pads may be dragging on the disc, causing the disc to overheat. Overheating also happens if there is unequal brake pad pressure on both sides of the disc. Four main causes of unequal pad pressure are:

   a. The floating caliper binds on the caliper shaft and caliper holder shaft, thus preventing the caliper from floating (side-to-side) on the disc.
   b. The brake caliper piston seal is worn or damaged.
   c. The small master-cylinder relief port is plugged.
   d. The primary cup on the master cylinder piston is worn or damaged.

1. Set the parking brake and block the front wheels so that the vehicle cannot roll in either direction. Support the vehicle with both rear wheels off the ground.
2. Remove the right rear wheel as described in Chapter Twelve.
3. Measure the thickness around the disc at several locations (**Figure 77**). Replace the disc if the thickness at any point is less than the service limit specified in **Table 1**.
4. Make sure the disc bolts are tight prior to performing this check. Using a magnetic stand, install a dial indicator and position its stem against the brake disc. Then zero the dial gauge. Slowly turn the hub to measure runout. If the runout exceeds the service limit in **Table 1**, replace the disc.
5. Clean any rust or corrosion from the disc, and wipe it clean with brake parts cleaner. Never use an oil-based solvent that may leave an oil residue on the disc.

BRAKE HOSE REPLACEMENT

Replace the brake hoses if they are worn or damaged. Refer to **Figure 78** when servicing the front brake hose. Refer to **Figure 79** when servicing the rear brake hose.

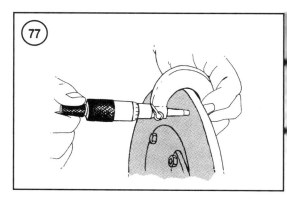

1. Place a container under the brake line at the caliper. Remove the banjo bolt and sealing washers from the caliper.
2. Place the end of the brake hose in a clean container. Operate the brake lever (front) or brake pedal (rear) to drain the master cylinder and brake hose of all brake fluid. Dispose of this brake fluid—never reuse brake fluid.
3. When replacing the front brake hose, repeat this procedure for the other front caliper.
4. Disconnect the brake hose from the master cylinder.
5A. When replacing the front brake hose, remove the bolts that secure the hose clamps to the control arms (**Figure 80**). If necessary remove the bolt that secures the hose union to the frame. See **Figure 81**.
5B. When replacing the rear brake hose, cut the cable tie that secures the hose to the swing arm.
6. Remove the brake hose, and note how it is routed through the frame. The new hose must be routed along the same path.
7. Install a new brake hose in the reverse order of removal. Install a new sealing washer on each side of each hose fitting.

78

FRONT BRAKE LINES

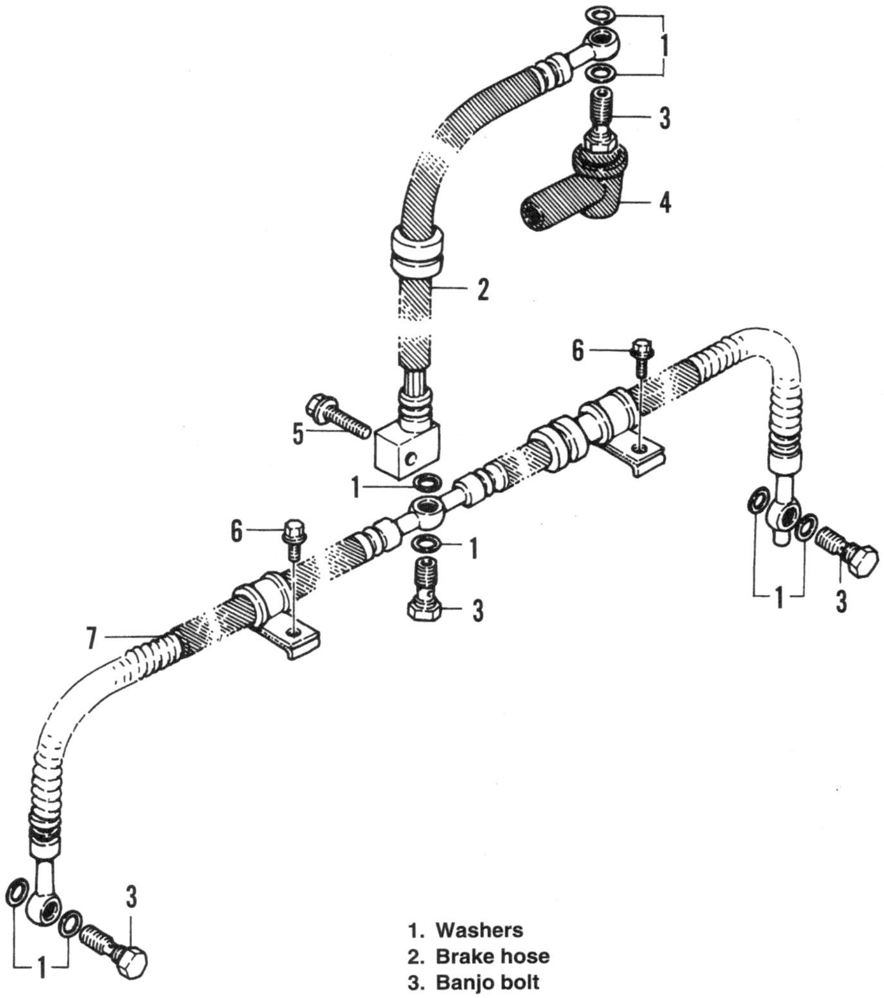

1. Washers
2. Brake hose
3. Banjo bolt
4. Cover
5. Bolt
6. Bolt
7. Brake hose

13

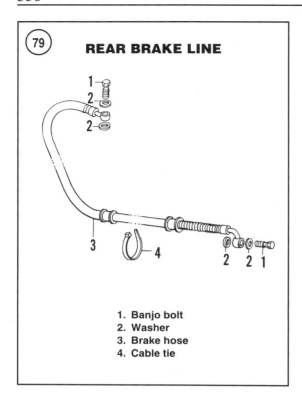

(79)

REAR BRAKE LINE

1. Banjo bolt
2. Washer
3. Brake hose
4. Cable tie

(80)

(81)

8. Tighten the banjo bolts to the torque specification in **Table 1**.

9. Refill the master cylinder with fresh brake fluid clearly marked DOT 3 and DOT 4. Bleed the brake(s) as described in this chapter.

WARNING
Do not ride the ATV until there is certainty that the brakes are operating properly.

PARKING BRAKE CABLE REPLACEMENT

Removal/Installation

1. Remove the front fender as described in Chapter Fourteen.

2. Loosen the parking brake cable adjuster nuts (A, **Figure 82**) on the parking brake housing, and create as much slack as possible in the cable.

3. Pull back the boot from the clutch lever assembly.

4. Pull in the clutch lever and hold it against the handlebar grip.

5. Pull the parking brake outer cable from the cable holder on the clutch lever, and then release the inner cable from the parking brake lever (**Figure 83**).

6. Remove the return spring (B, **Figure 82**) from the parking brake housing.

7. Disconnect the cable end from the brake cam lever (A, **Figure 84**) and remove the cable from the cable holder (B, **Figure 84**) on the parking brake housing.

8. Release the brake hose and parking brake cable from the cable holder (C, **Figure 82**) on the swing arm.

9. Follow the cable along the frame and remove all clamps and cable ties that secure the cable in place. If necessary, mark the frame in order to install new cable ties in the same locations during assembly.

10. Once the entire length of the cable is free, pull the cable from the frame. Note how the cable is routed along the frame. The new cable must follow the same path.

11. Installation is the reverse of removal. Note the following.

    a. Lubricate the new cable as described in Chapter Three.

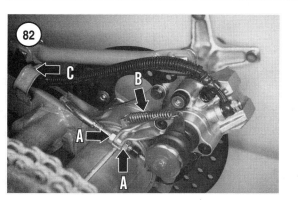

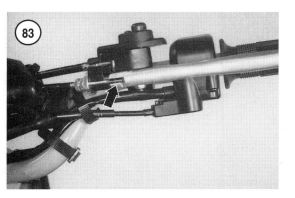

b. Connect the upper cable end to the parking brake lever (**Figure 83**), and route the new cable along the same path as the old cable.

c. Connect the lower cable end to the brake cam lever (A, **Figure 84**), and fit the cable into the cable holder (B, **Figure 84**) on the parking brake housing.

d. Install the return spring (B, **Figure 82**) so the hooks at the spring ends face toward the rear caliper.

e. Secure the cable to the frame with new cable ties.

f. Adjust the parking brake as described in Chapter Three.

PARKING BRAKE LEVER

Removal/Installation

Refer to **Figure 85** when performing this procedure.

1. Disconnect the upper end of the parking brake cable from the parking brake lever as described in this chapter.

2. Disconnect the clutch cable end from the clutch lever as described in Chapter Six.

3. Remove the nut, lift the pivot bolt from the clutch lever housing, and remove the clutch lever and the parking brake lever.

4. Remove the long and short pins, along with their springs, from the parking brake lever.

5. Installation is the reverse of removal. Note the following.

    a. Apply grease to the pivot bolt, the long pin and the short pin.

    b. Install the long pin in the outboard hole in the parking brake lever. Install the short pin in the inboard hole.

    c. Adjust the parking brake cable and clutch cable as described in Chapter Three.

BRAKE BLEEDING

This procedure is necessary only if the brakes feel spongy, there is a leak in the hydraulic system, a component has been replaced or if the brake fluid has been replaced.

> *NOTE*
> *During this procedure, all the hose junctions in the brake system are bled of air. It is important to check the fluid level in the master cylinder frequently. If the reservoir runs dry, air will enter the system and the procedure will have to be repeated.*

1. Remove the dust cap from the brake bleeder valve.

2. Connect a length of clear tubing to the bleeder valve on the caliper. See **Figure 86**. Place the other end of the tube into a clean container. Fill the con-

13

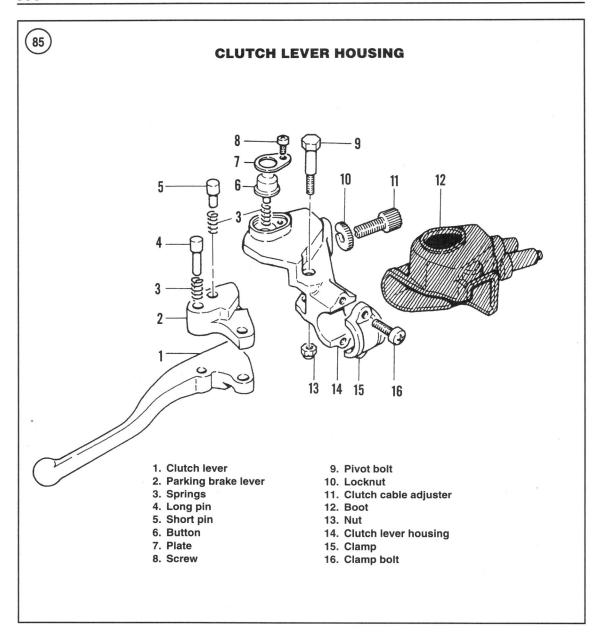

85

CLUTCH LEVER HOUSING

1. Clutch lever
2. Parking brake lever
3. Springs
4. Long pin
5. Short pin
6. Button
7. Plate
8. Screw
9. Pivot bolt
10. Locknut
11. Clutch cable adjuster
12. Boot
13. Nut
14. Clutch lever housing
15. Clamp
16. Clamp bolt

tainer with enough fresh brake fluid to keep the end of the tube submerged. The tube should be long enough so that a loop can be made higher than the bleeder valve to prevent air from being drawn into the caliper during bleeding.

CAUTION
Cover all parts that could be contami-nated by spilled brake fluid. Wash any spilled brake fluid from any surface immediately, as it will damage the fin-

86

ish. Use soapy water and rinse completely.

3. Clean the top of the master cylinder of all debris. Remove the cap and diaphragm. Fill the reservoir to a level about 10 mm (3/8 in.) from the top. Insert the diaphragm to prevent the entry of dirt and moisture.

WARNING
Use brake fluid clearly marked DOT 3 or DOT 4 only. Others may vaporize and cause brake failure. Always use the same brand and grade brake fluid. Do not intermix the brake fluids, as many brands are not compatible.

NOTE
During this procedure, it is important to check the reservoir fluid level periodically to make sure it does not run dry. If the reservoir should run dry, air will enter the system and the procedure will have to be repeated.

4. Hold the brake lever (or brake pedal) in the applied position and open the bleeder valve about a half turn—do not release the brake lever while the bleeder valve is open. When you open the bleeder valve, the lever will loosen and move to the limit of its travel. At this point, tighten the bleeder screw, and then release the brake lever.

NOTE
As the brake fluid enters the system, the level will drop in the master cylinder reservoir. Maintain the level at

about 10 mm (3/8 in.) from the top of the reservoir to prevent air from entering the system.

5. Repeat Step 4 until the system is bled. If replacing the fluid, continue until the fluid emerging from the hose is clean.

6. Remove the bleeder tube from the bleed valve. Torque the valve to the specification in **Table 2**, and install the bleeder valve dust cap.

7. If necessary, add fluid to correct the level in the master cylinder reservoir. It must be above the level line.

8. Install the cap and tighten the screws on the master cylinder.

9. Test the feel of the brake lever (or brake pedal). It should feel firm and offer the same resistance each time it is operated. If it feels spongy, air may still be in the system. Bleed the brake(s) again. When all air has been bled from the system and the brake fluid level is correct in the reservoir, double-check for leaks and tighten all fittings and connections.

WARNING
Before riding the vehicle, make certain the brakes are working correctly by operating the lever and pedal several times. Next, test ride the vehicle slowly until certain the brakes are working correctly.

13

Table 1 BRAKE SYSTEM SPECIFICATIONS

Item	Specification	Wear limit
Disc thickness		
Front	3.3-3.7 mm (0.130-0.146 in.)	3.0 mm (0.118 in.)
Rear	3.8-4.2 mm (0.150-0.165 in.)	3.5 mm (0.138 in.)
Disc runout	Less than 0.2 mm (0.008) in.)	0.3 mm (0.012 in.)
Brake pad thickness	4.5 mm (0.177 in.)	1 mm (0.039 in.)
Parking brake cable		
adjustment	42-44 mm (1.654-1.732 in.)	–

Table 2 BRAKE SYSTEM TIGHTENING TORQUES

Item	N•m	in.-lb.	ft.-lb.
Bleed valve	7.8	69	–
Brake hose banjo bolts	23	–	17
Caliper mounting bolts	25	–	18
Disc mounting bolt	36	–	26.5
Brake lever pivot bolt and nut	5.9	52	–
Front master cylinder clamp bolts	8.8	78	–
Rear master cylinder push rod locknut	18	–	13
Rear caliper holder shaft	18		13
Rear caliper shaft (Allen head)	23	–	17
Rear caliper pad holder bolt	18	–	13
Parking brake assembly bolt (Allen head)	27	–	20
Torque arm nut	34	–	25

CHAPTER FOURTEEN

FRAME

This chapter describes removal and installation procedures for fenders, footpegs, and other frame members. During disassembly, reinstall all mounting hardware (small brackets, bolts, nuts, bushings, collars, etc.) in their original locations. This will facilitate assembly. Kawasaki makes frequent changes during the model year, so the way parts attach to the frame may differ slightly from the ones used in these service procedures.

FOOTPEG
(1987-1988)

Removal/Installation

Refer to **Figure 1** for this procedure.

1. Remove the footpeg mounting bolt (**Figure 2**) and the footpeg mount from the frame.
2. Remove the cotter pin and washer from the clevis pin.
3. Withdraw the clevis pin from the footpeg, and remove the footpeg from the footpeg mount.
4. Installation is the reverse of removal. Note the following:
   a. Make sure the spring tang hooks over the footpeg mount.
   b. Apply grease to the footpeg clevis pin.

c. Torque the footpeg mounting bolt to 54 N•m (40 ft.-lb.).

FOOTPEG
(1989-ON)

Removal/Installation

On 1989-on models, the footpeg is equipped with a footguard assembly. Refer to **Figure 3** for this procedure.

1. Remove the footpeg mounting bolt.
2. Remove the two footguard mounting bolts (**Figure 4**) and the footpeg/footguard assembly. On 2000 models, the right side, lower footguard mounting bolt also secures the rear-brake-switch bracket (A, **Figure 5**) to the frame. If necessary, disconnect the switch spring (B, **Figure 5**) from the brake pedal, and tuck the rear brake switch safely out of the way.
3. If necessary, remove the footpeg from the footguard by performing the following:
   a. Remove the footpeg bolts from the nut plate.
   b. Lift the nut plate from inside the top of the footpeg, and remove the footpeg from the footguard.
4. Installation is the reverse of removal. Note the following:

14

① **FOOTPEG (1987-1988)**

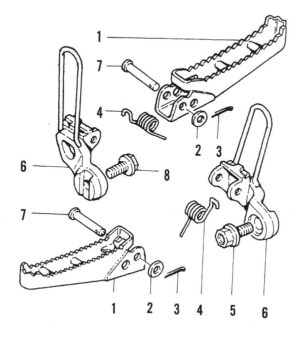

1. Footpeg
2. Washer
3. Cotter pin
4. Spring
5. Footpeg mounting bolt
6. Footpeg mount
7. Clevis pin
8. Bolt

a. Torque the footpeg mounting bolt to 54 N•m (40 ft.-lb.).

b. On 2000 models, install the switch bracket behind the right side, lower footguard bolt. See A, **Figure 5**. If removed, reconnect the switch spring (B, **Figure 5**) to the post on the brake pedal.

FRONT FENDER COVER

Removal/Installation

Refer to **Figure 6** when performing this procedure.

NOTE
The Mojave uses three different size front fender mounting screws: two 6 × 17 mm (A, Figure 7), two 6 × 24 mm (B, Figure 7) and two 6 × 13 mm (C,

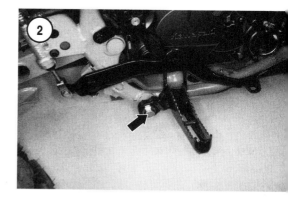

Figure 7). Note where these screws are installed during removal. Each will have to be reinstalled in its original location during installation.

1. Remove the six front-fender mounting screws (**Figure 7**).

③

FOOTPEG/FOOTGUARD (1989-ON)

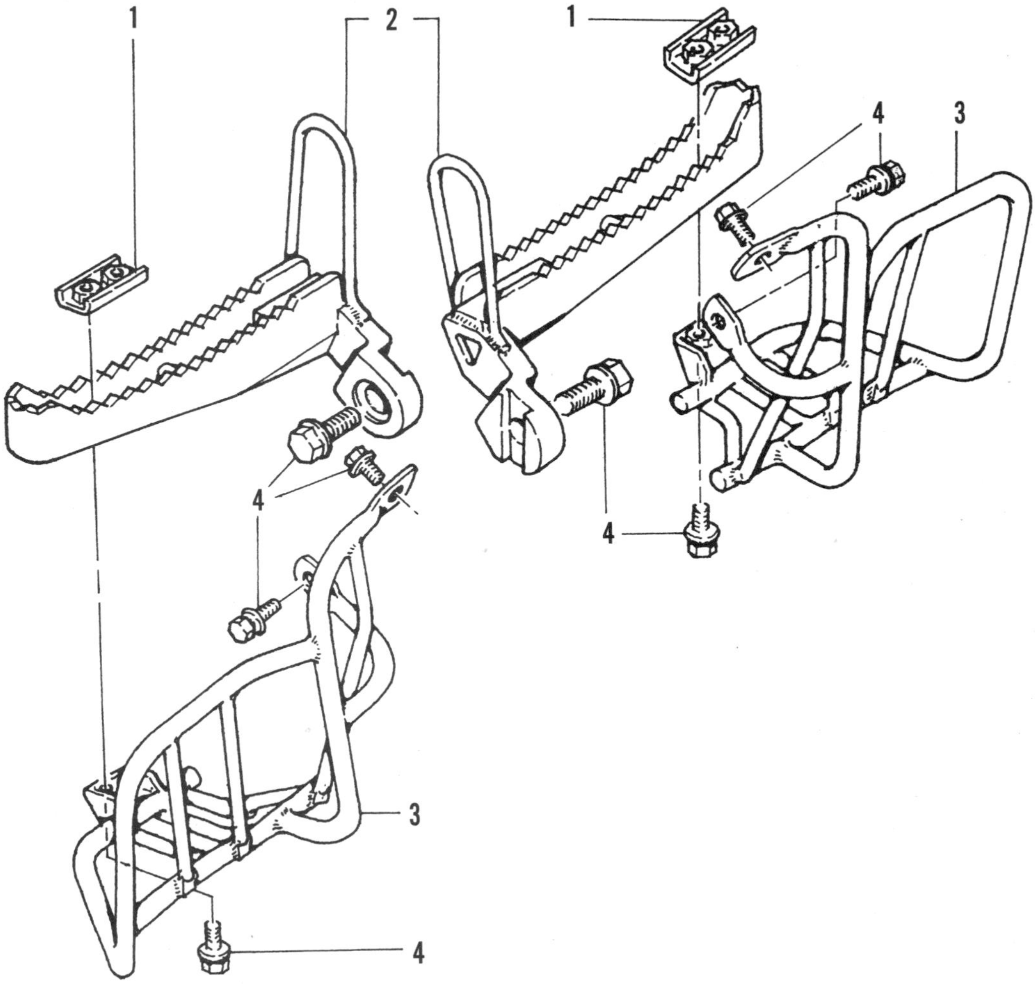

1. Nut plate
2. Footpeg
3. Footguard
4. Bolts

14

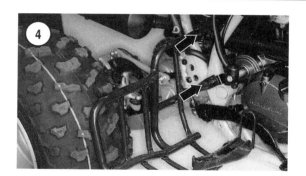

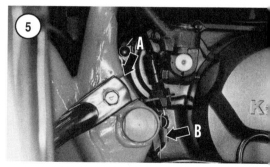

FRONT FENDER

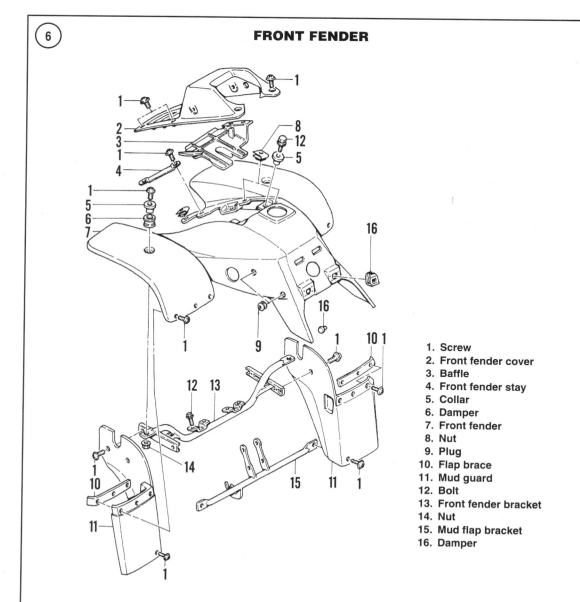

1. Screw
2. Front fender cover
3. Baffle
4. Front fender stay
5. Collar
6. Damper
7. Front fender
8. Nut
9. Plug
10. Flap brace
11. Mud guard
12. Bolt
13. Front fender bracket
14. Nut
15. Mud flap bracket
16. Damper

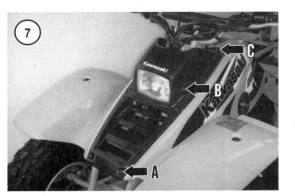

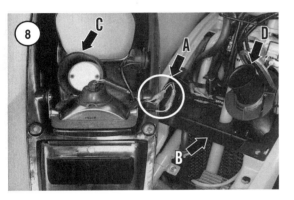

2. Lift the fender cover from the fender.

3. Disconnect the ignition switch connectors and the headlight connectors from the wiring harness. See A, **Figure 8**.

4. Remove the front fender cover.

5. Installation is the reverse of removal. Note the following:

    a. Make sure the baffle (B, **Figure 8**) is in place on the front fender.

    b. Install the front fender cover so the dust cap (C, **Figure 8**) in the cover fits over the snorkel duct (D, **Figure 8**).

FRONT FENDER

Removal/Installation

Refer to **Figure 6** when performing this procedure.

1. Remove the rear fender as described in this chapter.

2. Remove the front fender cover as described in this chapter.

3. Remove the baffle (B, **Figure 8**) from the front fender.

4. Remove the two 6×13 mm screws (A, **Figure 9**) and the front fender brace (B, **Figure 9**).

5. Remove the 6×21 mm screw (**Figure 10**) from the mount above each wheel. Account for the collar or damper on the mount.

6. Remove the two forward fuel tank mounting bolts (A, **Figure 11**) on each side of the tank, and remove the fuel tank cap (B, **Figure 11**). On 1988-on models, note that the fuel tank vent bracket is secured behind the left fuel tank mounting bolt (A, **Figure 11**). Reinstall the bracket beneath this bolt during installation.

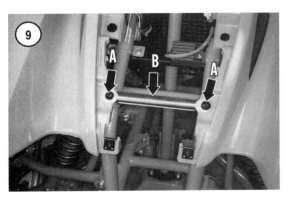

14

7. Remove the two screws (**Figure 12**) that secure each mud guard to the front fender bracket.

8. Remove the screw (A, **Figure 13**) that secures each mud guard to its mud flap bracket.

9. Pull each mud guard off its bracket (B, **Figure 13**).

10. Remove the fender by performing the following:

  a. Pull out the left side of the fender so it clears the fuel valve.

  b. Raise the fender so it clears the fuel tank filler neck.

  c. Pull the fender rearward to release it from the fuel tank tabs (A, **Figure 14**) and remove the fender.

11. Reinstall the cap onto the fuel tank.

12. Installation is the reverse of removal. Note the following:

  a. The fender must securely engage the fuel tank tabs (A, **Figure 14**).

  b. Make sure the damper and collar are in place in the mount above each wheel. See **Figure 10**.

  c. On 1988-on models, set the fuel tank vent bracket on top of the fender (C, **Figure 11**) and then install the left fuel tank mounting bolt (A, **Figure 11**).

  d. Check that the collar is in place on the two front fuel tank mounts (A, **Figure 11**).

  e. Tighten all mounting hardware securely.

FRONT MUD GUARD

Removal/Installation

Refer to **Figure 6** when performing this procedure.

1. Remove the two screws (**Figure 12**) that secure the mud guard to the front fender bracket.

2. Remove the screw (A, **Figure 13**) that secures the mud guard to its mud flap bracket (B, **Figure 13**).

3. Remove the three mounting screws (C, **Figure 13**) that secure the mud guard to the front fender.

4. Remove the flap brace that sits between the mud guard and the fender.

5. Pull the mud guard from its mud flap bracket (B, **Figure 13**) and remove the mud guard.

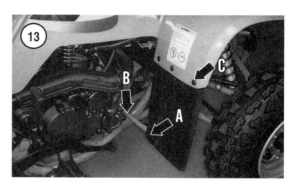
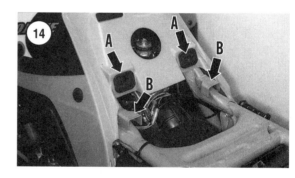

6. Installation is the reverse of removal. Be sure the flap brace is installed between the front fender and the mud guard.

REAR FENDER

Removal/Installation

Refer to **Figure 15** when performing this procedure.

NOTE
The rear fender can be removed with the seat and grab rail in place on the fender.

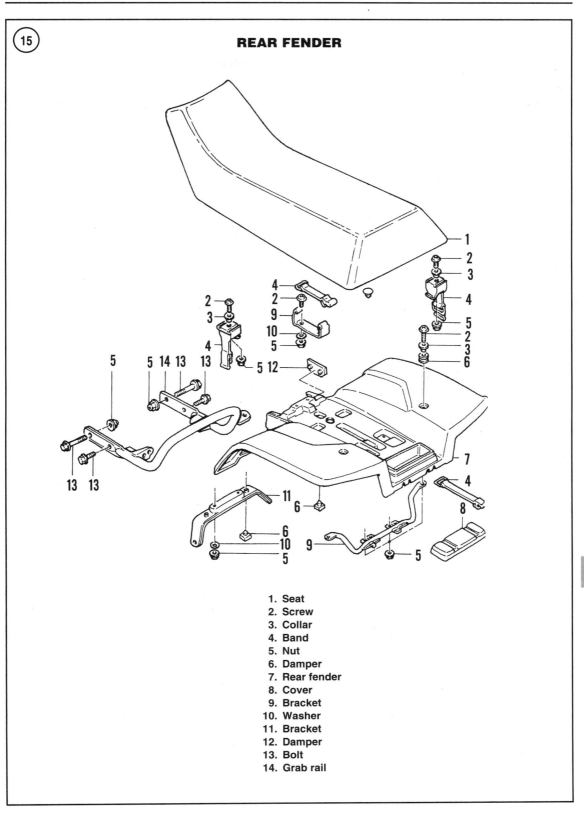

15 REAR FENDER

1. Seat
2. Screw
3. Collar
4. Band
5. Nut
6. Damper
7. Rear fender
8. Cover
9. Bracket
10. Washer
11. Bracket
12. Damper
13. Bolt
14. Grab rail

14

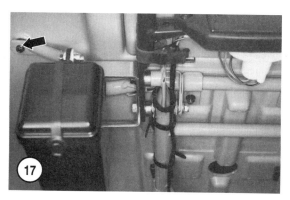

1. Disconnect the taillight bullet connectors (**Figure 16**).

2. Remove the rubber straps from the tool box.

3. Hold the nut (**Figure 17**) underneath the fender, and remove the screw (**Figure 18**) from the mount above each wheel. Do not lose the collar or damper from either mount.

4A. On 1987-1989 models, remove the two grab rail bolts (**Figure 19**) from the each side of the ATV.

4B. On 1990-on, perform the following:

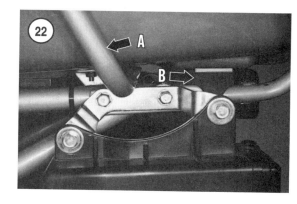

a. Remove the two grab rail bolts (A, **Figure 20**) from the left side of the ATV, and then remove the storage box (B, **Figure 20**) and its mounting bracket.

b. Remove the two grab rail bolts from the right side (**Figure 19**).

5. Pull the rear fender rearward, disengage the seat tabs from the braces (B, **Figure 14**) on the frame, and remove the rear fender.

6. Installation is the reverse of removal. Note the following:

a. Make sure the rubber damper and collar is in place on the mount (**Figure 18**) above each wheel. Replace them as necessary.

b. Slide the fender forward so the tabs on the seat engage the braces (B, **Figure 14**) on the frame.

c. Tighten the mounting hardware securely.

SEAT

Removal/Installation

Refer to **Figure 15** for this procedure.

1. Remove the rear fender as described in this chapter.

2. Set the fender on a bench with the seat facing down.

3. Remove the mounting hardware and the front brace (**Figure 21**) from the fender.

4. Remove the mounting hardware and the rear brace (A, **Figure 22**) from the rear fender.

5. Lift the fender off the seat.

6. Installation is the reverse of removal. Note the following:

a. Make sure the dampers (B, **Figure 22**) are in place on the seat.

b. Tighten all mounting hardware securely.

14

INDEX

15

15

KSF250 1987

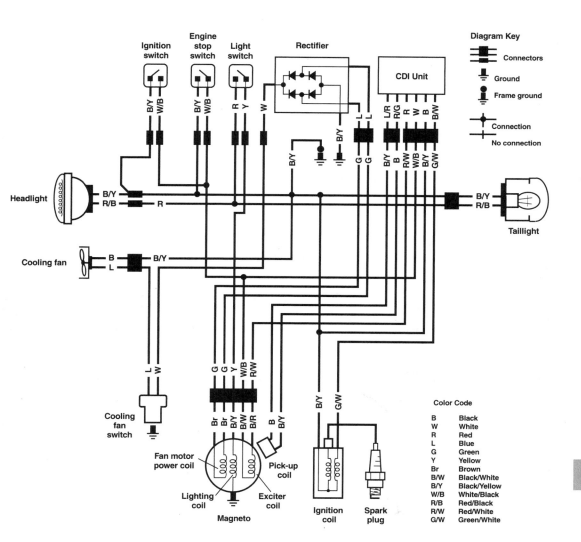

16

KSF250 1988-1989

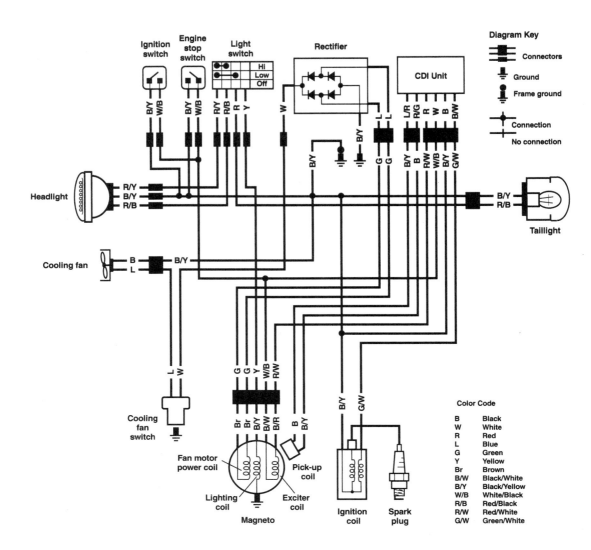

KSF250 1990-ON

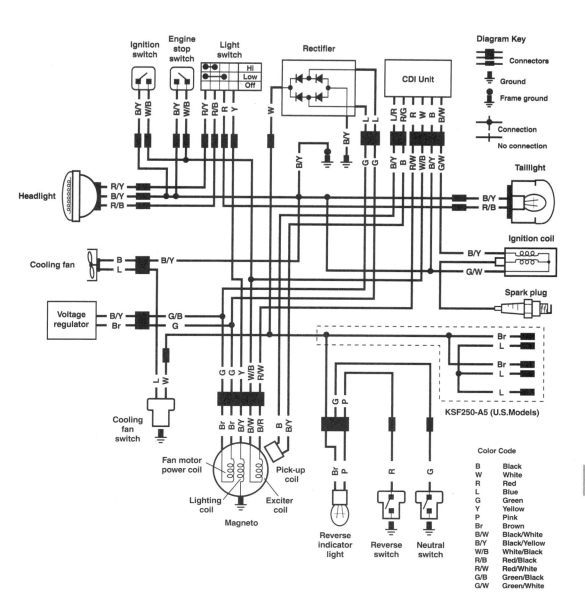

Diagram Key

- Connectors
- Ground
- Frame ground
- Connection
- No connection

Ignition switch

Engine stop switch

Light switch

	HI
	Low
	Off

Rectifier

CDI Unit

Headlight

Taillight

Ignition coil

Cooling fan

Spark plug

Voltage regulator

KSF250-A5 (U.S.Models)

Cooling fan switch

Fan motor power coil

Lighting coil

Pick-up coil

Exciter coil

Magneto

Reverse indicator light

Reverse switch

Neutral switch

Color Code

B	Black
W	White
R	Red
L	Blue
G	Green
Y	Yellow
P	Pink
Br	Brown
B/W	Black/White
B/Y	Black/Yellow
W/B	White/Black
R/B	Red/Black
R/W	Red/White
G/B	Green/Black
G/W	Green/White

16

NOTES

NOTES

MAINTENANCE LOG

Service Performed	Mileage Reading				
Oil change (example)	2,836	5,782	8,601		